Bodo the Apostate

Other Books by Donald Michael Platt:

A Gathering of Vultures
Rocamora
House of Rocamora
Close to the Sun

Bodo
The Apostate

Donald Michael Platt

PENMORE

www.penmorepress.com

Bodo The Apostate
by
Donald Michael Platt

Copyright © 2014 Donald Michael Platt

All rights reserved. No part of this book may be used or reproduced by any means without the written permission of the publisher except in the case of brief quotation embodied in critical articles and reviews.

ISBN-13: 978-1-942756-32-3(Paperback)
ISBN -13:978-1-942756-33-0 (e-book)

BISAC Subject Headings:
HIS045000 HISTORY / Europe / Spain &Portugal
FIC032000FICTION / War&Military
FIC031020FICTION / Thrillers / Historical

Ist Edition

Front Cover and Interior Design by Pam Marin-Kingsley
Website: pammarin-kingsley.com

Address all correspondence to:
Michael James
Penmore Press LLC
920 N Javelina Pl
Tucson AZ 85748
mjames@Penmorepress.com

For Pam Marin-Kingsley

... in the meantime, a credible report caused all ecclesiastics of the Catholic Church to lament and weep.
        Prudentius of Troyes, *Annales Bertiniani, anno* 839

For the Reader

Ninth century historical documentation for *Bodo*, the novel, is biased for the most part and at times confusing, with multiple names and years of birth for the same person and contradictory historians' speculations for motivations.

National languages in Western Europe did not yet exist in the first half of the ninth century. Old French was in its embryonic Francique stage, Old High German beginning to develop. In the Carolingian Empire, Latin continued to be the unifying language of the educated few who lived in monasteries, abbeys, or at Court.

Because most of the principal characters in *Bodo* are Franks, Alamanni, and Saxon, choices had to be made regarding names: the Frankish Pepin or Germanic Pippin; Aix-la-Chapelle or Aachen; Charles or Karl, the Bodensee or Lake Constance, Karolus Magnus, Charlemagne, or Charles the Great.

The Carolingians called the Iberian Peninsula Hispania, and the Muslims named it al-Andalus. Muslims were a mix of Arabs, Berbers, and Mauritanians, whom Christians referred to as Saracens or Moors.

For the reader's convenience, height and length are given in Carolingian feet, about a third of a meter, distances in modern miles, weights in pounds and ounces.

Childhood ended at age seven if not sooner in the ninth century. Royal and noble girls often wed when they became nubile, some at twelve or thirteen, and males generally at fifteen or sixteen. Teenage was a non-existent status and word until the 1920s, 1941, or 1950 depending upon the source.

At the end of *Bodo, the Apostate,* I have included Author's and Historical Notes, a list of fictional characters, and Church documents in Latin contemporary with Bodo that describe his origins and apostasy.

Donald Michael Platt
September, 2014

Abbreviated Carolingian Genealogy

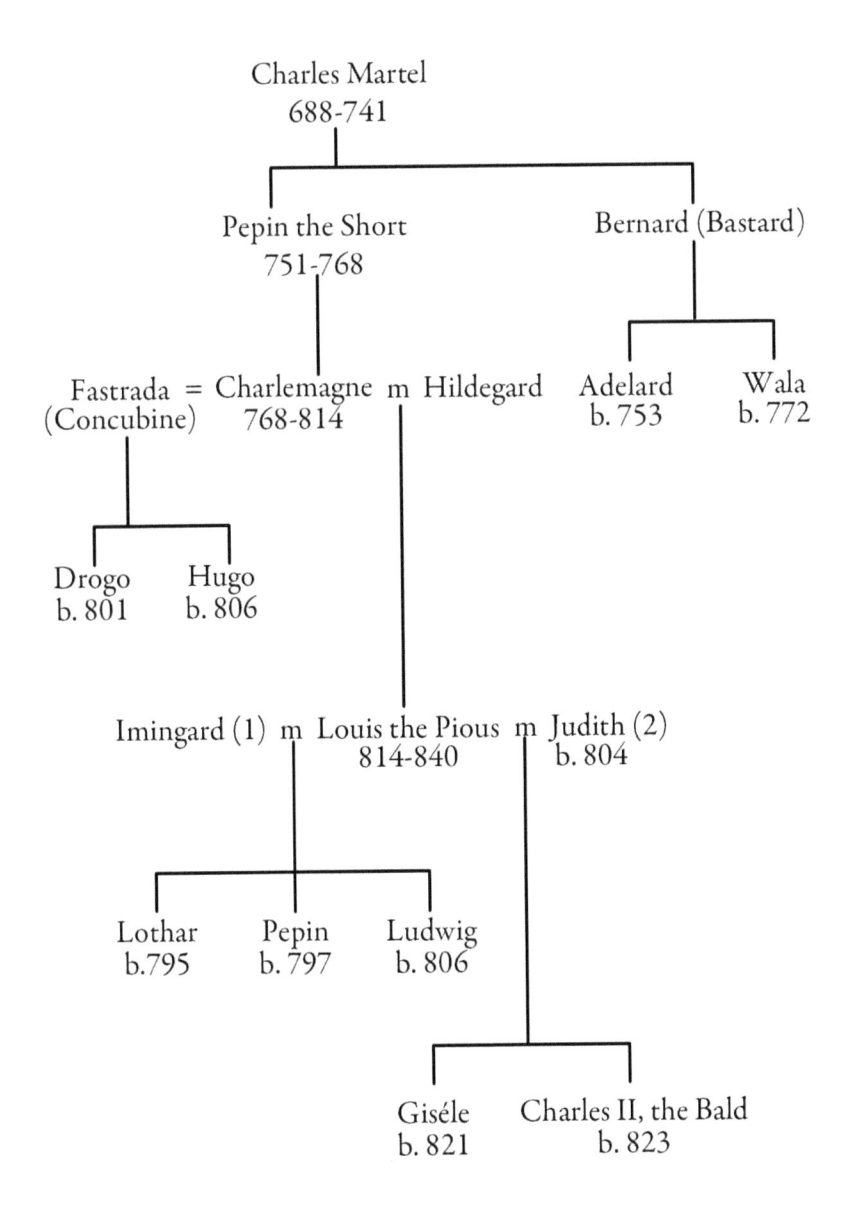

```
                        Charles Martel
                           688-741
                    ┌─────────┴──────────┐
            Pepin the Short         Bernard (Bastard)
               751-768                    │
                  │                  ┌────┴────┐
Fastrada = Charlemagne m Hildegard  Adelard   Wala
(Concubine)  768-814                b. 753   b. 772
     │
  ┌──┴──┐
Drogo  Hugo
b. 801 b. 806

    Imingard (1) m Louis the Pious m Judith (2)
                     814-840           b. 804
         ┌───────────┼─────────┐         │
      Lothar       Pepin    Ludwig       │
      b.795        b. 797   b. 806       │
                                    ┌────┴────┐
                                  Giséle   Charles II, the Bald
                                  b. 821      b. 823
```

... the reign of Louis the Pious was a golden age for the Jews of his kingdom such as they had never enjoyed, and were destined never again to enjoy in Europe.

Heinrich Hirsh Graetz, *History of the Jews, Volume III*

Part One
Bodo, the Boy
818-823

1. Great Tree of the Thunderer

"Donar ... Wotan ... I, Bodo ... son of Gunzo the Strong, Count of Hohentwiel, Count of Bodman, Count of the Aargau ... I command you ... show yourselves."

The old gods did not reply. Were they watching unseen?

Bodo also summoned trolls, lamias, and fairies, to appear and naiads to surface from their enchanted lakes and springs. None obeyed.

Were they lurking behind trees and foliage, inside caves, waiting for day to end? So everyone said. But was it true?

Bodo next challenged the Devil and his minions to rise from their hidden realm below massive oaks and firs obscuring the sky. The priests and monks said that was where they dwelled. Grown men and women believed it as truth.

Not Bodo. Born with innate skepticism and insatiable curiosity, he searched the woods for those strange creatures. Calling their names, he ran barefoot over clusters of fern, dry leaves, acorns, pine needles and cones deeper into the Black Forest west of the sprawling family villa at Bodman on the shore of the Bodensee.

The temperature high, Bodo wore linen trousers, no shirt or tunic. He carried a dagger and a boar-spear, each of weight and length adequate for a boy of six to hunt and skin small game or to defend against larger wild animals of the forest. Loyal Bardulf, his companion more wolf than dog, ran ahead.

Bodo had no fear. He held the talisman his father gave him to protect against maleficent spirits. Count Gunzo had taken it from a Viking he slew in battle. Its silver filigree curvilinear design represented Mjöllnir, war hammer of the Norse great god Thor the Thunderer, known as Donar by the Alamanni.

Again, Bodo challenged the old gods, strange beings, and Satan too to prove they existed. Not one appeared or spoke to him. He listened for mysterious noises in the forest but instead heard familiar sounds from harmless animals, birds singing, and calls from his older sister Adeltrud and Walafrid, son of a tenant farmer, to wait for them.

Bodo the Apostate

Bodo stopped running at a clearing by a pond. No spirits in sight, a swan and her brood glided along the surface toward reeds and clusters of lily pads. Bardulf barked. The swans ignored him.

Bodo's twelve year old sister Adeltrud emerged from the woods in a yellow linen blouse and billowing blue skirt. She carried a basket filled with berries and a bouquet of mixed flowers. Everyone said Adeltrud resembled their mother, said to have been the most beautiful woman in all of Alamannia, but Bodo could not remember Countess Huntrud's face. Their mother died when he was two, and his sister had raised him since.

Tall, lanky, and gentle ten year old Walafrid Strabo followed Adeltrud, dressed in a peasant's coarse blouse, short trousers of rough wool, and wooden shoes instead of his usual clerical robe and sandals. A brown hat shaded his eyes. All skin and bones, Strabo reminded Bodo of a migrating water bird.

He liked the young scholar, whose poor and humble parents tilled the soil on Count Gunzo's lands. Strabo studied at the abbey on an island in the Bodensee formed by the flow of the Rhine, which the Romans named Augia, and the Alamanni called Reichenau. The abbot gave Walafrid the name Strabo, a Latin word for distortion of the eyes, because of a drooping eyelid. Strabo had permission to enjoy the Midsummer's Eve festivities before he took the oath of an oblate, a first step toward becoming a monk.

"Bodo, look." Adeltrud pointed at an enormous wild boar snorting and rooting. "It is coming our way."

"Do not be afraid. Our father says their eyesight is poor. Bardulf, be quiet." Bodo wet a forefinger and pointed upward the way he had seen grown men test the direction of the wind. "The breeze favors us, and the boar is old and blind."

Bodo stepped in front of Adeltrud and Strabo and took a defensive stance with his small spear, Bardulf at his side. The boar passed. "Do you hear? Its snorting and grunting sounded like belching."

Adeltrud kissed Bodo's forehead. "You are wise and courageous beyond your six years, my handsome little brother."

He wanted to be wise, but there was so much to understand, so much to know. Bodo did not tell Adeltrud and Strabo about his dreams. He remembered few details but more the substance of them. Two things he did believe. His father was in danger, and he had to find a special oak of the Thunderer and there pray to Donar. Adeltrud often told him their mother had second sight. Did he? Adeltrud did not. Perhaps they were not dreams and instead visions.

Bodo missed his father. After the spring thaws in April, Count Gunzo left with his fit vassals to join the emperor's army in war against the rebellious Bretons. Bodo looked forward to the day when he became a knight, added prizes from war and trophies from the hunt to his father's weapons and animal heads on the walls of their home.

"Bodo, Strabo, listen. A storm is coming."

The forest became night black. Thunder shook the ground. Lightning illuminated the darkness. Rain came.

"Let us find shelter over there." Bodo led them to a great oak.

A lightning strike seared the nearest tree on their left. Adeltrud trembled. "The *tempestarii*, they have summoned a storm to harm us."

Bodo clutched his talisman. "I fear no storm. The Thunderer will protect us. I know he will."

A bolt charred an oak to their immediate right. The storm passed.

Strabo kneeled. "There will be no fire. Let us thank the Lord, blessed be He, who mercifully spared us."

"No." Bodo showed Strabo his talisman. "The Thunderer shielded us. I will pray to this tree. I will command Donar to protect my father."

Strabo lowered his voice. "But it is forbidden."

"Why?"

"The penalty is death if you are caught venerating or praying like a pagan."

"What is a pagan, Strabo?"

"A pagan is anyone who is unchristian and worships the old false gods."

"Why are the old gods false?"

"Because there is only one true faith."

Bodo chose not to question Strabo further and took his dagger from its scabbard.

Adeltrud came closer. "What are you doing?"

"Marking this oak. I want the Thunderer to remember that I Bodo, son of Count Gunzo, was here."

"Then do not pray to Donar aloud."

"Strabo, you taught me to recite the Latin alphabet. I can recognize the letters too. But I do not know how to write the words."

"I will guide your hand."

"I wish I knew how to read and write like you."

"You shall one day. The last letter. There. You have finished."

Bodo the Apostate

Bodo stepped away from the trunk and stared with pride at what he had carved with Strabo's assistance:

BODO
HIC
ERAM

Bodo was here.

2. Midsummer's Eve

The twenty-first of June was more than Bodo's day of birth. At sundown the annual Midsummer's Eve festival would begin and last for three days through the twenty-fourth of June, the Day of Saint John the Baptist. Tents and booths had been erected on the expansive grassy field in front of Count Gunzo's manse built upon the foundation of a Roman home Bodo had been told. Local landowners, free peasants, tenants, and servants converged from nearby villages and farms to celebrate the annual Midsummer's Eve festivities.

Proud he was now six, Bodo looked forward to lighting the bonfires in his father's place. He intended to stay awake throughout the night unlike previous years.

Dusk came late on the summer solstice. Beneath a full moon, Bodo lit the initial bonfire and joined the revelers with Adeltrud, who wore a garland of flowers on her braided flaxen hair, and Strabo. Peasants and tenants, whose one daily meal often consisted of gruel, gorged on roasted meats, pottages, and cakes. They drank their fill, some beyond, of wine, beer, or mead.

Vendors sold amulets and phylacteries for use against evil spirits and illnesses. Others offered to cast spells or interpret dreams. Adeltrud lingered behind a large number of men and women standing in front of a "wise woman" who offered love potions created from sperm, menstrual blood, and aphrodisiac plants.

With Bardulf at his side, Bodo accepted several small honey cakes from a crone. He ate his favorite treat at a fire where an elderly bard sang of oaths never to be broken, loyalty given to tribal leaders of yore, and great deeds of Alamanni heroes against monsters and the Romans. The bard also described the forbidden rituals of the Alamanni: worship of sacred trees, stone pillars, and rivers, fertile hills and mountain valleys. Many around Bodo voiced their belief that on this night fairies appeared in the forests and witches flew to their covens, and tomorrow on Midsummer's Day, the water spirits demanded human sacrifices.

Bodo next went with Adeltrud and Strabo to a bonfire where the stable master's son vaulted over the flames so his clan would be prosperous and suffer no harm during the coming year. Bad luck, he singed his feet. More men and boys challenged the bonfire. Most failed.

"My turn."

"No, Bodo, you are too small."

"I am not, sister. Father is away. Tonight I am Lord of Bodman. I will show you."

Too quick for Adeltrud and Strabo to restrain him, Bodo vaulted over the fire. "You see? I am untouched."

Couples holding hands jumped three times over a nearby bonfire to ensure a long and happy life together with wealth and many children. Peasants led cattle by ropes over cinders and ashes so their livestock would be safe from wolves and disease. Women collected embers to prevent injury and bad weather at harvest time.

Bodo tugged at Strabo's sleeve. "Do you believe all that?"

"My abbot and the monks at Reichenau disapprove of all such superstitions."

Adeltrud put her hand on Bodo's shoulder. "It is late, past your bed hour. I will take you home."

"If you can catch me. Come, Bardulf."

Bodo ran from Adeltrud and Strabo across the field and stopped when he reached the edge of the woods. He looked behind. No one followed. Where was Bardulf? He saw no fires. He heard no sounds of revelry coming from the field or from nocturnal animals in the forest.

Absolute silence.

An amorphous mist approached Bodo. Like clouds during the day its shape shifted. Bodo attempted to speak. No words came. Unable to move limbs or blink but more curious than afraid, he waited for something to happen.

The form transmogrified into a dense fog and engulfed Bodo in an embrace, not malignant but comforting. His sense of well-being continued when an unseen force lifted and floated him across the field until ....

3. Leader

"Bodo, did you hear me? You have been sleeping on your feet. It is late. You must go to bed."

As if he never left them, Bodo stood again with Adeltrud and Strabo. "I did?"

Bodo told Adeltrud he was ready for bed. In truth he wanted to be alone. He took two more honey cakes, a mutton leg for Bardulf, and left for the lodge. The great hall inside was dark. All servants were enjoying the festivities. Hounds in their kennels bayed at the moon. Bardulf settled near the hearth to gnaw on the mutton bone.

Bodo went outside through the back to a promontory jutting into the Bodensee. He sat at the edge, ate his honey cakes, and watched the moon reflect on still water. No water spirits or other strange creatures appeared. When the bells of Reichenau Abbey ten miles away tolled the hour, an owl soared above the Bodensee in the clear night sky, silhouetted against the moon. Was it an omen? If so was it for good or ill?

He returned to the great hall convinced his successful leap over the fire and prayers to the Thunderer would bring his father home from battle alive and covered with glory. Surely some superstitions had to be true. Why else did so many believe them?

Bodo fell asleep against Bardulf by the hearth. He had many dreams that night but in the morning remembered none.

Bodo spent the summer frolicking, playing leapfrog and other games with children close to his age, fighting with wooden swords, and swimming in the Bodensee. Each day he prayed at the great tree of the Thunderer in silence heeding Strabo's warning.

Late in September, Bodo continued to swim in the Bodensee to build his stamina. He ignored chills brought on by the colder water and weather of autumn. His father had described how young nobles trained to become knights. From age ten, boys underwent the same hardships of a soldier during war: lack of food and sleep, extreme cold, or unbearable heat while wearing armor, all to harden the body. The aspirants learned to master all weapons, hunt with hounds, cast off falcons, and leap onto a horse with ease while clad in armor.

Bodo remembered his father saying: "One who cannot achieve knighthood by age fifteen will never accomplish it."

When Bodo returned to the villa, he saw Adeltrud weeping. Why were their servants loading bags into a covered cart? Who were those two strangers speaking with Berend, their aged villa steward?

Bodo ran to Adeltrud. "Sister, why do you weep? What is happening? Who are those men?"

Adeltrud hugged Bodo. "Woe, woe, little brother. Our father is dead. We are orphaned. We are alone."

Bodo pushed his sister away. "No, it cannot be true. Father still lives."

"Alas, Lady Adeltrud speaks the truth. Your father's coffin awaits us for burial beside your mother at the church graveyard."

The man who spoke came closer. Bodo had not recognized his father's shield bearer. Englebert the Sturdy left Bodman a fit and healthy young man. He returned emaciated, bent, and yellow of complexion.

"Young master, it was not the Bretons who felled Count Gunzo and most of our men, but a fever caused by the miasma of their foul swamps. I was at your father's bedside when he died. I thought I was fortunate to survive, but I am so weakened and ill, I fear I may not see the end of this year."

Bodo believed Englebert. Enraged, he ran to the edge of the promontory and with all his strength threw the talisman into the Bodensee. If his father had taken it to war, he might still be alive. Or would he? Bodo recalled his daily prayers to the Thunderer at the great oak and successful leap over the fire during the Midsummer's Eve festivities. From this day, he would trust only what he could see or touch, not what anyone else said or believed.

When Bodo returned to the villa, Engelbert, Berend, and the stranger stood with Adeltrud by the covered cart. The shield bearer beckoned him.

"Bodo, this man is Dachs, one of your Uncle Welf's retainers. After Count Gunzo died, his brother, Count Welf of Altorf, commanded Dachs to bring you and Lady Adeltrud to his home in Aachen."

"No. This is our home."

"No longer. Count Gunzo was a vassal of the emperor. Hohentwiel, the Aargau, Bodman, and this villa, they all belong to His Majesty. He alone will decide who shall have the land and honors."

Bodo the Apostate

Bodo loved his home, the perfect order in his life. "No, I will not go."

"You have no choice. Your uncle is a good man. Count Welf promised your dying father he would welcome you and Adeltrud as a son and daughter. Now, get up on the cart. All your clothes and possessions are there. Dachs is eager to return to his family."

"Listen to him, little brother."

Bodo's emotions ran a gamut from anger to sadness. He bit his lip and struggled not to cry and run away. That was for cowards. His father often told him how much he despised weakness in men. Son of Gunzo, he too must be strong. His sister could shed tears for both.

At the cemetery, Adeltrud wept again when Count Gunzo was buried beside their mother at a ceremony attended by the entire village, Strabo, and the abbot of Reichenau. Bodo shed not a single tear, nor did he listen to the priest's prayers. Anger dominated grief. Bodo wished he could have given his father a traditional Alamannic warrior's funeral, immolation in fire. What good were Christian burials? Each time he stood over his mother's grave and spoke to her, she never answered.

After soil covered Gunzo's coffin, Strabo offered condolences. "I will write you, Bodo. I pray you will soon learn enough Latin to reply."

Bodo took his sister's hand. "Adeltrud, our father is dead. Now I am the man of our family. My name Bodo means Leader. I will lead us. I will protect you. Bardulf, come."

"No dog."

Bodo glared at Dachs, a big man, a hardened man whose scarred face and broken nose showed he had seen much of war. "Bardulf is my companion. My father gave him to me the day my mother died. He will come with us."

As if to emphasize all Bodo said, Bardulf growled at Dachs ready to attack. The soldier gripped the hilt of his sword. "He is more wolf than dog. A dangerous beast."

"That is why my father named him Bright Wolf." Bodo stood between Dachs and Bardulf. "Do not draw your sword. Bardulf will not harm you unless I tell him to."

Bodo leashed Bardulf, kneeled and hugged his wolf-dog tempted to let him attack Dachs. He heard the creature whimper. It sensed, it knew, and so did he.

"Young master, Bardulf must stay here."

Bodo praised Bardulf for his loyalty and companionship, stood, and handed Berend the leash. "Then treat him well." He stroked Bardulf's head. "I promise. I will return."

4. Welfings

> Count Welf the Shrewd of Altorf, b. ca. 765
> Countess Heilwig, Welf's wife
> Conrad, b. ca. 801, Welf's eldest son
> Judith, b. ca. 804, Welf's eldest daughter
> Hemma, b. ca. 807, Welf's youngest daughter
> Rudolf, b. ca. 811, Welf's youngest son

Bodo and Adeltrud worried they might never return to Bodman and the only home they had known. Bodo vowed somehow he would. Dachs did not answer any of their questions during the four hundred mile journey to Aachen. Shorter days left less daylight for traveling. Not until the hour before noon on the thirtieth day of October 818 did they arrive at Aachen to face an uncertain future.

Bodo wore tunic, cape, and boots, all too tight because he grew faster than most boys his age. A woolen hat protected his head from the cold. A heavy hooded cloak covered Adeltrud to her shoes. When they stepped from the cart in front of Welf's home narrower than their villa at Bodman, Bodo comforted his sister who trembled. "Do not be frightened."

"What if they mistreat us?"

"I told you. I am the man of our family. Adeltrud means Noble Strength. You must be strong." Bodo opened his mouth wider to show the gaps where his front teeth used to be. "See? They are gone. I am older." He gripped the hilt of his dagger. "I will never let anyone harm you. Remember what father said to us before he rode to war?"

"Yes, I think so."

Bodo had listened with pride when Count Gunzo told him and Adeltrud always to hold their heads high and how they should be known

Bodo the Apostate

throughout the empire. Lesser men were named by how they labored, the village where they lived, or some characteristic, often unflattering. One day after Bodo earned a county or frontier march and Adeltrud married a man of noble birth and accomplishments, they would be addressed by their titles. Until then, they would be known as son and daughter of Gunzo the Strong, Count of Hohentwiel and the Aargau, or as noble Hunfridings through their mother Countess Huntrud, and Udalrichings through their paternal grandfather. No one had greater lineage or nobler blood, no king, no emperor.

"Now, Adeltrud. Take my hand. We hold our heads high like father said."

Bodo often heard his father describe their Uncle Welf as shrewd. When he asked Strabo what that word meant, the scholar said it meant one who was wise, cunning, and never divulged his secrets.

Dachs knocked on the door, and servants led Bodo and Adeltrud into the great hall. Like their home at Bodman, the walls held heads of animals slain in the hunt between torches, arms, and armor collected from pagans and Saracens killed in battle. An elderly man who did not resemble their father sat on the center of a bench at a long table of wood flanked by his family and retainers drinking wine, nibbling on cheeses and nuts while awaiting venison to finish roasting over a hearth.

Count Welf the Shrewd of Altorf, influential member of the imperial council, and vassal to no man save the emperor, rose and approached Bodo and Adeltrud. His wife, sons, and daughters followed.

"You have arrived at last. I am your Uncle Welf. I welcome you to my home, which shall be yours. Son and daughter of my younger and beloved brother know that Gunzo fought heroically in Brittany and brought honor to our family. Not the Bretons, it was a vile fever that felled him."

Bodo spoke for himself and Adeltrud. "So we were told, Uncle."

Welf placed a hand on Bodo's shoulder. "Good size for your age, sturdy bones. I am now responsible for you and your sister. I shall soon learn of your abilities and plan your future. Are you hungry, thirsty?"

"Yes, we are, Uncle."

"Then meet your family and sup with us." Welf began the introductions. "Listen all. Here are my blood nephew and niece, son and daughter of my brother Gunzo. Bodo, Adeltrud, this is my wife, Countess Heilwig, and your cousins, my eldest son Conrad and youngest Rudolf, my daughters Judith and Hemma."

Bodo had thought Adeltrud to be the fairest of girls until he saw Judith. Hemma had Countess Heilwig's fine features but lacked her older sister's sweetness and charm. Mother and daughters wore wool dresses of different colors and a style Bodo had not seen before that conformed to their bodies, with trimmed high neckline, long sleeves, and decorated belts tightened at the waist. Would Welf give Adeltrud similar garb?

A commotion caught everyone's attention when a man wearing a cloak and cap of dark fur strode into the great hall accompanied by servants bearing a small chest of polished wood, a large terracotta amphora, and two smaller jugs. With that large nose, hair so black, and skin the color of tanned leather, he reminded Bodo of his father's falcons. From what land did he come?

Welf and the stranger embraced. "Abraham, I welcome you to my home."

"I thank you, Welf, and countess, young ladies, I do not know if even the greatest poets in the empire are capable of praising your beauty, grace and charm. Rudolf, you have grown since I saw you last, Conrad, they say you brought honor to your family well in battle against the Bretons. And who are this pretty girl and handsome little lad?"

"They are Adeltrud and Bodo, daughter and son of my brother Gunzo."

"I heard of his passing. My condolences. Children, your father Count Gunzo was a most puissant knight."

"Puissant, Uncle Welf?"

"Strong and mighty, Bodo."

He liked hearing his father remembered so well, but what meaning did Abraham have? Bodo never heard of any Alaman or Saxon called by that name.

Abraham studied Bodo's features. "Our emperor will be astonished when he sees your nephew. The boy has the same face and unusual green eyes of Good Queen Hildegard, Louis' mother. One winter when I journeyed across the Pyrenees, I saw a tarn of that rare color, which often appears on copper. Except for the color of his eyes, your nephew also resembles the emperor's eldest son Lothair when he was the same age."

Welf stared at Bodo anew. "By Donar's hammer, so he does. His resemblance to King Lothair can be explained. Bodo's mother Huntrud was the daughter of Hunfrid, Margrave of Rhaetia, and her aunt was Good Queen Hildegard, the most important of Charlemagne's wives and mother of Emperor Louis."

Bodo the Apostate

"It will be interesting to watch the emperor's reaction when he sees your nephew."

"I could not agree more. Now tell us, Abraham, what is it you have brought to our home?"

"Wine from my vineyards at Roquemaure on the Rhône. The jugs are filled with the best honey for your table and health. The chest contains rare perfumes for Countess Heilwig and the girls."

Judith and Hemma vied to take the chest from Abraham's servant. Heilwig chided her daughters for lack of manners to no avail, then relented and joined them when they sniffed at each small bottle of colored glass. The girls insisted Adeltrud participate with them, which pleased Bodo.

"We thank you, Abraham," Heilwig said. "Now that you have returned from your journey, we look forward to seeing more of your sweet wife and lovely daughter Deborah, whom Judith has missed."

Bodo touched the merchant's cloak. "Sire, I have never felt so fine a fur. From what animal does it come?"

"The marten, a rare creature found in the lands of the Khazars and beyond the Ural Mountains."

"What is a marten and where are the Khazars and Urals?"

Bodo thanked Abraham for his answers although he did not understand them. "Count Abraham, what lands are yours?"

"Bodo, stop bothering Count Abraham with so many questions."

"I do not mind, Welf. Bodo, the emperor has made me Count Palatine, Count of the Palace."

"Abraham is also the Merchant of the Palace," Welf said.

"I have another question. Uncle, who is Charlemagne? And I thought Ludwig was our emperor."

Bodo did understand Welf's explanation. The emperor was called Ludwig by the Alamanni and Saxons. Hludovicus Caesar was his formal name in Latin, and Louis in Francique, the language spoken by the Franks. Louis' father, whom the Alamanni called Karl der Grosse, was Karolus Magnus in Latin and Charlemagne in the language of the Franks.

"Then I must learn Francique."

Welf beckoned all to the table and escorted Abraham to the place at his right. Conrad sat beside the merchant, Bodo between Rudolf and Welf's steward. Heilwig took her place at Welf's left with her daughters and Adeltrud. A servant provided pillows for Bodo and Rudolf because the bench was too low for the boys to reach the food and drink.

Welf raised his goblet of wine to Abraham. "You are generous, my friend. I have missed your company and wise counsel."

"I have been thinking of all we must to discuss. Friend Welf let me express again how delighted I am you returned unharmed from the campaign against the Bretons."

"I am equally pleased you have arrived after so long an absence."

"Almost two years, but in these troubled times, it is best I stay at Court. My eldest son Nathan is now fifteen. He will leave in my place and head the next caravan. Aside from rare furs, perfumes, spices, and cloths from the east, I brought good news for the emperor. Our friendship with al-Mamun, the Caliph of Baghdad, continues without change from his predecessor, Haroun al-Rashid."

Bodo almost asked what Abraham meant by troubled times but sensed he should not interrupt the merchant.

Servants brought them trenchers of bread to absorb juices from the meat and soups. Bodo cut and tore at the food to make smaller morsels because his missing front teeth made it difficult for him to bite. He ate to bursting and drank wine Heilwig diluted for him, her youngest son Rudolf, and the girls.

Bodo did not understand the conversation about people he had not met and unfamiliar places. Nor did he comprehend Judith's wit, which provoked much laughter. He was surprised she and Hemma could read and write. Perhaps they might teach Adeltrud.

After the meal, Welf clapped his hands, and servants brought a cither to Judith. "Abraham, you will now hear a voice sweeter than any angel."

Judith tested the tone and sang in Latin a pleasing melody she had composed to the words of the Twenty-Third Psalm.

Bodo waited for the applause to end. "Cousin Judith, will you play it again so I can sing with you?"

"You know the Lord's prayer in Latin?"

"Yes, Uncle, I was taught the Latin alphabet, the Lord's Prayer, the Apostles' Creed, and some psalms by a scholar who studies at Reichenau Abbey on the Bodensee."

"Well, let us listen to you."

Bodo the Apostate

Bodo sang with Judith in perfect harmony. After they finished, she praised his voice and rewarded him with a hug and a kiss on his forehead.

"We must not wait until you are seven, Bodo," Welf said. "I shall take you to the palace and enroll you in the Academy. You can study with Rudolf."

"Will I learn to use weapons too, Uncle? I want to be a knight."

"In time, in due time."

5. The Palace

Early in the morning a week after his arrival, Bodo took in the sights and sounds of Aachen when his uncle walked him to the imperial palace less than a mile away from his home. He wore larger boots and new clothes, hand-downs from Conrad the girls shortened to fit better.

Along the way, Welf identified the great houses of magnates, bishops and abbots.

"Uncle, so many people in one place."

"Aachen is said to have a population of about twenty thousand when the emperor resides at the palace."

"It must be the largest city in the world."

"No, Constantinople in the east has over two hundred and fifty thousand inhabitants."

Bodo did not understand so large a number, nor could he visualize that many people.

Welf pointed to a long and high granite wall. "On the other side is the emperor's great hunting park and menagerie. He lets nothing interfere with his love for the chase and fishing."

"So did my father."

"And I. The emperor allows nobles and prelates to hunt there for sport, fur, and meat. We do the same throughout the empire. And over there you can see a gymnasium, a permanent camp for soldiers, a training ground for those who aspire to knighthood, and a hospice for the sick."

"Will I learn weapons and horsemanship so I can become a knight?"

"We have several years before we discover all your abilities." They approached another high wall ahead, behind which loomed tall towers. "We have reached the palace."

At the largest gate Bodo had ever seen, palace guards greeted Welf with deference and let them pass into a crowded courtyard. Bodo gaped at the structure and activity of people coming and going. He hurried to keep pace with Welf's long strides when they passed through the great wooden doors to a courtyard with a large statue of a king on horseback surrounded by his retainers.

"Is that Emperor Louis?"

"No, Bodo. He is the Ostrogoth conqueror Theodoric."

"Who was he?"

"You shall learn about him in good time. Remember, Bodo, we entered through the West Gate, and we are now in the middle of the Stone Corridor. Do you know the four directions?"

"North, south, east, and west. I can find my way here easier than in the forest because everything is square."

"I am impressed." Welf brought Bodo to Count Abraham and a half dozen men conferring in the Stone Corridor, each dressed for the cold weather in heavy hooded cloaks or mantles of varying colors with fur trim.

"This boy is my nephew Bodo, son of Gunzo the Strong."

Bodo thanked the men for praising his father and believed he would remember their names. Abraham introduced him to Priscus, a strange looking man in his twenties, with dark brown eyes of an unusual shape and skin that reminded Bodo of polished wood. Priscus was no taller than a typical woman, about five feet four inches of height. He wanted to ask from what land Priscus came, but Welf spoke.

"I warn you, Astronomer, my nephew will ask more questions than even you may be able to answer. Bodo, Priscus is a learned man in many areas of knowledge. I have arranged for him to familiarize you with the palace and introduce you to your teachers." Welf pushed Bodo closer to Priscus. "I must confer with my comrades now. Meet me here at the Western Entrance at midday after the bells of sext."

"Yes, Uncle. Priscus, what does your name mean?"

"It is of Roman origin and translates as Ancient."

"That is a strange name. You do not look ancient."

"It means of ancient family, lineage."

"Where do you come from?"

"Beyond Byzantium." Priscus smiled at Bodo's confusion. "I could name my land of birth, but you would not understand. Part of your education will be the study of geography, which includes the reading of maps."

Bodo the Apostate

"I want to see all those places for myself, not on maps." Bodo had trouble with more than unfamiliar vocabulary. Priscus spoke faster than the typical Alaman with an accent difficult to understand. "My uncle called you Astronomer."

"I study the planets and the stars."

"Are you a monk, a priest?"

Priscus bent his head to reveal straight black hair. "As you can see, I am not tonsured, nor do I wear clerical garb. I am a lay scholar who serves the emperor at his pleasure. Now, let us tour the palace. You should know that many centuries ago the Romans settled here because of the thermal springs and strategic location. They named their encampment and village *Augua Felix*, blessed water, because of its healing qualities. Our emperor's father, Charlemagne, chose this site for his winter palace and capital of his empire."

"I hear mostly Latin spoken."

"Do you understand what they are saying?"

"Some words."

"Good. How old are you?"

"I will be seven in June."

"More than eight months away. I have been told you are precocious, with a mind superior to children your age and some who are older. That is why you are being enrolled in our Palace Academy ahead of your birthday. Here you shall learn the trivium and quadrivium with other boys from the noblest families of the empire and others of lesser birth but who show promise. You will study Latin, which is the common language of the Court. The population of our vast empire speaks more tongues and dialects than any one man can learn. Latin is the first language you shall be taught, then Greek and Francique. Roman, Goth, Saxon, Breton, and others you must learn for yourself."

"I already understand Alamannic and Saxon. Who are all these people? Why are they here?"

"They are courtiers, scholars, clerics, and aristocrats, all seeking sinecures and benefices from the emperor. The poor come for redress of grievances or for charity."

"I do not understand some of the words you are speaking."

"In a short time you will. Now, stay close to me, Bodo, and be careful not to get lost. You should soon learn your way. This palace is an enormous square, each side with a length of three hundred and sixty feet. There are four clusters of buildings divided into four parts each by north-south and east-west lines."

"That is easy for me to understand."

"We are now at the northeastern end of the palace at the entrance to the *aula regia*, the great Council Hall."

"Can I see it?"

"Not today. Here is where the emperor welcomes dignitaries, emissaries, and holds a general assembly in May when he is not traveling to preside over regional assemblies. Of course you know that our emperor is sacred and his power comes from God."

"Really? Does he speak to God?"

"Of course he does."

"Where?"

"In his chapel at the south end of the palace and wherever else he prays."

"Does God speak to the emperor?"

"Only the emperor can answer that question."

"Then I will ask him when I see him. Where does he live in the palace?"

"The royal apartments are on the second floor above the Council Hall. Those steps to the right lead to the treasury and palace archives that are stored in a tower beside it."

"What are archives?"

"A room filled with church and historical records and legal documents."

"Can I see them?"

"Eventually, perhaps. You cannot see and learn everything in one day. You must obtain permission from the chancellor. He is responsible for the archives and scriptorium where scribes and notaries write diplomas, capitularies, and royal correspondence."

"Is the treasury filled with gold and jewels?"

"Yes, and much more." Priscus guided Bodo southward from the Council Hall. "Rare manuscripts. Gold and bejeweled weapons. Clothing of the finest material with threads of gold, all from tribute, the emperor's conquests, gifts from emissaries of other kingdoms and purchases from merchants."

Bodo walked with Priscus down the three hundred foot long Stone Corridor past buildings and rooms on each side: the royal library, a scriptorium where clerics created and copied precious manuscripts, workshops for gold and ivory, and a factory where artisans minted coins. Everywhere Bodo saw colorful mosaics representing scenes from the Gospels, Priscus explained, or symbols of the Orthodox Faith.

"Priscus, where is the Palace Academy?"

"Here, there, and everywhere. There is no specific place. You will meet wherever your teacher decides."

"What are those buildings?"

"The clerics of the chapel use them. If you had a seat in the sky, you would see they are laid out in the shape of a Latin cross. The Curia where the palace clergy meets is to the east of us, with offices and lesser chapels in the north and south, and an atrium with an *exedrae* in the west."

"*Exedrae*?"

"Come with me. It is best to learn sometimes by seeing instead of listening or reading."

They entered an atrium covered by a cupola decorated in gilt and supported by marble columns, with a semi-circular bench at the back. "Who sits there?"

"Clery who conduct hearings and trials."

At the south end of the palace, they entered the great octagonal chapel. "Bodo, because it was consecrated in 805 by Pope Leo III in honor of the Virgin, this chapel is also known as the Church of Saint Mary."

Bodo counted sixteen arches supporting galleries above. "The ceiling is so high. How many feet is it?"

"It is called a cupola and is almost a hundred feet high and about fifty feet wide."

Bodo counted the cupola's colorful mosaic of twenty-four men flanking a man on a throne. "Who are they, Priscus?"

"Jesus Christ and the Elders of the Apocalypse."

"What is the Apocalypse?"

"The End of Days."

"Is that the same as the Raganarök our bards sing of?"

Priscus put a finger to Bodo's lips. "Speak not of pagan gods and practices. You will learn about the Apocalypse in good time. Now look. Here in this marble sarcophagus lies Charlemagne, who created the greatest empire since Rome at its apogee, height of greatness."

Bodo stared at a carving Priscus called a bas-relief. It depicted a woman struggling against a bearded man. "Who are they?"

"Mere decoration."

"Why is that big book chained to the altar?"

"It is a complete Bible with both Old and New Testaments. Very rare and valuable. Look, here let us go to the baths."

"It steams, Priscus."

"The baths are fed by a hot spring the Romans named Quinius. Charlemagne restored and added that smaller soaking pool at the far end and those marble benches. He swam almost daily when he held court in Aachen. Often, more than a hundred men joined Charlemagne in the pool while he consulted with his advisors and issued decrees."

"But no one is here except the two of us." Bodo stood over the thermal water. "May I come here whenever I want to swim?"

"You swim?"

"My father threw me into the Bodensee when I was three and taught me how to move in the water. Can I show you now?"

"Not today, Bodo."

"How long and wide is the pool?"

"Sixty feet by sixty feet, a perfect square."

"When do I begin my classes? What hours are they?"

"After the Calends of January. The hours are not fixed."

"Will you be my teacher?"

"I believe I must, for I may be the only one in the palace who has the patience to answer all your questions without going mad."

"Can I come here to swim every day?"

"If your uncle gives his assent."

"And can I go to the gymnasium and field where the knights and soldiers train?"

"Again, ask your uncle."

"When can I see the emperor?"

"When he summons you or encounter him by chance. I look forward to seeing how His Majesty will react to all your questions."

6. Family Above All

The man of their family, Bodo consoled his sister whenever she grieved, but he would never reveal to anyone how much he missed his father, Bardulf, their home in Bodman, and a life of order. Although Welf and Heilwig treated him and Adeltrud the same as their own children, Bodo did not trust his uncle. Despite a genial mien, Welf's eyes resembled those of a sly fox.

Heilwig ran an efficient and orderly household. She made sure all washed their hair once each week with chalk to be rid of lice and trimmed their nails. She provided sticks for cleaning teeth. Each week servants washed their clothes and changed the bedding. Each Saturday, they bathed, which was an Alamannic and Saxon tradition.

Bodo adored Judith for her beauty, cheerfulness, and charm. She taught him to play the cither and lute. Bodo believed Judith when she told him he was her favorite cousin and one day would be a handsome noble knight.

Hemma, a well-mannered strong-featured girl who resembled her mother, was more distant than Judith, and Bodo suspected she might be shrewd like her father.

Both Judith and Hemma included Adeltrud in all activities: spinning, gossiping, and moments of vanity. One day, Bodo saw the girls plaiting each other's hair. When he made fun of the girls as they applied small pincers to their eyebrows to make them narrow, they threatened to pluck his and chased him.

Conrad, who was away much of the time hunting and carousing with his fellow knights, paid little attention to Bodo and Rudolf except when they asked questions about weapons and knighthood. Closer in age, Bodo and Rudolf developed a friendly physical rivalry. They wrestled, fought with wooden swords, and raced against each other.

Like Bodo's father, Welf encouraged the children to take pride in their caste and lineage. Family came before all others. Welfings and Hunfridings must never forget they were *geboren*, born human, and of the warrior caste, whereas those not of noble blood were merely foaled like animals and to be treated as such, even if they rose to high station through merit in royal administration or the church.

"We of noble birth are warriors. All others in the empire are foaled and either pray or labor."

One afternoon, Welf unrolled a map and showed his sons and Bodo the Welfing domains from Bavaria and the north of Lake Constance to Strasburg and beyond into Alsace. He identified Gunzo's former lands when his forefinger moved from Hohentwiel to Bodman and the Aargau.

"When I am of age, will they be mine? They belonged to my father."

"That will be the emperor's decision."

Bodo learned from Welf that Louis inherited the empire Charlemagne had structured into counties administered by counts and margraves. Warrior margraves ruled the marches: lands on both sides of the Pyrenees contested by Muslim Saracens and Moors, Basques, and Visigoth Christians in Navarre and the Asturias; Alpine regions populated with rebellious Rhaetians; Brittany where Celtic Bretons fought for independence; and eastern borders threatened by Wends, Sorbs, and other pagan tribes.

Welf explained why titles and honors were not permanent. The emperor moved nobles to different counties and marches based upon need or stripped them of lands and honors when disloyal. Louis also created bishops and bestowed abbeys to many from the laity.

Welf lit a candelabrum and led them to the cellar. He unlocked a door and lit wall-torches inside illuminating ornamented swords, scabbards, baldrics, helmets, and various types of armor.

"Remember, it is essential we use part of our wealth for gifting. Generosity is a quality of nobility equal to bravery, whereas avarice and cowardice are the most grievous faults of aristocrats."

"My father said the breaking of an oath is worse than cowardice."

"Gunzo may have been right, for it is perhaps the most difficult virtue of all to sustain."

"Why is that, Uncle?"

"Because of unexpected events and changes in the behavior of those to whom you have sworn an oath."

"I shall always keep my word."

Bodo the Apostate

"Perhaps and perhaps not." Welf took Bodo to a pile of weapons and armor. "These belonged to your father. One day if you are worthy, you will become a knight. Gunzo's sword is too heavy for you to wield now, but I can give you his dagger and scabbard."

Bodo admired the weapon even though the decorations on its silver hilt and gem encrusted scabbard represented Donar's hammer. He hated all pagan beliefs and superstitions. None had saved his father.

"This bag of coins contains the price paid for your father's horse, which I sold to a knight who had lost his. The money will be yours when you reach the age of fifteen."

"And my father's lands."

"Bodo, I told you. Hohentweil, Bodman, and the Aargau belong to the emperor who has given them to me to hold in trust, except for the villa at Bodman. He enjoyed his visit there the year after you were born, and I suggested he should have it for a palace. You will have to earn your lands the same as your father did."

Bodo suspected Welf the Shrewd had more unpleasant surprises yet to be revealed.

7. Insatiable Curiosity

Bodo swam in the thermal pool whenever he visited the palace with Welf. His uncle told him the emperor, his sons, and ranking nobles bathed there each Saturday before donning fresh clothes for the week ahead.

Bodo became known to the guards and certain notables who respected his father. He had the run of the palace and more opportunities to learn from Priscus before his formal studies began. One frustration, Bodo had yet to see the emperor. Louis either hunted or met with his advisors *in camera*, , which is Latin for in private chambers the Astronomer told him.

On a day in November, Bodo shared the pool with Welf and Abraham, who conferred at one end, and he saw something odd. The Merchant of the Palace's *membrum virile* was different from his and others he had seen. After Welf and Abraham left for important meetings, Bodo dressed and hurried to Priscus' observatory.

"What is it, Bodo? You are out of breath."

"I saw the strangest thing at the pool."

Priscus listened to Bodo's description of Abraham's genitalia. "The explanation is simple. It is called circumcision, the removal of one's foreskin."

"That must be painful."

"They do not remember the pain. All Jewish males are circumcised eight days after birth when they are given their names. So was Baby Jesus, who was born a Jew."

"He was? No one ever told me that."

"That is why the Calends of January is still remembered by many as the Feast of the Circumcision even though it is now called the Octave of the Nativity for the eighth day after Christ's birth."

"If Baby Jesus was circumcised like the Jews, why are all Christians uncircumcised?"

"Fewer pagans would have converted if circumcision had been a requirement to be a Christian, and the Church decided to distance itself from its Jewish origins."

"I do not understand."

"Bodo, the answer is complicated. One day you will discover why on your own."

"That's what you always say. Is it because you do not know the answers?"

"Sometimes, but not always. Think of the thermal pool. What happens to a pebble if I drop it into the water?"

"It sinks to the bottom."

"Exactly. Now, Bodo, think of that pebble as a fact."

"Like Jesus was circumcised?"

"Yes, and to understand why Jews are and Christians are not, you would need many more pebbles of knowledge to fill the pool and prevent yours from sinking. That is what an education provides. That is why it takes time to fill the empty pool inside your head."

"It must take a long time to fill a head with so much knowledge."

"Many years. Even then, one may gain knowledge without the wisdom of understanding."

"How do you learn to understand and to be wise?"

"Those, Bodo, are rare gifts bestowed upon us by our Creator. They cannot be taught."

"Priscus, will I be wise?"

Bodo the Apostate

"Continue questioning. Keep your mind open, and you may indeed become wise."

Not only Priscus, Bodo had been asking questions of everyone from the day of his arrival in Aachen. He forgot nothing even if he did not always understand. Bodo believed he now comprehended what Abraham meant by "times of troubles." The emperor mourned the death of his wife, Queen Irmingard, who died of fever the previous month. Louis had recurring nightmares because he blinded his nephew Bernard, King of Italy who died two days after.

Welf and Abraham worried how best to prevent Louis from abdicating and retiring to a monastery. Welf feared losing power and influence if Lothair became emperor. Abraham worried that he and the Jews might lose their privileged status in the empire.

Bodo learned several things about Jews, which provoked more questions.

They once ruled a land called Israel. Where was it?

They were neither *geboren* nor foaled. Jews were descended from men called patriarchs. Who were they? Jews did not believe Christ was the Son of God. Why?

Priscus would not tell him why Jews circumcised male children. When Bodo changed the subject and asked why Louis' eldest son Lothair was co-emperor, the Astronomer explained Salic Law with a map of the *Ordinatio Imperii* of 817 that divided the empire among Louis three sons: Lothair, Pepin, and Ludwig.

Bodo also added another new word to his vocabulary, primogeniture. Bequeathing one's lands and wealth to an eldest son made more sense than apportioning it to several.

8. A Bold Stratagem

After a heavy midday repast, Adeltrud and the girls retired to their quarters with Countess Heilwig. Conrad left for a liaison with one of the servant girls. Bodo fell asleep under the table with Rudolf against several hounds until a conversation between Welf and his guest Count Abraham awakened him.

"I have decided that I shall speak to Louis and seek his consent for a marriage between my Judith and King Lothair."

"So you can manipulate the co-emperor through your daughter."

"Of course. As you have seen, Judith is nubile. She will be fifteen this coming January after the Epiphany. My younger daughter, Hemma, who is but eleven years old, may also develop into a beauty and perhaps wed King Pepin or Ludwig."

"You have similar nuptial plans for your sons?"

"I have. Conrad, my eldest, distinguished himself in battle. There are many noble families with available daughters. I have more time to choose a wife for Rudolf. He is but a boy of seven and attending the Palace Academy for the finest education in the empire."

Bodo looked at Rudolf still asleep and waited for his own name to be mentioned.

"Welf, you are the most fortunate of men. Four potential alliances with the greatest families."

"I am responsible for two more children who may yet prove to be useful. Before my brother Gunzo died, I promised to raise his son and daughter equal to my own children. Bodo, the boy, is but six, and his sister Adeltrud twelve. When the time is right, I shall arrange a suitable marriage for Adeltrud and the best education for Bodo so he might one day earn a high position at Court."

What high position? What did Welf mean? Could one be a knight and also have a high position at Court?

"Welf, your plan is an excellent one, but Louis may abdicate before you can carry it out."

"My greatest fear. Louis listens to you, Abraham. Perhaps you can embolden him not to abdicate."

"It will take more than one man and one meeting to prevent so terrible a calamity."

"That is why I have decided. Whether the emperor abdicates or not, Judith must marry Lothair in haste. It is no secret my family's great rival in Alsace, Hugh of Tours, has been scheming for his daughter Irmingard to wed Lothair. I know I can count on your support when I also ask the emperor to give permission for Conrad to wed her instead. But, why do you frown?"

Bodo the Apostate

"I believe there is a better alternative to Lothair. It contains much risk, but the prize is greater."

"Continue, Abraham. Do not tantalize me."

"In the east, when it is time for a ruler or his heir to wed, the most comely girls from the greatest families are brought to court so he can select the one who pleases him most. Why should we not entice our emperor to do the same? Only if Louis' eyes and ears are failing him will he choose another than your Judith."

"That is a bold gamble you propose."

"True, our emperor is inclined towards monasticism, but he is not one to be celibate for long. He always had an eye for a pretty face and form. Remember, his *concubita*, Theodelinde, gave him two children by the time he was fifteen, a son, Arnoul, whom he made Count of Sens, and a daughter Alpaiís, who wed Beggo, Count of Paris at age thirteen. After Beggo died early the previous year, Irmingard pressured Louis to make Alpaiís Abbess of Saint Peter at Rheims to keep her away from Court."

Bodo frowned. More names to know and words to understand.

"Yes, we all know that Louis' great love for Theodelinde is the reason why Charlemagne forced him to wed Irmingard at age sixteen."

"And nine months after that Irmingard presented him with Lothair, the eldest of his three sons. Remember, friend Welf, the emperor had not shared his wife's bed in over a decade before she passed on and instead continued to enjoy the company of Theodelinde, and would be doing so this day if she had not died before the campaign against the Bretons. That is why Louis is likely to seek another beauty to warm his bed. Once he sees your Judith, he will desire and wed her."

"You may be right. Judith has more than youth, beauty, and grace. My eldest daughter is intelligent for a female, well read, conversant in Latin and Greek, and able to compose verse and music. When Louis discovers Judith's accomplishments and depth of mind, he may well become her captive. But how best do we encourage His Majesty to summon the most beautiful noble maidens of the empire? And when?"

"I shall do my part, and so must our allies. Present your Judith to them, and they shall praise her beauty, virtues, and accomplishments in the emperor's presence. Then, when the time comes for Judith's appearance at Court, I will supply your daughter with the finest raiments and proper colors to emphasize her form and complement her eyes, hair, and complexion. I shall do the same for Countess Heilwig and your sons, your daughter Hemma, niece Adeltrud, and nephew too."

Bodo listened to Welf's and Abraham's speculations, almost falling asleep again, until he heard Abraham mention his name.

"Priscus is impressed with Bodo's mind."

"The boy does ask many questions."

"Boy? Have you not observed how Bodo carries himself? He is like a little man."

"Now that you mention it, he does. Perhaps Bodo is a prodigy."

"He may well be."

Bodo wanted to know if prodigy was a compliment. He had to wait until the morning to ask Priscus its meaning.

9. To Convince a Daughter

In the great hall, Welf recounted his satisfactory meeting with the emperor and the imperial council earlier in the day. Louis assured all he would not abdicate, and he expressed his desire to wed again. The emperor then delegated Royal Chamberlain Helisachar to invite all marriageable daughters from the highest nobility to appear in "A Pageant of Favorites."

"You should have seen them hurry away to prepare their daughters for the great event." Welf raised his goblet of wine to Judith. "No family has a daughter more beautiful and accomplished than you."

Bodo agreed when he looked at Judith. How could the emperor not select his cousin? Then he saw Hemma frowning. Was she envious of her more pleasing older sister?

Countess Heilwig drank before speaking. "How did the emperor's sons take his decision?"

"Lothair left immediately with Hugh of Tours. Pepin sulked alone, and young Ludwig seemed confused. Judith, should you become empress, you will have a difficult task gaining their approval, but I believe you can charm your future stepsons into accepting you."

"What if I do not like the emperor? Is he not an old man?"

"He is forty, my daughter, thirteen years younger than I."

"Father, I did not mean …."

Heilwig touched Judith's arm to silence her. "Husband, you are the most observant of men. Describe the emperor for our daughter."

Bodo the Apostate

"Tell me the truth, father, for I do not want to be surprised or disappointed."

"I shall do my best, Judith. I take pleasure in calling you by your Christian name now. If all goes well as I believe it shall and you wed the emperor I, all of you ... we must then and forever after address Judith as Your Majesty." Welf waited for his sons and Bodo to cease their laughing and the girls to stop giggling. "Louis is strong and muscular, about five feet ten inches of height with the handsome pleasing countenance and manly voice of his father Charlemagne. He is well coordinated and loves the chase more than anything. Like you, Judith, he enjoys reading poetry, plays, stories of the Greeks and Romans, and writings of the church. He is deservedly praised for his understanding of scripture and exegesis."

"Surely the emperor has flaws, father."

"Of course. No man is perfect. Louis is physically courageous in battle and the hunt, but he lacks the confidence of Charlemagne to rule with strength and consistency. The emperor becomes enraged at the wrong time and later regrets his harsh actions, which he did and still does after blinding his nephew Bernard. He tends to be too introspective and unnecessarily humble before ranking men of the Church. He questions his abilities and decisions and often follows the advice of the last person who has his ear. You must be that person each night in your marriage bed."

"I will advise our daughter in such matters," Heilwig interrupted.

Welf raised his goblet to Heilwig. "I am content to leave that to you, wife, but I shall instruct Judith how best to give him confidence. To continue, Louis can be quick to anger and quick to forgive. He is inclined to brood alone and has monastic tendencies. He is temperate in food and drink. He is modest in dress except for the most formal of occasions. He does not laugh or smile even when all around him do so at the antics of fools and mimes."

"No smiles, no laughter? How can I live with such a man if I become his empress?"

"An emperor should never laugh in public because the body and behavior of a man of rank and authority must reflect power, which laughter diminishes. Louis agrees with Saint Augustine, who wrote that laughter, although human, reflects a person's lower nature and can lead to loss of self-control."

"Impossible."

"Judith, listen to me. An emperor must maintain an aura of gravitas and authority before his subjects. And so must his empress. That is why he avoids excesses of uncontrollable undignified laughter. That is why he dislikes *poetica carmina gentilia,* the secular and pagan songs so popular at Court that Charlemagne enjoyed."

Bodo had not known until now that the *poetica carmina gentilia* were the same stories the bards sang at Bodman. They included battle cries, historical and mythological poems that celebrated heroic deeds in battle, and the most important virtue, loyalty to one's family and chieftain.

Welf continued, "Understand that Louis derives his concept of rule from the Old Testament Kings of Israel. He also emulates the court protocol of the Roman and Byzantine Emperors. Louis believes, no less than his father and grandfather, that his empire is New Israel and Aachen the new Rome. All who come before him must follow the custom of *proskynesis*, bowing and genuflecting. Even Queen Irmingard had to request an audience if she wished to speak with him."

Judith's face reddened. "Intolerable. If the emperor continues that practice, I shall make him request an audience with me."

"You may well succeed in that endeavor, daughter. I also have grand plans for you, my lovely Hemma. Ludwig, the emperor's youngest son is King of Bavaria. He is fourteen and a sturdy, fine looking young man. If Judith becomes empress and when you are nubile, I shall arrange your marriage to him."

"Then I will be a queen too."

"Yes, and my sons, I shall ensure that you also marry well."

Bodo worried why Welf did not mention him and Adeltrud, and again he wished he understood all the words spoken by Welf and other adults.

10. Octave of the Nativity

"The meat is cooked."

Smoke and the aroma of wild boar and venison roasting in the hearth intensified Bodo's hunger. At the long table, he sat alongside Rudolf and Conrad. Heilwig, Judith, Hemma, and Adeltrud

Bodo the Apostate

sat at Welf's left. The count's mayordomo, masters of hounds and stables, falconer, and other vassals took places farther down the table on both sides. Servants and slaves stood awaiting their master's commands.

Bodo enjoyed the entertainment provided by Welf's fool, mime, and musicians throughout the meal. The punishment of a thief was part of the amusements on the Octave of the Nativity. Having been flogged earlier for attempting to steal and sell one of Welf's best hunting hounds to another noble, the unfortunate young man trembled between two burly servants. The stable master held the hound in question.

Welf stood. "You have been given thirty lashes, and before I banish you, foaled Visigoth that you are, I gift you with our traditional Alamannian punishment for stealing a hound."

The two servants brought the thief to his knees and despite the young man's struggling forced his face to the dog's posterior.

Welf commanded the thief to kiss it and shouted a common insult: *"Undes ars in tine naso,* a hound's ass up your nose."

Winter darkness came early. Servants lit more torches and candles. Drinking and levity increased. Masters of the animals and servants alike competed for a prize. The first to offer *unum saltum et siffletum et unum bumbulum*, a simultaneous salute, whistle and fart, while leaping over a fire would win the coin. All present made ribald comments when the competitors accomplished one or two of the feats but failed in all three until Welf's falconer succeeded.

Welf threw him the coin. "The Thunderer has spoken and favored you. Now, what shall be our next amusement?"

"Riddles," Judith suggested.

Everyone enjoyed riddles, and Bodo vowed never to forget them.

Conrad posed his. "I saw a woman flying and carrying death. She had an iron beak, a wooden body, and a feathered tail. What is it, Rudolf?"

Rudolf furrowed his brow. "You know I have no head for riddles. Let Bodo answer."

Judith saw his confusion. "I will help you, Bodo. She is a woman beloved by soldiers."

"Iron beak, wooden body, feathered tail." Bodo closed his eyes. "Is it an arrow?"

Judith applauded. "Well done, my little angel."

The adults posed more riddles favored by the Romans centuries earlier, which Judith translated for Bodo from Latin to Alaman:

"*Quis occidit hominem impune?* Who can kill a man with impunity?"

"*Medicus.* A physician."

"*Quae mulieres maritis sunt utiliores?* Which women are the best to marry?"

"*Divites quae cito moriunt.* Rich ones who will die quickly."

When the festivities ended, Welf raised his goblet. "I have saved a surprise for last. Abraham has promised to gift Judith with the finest silks, velvets, and furs so she may shine above all other young women. He will also provide suitable garments for each of us to wear at the emperor's pageant of favorites. To success."

Bodo raised his goblet of watered wine toward Judith. "To the next empress."

11. "Pageant of Favorites"

Several hundred people, Bodo guessed, when he and Rudolf carried the train of Judith's long cloak of lush dark brown sable into the great Council Hall of the emperor's palace. Welf and Heilwig flanked Judith. Behind the boys Conrad, Hemma, and Adeltrud followed. Pages escorted the Welfings to the front right side of a dais with an empty high-back throne chair. They were the last of the great families with eligible daughters to take their places by rank.

True to his word, Abraham provided vivid silks and velvets for Welf and his family to wear. Beneath fur trimmed mantles, the edges of their tunics were embroidered with gold and silver threads. Garbed identical to adult males in their finest clothes, Bodo wore a forest green tunic with tightly cut sleeves and a stitched belt to hold his dagger and scabbard. Brown trousers, a slit brown mantle that fell from neck to heels, all of fine wool, and pairs of soft deerskin gloves and boots completed his ensemble.

The variety of women's clothing fascinated Bodo, some in mantles, others wearing floor length tunics with billowing sleeves and jeweled belts, with gem covered pendants or crosses hanging from their necks. All wore gold headbands over headdresses securing veils and collars. Bodo amused himself counting the great variety of hair styles while inhaling a plethora of different perfumes.

Bodo the Apostate

Welf's greatest rival for power, haughty Count Hugh of Tours, stood with his family opposite the Welfings. Bodo's uncle reassured Judith. "Count Hugh's eldest daughter Irmingard is comely. I give her that, but she cannot match your beauty and charm. Nor can the daughter of any other noble."

Conrad lowered his voice. "I prefer the younger sister Adelaide to Irmingard."

Welf pointed out another noble whispering with Count Hugh, his sister's husband Count Matfrid of Orléans.

They mentioned so many names, Bodo decided the best way to remember them was by physical appearance. Counts Hugh became Jug-ears and Matfrid, Rabbit-teeth.

Bodo evaluated the other candidates to become empress. Both Adeltrud and Hemma were prettier than any of the others vying to be Louis' wife, excepting Judith, who hid her face and form behind a diaphanous veil and fur cloak. He looked forward to the emperor's reaction when she bared her face.

"Father, where is His Majesty?"

"You have much to learn about life at court, Judith. Making us wait is how Louis displays the majesty of being an emperor. Punctuality is for his subjects."

Excitement passed. Boredom arrived. Bodo yawned and fidgeted while they waited for Louis to appear. He stayed alert admiring weapons carried by the emperor's guard until horns sounded. A parade of palace notables entered the Council Hall and proceeded towards the dais. Although Bodo admired their beards of varying lengths, he intended to grow one exactly like his father's.

Bodo listened to Welf identify each man for Judith. "That is Helisachar at the head of the procession. He is Chamberlain of the Palace the same rank he held in Aquitaine when Louis was king there during Charlemagne's reign. Be sure to charm and win him over."

Cherry-nose was how Bodo would remember Helisachar.

"That short, round shouldered man behind him is Ebbo, Archbishop of Rheims and the emperor's foster brother."

Ebbo's face seemed graven into a permanent sour expression. "What is a foster brother, Uncle Welf?"

"Ebbo was foaled not *geboren*, the son of serfs, Bodo. His mother wet-nursed him and Louis at the same time. Later, Charlemagne freed

Ebbo and had the boy educated in the Palace Academy. After Ebbo was ordained, Charles sent him to serve Louis in Aquitaine as librarian. Now he is an archbishop. Ebbo bears watching, Judith. He is too ambitious for one so low born."

Abraham and Priscus entered the Council Hall with the other palatine notables. After the merchant paid his respects to Welf's family and stood with them, a tall, muscular young man with the bearing of both soldier and arrogant magnate led a procession of counts and margraves into the hall. His presence dominated the room. He stopped for a closer look at Judith and tried to peer through her veil.

Welf introduced the noble to his family. "This is Count Bernard of Septimania, Barcelona and Gothia-Narbonne."

Bodo watched Bernard's eyes linger on Judith before the count noticed Abraham. The two men embraced. They resembled each other in appearance, dark of hair, swart of complexion, but with two exceptions: Bernard's great nose was larger than Abraham's and his vivid blue eyes lacked the merchant's warmth.

When Bernard moved to the edge of the dais, Bodo asked Abraham, "Is he your son?"

"Your keen eye has seen a family resemblance. Bernard is my cousin. He is the eldest son of the great Guillaume of Gellone and both cousin and godson of the emperor. Bernard's grandmother Alda was a daughter of Charles Martel and, therefore, Louis' great-aunt."

Those unfamiliar names and genealogies confused Bodo, but he marked Bernard as a cold man, hard and dangerous, not to be trusted. Before he could ask more questions, horns blared a second time. A trio of young men entered the Council Hall. The assemblage genuflected when they passed.

"The tallest is twenty-three year old Lothair," Welf informed his family. "He is the eldest of the emperor's three legitimate sons and co-emperor. Twenty-one year old Pepin, King of Aquitaine, is at his right, and fourteen year old Ludwig, King of Bavaria, to his left. All three are unmarried."

Bodo sensed something odd about Pepin's eyes. Slighter than both Lothair and Ludwig, darker of hair, the King of Aquitaine looked about the Council Hall with an expression of fear and suspicion.

"My friend Welf, observe how friendly Lothair is with Hugh of Tours. When our emperor selects Judith, you can be certain he will wed Irmingard."

Bodo the Apostate

"But look over there, Abraham, how uncomfortable Hugh and the other magnates are whenever they look at my Judith. They know their daughters cannot surpass her in beauty, charm, and accomplishments."

Bodo addressed Abraham, "Sire, do you think the emperor will select my cousin Judith?"

"How can he not?"

At another blast from the horns, Helisachar thumped his staff of office on the marble floor. "All bow before his Imperial Majesty Hludovicus, Caesar Augustus by grace of God."

Bodo had a better view of the emperor when all prostrated before him. Unlike the vast assemblage of nobles and clergy glittering in their finest garments and gems, Louis, a sturdy handsome man with a trimmed dark blond mustache and beard, wore plain unadorned tunic and mantle of grey and brown wool. His crown of gold had a jeweled band around the temples, two more crossing over his head over scarlet satin with a hoop topped by a cross. Lappets covered with a line of pearls hung from the crown to a few inches below his shoulders. The emperor looked neither to the left nor right during his progression, his facial expression frozen.

After Louis reached the dais, Helisachar rapped his staff again. "All rise. Distinguished nobles, prepare your daughters for His Majesty's inspection."

Hemma and Adeltrud removed Judith's cloak. Bodo and Rudolf held the heavy fur. Bodo thought Judith had never looked more beautiful than on this day. She wore a neck-high tunic of blue velvet cinched at the waist by a jeweled belt of gold, with sleeves trimmed in sable fur. It clung to her body revealing every womanly curve. A golden chain and Byzantine cross hung from Judith's neck. A diaphanous veil of pale blue fell from a jeweled headdress atop her braided hair.

Louis left the dais, and followed by his sons began an assessment of the young women, beginning with Tours' daughter Irmingard. That meant Judith would be last.

The emperor acknowledged each noble family and next asked questions of the candidate. After what seemed long hours, the emperor and his three sons stood before the Welfings. Bodo took an instant liking to Louis. His Majesty had kind eyes. Bodo next formed an impression about each of the emperor's three sons. He thought Lothair, King of Italy, to be the most regal and warrior-like of the brothers. Louis' eldest did not smile at Judith. Pepin, King of Aquitaine, half a head shorter than Lothair, had strange eyes, not distorted like Strabo's, but odd, unfocused. Clean-shaven fourteen year old Ludwig, King of Bavaria, had noble features and blushed when he saw Hemma staring at him.

Helisachar nodded permission for Welf to address Louis.

"My daughter, Lady Judith, your Imperial Majesty."

Louis faced Judith without altering his expression even when she removed the veil from her face. "How old are you, Lady Judith?"

"I reached fifteen this past Epiphany."

"What are your accomplishments?"

"I compose music on my cither and lute. I know the languages of the Alamanni, Saxons, Bavarians, and the Franks. I read, write, and speak Latin and Greek. I am skilled with bow and arrow, and I enjoy the chase."

"The chase you say? As a spectator or participant?"

"I sit a horse well, Your Majesty."

The emperor did not smile at Judith, and Bodo feared Louis thought her to be displeasing until he remembered Welf's explanation of the man's gravitas.

"And your religious upbringing?"

"I am devout, Your Majesty. I can recite the Lord's Prayer and the Apostles' Creed. I have read works by the Church fathers."

Louis whispered to Helisachar, and the chamberlain identified each member of Welf's family. The emperor's sudden softness of expression puzzled Bodo. Louis again whispered to Helisachar, who said, "His Majesty demands to know your lineage."

Welf had prepared Bodo how best to respond to this eventuality. "Your Majesty, I am the son of Gunzo the Strong and Count Welf's nephew. My mother was Huntrud, daughter of Margrave Hunfrid. Her aunt was your mother, Good Queen Hildegard."

"Yes, you have her eyes. Now that we look closer, you have the identical features and hair of our eldest son Lothair when he was your age." Louis patted Bodo's cheek. "Most unusual, most unusual."

The emperor stiffened and froze his face again. After one last look at Judith, he went to his throne on the dais and whispered to Helisachar. It seemed to Bodo that each person present stopped breathing in anticipation of the chamberlain's next words.

"The following noble ladies will approach his Imperial Majesty. Irmingard of Tours. Rosamund of Lyon. Cunegunde of Mainz. Judith of Altorf."

Bodo the Apostate

Louis scrutinized each young woman when she walked, genuflected, and stood before him. After many long minutes, Helisachar told Judith and the others to return to their places. Horns sounded a fanfare at a gesture from the chamberlain. Louis and his sons left the Council Hall followed by the throng.

While Bodo carried Judith's train with Rudolf, he heard Abraham reassure Welf. "The emperor postponed his decision because he does not wish to humiliate the families whose daughters he rejects."

"I hope he can decide before our rivals sway him otherwise."

"I will stay here in the palace and do all I can to prevent that from happening."

Bernard of Septimania approached never taking his eyes from Judith. "Count Welf, were I emperor and unwed, I would choose your daughter."

"So would all men here."

"And I," Bodo said, which brought on much laughter from the men and reward of a kiss from Judith.

12. Semper Augusta

Bodo shared Welf's optimism that the emperor would select Judith to be his wife. As if celebrating in advance, the Welfings drank large amounts of wine and gorged on pottage filled with more meat and vegetables than common folk ate in a lifetime.

"To answer your question, Conrad," Welf said, "after Louis chooses Judith, he will grant me more honors and lands. Then, I shall be, through our Judith, the emperor's chief advisor. My sons, you will have titles, rewards, and suitable wives. I will see to it when the time is most proper that each of you will be given a prosperous abbey. I will ask to be Duke of Bavaria and rule in Ludwig's name until he is of age."

"Hemma likes King Ludwig."

"Judith, you promised not to tell."

Welf calmed his daughter. "Hemma, you and Ludwig are close in age. I believe you are the stronger person and can dominate him. We will ensure you see much of each other. Bodo, I will make a fine marriage for your sister Adeltrud."

"And I, Uncle?"

"It has already been arranged. You shall live a life of privilege in the palace beyond your imagination. You are to be as one of the *nutritii*, the nourished ones. The Palace Academy will prepare you to serve the emperor. I saw how Louis reacted to your resemblance to his mother and Lothair. I believe he will favor you, no less than Judith does now."

Before Bodo could digest all Welf said, he heard a loud rapping at the front door. Welf's mayordomo opened it, and Helisachar strode into the hall. "My compliments, Count Welf, Countess Heilwig." He bowed before Judith. "His Imperial Majesty has selected you, Lady Judith, to be his wife. Your wedding will take place before Lent. Count Welf, on that day, you shall become Duke of Bavaria with authority to govern the kingdom until His Majesty King Ludwig is of age."

Helisachar politely refused Welf's offer of hospitality and left for the palace. Bodo sensed for reasons he did not yet understand that Helisachar disliked Judith. He felt an equal animus toward the chamberlain, whose one feature resembled descriptions of male sorcerers: three long coarse black hairs protruded from the tip of his cherry nose.

After receiving congratulations from her family, Judith said, "Father, mother, I know you will be my eyes and ears at Court. Hemma, Adeltrud, you will be my principal ladies. Conrad, Rudolf, I want you close by my side, and you, my adorable cousin Bodo, when you are not participating in your lessons and studies, you will attend me and be my principal page."

Welf commanded attention and raised his goblet. "To my daughter, Empress Judith."

After Bodo took his turn congratulating Judith and calling her "Your Majesty," he went to Adeltrud. "You will live in the palace with Judith. If anyone mistreats you, let me know."

Adeltrud hugged and kissed Bodo. "I shall, my brave brother."

Bodo chose not to speak his thoughts to Welf because his uncle had crossed the line of sobriety. Was he the only one to observe that Helisachar seemed displeased by the emperor's selection of Judith?

In February before the beginning of Lent, Bodo and the Welfings marched through the massive bronze doors of the great palace chapel down a long aisle between a gathering of the most powerful magnates, their wives and children, court notables, and clergy. During the long wait before the wedding ceremony and an interminable sacrament in Latin, Bodo fidgeted

Bodo the Apostate

and counted the marble and multi-colored stones that made up the chapel walls. He admired the eight great pillars covered with gold, silver, and intricately designed lamps supporting the thrust of large arcades.

Bodo could not see Charlemagne's marble sarcophagus because the throng blocked his view. He focused instead on the two higher galleries and their choirs above at the eastern and western ends filled with spectators except for the emperor's unoccupied marble throne at the western end.

The previous December, Bodo had sneaked into the gallery and sat on Louis' throne when no one observed him. From that vantage he saw an altar of the Savior in front of him, another of the Virgin Mary below, and a third of Saint Peter at the far end of the western wall.

After the ceremony, Welf and his family followed Louis and Judith from the chapel along the Stone Corridor to the Council Hall. Bodo suffered through another long ceremony that culminated when Louis placed upon Judith's head a smaller bejeweled hoop crown. He joined the assemblage when all shouted *"Semper Augusta"* three times.

Ever curious about the reactions of others, Bodo noted that Lothair, Pepin, Ludwig and certain nobles did not cheer their new empress. Bodo understood why Hugh of Tours and other magnates whose daughters had been rejected might be unhappy, but he could not understand how anyone could dislike Judith.

During the feasting that followed, Bodo observed Priscus enjoying the company of a woman dressed in a fur lined brown mantle and white headdress with a veil lifted to expose a face no less lovely than Judith's, but of different features and complexion. Beneath her open mantle, a gold pectoral cross covered the front of her tunic.

Bodo went to Count Abraham. "Sire, who is that pretty lady Priscus is speaking to? Is she his *concubita*?"

"No, Bodo, she is Alpaïs, Lay Abbess of Saint Peter in Rheims. She is the emperor's daughter through his now deceased *concubita*, Theodelinde."

Priscus and Alpaïs stood close to each other. Smiles never left their faces.

"Count Abraham, it is obvious they like each other. Are they going to wed?"

"I suggest you wait for Priscus to bring up the subject of Alpaïs, if he so chooses."

13. Palace Academy

After Judith and Louis wed, Bodo began his studies in the Palace Academy. His classmates included sons of nobles and foaled intelligent boys like Strabo who had been recommended by their abbots and bishops. The palace supplied their shirts, drawers, trousers, tunics, mantles, cloaks, stockings, gloves, boots, and shoes all of the same brown and beige colors but of good quality. Judith provided more colorful clothes for him when he served as principal page at her functions.

Bodo took instruction in sacred and secular learning from members of the clergy and lay scholars under the general supervision of Chamberlain Helisachar. The *Nutritii* had to memorize The Lord's Prayer and The Apostles' Creed in Latin, which Bodo had learned from Strabo, passages from the Gospels, and writings of the Church Fathers.

Priscus taught Bodo Latin from the Romans and Gallican vulgate *biblia*, individual illustrated books from the Old and New Testaments, lives of saints, and psalters containing the Psalms. Textural debates and investigation into Old Testament books the older students studied interested Bodo the most, but battles fought by the Hebrews were his favorite stories. The priests and monks would not explain why rabbis came to the palace to explain Jewish biblical exegesis so the clerics could better understand the historical context of the Old Testament.

Bodo thrived in the Palace Academy. Outstanding in studies, he became popular with his fellow students, whom he helped with their lessons. He preferred the secular curricula derived from the Seven Liberal Arts of the Greeks and Romans over the religious. The Trivium, or the Three Roads, consisted of Latin Grammar, Rhetoric, and Logic also known as Dialectic. The Quadrivium, called the Four Roads, included Arithmetic, Geometry, Music, and Astronomy.

Priscus gave Bodo most lessons in the palace observatory, library, or the archives whenever possible and introduced him to the rudiments of meteorology, astronomy, and historical research. The Astronomer taught better than the priests and monks. Whenever Bodo questioned the clerics'

Bodo the Apostate

assertions, they refused to answer or became annoyed and told him he was going to Hell.

"Priscus, how can I learn if I do not ask questions?"

"You cannot. Memorizing without understanding is not knowledge. Always feel free to question me. Now, back to the subject at hand. Bodo, philosophy integrates and unites all branches of education. It nourishes the Seven Liberal Arts. You must be exposed to every possible endeavor to learn for which you are best suited."

"For which do you think I am?"

"It is too soon to tell. You alone must answer that question. Where do your inclinations lead you?"

"To be a knight like my father and rise to the rank of count, margrave, or duke. I would like to be a captain of the palace guards too. But I also love learning."

"Consider this. Is it not better to live for the emperor than to die for him in battle?"

"The way you do as his astronomer and advisor?"

Priscus let a slight smile suffice for a response.

During the pause Bodo showed Priscus a letter. "It is from an older boy, a peasant from Bodman, who is studying to be a monk at Reichenau."

"He must like you, for he addressed you as 'My little blond lad.'"

"He always calls me that. One day, I will not be little."

"And he signed it 'Your friend with the twisted-eye.'"

"That is why everyone calls him Strabo."

"An interesting name. Do you understand all he wrote?"

"I think so. Strabo enjoys all he is learning about history, the Gospels, the Greek language, and he likes most his study of metrical verse."

"Poetry."

"Yes, and he advises me to be moral, honorable and a good student. He also writes he is happy to be so well clothed."

"Strabo is fortunate, for it is different at each monastery."

Bodo looked at the letter. "For the year, he is given two shirts, two long cloaks, a hooded vestment, two pair each of drawers, mantles, stockings, and gloves."

"Well done, Bodo. And have you written a response?"

Bodo showed Priscus another paper. "It is the best I could do."

"Not bad, but it needs some corrections. Let me show you."

Bodo had access to every room in the palace and its environs and lived a well-fed pampered life second only to the royals. Although a dormitory had been set aside for the *Nutritii*, he often slept in the empress' suite, Priscus' observatory, or at Welf's home.

Judith told Bodo the emperor favored him because of his charm, manners, and resemblance to Louis' beloved mother, Good Queen Hildegard, and eldest son, King and Co-emperor Lothair. Having assumed responsibility for Adeltrud, Bodo spoke with his sister each day for reassurance that everyone treated her well.

Bodo familiarized himself with the palace hierarchy. The Seneschal supervised the emperor's table, the Butler palace finances, the Constable or Count of the Stable provisioned the horses, and Chamberlain Helisachar, "the second man in the empire" was responsible for securing Louis' treasury of coins, gold, silver, gems, silks and luxury goods.

Priscus introduced Bodo to the palace archives where clerks wrote in cursive Latin and Francique for their correspondences, reports, and royal diplomas. They also guarded the holy relics Louis took with him on his journeys from palace to palace during the year, the most favorite being Saint Martin's cape. Bodo had many questions he wanted to ask about the cape, saints' bones, and splinters from the cross on which Christ was crucified. The priests said they had miraculous powers and answered prayers, all of which seemed identical to the paganism condemned by the Church.

Bodo next followed Priscus into a room the Astronomer called the scriptorium. He admired the illuminated writing on parchment created by monks bent over their desks. Priscus exchanged greetings with several whose names sounded odd to Bodo's ears: Ciaràn, Daíbhi, and Tighearach.

"Such strange names. What land are they from?"

"These men are Celts and come from Ireland across the western sea. Their monks are the best educated and most gifted."

Priscus explained to Bodo that the Carolingian Bible was a revised Vulgate translation by the great scholar Alcuin, who founded the Palace Academy, that he based on Old Latin and Greek. Psalters and *ta biblia*, books, were Gallican versions of individual books of the bible separately bound and commonly used by abbeys, cathedrals, courtly institutions, and literate individuals.

Bodo the Apostate

Massive single-volume Bibles called pandects were expensive to obtain, laborious to produce, rare, and difficult to store. Many abbeys did not have one, and those that did kept the pandect chained and locked in a central area for consultation.

Priscus peered over the shoulder of one elderly illustrator, whose eyes almost touched the parchment. "Precise and excellent work, Tadgh."

"All in the service of our Lord, good Priscus, but this drudgery comes at the expense of my vision."

Bodo did not understand the Irishman's Latin, which had a pleasing musical cadence, until Priscus translated it for him. "I must study harder."

"Bodo, you cannot learn everything at once. Give yourself time, and perhaps you shall eventually."

Bodo hoped to equal Priscus' many interests and wide range of knowledge. Except when observing the heavens, making notes in his study, and mentoring, Priscus advised the emperor on military strategy, tactics, and fortifications and consulted with the royal physician about the efficacies of healing herbs and spices.

"You know much about Medicine. Why is it not included in the Seven Liberal Arts of the Trivium and Quadrivium?"

Priscus reminded Bodo that the Seven Liberal Arts were single subjects each. "To understand and apply healing medicines, a man must know all of them:

"Grammar to explain what he read.

"Rhetoric to support his conclusions with sound arguments.

"Dialectic so that by use of reason he could investigate the cause of sickness for healing purposes.

"Arithmetic to calculate the times of day.

"Geometry so he may teach what a man should know about different places.

"Music for whatever may be done for the sick by this Art.

"Astronomy by which to calculate the stars and changes of seasons because they affected the human body.

"And so, Bodo, that is why Saint Isidore called Medicine the second Philosophy."

"Then I must learn the Art of Medicine too."

"Best you leave that to the physicians, but over time I shall enlighten you about the efficacies of certain herbs and plants." Priscus anticipated Bodo's next question and added, "Efficacy means usefulness in healing."

"Another word for me to remember. Can you spare some paper for me?"

"For what use?"

"I want to list all the words I do not understand and write their meanings so I will remember them."

Priscus opened a cabinet. "Bodo, here are several quartos of paper and a leather envelope to store them, but I doubt if enough paper exists in all the world to satisfy your logophilia, a Greek word for love of words."

Bodo took a writing instrument from Priscus' desk and on one fold of a quarto wrote all the new words he learned today, ending with, efficacy, logophilia, logophile, and their meanings. "There. Now I shall never forget them."

14. Practical Lessons

Bodo's special status and natural curiosity provided a useful education beyond the Trivium and Quadrivium. He had more opportunities than most to be in Louis' presence during informal occasions and festivities, and he attended Judith at banquets she arranged. The empress supervised the decorations and required Hemma, Adeltrud, and other ladies to appear before the guests in Roman dress with garlands in their hair and carrying bouquets of flowers and bowls of fruit.

All said that from the day of his marriage to Judith, the emperor became livelier and less severe although he never showed pleasure or the slightest smile during the entertainments she arranged for him. The behavior of palace officials and great nobles at the emperor's table amused Bodo whenever each proud man groveled and vied for the privilege of drinking from Louis' cup. So did the musicians who played and sang profane music on pipes, cithers and lyres. Mimes made everyone laugh. Jugglers, acrobats, and tumblers thrilled all with their skills.

Bodo often fell asleep when poets competed with long incomprehensible rhymes in the Greek and Latin style to praise Judith's exceptional beauty, vivacity, and grace. He promised himself that after he mastered those two languages whatever he wrote would make sense.

The palace had everything to stimulate Bodo's mind and senses. Were

Bodo the Apostate

it not for his genuine interest and compliments for their skills, his questions might have driven the artisans of the palace to distraction. Instead, they were delighted to show him how they achieved the quality of their work.

At the treasury, minters showed Bodo how to form silver ingots into pound weights and flatten them to the thinness of a silver denarius. They cut the metal into measured squares and hammered them to a round shape. Engravers imprinted a portrait of the emperor, royal seal, or name of the minter on either side. One minter told Bodo if someone was proven guilty of creating false or debased coinage, the authorities cut off a hand. Further disobedience led to a fine of sixty solidi if a free man, sixty lashes if a serf.

Here and not the classroom Bodo learned the three values of money resulting from the reforms of Charlemagne and Louis. They based the pound on the Latin weight for a silver ingot but never minted it for coins. From the ingot, the minters cut with precision two hundred and forty pure silver denarii, the only coin of the realm.

The solidus, worth twelve denarii, became the principal money of account. One pound of silver was worth twenty solidi.

Bodo found it easier to write I solidus than XII denarii and I pound or XX solidi than CXL denarii. Those fixed values helped him understand the bartering system common throughout the empire and how taxation became better regulated. Although prices often varied by region or because of good or bad harvests, one denarius usually could purchase 23 two pound loaves of oats, 20 of barley, 15 of rye, or 12 of wheat. Bodo paid little attention to the prices for farm animals and clothing because he had no land and the palace garbed and fed him.

With his new knowledge of money, Bodo better understood the great cost of becoming a knight when he spoke with the armorers. They confirmed what Conrad had told him. Only the wealthy could afford to be armored, well-armed and own a steed.

Iron helmets might cost seventy-three denarii. Wooden shield with metal strips and lance together seventy-two. A long iron sword, sixty. Scabbard of wood and leather forty-eight and more depending upon decorations. A cuirass, metal armor hammered to conform to a knight's torso, one hundred and forty-four. A knight's horse three hundred and sixty. Lance and buckler fourteen.

Bodo worried not about his ability to achieve knighthood or those costs. Welf promised that when he reached age fifteen, his father's armor, weapons, and money to purchase a steed would be his.

15. Royal Progress

In the spring of 819, Bodo's wish to learn geography through travel instead of reading maps came sooner than he expected. Judith commanded him to serve as her principal page while she accompanied Louis during the annual royal progress that lasted from the week after Easter to the end of October. Between hunts in the vast uninhabited forests, the emperor presided over annual Diets and ceremonial feasts throughout Francia, Alamannia, and Neustria. Bodo's lessons with Priscus continued when the Astronomer was not advising Louis in matters of diplomacy, military tactics, and what the heavens revealed.

Couriers announced Louis' itinerary well in advance of his arrival because several hundred courtiers, provisioners, servants, and soldiers accompanied Their Majesties. Between the royal residences, local lords, bishops, and abbots needed time to prepare ample food and drink, clean lodgings, and have streets and paths swept.

Louis and his predecessors ensured their kingdoms had well cared for roads to speed movement of soldiers, merchandise, and messengers. In good weather when days were longest, the progress averaged twelve miles a day. Delays occurred whenever heavy downpours muddied the roads and caused ruts that damaged wheels and axels. Mansions of great nobles, abbeys, and episcopal palaces could not accommodate Louis' entire retinue, and those of lesser rank lodged in inns and homes of villagers, nearby farms, or in fields.

Each night Bodo slept near the empress' quarters. The diocesan palaces impressed him most. Instead of living in the humble austerity they preached during sermons, bishops lived lavishly in luxurious rooms and interiors painted in bold colors brightened further with glass windows. Their households of servants, lectors, canons, notaries and keepers of hospices numbered greater than those of many lay lords. Prelates hunted the same with weapons, hounds, and falcons and gave feasts with performances by actors, mimes, and poets. Although canon law forbade them to shed

Bodo the Apostate

blood, bishops and abbots donned armor and rode to war.

Bodo discovered that geography and diverse languages divided the empire more than any man-made boundaries. Mountains, dense forests, and rivers separated populations that seldom ventured beyond their farms and villages.

If Alamanni, Saxons. and Bavarians went twenty-five miles in any direction from their homes, they could not understand their fellow tribesmen. Different tongues prevailed throughout the empire. Aquitainians and Alamannic Franconians spoke *lingua romana*, a variation of Latin. Saxon Salzburgers communicated in Roman, and Tyrolians in Ladin. Basques and Bretons had their own unique languages.

Bodo followed Priscus' advice. With Latin and Greek, he concentrated on learning Francique. Government functionaries had to be bi- and tri-lingual. Although Latin, the unifying language of the educated few, was used for administrative documents, Louis preferred to speak and issue edicts in Francique, the dominant regional language of the Franks.

Throughout spring, summer, and autumn, Louis spent most of his time in the chase. Artisans and servants set great tents or built thatched lodgings for Their Majesties' comforts during the annual hunts in the dense uninhabited Charcoal Forest, the Ardennes, and mountains of the Vosges. More chases took place through fir, oak, birch, and maple woods of Alamannia, northern Bavaria and Thuringia.

The emperor and his vassals hunted for more than sport. Their palaces, manses, and villas needed to be well-stocked with meats and furs for the long often harsh winter months. No animal was safe. Louis, Judith, nobles and high clergy hunted stags, boars, aurochs, bears, bison, beaver, and wolves. Falcons brought down scores of game birds. Each night they retired to thatched lodges or leaf and branch covered huts to feast and drink.

Too small and too young to ride, Bodo and other noble boys set traps for small game and ran with the hounds carrying daggers and short boar-spears. He helped skin animals for pelts. Louis and Judith praised him whenever he brought down a faun, a young bear, or a wild hog. Whenever possible, Bodo swam in thawing lakes and rivers despite the biting cold and slept outside to toughen himself for knighthood like the older boys.

From Priscus, who always accompanied the emperor, Bodo learned the names of trees, plants, and flowers and which almonds and mushrooms were safe to eat or poisonous. The empress sent Bodo into woods and fields to gather seasonal fruits and nuts for her table. Adeltrud, Hemma, and other ladies of the Court collected flowers for scent and decoration.

Wherever the emperor stopped, his men foraged for food to supplement the meat and birds they consumed during the hunt and for hay to feed their horses. Climate and soil determined what people ate. Bodo tasted everything, regional potages and broths, even an Alamannian soldiers' stew of greens and vegetables boiled in animal stomachs or intestines. Most of all, he enjoyed roasted meat and fish prepared with creative sauces, bread with generous portions of butter and honey, apples, pears, chestnuts, and fruit pies.

Because grapes did not thrive in harsh northern climates, beer, ale, and mead replaced the wine commonly imbibed in the south. The same held true for olives, an expensive import, and the populations extracted oil instead from the poppy and nuts.

Along with hunting and feasting, Bodo looked forward to the legal courts held in fields or public squares, where Louis or ranking magnates and prelates heard cases and meted punishments, most often fines to prevent feuding and vengeance by the offended parties:

12 solidi for cutting off an entire thumb, 6 if only the first joint is severed.

10 solidi for cutting off the second finger, 3 for the third, 5 for the fourth, and 10 for the fifth finger.

A grave robber had to return the stolen goods and pay 80 solidi.

Bodo found fines for mistreatment of women to be the most curious: 6 solidi for uncovering the head of a free unmarried woman, 12 solidi for lifting her dress and exposing her genitalia or buttocks, 40 solidi for rape if she was single and 80 solidi if married.

Even at pilgrimage centers, women sold their favors despite Louis' capitulary: any man caught housing a prostitute had to carry her on his shoulders to the market place where she faced a public scourging. If the man refused, he suffered the same punishment. Some sentences were designed to shame and humiliate the guilty party such as the Alamannian *hamscara*, when the judge ordered a criminal to be saddled and ridden like a horse. The imperial legal system made Bodo more impatient to master Latin so he could read and understand his tribe's written codes, *Lex Alamannorum* and *Pactus Alamannorum*.

More than at Court, Bodo saw for himself during the progresses how favored and privileged a life he led. He passed farms where serfs, freemen, and slaves worked the soil from sunrise to sundown, driving oxen ahead of crude plows, swinging their scythes at grains, and digging the ground for planting. Most lived in hovels with diets that barely gave them sustenance while he lived at Court well fed and clothed free to study and prepare for knighthood.

At Mainz and Verdun, Bodo watched slave traders bring chained and miserable pagans from conquered lands of the Slavs and others farther east to be auctioned for local magnates and prosperous landowners, or continue south to Muslim Hispania. Bodo thanked the Thunderer he had been *geboren* unlike boys close to his age selected to be castrated for their future Saracen masters.

Bodo heard certain clerics complain that Jewish counts and landowners in Septimania and the environs of Lyon had Christian serfs and pagan slaves whom Louis' charters forbade the Church to proselyte. By now Bodo noted that Count Abraham did not participate in the hunts or appear whenever Louis met with the bishops. If the population of the empire made war, labored, or prayed, what place did the Jews have?

16. Return to Bodman

Late spring of 820, Louis moved his court to Bodman for a month of boating and fishing in the Bodensee. Even at Bodman the business of ruling an empire continued. No matter where the emperor resided or hunted, he dispatched couriers and sent *missi*, emissaries, to carry out his commands.

Bodo did not recognize his former home, which royal architects and artisans had transformed into a luxurious palace. A visit to the graves of their parents with Adeltrud further saddened him. Bodo questioned why his mother had to die so young and lamented his father's passing. He should have been at Count Gunzo's bedside to comfort his father.

At the kennels, his bleak mood vanished. Bardulf barked recognition, leaped into Bodo's arms almost knocking him down, and licked his face. They played throw and retrieve with a stick and wrestled.

Bodo ran with the wolf-dog across the field and into the woods chasing hares and squirrels. When exhausted, they slept together against the great oak on which he had carved his assertion and name.

Bodo had a second joyful reunion when he accompanied Louis and Judith to Reichenau Abbey and visited with Strabo. His friend seemed happy studying and working in the vegetable and herb gardens. Bodo surprised Strabo with his progress in Latin, Greek and various subjects of the Trivium and Quadrivium far beyond what most boys of eight learned.

Bodo romped and hunted daily with Bardulf in the woods, and after tiring they slept at their usual place under the great oak. He often dreamed but remembered nothing afterward.

No dream today, barking and grunting awakened Bodo. He opened his eyes and saw Bardulf battling a wild boar twice the wolf-dog's size. Bodo watched horrified when the swine's tusk ripped open Bardulf's gut. In a blind rage, Bodo thrust his spear deep into the boar's throat and stabbed the animal again and again long after it died.

His clothes soaked in boar's blood but calmer, Bodo went to Bardulf, still alive and suffering on the ground. He hesitated even though he knew what had to be done. Bodo had seen strong men weep when they dispatched their beloved injured horses and hounds with mallet blows to the head. Best he end Bardulf's suffering in an instant. Bidding farewell to his loyal companion, Bodo slit the wolf-dog's throat.

What to do next? Bodo did not want to leave Bardulf to be found and devoured by carrion or buried to become food for worms and maggots. Grieving and remembering all the times they wrestled, swam, and ran in the woods Bodo cut enough branches to make a small raft and tied them with vines. He set Bardulf atop the bier, secured the wolf-dog as well, and covered its carcass with dry brush.

Bodo needed all his strength to drag the burden to the Bodensee where he lit a fire, set the branches aflame, and undressed. Naked, Bodo pushed the raft into the water and swam beside the craft until it sank.

Companion of my boyhood, I have given you the warrior's funeral you deserve. I shall never forget you.

The fire must have caught the emperor's notice. By the time Bodo swam to shore, Louis, Judith, and several Court officials stood by his clothes.

"Bodo, why are your clothes bloodied? What is it you have burned?"

"Sire, I gave Bardulf an Alamannic warrior's funeral."

"Why?"

Bodo dressed and recounted how Bardulf died and his slaying of the boar.

"Show us your kill."

"Follow me, Your Majesties."

When they reached the boar, all praised Bodo for his courage. Louis counted the dagger wounds. "So many, Bodo. You must have been fierce as a Viking Berserker."

"It killed my dog."

Louis summoned his forester. "Behead the boar. Add it to the others on the walls in the great hall. We shall feast on its meat. Well done, brave lad, well done."

When the time came to depart Bodman, Bodo bade silent farewell to Bardulf surprised that this time he did not regret leaving his former home. A wider more exciting world lay before him.

17. Contra Human Nature

Bodo preferred his lessons from Priscus to the dogmatic instructions given by monks and priests. In corridors and rooms at Aachen, certain clerics disgusted Bodo when they begged and bribed to gain a monastery or abbey, not for spiritual reasons, but for the income the sinecure provided. Others ridiculed and condemned noble knights for the sins of fighting, gluttony, drinking, and lust. Yet, at many a feast, Bodo saw the same bishops, abbots, and priests gorging and imbibing beyond capacity. Many broke their vows of celibacy and had wives or *concubitae* and children both legitimate and illegitimate.

Worse, on several occasions Bodo encountered clergy fornicating in the palace at Aachen like dogs in heat, even in the royal chapel. All those transgressions confused and appalled Bodo because he valued oaths to the emperor and God to be inviolable. When he complained about it to Priscus, the Astronomer taught him a new word in all its grammatical forms: hypocrisy.

A personal confrontation alienated Bodo from the clergy. One occurred when a friar gave the *Nutritii* lessons about the Apocalypse in the royal chapel at Aachen. Some cowered in fear at their instructor's vivid descriptions of the Beast and horrors to come, but not Bodo. The Apocalypse was similar to the Ragnarök, old folk tales sung by the bards describing destruction by the gods, submersion of the earth in water like the story of Noah, and its regeneration.

When the friar pointed a finger at the cupola to name and identify the Elders of the Apocalypse portrayed there, a classmate emitted an extended fart, which infuriated the cleric. He chided the culprit for disrespect, the entire class for laughing, and concluded his tirade with a common monkish homily, "Remember this, children, Christ never laughed."

Bodo stepped forward. "You friars and priests always say that. Where is it written in the Gospels that Christ never laughed?"

"How dare you question me."

"I question everyone and everything because I want to know. You say Christ never laughed? Show us proof in the Gospels."

"Foolish child. Nowhere in the Gospels does Christ laugh. That is the proof."

"But do they say He forbade laughter? Does God forbid laughter? If we are made in His image, and we laugh, then God must laugh too."

The monk screeched over the boys' laughter, "You blasphemous puppy. You deserve a severe beating for your insolence."

"At your peril," Bodo countered and unsheathed his dagger, the way he had heard and seen knights respond to a challenge. "Is that how you teach? The way the Church forced the Alamanni and Saxons to be Christians? By the sword?"

The monk shrank before Bodo and pointed to an exit. "You. Out. Leave this chapel now. I shall see to it that you are removed from the Palace Academy."

"It is you who should be removed. You do not know how to teach."

Bodo the Apostate

In the observatory, Priscus listened to Bodo's account of his confrontation with the monk. "You asked an honest question and instead of answering he threatened you with a beating?"

"Yes. That's why I drew my dagger."

"The friar has demanded your expulsion from the academy."

"My Uncle Welf and Empress Judith will prevent it."

"Yes, I am sure they will because you are under their aegis."

"Aegis?"

"A Greek word, meaning shield, protection."

"How do you spell it?"

"Alpha, epsilon, gamma, iota, sigma."

"Then I must learn more Greek too. That monk never answered my questions. Can you?"

Priscus lowered his voice. "I can assure you that in His human form Christ would have laughed, but at what, no one can say. However, there is something you should know about priests, friars, and monks. I shall try to explain it in words an eight year old can understand. Ask me questions if you do not."

"I will, Priscus. You know I will."

The Astronomer explained that the followers of Benedict were known as black monks because of their garb. Their obsession with mastery of the self and fear of immoderate laughter threatened their ability to control the body. Although they believed joyful laughter happened in heaven, it would be laughter of the soul, not lascivious, corporeal laughter.

Bodo did not understand how a soul could laugh without the body, but he chose not to interrupt Priscus who further explained that the monks permitted laughter provided its object was pious and dignified. They taught that insulting, abusive, and defamatory laughter was idle and pointless, incompatible with prayer and proper reverence for the suffering of Christ, for it illustrated lack of moderation and loss of self-control.

Bodo detested most of all the monks and friars because they attacked something most dear to his heart, a good laugh. He remembered the fun he had with Strabo at Bodman, Impossible his friend would disapprove of a hearty laugh.

"Bodo, many aspire to emulate Saint Martin, of whom it is said, no one ever saw angered, excited, grieving, or laughing. You must understand that Louis' spiritual advisor, Benedict of Aniane, preaches that laughter exemplifies the sin of pride."

"I was not prideful when I laughed at my classmate's fart. It happened without my thinking."

"Of course it did. And at what else do you laugh?"

"That is easier to answer. Mimes and jesters make me laugh. So did my classmate Santfrid's fart in the chapel … and the expression on the friar's face when he did. Everyone laughed."

Priscus wrote four words in Latin and their various forms. "You must add these to your vocabulary and remember their meanings. We laugh at the absurd, the ridiculous, the satirical, and incongruity."

Bodo listened to Priscus' explanation of each word. "I think I understand."

"Then consider this. Your monkish teacher, enters the chapel, slips, and falls on his posterior. Ah, you laughed. But, what if your sister, Empress Judith, or someone else you love or have befriended had the same fall. Would you laugh then?"

"No, I would run to help them."

"Of course you would, so why we laugh is a matter of perspective, another word for you to know and understand. We laugh at incongruities and the unexpected."

"Priscus, will I ever know as much as you?"

"My greatest wish is for you to know more."

"I wish books existed that contained all words with their definitions."

Priscus gave Bodo several blank quartos of paper. "To add to your compilation."

"Thank you."

"Is there something else?"

"Yes, you said one day you would tell me how you came to Aachen from a land so far away."

"I might as well, or else you will continue to ask me the same question each day."

Bodo moved his chair closer to Priscus so he would not miss a single word.

Bodo the Apostate

Born in 790, Priscus came from a pagan family that lived in a land beyond Persia near a river called the Indus. A Master of Elephants, his father served the great Caliph, Haroun al-Rashid, who brought people of all religions to his court based upon merit. Priscus revealed to Bodo his fitting birth name Ganapati, Leader of Elephants in his peoples' language.

At that time, Count Abraham's father Isaac was both Merchant of the Palace and Charlemagne's ambassador to Haroun al-Rashid, Caliph of Baghdad. Their purpose was to ally with the Abbasid Muslim Caliphate against their mutual enemy, the Ummayad emirs, who controlled North Africa and Hispania.

During an exchange of presents Caliph Haroun al-Rashid gifted an elephant for Charlemagne named Abul-Abbas. Priscus' father rode and cared for the beast during the journey from Baghdad to Aachen. He took his only child, Ganapati, with him because he had no wife.

The difficult journey included transporting Abul-Abbas by boat across the Mediterranean. Priscus' father and all court officials who accompanied Isaac and Abraham died along the way from mishaps and sickness.

Twelve year old Priscus rode and cared for Abul-Abbas from Marseilles to Aachen. After the elephant caused a sensation at Court, Charlemagne installed the beast in his royal menagerie. Impressed by Ganapati's intelligence, he had the boy baptized Priscus and educated in his Palace Academy. By age fourteen Priscus became renowned as a prodigy who understood the stars and planets better than anyone at Court. Shortly after Louis' accession, he made Priscus the Royal Astronomer.

"So, Bodo, that is how and why I came to Aachen. Have I satisfied your curiosity?"

"What happened to the elephant?"

"In 810 Charlemagne took us on a military campaign. Abul-Abbas was ill with rheumatism and had more than forty years of age. He died before any battle began. Anything else you want to know?"

"Almost. Is there one you love? Have you ever married, or do you have a *concubita*?"

Bodo's abrupt change of subject caused Priscus to frown. "There are private matters of another's personal life you should never know."

Despite Priscus' admonition, Bodo hoped to learn why each time the royal progress stopped at Rheims Priscus visited the Abbey of Saint Peter.

Was it to meet with Alpaiïs, its beautiful Abbess and illegitimate daughter of Louis? He never forgot how they had looked at each other during the feasting that day when Judith wed Louis.

18. "Sweet Cheeks"

Bodo's second unpleasant encounter with a cleric occurred during a chilly February morning in 821. Torches and candles everywhere made the short grey days and long nights bearable. So did the thermal pool where he bested his cousin Rudolf in a swim along the sixty foot length of the great pool.

"Your mind is elsewhere, Dolfo, otherwise you would have won."

"No, you always do."

"What troubles you?"

"I will never be able to count the way you did in class today."

"Let me show you." Bodo sat with his cousin on the edge of the pool. "Observe how I fold the last three fingers of my left hand on the palm. Each way I move my forefinger and thumb indicate the numbers. Now, on my right hand, I fold the fingers like this for hundreds and this way for thousands. For tens and hundreds of thousands, I touch my chest, navel, and thigh. In that way, I can reach one million."

"I cannot picture a million of anything." Rudolf scratched his head. "Bodo, I will never learn large numbers. Those problems posed as riddles confuse me more. I still do not understand how to answer to the one our teacher posed today."

Neither had most students. The problem was simple for Bodo. Three boys each had a sister. The six of them arrived at a river where a single boat could transport only two. Because morality dictated each sister travel with her brother, how were they able to accomplish it?

"Let me show you, Dolfo. "Two boys row ...."

"No, Bodo. It will do no good. My head is spinning." Rudolf stood. "I am going to the gymnasium to take an easier lesson from one of the masters of arms. Are you coming with me?"

"Not this time. I prefer the pool on so cold a day."

While Rudolf dressed, Bodo swam the length of the pool and back. By then, his cousin had left, but he was not alone. A handsome young

Bodo the Apostate

priest Bodo had not seen before stared at him with the same expression he had seen on the faces of men when they desired a woman. When the cleric licked his lips, Bodo left the pool and dressed.

"You swim like a fish, Sweet Cheeks."

Bodo ignored the priest. He hurried from the baths and found Priscus in the palace observatory making charts of the stars from a strange device.

"What is that, Priscus?"

"An astrolabe."

"Star-taker?"

"You are learning your Greek well, the same as you have done with Latin and Francique. Bodo, Count Bernard brought this astrolabe to the emperor for a gift. He seized it with other booty in a raid against the Saracens south of Barcelona. It is more precise than anything I have seen. Look here, Bodo, this astrolabe has angular scales and circles to indicate azimuths on the horizon. I can now record with more accuracy the times of sunrises, rising of fixed stars, to locate and predict the positions of the Sun, Moon, planets, cast horoscopes, and use it for navigation and surveying. We must make copies. But what are you doing here? We have no lesson scheduled today."

Bodo told Priscus about the priest. The Astronomer frowned. "Sweet Cheeks he called you? Beware of such men who prefer boys to women. The sin of lust clouds all judgment."

"I shall report him to Judith and the emperor."

"No, Bodo, the emperor and empress have gone into mourning. An hour ago, Louis learned that his spiritual mentor, Benedict of Aniane, passed on. Anyway, from your description, I believe the priest is Theobald, kin to Helisachar. He has other powerful patrons at court who are seeking a benefice for him."

"But I am kin to the emperor and empress."

"Were there witnesses?"

"No."

"He will deny he spoke to you."

"Then what can I do?"

"Be alert. Have your dagger at the ready, especially when you are in bed at night. Try always to be in the company of other boys or men you trust."

Bodo often saw Theobald lurking near the *Nutritii* and eying him, but several months passed without another incident until one evening after Lent. Before he fell asleep in the student dormitory, Bodo found a sheet of paper under his pillow. He took it to the nearest candle and read an unsigned poem written in Latin addressed to Sweet Cheeks. It contained many words he had not learned but was able to make sense of it. The priest described him more beautiful than any girl and praised every aspect of his hairless physicality. Bodo became angry at being called beautiful and compared to a girl. He read further that his hair was brighter than gold, green eyes more luminous than any gem, the sight of his face radiant and so filled with beauty, it set the priest's heart aflame with love.

The last part of the letter was filled with advice and a plea. Bodo's flowering youth would soon wither, his smooth, milky, tender flesh covered with coarse ugly hair, and skin become rough, so now was the best time to grant an eager lover his wish.

Bodo did not understand other words and phrases. He lay awake until morning, and after lauds, he showed the letter to Priscus. "It is from Theobald."

"Despicable. Did you understand everything?"

"Most of the words."

"He used some you are too young to understand. Theobald has not bothered you since?"

"Not yet. What shall I do?"

Shouting outside and sounds of people running interrupted them. A servant rushed into the observatory. "My Lord Priscus, the emperor summons you. Her Majesty has gone into labor."

19. Lothairians

A new order in Bodo's life replaced his comfortable years at Bodman with the seasonal regularity of royal progresses and hunts, festivals, feast days, and lessons. At the same time, he studied the behavior of men no less than the academic curricula and geography.

On instinct, Bodo judged people at first meeting or observation and separated them into three categories: those he liked and who meant him

Bodo the Apostate

well such as Louis, Judith, Priscus and Count Abraham, those he disliked or mistrusted, mostly clerics, and those who left him indifferent or beneath notice.

Concerning his family, Bodo loved Adeltrud and trusted her with his life. He adored Judith who did so much for him. He liked Rudolf even though the boy lacked swiftness of mind. Bodo could not warm to his oldest cousin Conrad, who reacted to his questions with obvious annoyance and whose arrogance made many enemies when he inserted himself at tables and in processions ahead of greater nobles and prelates. Aunt Heilwig had no impact on his life after he became one of the *Nutritii*. Hemma used him as a messenger in an exchange of notes with King Ludwig. Welf continued to baffle Bodo without clear cause. He liked his uncle but instinctively mistrusted him.

Bodo did not have time to dwell on his uncle. In May of 821, Judith gave birth to a girl baptized Giséle, which disappointed the empress, Louis, and Welf. While the empress lay abed unable to advise the emperor to the contrary, Louis made concessions to ecclesiastic and lay supporters of Lothair during the annual May Diet convened at Nijmegen. These men, whom Bodo now labeled Lothairians, feared the young empress might give birth to a son next time and demand he be given a portion of the empire.

To prevent a further partition of lands should that happen, Chamberlain Helisachar led a majority of prelates and nobles to Nijmegen. They pressured Louis to confirm for a second time the 817 Division of Empire and Lothair's status as co-emperor. They went further, and Louis agreed to their other demands. He summoned to court those he exiled or banished to monasteries in 818 for conspiring against him and restored their titles and honors.

One former exile impressed Bodo above all others by his regal bearing and reputation, forty-nine year old Count Wala, a grandson of Charles Martel. During Charlemagne's last years, Wala served as both Steward of the Royal Household and Administrator of Royal Justice, counsel for the emperor, commander of the army, and regent for Lothair's predecessor, ill-fated King Bernard of Italy, when Louis' nephew was a minor. In essence, Wala had been de facto ruler of the empire, and he had expected to continue as such during Louis' reign.

At Nijmegen Louis made Count Wala Abbot of Corbie near Amiens and his cousin's elder brother Adelard Abbot of Corvey in Saxony. He gave permission for Lothair to wed Irmingard, daughter of "Jug ears," Count Hugh of Tours, lay leader of the Lothairians. The emperor arranged another marriage for his second son Pepin of Aquitaine to Ingletrud of Madrie, daughter of a distant cousin.

Louis ended the monastic exiles of twenty-one year old Drogo and sixteen year old Hugo, his loyal bastard half-brothers, sons of Charlemagne. Queen Irmingard had pressured her husband to tonsure and imprison the brothers because she feared he favored them over her sons. When Drogo and Hugo arrived at Nijmegen, the emperor prostrated himself at their feet and begged for forgiveness.

Separate from his list of new words and their meanings, Bodo wrote cursively in idiomatic and phonetic Alaman the name of each prelate and noble who sought Louis' abdication. Many Lotharians came from the clergy. Led by Bishop Agobard of Lyon, they had specific goals: diminish the influence and power of Jews, expand the authority of the Church over the emperor, and institute monastic and diocesan reforms. Bodo believed the emperor's foster brother Ebbo bore watching. Although the Archbishop of Rheims had not indicated support for the Lotharians, Bodo saw hatred in Ebbo's eyes whenever the prelate looked at Louis.

The clergy's lay allies included Louis' sons.

Lothair aspired to be sole emperor.

Pepin sought more autonomy.

Now seventeen, Ludwig confided to Bodo his impatience to reside in his Kingdom of Bavaria, govern it independent of his father and Welf, and wed Hemma.

Bodo labeled the most prominent Lotharian lay nobles, Counts Hugh, Lantbert, and Matfrid, as "the Unholy Trinity," so virulent was their hatred of Louis and Judith. Hugh of Tours had served as Charlemagne's advisor and envoy to the Byzantine Emperor but held no equivalent position under Louis. Matfrid of Orleans, a protégé of Bishop Agobard and a current member of Louis' council, and Lantbert of Nantes, typical of other great magnates, believed they would gain more honors and autonomy if Louis abdicated.

As best Bodo knew, the emperor's faction included the Welfings, nobles and clergy favored by Louis and Judith, Priscus and other Court officials, Count Bernard of Septimania and his kin, Abraham and the Jews. He added Drogo and Hugo because they bore no animosity and professed loyalty toward Louis.

Bodo the Apostate

Bodo was not certain which faction would prevail. Despite his loyalty to Louis, he concurred with the Lothairians that the emperor tended to vacillate, another new word he learned from Priscus, but he did not think it was reason enough for Louis to abdicate.

To his regret, Bodo believed what many said of Louis to be true. No ruler before him was ever so generous with grants of land and abbeys to those who professed loyalty even though they had gone back on their word before. Bodo lost count of offenders whom Louis punished severely when angered, yet forgave and restored their titles and lands.

20. Two Clerics

Not until early April did the winter of 821-822 end and spring thaws begin. Louis' mood changed with the weather from one of contrition to anger. He blamed Helisachar for pressuring him to renew the Division of 817, removed his chamberlain from office, and proclaimed a sentence of banishment from Court. Yet, he gave Helisachar the Abbey of Saint Riquier in Picardy. Then, against advice from Judith and Welf, Louis appointed the Lothairian Hilduin, Abbot of Saint-Denis and Saint Medard, to be Arch-chaplain of the Palace with duties to rule over the clergy and be the emperor's chief advisor in religious matters.

Hilduin's arrival at Court distressed Bodo, who abhorred any change in the order of things. A muscular man who seemed to be more warrior than abbot, the new arch-chaplain accepted added authority and a second title from the emperor, Archbishop of the Sacred Palace. Hilduin became responsible for recommending candidates to be bishop and abbot and for presiding over assemblies during religious and liturgical debates.

Hilduin brought with him to Court his protégé Hincmar, a sixteen year old priest who came from a noble family connected to Hugh of Tours. Intelligent, scholarly, and soft of face and body, Hincmar gave lessons to Bodo and the *Nutritii* in Canon Law, the Gospels, and writings of church elders. The well-fed priest held extreme prejudices against Judith. So did Hilduin, who within days of his arrival at the palace summoned all academy students to the smaller clerical chapel.

Bodo fumed while the arch-chaplain sermonized:

"You are the great hope of the future because impurity, adultery, and sacrilege have turned the empire into a cesspool of immorality. Dioceses and abbeys have been awarded to coarse drunkards. They are given from father to son. That has led to venality, corruption, without any sense of clerical morality and calling. How can it be otherwise when these brutish lustful men set the worst possible examples for the clergy who serve under them?"

Bodo already lacked respect for Hilduin because the arch-chaplain collected saints' bones, pieces of their clothing, splinters from the True Cross, icons, and believed they performed miracles. More than anyone in the empire Hilduin looted holy relics from churches and abbeys to expand his enormous collection. Now Bodo despised the arch-chaplain for his ingratitude and disloyalty to Louis who had raised him to a great height.

After the sermon, Hincmar confronted Bodo while Hilduin watched and listened. "The priests and monks have warned us about you and your blasphemous questions. We will not tolerate any more of that or spying for your kinswoman, that wicked Jezebel."

Tempted to strike the priest for slandering Judith, Bodo thought better of it. He walked away without a word and later added Hincmar's name to the Lothairians.

But what about Lothair? Bodo had yet to have direct contact with Louis' eldest son. Did Lothair aspire to replace Louis as much as his supporters wanted? Bodo looked forward to meeting the King of Italy so he might judge for himself who would be a better emperor.

21. Unexpected Foe

Late spring before his tenth birthday, Bodo began training for knighthood at Bodman where Louis and Judith resided for several weeks of fishing and boating. Masters of Arms instructed Bodo and Rudolf in the sword, bow and arrow, battle ax, dagger, wrestling, horsemanship, and the chase. This day it was the sword, and the Master of Arms' voice beat a steady rhythm for Bodo and Rudolf: "Strike, raise shield to defend. Strike. Defend. Strike ...."

Bodo's blows drove Rudolf across the field until his cousin fell and cried out, "I yield."

Bodo the Apostate

The Master of Arms praised Bodo and set him against several older boys who fared no better than Rudolf.

Conrad, drunk as usual, intervened and took Rudolf's wooden sword. "Let us see how well you can do against a real knight."

The Master of Arms stepped between them. "Count Conrad, Bodo is still a boy. You are taller, stronger, and more experienced with weapons. It is not knightly to challenge Bodo and unwise too, for there is no glory for any knight if he defeats a mere boy. And there is the potential for you to be humiliated if he wins or fights to a draw."

Conrad cuffed the Master of Arms, pushed him aside and slurred, "I am brother of the empress. No lowborn oaf can tell me what I can or cannot do."

Bodo measured his reeling older cousin, half a head taller at five feet six inches and remembered his father's advice: "When someone threatens you, strike first and hard. Better to make a mistake and apologize than to lose and beg for mercy."

Bodo did not wait to be attacked. He summoned all his strength and struck Conrad's sword arm. The weapon fell, and so did Conrad when Bodo tripped him.

"Yield, cousin."

Enraged by his defeat and the ridicule coming from other knights, Conrad brushed aside Bodo's sword. He stood and reached for his dagger. "I will teach you a …."

A larger more powerful man seized Conrad's arm. "Bodo can learn nothing from you, but perhaps you should become his pupil. Now, I command you. Apologize to the Master of Arms. You had no right to strike him."

More laughter came from all who witnessed Bodo's triumph, but Conrad did as told before he fled the field with Rudolf.

"Well done, Bodo. You are truly Count Gunzo's son."

Bodo heard familiar sounds in the distance. Had the Thunderer granted his wish to meet Lothair, a strapping blond with intense blue eyes?

The King of Italy gripped Bodo's shoulders. "Your father, Count Gunzo, would have been proud of you. He was a great warrior and taught me how better to wield my sword. Your face, it must be true. Everyone says you look as I did when I was your age. Refresh my memory and remind me how we are related."

"My maternal great aunt was the sister of your grandmother, Good Queen Hildegard."

"Now I remember. How old are you?"

"I shall be ten next week."

"Five years away from knighthood, yet tall and strong for a boy your age."

At about five feet, Bodo aspired be to be six feet, the same height Gunzo his father had been.

"Well, young Bodo if you realize your potential, I would be pleased to have you at my court and ride beside me into battle and during the chase."

"You honor me."

Bodo did not speak his true thoughts. He liked Lothair but could serve only Louis and Judith. To do otherwise would be dishonorable.

"In the meantime, beware of Conrad. Men of his reputation and behavior such as we saw moments ago can be dangerous enemies even to their own kin."

Bodo had marked Conrad as a foe the moment his cousin threatened him. The only question was why. They never exchanged harsh words until today. Was it because he bested Rudolf at studies and arms?

Conrad absented himself from Court and returned to his lands rather than face more ridicule. Judith never questioned what happened between Bodo and her eldest brother.

22. Stimulating Summer

Another cleric arrived at Court. Bodo did not yet know if Helisachar's replacement as Louis' *camerarius*, Abbot Fridugis of Saint Martin in Tours was loyal to Their Majesties or a Lothairian. That was the question he asked Priscus.

The Astronomer offered Bodo a pear from a basket of fruit on his desk. "Time will tell. Fridugis was the favorite pupil and later a protégé of Alcuin, who founded the Palace Academy. He replaced Alcuin upon his mentor's death and taught me."

Bodo waited to hear more about Louis' new chamberlain, but Priscus seemed lost in thought, a pleasing one to judge by the Astronomer's smile. "What amuses you so?"

"I was remembering an interesting mental exercise Fridugis created."

"I should like to hear it."

"I always enjoy testing the limits of your intelligence. I shall ask you the same question Fridugis posed for me. Is nothing something or not?"

"That is silly. How can nothing be something?"

"Nothing is a noun, and according to Aristotle that means it is the name of *some thing*. Fridugis then asked us what type of thing is Nothing, the implication being this. Nothing must be something great, because our world, each creature, each man, everything, was created *ex nihilio*, out of Nothing. That is why one must conclude Nothing is remarkable, the source of something and everything."

"Please stop, Priscus. Your description of nothing, something, and everything has turned my brain to gruel. Such exercises do not help me learn to which faction Chamberlain Fridugis belongs."

"Perhaps it is best you consider him to be a cypher when it comes to factions. Bodo, why do you laugh?"

"If a cypher is nothing, does it not imply that Fridugis must be someone great?"

Bodo left Priscus still confused by their discussion of Nothing and whether to place Fridugis as a Lothairian or not. Perhaps Louis made the abbot his chamberlain in name only to avoid giving so much power to a more ambitious man, and Judith was the true "second person" in the empire.

Bodo's training for knighthood, his continuing lessons from Priscus, and serving Judith prevented him from visiting Strabo at Reichenau Abbey. Just as well. He had not changed his mind about abbeys and monasteries, all of them gloomy places filled with humorless clerics unlike certain episcopal palaces that were true dens of pleasure. At Aachen and other palaces, Bodo did not allow dour clergy to spoil his enjoyment of a jest, riddles, playing and listening to music, or watching mimes, jugglers and acrobats. That was why he sought the company of those who enjoyed a good laugh, and he looked forward most to the empress' feasts and entertainments.

Mastering arms, free to expand his knowledge and vocabulary, and favored by Their Majesties and King Lothair, Bodo could not imagine anyone leading a better life. Still, he faced frustrations, minor though they might be.

Throughout the summer of his tenth birthday, Bodo wished he had the ability to write poems or compose songs when Judith's admirers vied to create laudatory odes and ballads to her beauty. Painters and sculptors also competed to reproduce the empress' perfection of face and form. None succeeded, and she had their efforts destroyed.

Bodo continued to find it odd that the empress' devotees never offered comparisons to women from the New Testament or any of the saints. Instead, they likened her to Helen of Troy, Aphrodite, and Venus from the Greeks and Romans, and from the Hebrews Miriam, Esther, Rachael, the biblical Judith, and many more.

For those reasons, Bodo wanted to learn more about the Jews, whose history and presence Louis and many at Court admired but repelled a hostile minority in the clergy. Several of the empress' ladies in attendance and favored by Judith came from Jewish families, including Count Abraham's eldest daughter Deborah, whose nose was too big and skin too dark for Bodo's standard of female beauty.

One evening during a feast, Judith's sister Hemma, with a wicked expression, read aloud to the empress and her coterie the poet Sedulius' praise of Lothair's bride Irmingard, eldest daughter of Count Hugh of Tours:

"Her voice is pure as gold and clear as the note of a cither.
Her skin is as roses mixed in snow.
Her blonde hair circles her head like a chrysolith.
Her eyes are lively.
Her white neck like milk, lilies, ivory.
Her graceful hands are like the snow."

Judith's adoring poets, musicians, and admirers heaped scorn upon Sedulius' efforts:
"So much snow."

Bodo the Apostate

"A chrysolith? He does not know his colors."

Bodo contributed: "Sedulius is one blind poet who is no Homer."

Judith beckoned Bodo closer and tapped his shoulder with a rose. "Such wit and humor for one so young. We hereby knight you our principal courtier."

Bodo responded with an exaggerated bow and kissed her hand. "And one day, Your Majesty, I shall be your first knight and champion."

23. Self-Mortification

In August of 822, Bodo and Priscus accompanied the emperor and empress to Attigny on the Aisne in the Ardennes, but not for a typical season of hunting. Louis' capitulations at Nijmegen left the Lothairians unsatisfied and emboldened. Helisachar and Count-Abbots Wala and Adelard sermonized and insisted Louis atone for causing his nephew Bernard's death, for their own mistreatment, and for all woes his policies brought upon the empire and its subjects. Arch-chaplain Hilduin warned the emperor he faced eternal damnation unless he acceded to their demands at a Diet in Attigny.

Despite Welf's and Judith's cogent arguments to disregard the prelates' attempts to gain supremacy over the Crown, the emperor's irrational piety dominated all reason. Judith expressed her concerns about emperor's recurring nightmares in which Bernard's ghost appeared with blood oozing from the blinded king's eyes. Was remorse the cause of Louis' tears during prayers in the chapel?

The Lotharians planned well. Louis' three sons would be present, and Lothair brought Pope Paschal I from Italy to pronounce all penances. Judith refused to be present at the emperor's submission to His Holiness and witness his chastisement.

At Attigny, Bodo stood beside Priscus in a square filled to capacity outside a centuries-old Merovingian palace. A three-step canopied dais had been erected, upon which dour Pope Paschal I sat on a throne attended by cardinals and Vatican officials.

Paschal's Papal finery held Bodo's interest before Louis arrived. The Pope's helmet-shaped frigium, a white linen miter, had stiches of gold thread decorating the edge. Over an alb, His Holiness wore a gold and scarlet tunicle, a white amice oblong collar, a dalamtic stole, a chasuble, and a Y-shaped white pallium decorated with blood red crosses.

Barefoot and wearing a penitent's robe of coarse wool, Louis walked between rows of clergy and kneeled before the Pope with crossed arms against his chest. Helisachar had left his abbey to play an important role for the occasion and hovered over the emperor. Louis' foster brother Archbishop Ebbo of Rheims and other bishops held their shepherd's crooks of authority. Hard and self-righteous expressions creased their faces and those of Louis' three sons and ranking nobles. Chamberlain Fridugis' expressed sympathy whenever he looked at Louis, definitely not a Lothairian but ineffectual, Bodo concluded.

Helisachar, Ebbo, and other prelates took turns reading from scrolls. They accused Louis of a plethora of crimes and sins, most prominently the blinding and death of Bernard and the tonsuring and torturing of his innocent half-brothers and sons of Charlemagne, Drogo and Hugo. They named more men the emperor banished to monasteries or exile without just cause or fair hearings.

Bodo cringed, mortified for the emperor, when Louis accepted guilt for each transgression and further acknowledged culpability for crimes of which he had not been accused including his father Charlemagne's supposed cruelties, sins, and encroachments against the Church. Pope Paschal then decreed harsh penances, which Louis accepted: long periods of fasting, prayers, vigils, abstentions, and self-flagellation.

Why did the emperor allow the Church to assert supremacy over the Crown? Why did Louis restore to the Lothairians their honors, offices, and promises of reforms they wanted? The emperor even appointed Count-Abbots Wala and Adelard to his council and promised to follow their advice implementing reforms for both Church and State.

Still distressed over Louis' self-mortification, Bodo took comfort that the Lothairians failed to achieve their main goal, the emperor's abdication and retirement to a monastery. The only question remaining was how much time would pass before Louis regained control of the empire and punished those who humiliated him.

Louis' sons disappointed Bodo because they did not defend their father. After His Holiness penanced the emperor, Pepin hurried home to his Kingdom of Aquitaine, Ludwig to Aachen, and Lothair to Italy with Pope Paschal and Wala. What new schemes against Louis and Judith would they plan there?

24. Signs and Portents

Gloom infused the Court after Attigny. All expected the celebrations of the Nativity, Calends of January, and the Epiphany to be muted if not cancelled. Then in mid-December the pall disappeared when Judith countered with the best weapon she had against her foes, herself. The empress announced she was three months with child. Louis' penance of abstinence had not lasted for long.

Also gone were the emperor's lassitude and contrition in the spring of 823 when a messenger from Italy brought word that Pope Paschal crowned Lothair as co-emperor to demonstrate the Church in Rome held supremacy over emperors and kings. Furious, Louis sent a courier to Italy with a summons and threats of dire consequences should Lothair and Wala disobey his command for them to return to Court.

On his way from Priscus' observatory where he had discussed with his mentor the significance of Pope Pascal's defiance, Bodo hesitated before entering the Stone Corridor. Odd, how the air outside felt so heavy. And that unnatural baying of the hounds coming from the kennels. What did it all portend?

A sustained roar. The palace swayed. Bodo lost his balance and fell to the floor of the Stone Corridor. Statues overturned. Cracks split walls. Stones dropped from the ceiling injuring many. So did a beam that crushed one man and injured another.

Amidst screams from the frightened, cries for help from the injured, and calls to God from the religious, Bodo's curiosity dominated fear while the palace swayed.

Has the Thunderer allied with "Earth Shaker" Poseidon?

The shaking and the roaring ceased. Bodo regained his footing. Barriers of stones, beams, the dead and injured lay before him. Loosened debris continued to fall.

Worrying about Adeltrud, Bodo leaped over the moaning injured, shattered statues, and cracks on the floor. He ran along the Stone Corridor toward the stairs leading to Judith's apartments. Bodo pushed upward against terrified courtiers and officials fleeing down the steps. and hurried into Judith's suite. Adeltrud rushed to him.

"Bodo, I thank God you are unharmed."

"And the Thunderer spared you." Bodo embraced Adeltrud and looked past her shoulder. Louis, Welf, and Abraham stood at Judith's bedside blocking his view of the empress.

"Judith is well, Bodo. She did not lose the baby. She is in the best of hands."

A powerful aftershock brought more screams, damage, and injuries. Bodo maintained his balance and held Adeltrud. Now he was able to see Judith. A servant tried to calm Giséle, but the two year old would not stop crying.

Judith beckoned Bodo. "No one can quiet my daughter. She adores you, Bodo. See if you can stop her weeping."

The moment Bodo took Giséle from the servant the toddler stopped wailing, pulled at his hair and giggled. "What shall I do with Princess Giséle, Your Majesty?"

"Distract my daughter until she falls asleep."

Louis kissed Gisela's forehead. "You have a calming manner, Bodo. We hope to see more of you."

The great earthquake killed and maimed many inhabitants. It leveled homes, abbeys, and churches throughout Aachen and environs. Better constructed homes like those owned by Welf and Abraham sustained minor damage. Louis ordered fasts to be observed and repairs begun. He commanded priests to pray for surcease and all to be generous with alms in the hope of preventing greater calamities. He sent couriers to all parts of the empire to learn if other towns and counties suffered damage.

During the following weeks, priests and bishops sermonized that God was punishing all for their sins but could not explain to Bodo's satisfaction why the good suffered with the wicked. Lesser but still severe earthquakes continued to shake Aachen and much of the empire. Messengers arrived and described how the great earthquake obliterated many villages, caused lakes to disappear, and altered the course of rivers.

The superstitious saw signs and portents everywhere. Even Bodo had many questions for Priscus, who survived the quake with minor scratches and bruises. "Can you explain those strange sounds we are hearing at night?"

"I believe they are caused by wild animals and birds not common to our geography. They might be migrating for any reason, perhaps famine or disease."

"You make sense as always Priscus. Do you believe those reports coming from all over the empire? Lightning appearing from clear skies. Great stones falling with hail during storms that have killed man and beast and destroy homes. And chunks of ice so large some are said to be fifteen feet long and wide."

"They are true."

"But what are the causes? Were I superstitious, I might believe the Thunderer is hurling them at us."

"No Thunderer, Bodo, and no angry God. I have read manuscripts that describe volcanoes capable of sending such things into the air by the force of their eruptions and their being carried everywhere by the winds."

"Where are those volcanoes?"

"Italy, but they have been dormant of late. Perhaps there are volcanoes in faraway unknown lands to the north or west."

"The earthquake has given the Lothairians more weapons to use against Their Majesties. I want to speak out against the priests and bishops when they sermonize that every disaster, sign, and portent has been caused by the sins of our emperor and empress."

"It is best you do not. There may be something greater than an earthquake that could shatter the empire."

"You mean if the empress gives birth to a son."

"That would be the greatest calamity of all."

25. Judith Victorious

Bodo stood with Louis, Judith, and palace officials over a vast pit where the earthquake demolished an abbey a few miles outside Aachen and exposed the foundations of a Roman villa. Below under Priscus' supervision, laborers and artisans excavated what had lain beneath the abbey for several centuries: marble busts, household utensils, weapons, sections of mosaics and bas-reliefs, pottery, and amphorae. They placed gold, silver, and valuable artifacts on separate canvases.

Workmen brushed soil and debris from what appeared in the distance to be marble. Priscus waved at Louis and Judith. Given permission by the empress to learn what it might be, Bodo leaped into the pit and ran to the Astronomer where the base and lower section of a statue lay face down in the soil.

"Priscus, what is it?"

"Perhaps a masterpiece of sculpture. Careful men, do not damage the marble with your tools."

Bodo recognized the edges of wings. "Priscus, is it an angel?"

"Unlikely, because the sculpture is of Greek origin."

"How can you tell?"

"Greek statues are free standing on their pedestals without added pieces for balance. The Romans never learned how they accomplished it, nor have we."

Priscus became more exited. "Bodo, I know who this statue represents. Look at the raised right arm and the hand holding a wreath. Let us pray there is no damage to the front, especially its face."

Priscus told the men to tie ropes around the statue and at the best moment in his judgment commanded them to pull. After the life-size statue was vertical and secure, all stood in awe of its perfection of female form and symmetrical beauty.

Bodo could not take his eyes from the statue's face. "Priscus, do you not see? It is Judith, our empress. Why, she might have posed for it herself."

"You are right, Bodo. Uncanny how it resembles Her Majesty in every feature and form of body. Why are you laughing, Bodo?"

"The Greeks accomplished what no living artist has done. They have portrayed the empress in all her perfection. Which goddess does she represent? Aphrodite?"

"No, Bodo. Not Aphrodite. She is Nike, the winged Greek Goddess of Victory."

Bodo shouted from the pit at Their Majesties. "It is a statue of Nike, and when you see it, you will believe the empress posed for it."

"We must see for our self."

Louis attempted to prevent Judith from going into the pit because she was too close to giving birth and might endanger their child. The empress had the stronger will. Servants and workers brought planks of wood and ropes so Judith and Louis might descend without falling into the pit. Adeltrud and Hemma assisted the empress. Palace officials followed. When

Bodo the Apostate

Judith stood face to face with Nike, all agreed it was as if the empress faced an identical twin.

Priscus addressed the royal couple. "Your Majesties, where do you want this masterpiece taken?"

Louis deferred to Judith. "The empress shall decide."

Judith walked around the statue. "You say she is Nike, Goddess of Victory. Then it is a portent. We shall be victorious over those who oppose us. We shall give birth to a son. Priscus, take the greatest care. Nike must be ensconced at the entrance to our suite as a warning to certain prelates and nobles we shall prevail."

Judith was indeed victorious. On the thirteenth day of June 823 she gave birth to a boy. In the empress' apartments, Bodo saw nothing special. All babies looked alike to him. He took his turn to congratulate Judith and Louis. "What name will you give His Highness?"

The little prince slept against Judith, and she kissed her son's forehead. "He shall have the name Charles for His Majesty's father."

Bodo chose a place of vantage from which to observe the Lotharians' reactions when Louis' three older sons, palatine nobles, and high clergy came to pay their respects. The Lotharians had to pass the impressive statue of Nike, and its likeness to Judith unsettled all. The expressions on the faces of Lothair and Irmingard, who had returned from Italy, could not have been more sour or their pro forma smiles more forced.

Magnates, bishops, and abbots arrived from all parts of the empire for the infant's baptism, most prominent of all, Bernard of Septimania. Judith's face shone with pleasure when the count congratulated her.

Bodo stood beside twenty-two year old Drogo and seventeen year old Hugo, Louis' bastard half-brothers now living at Court. Both had similar slight physiques, short stature, and button noses, most likely inherited from their mother Bodo surmised. He admired Drogo and Hugo for their unwavering loyalty to Louis even though the emperor tonsured, tortured, and falsely imprisoned them.

Louis beckoned Lothair, and Bodo relished what was about to happen. Because Judith had given birth to a boy, her sway over the emperor became stronger. Disappointed by the defiance of his three sons, Louis gave consent to her wishes.

"Lothair, our eldest son, we ask you to be your new brother's sponsor at his baptism."

Lothair stiffened. His lips disappeared. "You honor me, Sire, more than I deserve."

The emperor had more to say. "To celebrate the birth of our son, we appoint you, our loyal brother Drogo, Bishop of Metz, and upon you, our loyal brother Hugo, we bestow the Abbeys of Saint Quentin in Picardy and Laubachon on the eastern side of the Rhine."

Bodo did not miss Louis' emphasis on the word *loyal* nor Hilduin's repressed anger. The emperor had usurped the arch-chaplain's authority to recommend candidates for bishop and abbot.

Louis commanded silence. "Conrad, our steadfast brother-in-law, we appoint you lay Abbot of Saint Germaine-des-Prés outside Paris where the Merovingian kings of Neustria are buried."

Another affront to Hilduin.

The emperor had not finished. "Conrad, we are pleased also to make you Count of both Auxerre and the Aargau."

Bodo stifled an urge to cry out, "No, anyone but Conrad, not the Aargau, not my father's county." Everything became clear. Welf gave Bodman to Louis. Then, shortly after Bodo and Adeltrud arrived at Aachen their uncle said that Count Gunzo's counties reverted to the emperor while scheming to give them to Conrad.

Why had he not foreseen Welf's duplicity? And if he had, what could a boy almost eleven have done to prevent it? Nothing was the answer.

What other disagreeable surprises might Welf the Shrewd be planning? And there would be more. That much, and his inability to anticipate the specifics, Bodo did foresee.

Despite his disappointment, Bodo affected a cheerful mien and congratulated Conrad, who responded with an infuriating smirk. One consolation, in a few years he would reach and then surpass his older cousin's height.

Eight days after Charles' birth and on Bodo's eleventh birthday, a great assemblage filled the palace chapel to capacity for the infant's baptism. Before the ceremony began at the font, Louis placed Lothair's hand on the great Holy Book chained to the altar.

Bodo the Apostate

"In the presence of Arch-chaplain Hilduin and all witnesses here, do you Lothair, King of Italy and co-Emperor consent to whatever part of the realm we shall apportion to your brother Charles?"

"I so consent."

"And do you also swear that you will do everything in your power to defend your brother Charles against all enemies?"

"I so swear."

Two oaths falsely sworn, Bodo judged from Lothair's tone of voice.

"Count Bernard of Septimania, approach. As we are godfather to you, so do we ask you to be godfather to our son, Prince Charles."

"I am humbled to accept that great honor, Your Majesty."

The ceremony began. Each word Hilduin spoke over Charles' crying sounded to Bodo like those of a constipated man forcing his bowels to work. So innocent and helpless, the little prince's mere existence might well doom the empire. Bodo wanted to know what the chart Priscus created for Charles presaged, for good or for ill.

26. Judith's Champion

After Charles' birth, the Lothairians intensified their defamation of Judith. Bodo failed to understand why Louis allowed a nest of viper clergy to thrive at Court. Led by Hilduin, they slandered the empress and calling her a witch, sorceress, and seductress who betrayed Louis with Bernard of Septimania and other men, always suggesting the emperor was not Charles' father.

In the chapel after matins, Hincmar read aloud to the *Nutritii* a letter Bishop Agobard of Lyon circulated throughout the empire: "Young men laugh, and old men suffer to see the paternal couch smirched, the palace dishonored, the lady of the palace delivered up to puerile games in the very presence of men in sacerdotal orders."

Bodo seized the letter from Hincmar and ripped it into small pieces, which he then threw in the priest's face. "Lies, all of them lies."

"Are you saying the Bishop of Lyon is a liar?"

Having grown to a height level with Hincmar, Bodo stood eye-to-eye with the priest. "If Agobard wrote this, yes, he is a liar."

Hincmar turned to the *Nutritii*. "You have all heard. Bodo has blasphemed our Church and our faith. Arch-chaplain Hilduin has said it himself, and we all know it is true that Judith is better named Jezebel as the Bishop of Lyon had written. She practices witchcraft and sorcery taught by the perfidious Jews."

"Liar."

Bodo struck hard and fast. He pummeled Hincmar and bloodied his nose in defense of Judith until classmates pulled him away from the young priest weeping on the chapel floor.

Later in the day, Bodo genuflected before the empress who reclined on a divan in her apartment. A wet nurse cared for Charles, whom Louis and Judith had begun to call "our Benjamin" for the youngest and most beloved son of the Hebrew Patriarch Jacob-Israel.

"Bodo, we have heard that you defended my honor like a knight in trial by combat."

"I might have slain Hincmar if others had not interfered."

"So it has been reported. Arch-chaplain Hilduin demands we remove you from the academy and send you to a monastery, but he shall not have his way. We suggested, and he took our advice, that Hincmar would better thrive at Saint-Denis. The priest has left the palace. You have performed well as my champion."

"When I am knighted, I shall champion you against all enemies and their calumnies."

"We expect no less from you, my favorite cousin."

In the archives, Bodo studied a map of the empire based on the Division of 817. What portion of the empire might Prince Charles have without causing great discord? Louis' three sons by Irmingard would scheme and do battle to keep their lands. Each coveted portions of the others' provinces. Dame Fortune might intervene again. By the time Charlemagne died, Louis was his sole surviving heir, which left the empire whole. Many officials, now Lothairians, wished his brother Carloman had been the one to survive.

Bodo reflected upon his encounter with Hincmar and why certain clerics and nobles spread vile rumors about the empress and accused

Bodo the Apostate

her of every evil. By attacking the empress, they hoped to weaken Louis' authority.

Many nobles out of favor resented Louis because of their human frailties of ambition and greed. They also believed Lothair would be a better ruler. For the clergy it was both individual lust for power and a collective insistence that the Church must have supremacy over the emperor.

Bodo saw a contradiction between Louis' belief in the priestly nature of his royal power and his supremacy over the Church, which sought to place itself between the emperor and God. One significant area of dispute had not been resolved: who had the authority to appoint bishops, abbots, and deacons, the emperor or the Church hierarchy?

The Franks believed a king's power to be sacred, the Church and Papacy subservient to his will. Upon inheriting the throne, monastic inclined Louis initially obeyed the bishops and divided the empire in 817. The emperor regretted doing so ever since. Bodo did not doubt that Judith could persuade Louis to abrogate the *Divisio* and give a substantial portion of the empire to Prince Charles.

As Bodo grew from boyhood to youth and young manhood, he became a favorite of the imperial household ....

> Allen Cabaniss,
> *Judith Augusta, A Daughter-In-Law of Charlemagne*

Part Two
Bodo, the Favored
824-830

Frankish liturgy, morality, religious laws, and even the politico-religious system resembled Jewish custom so closely that some historians have conceived of an "occult influence of Judaism on the Christian conscience."

> Pierre Riché,
> *Daily Life in the World of Charlemagne*

27. Confusion of Names

"Priscus, here is another letter from my friend Walafrid Strabo. He told me he is writing a poem about Saint Mammes, a martyr monk of Caesaria. Have you knowledge of Mammes?"

"No." The Astronomer put aside his writing in the observatory. "There may be more canonized martyr saints than all the stars in Heaven for me to know who they are. Let us go to the archives and find what we can about this Mammes."

The Keeper of the Archives brought a worn manuscript to their table. Priscus read and summarized for Bodo. "Mammes lived in the third century. He was arrested and tortured by the governor of Caesarea for being a Christian. When Mammes refused to deny Jesus, the governor sent the monk to Emperor Aurelian who also brutalized him. Mammes clung to Christ. While in the dungeon, an angel set him free, and he returned to Caesarea at God's direction. He was again arrested and thrown to the lions. Instead of devouring Mammes, the lions became docile."

"As the tale is told."

"As all are, my skeptical student."

"And how was he martyred?"

"In the end, the ruler of Caesaria had Mammes gutted with a trident."

"Then neither an angel nor God saved him. I cannot see myself believing so strongly in any religion to give my life for it. Is that not why my Alamanni and Saxons ancestors converted to Christianity rather than die by the sword?"

"Some would be more likely to say that saving the martyr's life was less important than for his soul to be saved."

"I cannot see myself believing so strongly in any religion to give my life for it. Is that not why my ancestors converted to Christianity?"

"To submit to conversion by force is an easy choice for all but the most fanatical. But remember, Bodo, who can know what anyone truly believes."

In the adjacent scriptorium, they encountered Einhard, called "Little

Bodo the Apostate

Nard" because of his lack of height, an eminent scholar, former Director of the Royal Works, and Louis' private secretary. He wrote on parchment oblivious to his surroundings.

"Is he copying a manuscript?"

"No, Bodo. Einhard is completing his *Vita Karoli Magni*, a biography of Charlemagne. I fear it will please those who want our emperor to abdicate."

"Why is that?"

"Einhard believes Emperor Louis is too apathetic, unwise, and does not know how to wield power. He tutored Lothair and believes his protégé can better unify the empire."

Priscus approached the scholar. "How progresses your *Life of Charles*?"

Einhard stopped writing and rubbed his eyes. "Good morning Astronomer, and you, young Bodo." Einhard stood and stretched, the top of his head level with Bodo's shoulder. "After another two or three months it will be completed."

"We all look forward to reading it. Will you credit yourself as Einhard or Bezaleel?"

"Alas, Priscus, I am afflicted with the sin of Pride, so it shall be Einhard."

After they left, Bodo had yet another question for the Astronomer. "Who is Bezaleel?"

"Do you remember I told you that like his father Pepin the Short, Charlemagne called his empire New Israel and himself King David?"

"Yes."

"Charlemagne also bestowed Hebrew names from the Old Testament on his sons and favorites according to their characters. He gave Lothair the name Joshua for his warlike qualities."

"I have read about King David and Joshua in the Old Testament, but who was Bezaleel?"

"As described in the Old Testament, Bezaleel designed and built the Ark of the Covenant under instructions from God."

Bodo had long been aware that many high ranking members of the clergy had baptismal Hebrew names and not those of apostles and saints: Bishops Elijah of Troyes, Solomon of Constance, and Jeremiah of Sens as a few of many examples. Christian women too had Old Testament names, and Judith's admirers praised her as Miriam, Esther, and Rachael according to their perceptions of the empress.

"Priscus, why do the bishops and abbots not take names from the New Testament?"

"Because they study the Old Testament more or cling to tribal traditions of naming. The emperor, many nobles, scholars and clerics feel a strong kinship to the Hebrews. You will learn that the Frankish liturgy, morality, and religious laws, are similar to those of the Jews."

"Why do you laugh, Priscus?"

"There is a delicious irony in it all, for many Jews have taken the Latin names Donatus, and Gaudiocus for example, and more than a few Franks have assumed Latinized Hebrew names Abbo for Abba and Haimo for Chaim."

"Priscus, do you know Hebrew?"

"A little."

The course of their conversation emboldened Bodo to ask a question he had long suppressed. Many Jews had Roman names such as Marcus, Domatus, and Taurus. "Priscus is a Latin name. Are you a Jew?"

"I am simply Priscus, the Astronomer."

His mentor's answer left Bodo unsatisfied. By now, he had observed something else that angered a powerful minority of clerics more than Louis' weaknesses and palace licentiousness. Many great magnates including his Uncle Welf did not always attend Sunday services in the chapels. More often than not, they instead went to synagogues on Saturdays to hear rabbis' sermons, participate in Jewish prayers, and to be blessed. Judith and other women of the Court showered gifts upon Jewish wives and daughters of scholars and landowners, whom they welcomed into their circles. That favoritism and interest in Jewish rituals was made evident to Bodo six weeks after Charles' birth.

28. Adeltrud's Confession

Adeltrud sent a message for Bodo to meet her in the palace garden after sext, He found his sister cloaked, hooded, and shivering in the wind on a stone bench by a sundial.

"Would it not be better to go somewhere inside?"

"There is something I have to confide, but you must never tell anyone about it."

Bodo the Apostate

"You have my word, but why are you so furtive?"

"I fear the priests and bishops may accuse me, Empress Judith too, of blasphemy and heresy, if they discover what we have done."

"What have you done?

Adeltrud looked in all directions and lowered her voice so strollers could not hear. "Bodo, not even the emperor knows what Judith, her mother, Hemma, and I did."

"Adeltrud, please, calm yourself and tell me all."

"You know that each second day of February we celebrate the Purification of the Blessed Virgin and Feast of the Presentation of Christ in the Temple."

Bodo listened to Adeltrud, puzzled because of her natural inclination toward circumlocution, a new word he learned the day before, until her narrative became clear. On the fortieth day after Charles' birth, Welf arranged for Judith to take her son to Count Abraham's home. It had a small thermal bath spacious enough to accommodate eight people if they stood. The empress' mother, Countess Heilwig, Hemma, Abraham's daughter Deborah, and Adeltrud accompanied Judith.

"Bodo, today I learned that Jewish women must go to a monthly ritual bath they call a *mikvah*. Lady Deborah explained what it was, but Judith knew all about it. She goes to Count Abraham's home whenever possible with her mother and Lady Deborah after her monthly time. Today, like Saint Mary, the empress cleansed herself of bodily and spiritual impurities caused by the birth of her male child. Is that not heresy, Bodo? And I was both witness and participant."

"How many times have we sat with Welf and his family and listened to rabbis' sermons in the Aachen synagogue on the Jewish Sabbath? How many times have we been given their blessings? Were there not other great nobles and bishops in attendance?"

"Yes."

"Then you have nothing to fear if anyone finds out that Judith replicated the Purification of Mary."

After Bodo reassured Adeltrud no harm would come to her and they parted, he decided to learn more about the *mikvah*. In the archives, Bodo read relevant passages from Exodus, Leviticus and other sources describing the ritual. Jews believed a mother who gave birth to a male child was unclean for seven days afterward and had to wait thirty-three more days for her blood to be free of impurities. After her monthly menses, the *mikvah* returned a woman to a state of purity by washing away her past and cleansed the woman spiritually, similar to the Sacrament of Baptism.

The Gospel of Luke: 22-40 stated that forty days after Jesus' Nativity, Mary and Joseph took Him to the Temple in Jerusalem to complete his mother's ritual purification after childbirth, which redeemed the Christ-child in obedience to the Law of Moses.

Was Christianity a variant of Judaism with pagan compromises?

The *mikvah* took place at Abraham's home. Who better to ask than The Merchant of the Palace?

29. Jewish Influences

Abraham invited Bodo to sit beside him on a bench inside the thermal baths. "Priscus tells me you are his most brilliant student."

"I remember overhearing that evening we met at my Uncle Welf's home that you told him I might be a prodigy."

"So everyone believes, but you are also an anomaly."

"That is a new word I do not understand."

"It means an incongruity. You have an adult mind in a boy's body."

"I am pleased to hear that, but there is so much I still must learn."

"Is that why you have sought me?"

"Yes, I want to know more about the Jews."

"Our religion?"

"That, and more. I want to know everything about your tribe here in the empire."

Abraham described how Pepin the Short, Charlemagne and now Louis allowed Jews to control the trade with Muslim Hispania, Byzantium and the East to ensure a flow of wealth. That was why Jew and merchant were interchangeable words. Jews and their goods were exempted from all river, bridge, and gate tolls. They obtained the right to live by their own laws. If a Jew was accused and tried in the royal court, the Christian plaintiff had to present Jewish witnesses.

Abraham confirmed what Bodo had observed that Jews clustered in communities along the Rhine, Rhône, and Moselle Rivers, and at the Mediterranean seaports of Marseilles, Narbonne, and Barcelona. Primarily, they were artisans and traders, but several owned great tracts of land around Narbonne and vineyards along the Rhône. The diocese of Lyon had so large and influential a Jewish population, their representatives had direct access to the emperor and other royal officials. Because Jews dominated the trade around Lyon and the Rhône in meat and wine, Louis changed the market day from Saturday to Sunday.

Under Louis' special protection and favored above Christians, Abraham led the great network of Jewish traders based in the Rhône valley. For those services, the emperor made him Count Palatine, Count of the Palace.

Abraham, a cousin of Count Bernard of Septimania, told Bodo a near unbelievable story. Because the Jews of Narbonne allied with King Pepin the Short to drive the Muslims out of Septimania, he sent for an exilarch, a descendant of King David from the Bustanai family in Baghdad, to rule over Septimania and gave the Jewish *Nasi,* which they called their prince, his sister Alda for a wife. Because the *Nasi* became his vassal, Pepin believed he had a right to the Davidic succession and to create New Israel.

Abraham's nephew Viscount Taurus of Roquemaure on the Rhône, managed and protected the merchant's allodial tracts of land and vineyards in Septimania and Burgundy, property independent of vassalage to local lords and kings. Taurus produced wines for Jews planted, gathered, crushed, and casked only by Jews according to Talmudic laws of *Kashrut* and high quality non-kosher wines for the nobility and clergy by Christian laborers.

Abraham traded in gold, silver, weapons, salt, papyrus, and expensive wines, content to leave most of the trade in grains, cheese, and fish to Christians. His ships and caravans brought to the emperor and wealthy nobles desired luxuries and necessities from Africa and lands beyond Byzantium and Baghdad to Frankia, Hispania, and Constantinople, which included silk, spices, furs, and dyed textiles.

Abraham surprised Bodo when he said the Jews had a prince in Narbonne. Vassal only to the emperor.

"Who is the Jewish Prince, Count Abraham? Have I seen him at Court? Are you that Prince?"

"He is Bernard of Septimania."

"How can Bernard be a Jewish Prince and a Christian?"

"Through blood relationship to Charlemagne and Louis. If you wish to learn more about the Prince of the Jews, I suggest we speak of it another day. I must leave now to confer with the emperor about a most serious matter. Bishop Agobard of Lyon has come to Court to complain about the Jews."

Bodo heard Agobard's name mentioned often. A proponent of clerical reform, the Bishop of Lyon presided over most religious councils, led the Church's orthodox faction, thus by default a Lothairian.

"What is Agobard's complaint?"

Abraham stood, and a servant dressed him. "I have enough time to tell you this. The Lyon Affair began last year when Agobard attempted to convert Jewish children to Christianity. After he decreed a great baptism of Jewish children would take place on the approaching Easter Sunday, a delegation of Jews petitioned the emperor to prevent it. The bishop ignored Louis' written command to desist. The emperor next dispatched his *Magister Judaeorum*, Guardian of the Jews, who ordered the bishop in the emperor's name to cease meddling with the Jews. And so, Bodo, Agobard has arrived at Court to defend his actions."

"Then he is meeting with the emperor now?"

"No, Agobard has not been given direct access to Louis. The emperor delegated Bishop Drogo, Abbot Hugo, and Count Welf to listen to Agobard's complaints. They will decide if he can have his audience with the emperor."

Bodo's wish to be present when the meeting with Agobard took place was granted when Judith and Welf commanded him to attend the meeting as his uncle's page.

30. A Lesson in Bigotry

Welf, Drogo, and Hugo sat in high back chairs at a table on a dais in one of the smaller conference rooms. Agobard stood before them, forced to look upward at the trio as a lowly supplicant.

Bodo studied the forty-four year old bishop's features. Age, sunken cheeks, and an ascetic temperament created deep lines like angry scars to mar Agobard's face. The habitually genial Drogo glared at the bishop, Hugo's face expressed disgust, and Welf's expression was one of annoyance because of Agobard's hostility toward Judith and a severe case of piles.

Welf glared at the defiant bishop. "Speak."

Bodo the Apostate

"We must eliminate all Jewish privileges and access to the emperor. I demand we apply all restrictive laws of the Visigoths and Merovingians, end the great emphasis and examples from the Old Testament that support the primacy of imperial rule over individual salvation. I want a Christianity of the Son rather than that of the Father.

"I call for a return to the separation between Jews and Christians. No Christian should buy meats sacrificed and butchered by Jews, nor should they drink their wine. No Christian should dine with a Jew.

"In my diocese, Christians and their wives prefer to listen to rabbis' sermons in synagogues than those of Christian preachers. There they are told the Jews are descendants of patriarchs and prophets, God's own people who practice the true religion. It is scandalous that many Christians have no fear of converting to their false faith."

Bodo guessed what Welf must be thinking. His uncle often expressed resentment, like many Alamanni and Saxons, that their forebears had been converted to Christianity by threat of death and not by faith.

Agobard increased the volume of his tirade. "Why are there so many Jews at Court? How can we tell who they are? They wear no marks of shame to identify them. They dress and speak the same language as everyone else. Why must our emperor, who is so pious and generous to our monasteries, give so much favor to the Jews? He ignores all restrictions against them stated in canonical laws from the time Christianity became the official religion of the Roman Empire. He appoints Jews to high government positions, and they are tax collectors and ....."

"Because they can read, write, and understand numbers better than the clergy," Welf interrupted.

"... and those illegal and immoral charters between Louis and the Jews give them specific privileges including the right to acquire and sell property and moveable goods.

"They exempt Jews from labor on government projects; tolls and foraging by government officials, high ranking clerics, and soldiers; and from responsibility for any damage their caravans might do to fields during their travels.

"Their taxes are one percent lower than those paid by Christians.

"A Jew accused of a crime cannot be tortured or face trial by ordeal. If a Jew is a defendant against a Christian, he stands with a Torah in his right hand and recites a superstitious plea to Moses for help, a demand for God to afflict him with leprosy and may he be swallowed by the earth if he lies.

"Jews may live anywhere in the empire. They employ Christians and import slaves. Our clergy may not baptize the slaves of Jews. That sacrament would free them and save their souls.

"Jews alone try Jewish offenders. They may not be scourged or face ordeals by fire or water.

"Jews collect taxes from Christians in violation of canonic law.

"Why must our scholars prefer to read Jewish historians in preference to the apostles? And they do not attempt to refute them.

"As I wrote in my epistle *De insolentia Iudaeorum, On the Insolence of the Jews*, why am I being publicly humiliated when my only offense is trying to save Christian souls? Jews are like whores and pollute Christians. Jews are worse than any heretic. They are in fact antichrists.

"Can you not see that the Jews behave with outrageous arrogance? They say the emperor esteems them because they are descended from the biblical patriarchs. The most eminent members of the imperial court attend synagogues because they find their services more attractive than ours.

"Is it not true what I have heard, that educated ladies and nobles here at Court shamelessly proclaim they venerate Moses the lawgiver above our Savior and listen to lectures in synagogues where readings from the Torah are explained? Is it not true they ask the rabbis to bless them? Too many nobles prefer rabbis to be their chaplains instead of priests."

Bodo, Welf and his family did the same, and his uncle like more than a few nobles, had a Jewish chaplain at their villa in Altorf. Welf whispered to Drogo and Hugo, "Let him continue and hang himself with a rope spun by his words."

Agobard continued without pause, "Jews are presumptuous and ostentatious. Their women parade about in gowns said to be gifts from ladies at the court and even the empress herself."

Welf became livid at Agobard's mention of Judith. "Be careful ...."

"Jews boast that they can build all the many synagogues they need, despite legislation to the contrary."

Bishop Drogo forced a loud yawn. "You repeat yourself like an unwanted belch."

"Then let me say this. I spoke with a young man who escaped from slavery in Hispania. He said the Jews kidnaped him when he was a child. Everyone knows the perfidious Jews are still capturing boys who suffer abuses and mutilations too terrible to describe."

Bodo the Apostate

Welf pointed a finger at Agobard. "Then why did you not bring the boy and other so-called victims here to prove your assertions?"

Agobard ignored Welf's question. "We, of the Church, with all humility and goodness which we use toward the Jews, have not succeeded in converting a single one to our beliefs. Yet a large number of Christians have been converting to Judaism so they might be untaxed, exempt from feudal service, and free from trial by ordeal of combat. And not only in my diocese. Archbishop Julian of Toledo says Septimania is a brothel filled with blasphemous Jews."

Tears from frustration wet the bishop's cheeks. "Why do Jews more than Christians have direct access to our emperor? In violation of our canonical laws they can build synagogues and speak freely about the meaning of Judaism in the presence of Christians. They reject our Savior Jesus Christ as the true Messiah. They ridicule the miracles and veneration of our saints. They say our relics are examples of idol worship."

"Have you not also attacked praying to icons and relics?" Hugo reminded the bishop.

"That is a different matter, for I war against all heterodoxies. If there is one emperor, there must also be one church, our Orthodox Church. Too many Christians revere and call Judaism the true religion. I can name bishops who use Jewish expositions of Holy Writ for their sermons. I repeat to you what I wrote in my letter to the emperor. I want to isolate the Jews, convert their slaves and children, and save their souls.

"Count Welf, Bishop Drogo, Abbot Hugo, my greatest wish is to protect Christians from the pernicious Jews. I should be saying all I have said and more to the emperor himself." Agobard crossed his arms against his chest and softened his voice to a plea. "I humble myself before you. All I desire is the unification and stabilization of the empire with Orthodox Christianity supreme. The Jews by their evil examples have led to moral laxity and love of material splendor at Court …."

Again Welf pointed a finger at Agobard. "I warn you …."

"… where all have forgotten eternal life is given only to those who seek and deserve it."

While Welf conferred with Drogo and Hugo, Bodo reflected upon Agobard's screed against the Jews. The Bishop of Lyon's venomous eloquence far surpassed that of Hilduin. Agobard's hatred of Jews, if not murderous, could well lead to violence by those who heard or read his rants. Or worse. Despite his generous charters and capitularies favoring the Jews, Louis had not abrogated the canonical laws against them. A different emperor or king might enforce them in an instant.

"Then we are in agreement." Welf said. "We must allow the audience, unpleasant it might be for the emperor."

31. Agobard's Humiliation

Bodo sneaked into the gallery above the Council Hall to witness Agobard's appearance before the emperor. Below, Welf, Abraham, Priscus, Louis' half-brothers Drogo and Hugo, and Count Bernard's brother Evrard, a swart muscular man with a prominent nose, flanked the emperor on the dais. Arch-chaplain Hilduin and Count Matfrid of Orleans, "Rabbit tooth," stood beside Agobard and behind them a quartet of austere clerics who accompanied the bishop from his diocese.

Chamberlain Fridugis deferred to Drogo who repeated all previous imperial reprimands sent to the bishop:

"… and furthermore, his Imperial Majesty, Hludovicus Caesar, issues new separate charters of security for the Hebrews Rabbi Domatus and his kin Samuel, David and Joseph, the Hebrew congregation, and Jews all living in the city and environs of Lyon and your diocese.

"They may own buildings, fields, orchards and vineyards, garden farms, and mills.

"They are exempt from tolls on merchandise passing over bridges and into and out of towns.

"They may worship their religion freely in the city and all palaces under His Majesty's protection and continue to hire Christians to work in their businesses, on their lands, and in their homes."

Agobard paused, opened his mouth to speak further, but gulped for air when Drogo said, "Be silent until our emperor gives permission for you to respond. This nobleman beside me and cousin of our emperor is Evrard of Septimania. He is the brother of His Majesty's godson, Count Bernard and son of the great Guillaume of Gellone. Our emperor has raised distinguished Evrard to the rank of Count and to be his new direct imperial administrator and *Magister Judaeorum*. Count Evrard will prevent further

Bodo the Apostate

mistreatment of the Jews by you, your minions, and anyone else so inclined. You may now return to Lyon, Bishop Agobard."

Louis rose, and all followed the emperor out of the Council Hall. Bodo left the gallery and chased after Agobard eager to learn what he would do next. He hid behind a column in the chapel where the bishop met his supporters.

"What happened to me in the Council Hall ... never in my life have I been weighted with so much humiliation and shame, but I promise you this. I shall continue our struggle against the Jews."

Bodo believed Agobard would fail while Louis ruled, listened to Judith, and accepted advice from men like Welf, Abraham, and Priscus. But no one lived forever. Bodo did not know what opinions Lothair, Pepin, and Ludwig held about the Jews. He liked those he had met. Their rabbis' sermons had been instructional whereas those of the Christian clergy, when not erroneous, condemned human behavior, accused all of original sin, and threatened eternal damnation. Jews embraced life. Most priests and monks seemed to hate mankind for its sinning, but rabbis did not. He sought Count Abraham for an explanation but instead encountered Conrad outside the chapel.

"Come with me. The empress has something of great importance to tell you."

A premonition alerted Bodo that the empress had something unpleasant to say, but he could not guess what it might be.

32. Mother Love

Judith beckoned Bodo closer. Wearing a sable cloak, the empress reclined on a divan in her reception room by a brazier. A wet nurse sat beside Judith holding Charles who slept. Welf, Conrad, and Rudolf stood on one side of the empress, Hemma and Adeltrud on the other, her eyes red from weeping.

Who had caused his sister to cry?

"Bodo, because of your indubitable loyalty, we have decided which role you must play in the service of the emperor, our self, and our son. We are well aware you began to train for knighthood last summer after your tenth birthday. It is what your father, Gunzo the Strong, wished for you.

All instructors at the gymnasium and King Lothair praise your skills with weapons and the hunt."

"I am pleased to hear that, Your Majesty."

Judith clasped Bodo's right hand. "Do you swear to serve us, your emperor, and Prince Charles as we so command from this moment?"

"I so swear."

Judith warmed Bodo with a pleasing smile. "Priscus tells us you have progressed with your learning far beyond your classmates in the Palace Academy and even many priests who pretend to be scholars. We have discussed your place with our father, brothers, and the emperor, who looks upon you with much favor. Conrad suggested and we agree. We have knights aplenty in our empire but too few in the clergy whom we can trust. That is why on the morrow, you shall enter the minor orders. I consulted with Priscus who said you qualify to be a lector."

A lector? The clergy? Not a knight?

Bodo had no one to whom he could appeal against the command of Their Majesties. He stifled an unmanly urge to weep and instead found his voice. "Your Majesty, I do not want to be a monk or a priest. You said so yourself that I am training to be a knight and warrior like my father."

Welf placed a hand on Bodo's shoulder, his tone unctuous. "Nephew, please understand we are not sentencing you to some grim cell in a monastery. In essence, your life will continue as before. You may still go to the gymnasium and train as if for knighthood. You may yet ride to war. I can name a dozen bishops and abbots who have. When you are fifteen, I will give you your father's armor, weapons and the money for his horse."

Judith continued to hold Bodo's right hand while smiling. "My most cherished cousin, you believe we are punishing you, which could not be farther from the truth."

"It will be a punishment." Bodo touched the top of his head. "I shall be tonsured, shorn like a lamb."

Judith ignored Bodo's complaint and released his hand. "All agree you are wise and mature of mind beyond your age. We promise that you shall progress rapidly to subdeacon, deacon, and shortly after that the emperor, may His Majesty live that long, or our son will appoint you bishop, then in time Arch-chaplain of the Palace and *camerarius*. Our plan is for you to be one day the second man of the empire and our son's chief advisor. Do it for our Charles, Bodo. Do it for us. For your family."

"Why not prepare Conrad or Rudolf to be Prince Charles' *camerarius* and second man in the empire?"

Bodo the Apostate

"You are better qualified than our brothers."

Judith's praise removed the smirk from Conrad's face. She took her precious Charles from the wet nurse and kissed the boy's forehead. The empress' features transformed and hardened as if some demon had taken possession of her. If Bodo had not seen it, he might never have believed it. Judith's beauty disappeared and with it her familiar sweet voice when she looked upward.

"We vow this, our Lord God. We shall dedicate our life to ensure that you, my handsome son, shall have the greater portion of the empire and be its sole emperor. Nothing and no one will stand in our way. For you, our Benjamin, we shall stir the waves and the seas and drive the winds. We shall bend the hearts and minds of men to our will. We shall move all people and things at our command to achieve that goal."

Bodo did not doubt she would. Dismissed by Judith, he lingered outside her suite by the statue of Nike to calm himself and collect his thoughts. Somehow, he had to find a way to avoid a life in the clergy. Bodo cursed all those he trusted and betrayed him. And what about Judith's transformation from sweet, playful empress to ferocious possessed mother determined to advance her son's interests at all costs regardless of the consequences? Bodo traced Nike's forever frozen perfect features with his fingers, but from what he had seen of the empress this day, Judith's face no longer seemed beautiful.

Bodo later met with Adeltrud in the royal chapel. "Now I know why your eyes were red."

"I still weep for you, my brother. I had no way to warn you."

"When I swore the oath, I had no idea Judith wanted me in the Church. Honor prevents me from violating it. I should have been more suspicious of our shrewd uncle when he arranged for Conrad to have the Aargau. Only you, my dear sister, I can trust no one else here at Court."

"What about Priscus, your mentor?"

"The empress said she spoke to him about her plans for me. He should have warned me. I cannot understand why he did not. I will confront Priscus now."

"Let him explain. Do not speak words you may regret. And beware of Conrad. Only today did I learn how much he envies you."

"Why? He is a knight and has one of our father's counties. And now he is a member of His Majesty's council."

"Because both Judith and the emperor value you more."

Bodo found the Astronomer in the observatory conferring with Abraham. "I am sorry. I did not mean to intrude."

"Your protégé seems to be distressed, Priscus."

"Yes, I can see that. What is the matter, Bodo?"

"Did you know?"

"Know what?"

"About the empress' plans for me." Bodo described the oath he swore and all Judith said. "Why did you not warn me? You know how much I trust you."

Priscus recoiled at the rebuke. "Calm yourself, Bodo and lower your voice. The empress asked me about your scholarly progress. She never spoke of her intent for you to enter the Minor Orders."

"But you are wise enough to have suspected her intent."

Abraham's expression was sympathetic, his tone soothing to the ear. "Priscus, it is obvious that Welf and Judith tricked the boy into swearing an undefined oath before they revealed the specifics. Most unethical of them."

"I agree. Bodo, I have always wished the best for you and still do. Even if the empress had so informed me and I alerted you, what could you have done? Go to Judith and try to dissuade her? Speak to the emperor? Do you really believe you would have swayed either?"

"No."

"Will you run away from Court?"

"I can still do that."

"Bodo," Abraham said, "you must think carefully about the course the empress has set for you and consider the alternatives. If you let him, Priscus will continue to advise you, well, I am sure, and you may always seek my counsel. You are still a youth. Time is your ally. Future events may alter the course of your life and that of the empire for the better or the worse. You can still exercise free will at the appropriate time."

Bodo appreciated Abraham's support. One day he must ask the merchant how Jews honored the oaths they swore.

Bodo the Apostate

"Things could be much worse for you, Bodo."

"How, Priscus, how could they be worse?"

"You are well fed, clothed, and pampered, one of the *Nutritii*. Despite what you may think, their Majesties favor you. They did not make you an oblate, the first step toward becoming a monk, those hateful men in their cowls and scapulars who hide from the world in anxiety."

Priscus assured Bodo that everyone respected the lectors, whose advanced education was limited to a select few. Although bishops sermonized, lectors were more skilled at exegesis and expounded on what the prelates read to their congregation.

"Bodo, you love to read and expand your knowledge. Now, you will have access to all books and manuscripts in the palace, many of them forbidden to most of the clergy, and other archives throughout the empire."

"And I offer you access to my library," Abraham added.

Bodo thanked the merchant, but he now faced a new problem. How could he be a lector without becoming a hypocrite? No longer a boy who believed in the pagan ineffectual gods and talismans, in mind and heart he had yet to be converted to Christianity.

33. Lector and the Art of Exegesis

A clerical barber tonsured Bodo less extreme than was done to monks and oblates. Cropped hair replaced his long blond locks and ringed a shaved circle the size of a wafer. A priest gave Bodo the surplice, a loose white outer vestment to wear when he read and explained passages from the Holy Bible at Mass.

Biblical exegesis, a method, some called an art, explained the historical context of a selected passage a lector read to a congregation. Not the bishops and priests, Bodo admired most the rabbis, whose sermons offered more clarity. When he asked Abraham who might provide the best lessons in exegesis, the merchant invited him to his home, the most impressive in Aachen, having been repaired after the great earthquake of 823, with a stone and brick exterior, many windows of glass, marble portico and columns in the Roman style.

Instead of weapons or heads of prey slain in the hunt, typical of Bodo's former home and those of the nobles, silk tapestries decorated with colorful animals, flowers, and Hebrew writings in threads of gold hung on the walls. Velvet fabrics of vivid colors and stuffed pillows covered chairs and divans. Between woven carpets, marble tiles glistened.

Abraham answered Bodo's many questions with genial patience. "Those tapestries represent the symbols of the Tribes of Israel. The writings are passages in Hebrew from Scripture, what you Christians call the Old Testament. The windows? Those are lead molds that hold the glass in place."

Abraham invited Bodo to sup with his family and introduced him to his wife Channah, a woman deferential to her husband, whose hair was covered by a black opaque cloth. The merchant's eldest son Nathan, a sturdy young man of fifteen, suggested how Abraham might have looked at the same age. He would be leaving in the spring on behalf of his father for a journey to faraway lands. The merchant's two shy daughters about seven and five years of age hid behind their mother, and Bodo smiled at lively two year old Judah. Deborah, Abraham's eldest daughter, who had attended Judith until she wed a rabbi the previous year, now lived in Narbonne.

Savory aromas wafted from a separate kitchen. In the great room, Abraham and Channah settled in a pair of high back cushioned armchairs in the center between pillowed benches at a long table of polished wood. The merchant sat Bodo in the place of honor on his right. Servants brought them food on gold and silver platters, wine in glass goblets covered with gold engravings, and porcelain bowls decorated with dragons and peacocks from a land far to the extremities of the east.

After Abraham recited prayers in Hebrew for wine and bread, Bodo ate lamb seasoned with rare herbs and spices instead of mutton, salmon in ginger oil, and dried figs that came from Hispania. He noted the affection Abraham and Channah gave their children, and learned that unlike the noble Alamanni, Saxons, and Franks, Jews did not send their sons to live and be educated with another family when they reached the age of seven.

When the meal ended, Abraham invited Bodo to his study. Along the way, they crossed a patio with a garden and fountain, and the merchant showed him a room that resembled the palace thermal pool on a much smaller scale and warmed by the same spring that fed heated water into his home. Bodo recognized the bath from Adeltrud's description as the *mikvah* where she bathed with Judith, Heilwig, and Hemma.

Bodo the Apostate

In the study, he entered a paradise of books and manuscripts. They filled many shelves, most written in unfamiliar languages. Bodo aspired one day to match Abraham's linguistic skills. The merchant was a polyglot who knew the Hebrew, Arabic, Persian, Greek, Latin, Frankish, and Alamannic languages, and some Slav dialects, a necessity for his journeys and various enterprises.

A rectangular chest carved with tendrils and flowers held Abraham's writing tools, quartile folios of blank paper and papyrus. Records of accounts burdened the open folding top. A scroll of what Jews called their Torah lay on a nearby lectern high enough for one to read while standing.

"Count Abraham, all those books and manuscripts, have you read every one of them?"

"Yes, several more than once, and our Torah continually."

"Maybe I will learn Hebrew one day."

"I expect you will."

"Are you also a rabbi?"

"No."

"But you are so literate and knowledgeable about your religion."

"Most Jews are literate so we can read and understand the Torah. You should also know that we called our sacred Bible Scripture because it is the only Testament. We do not acknowledge the New Testament."

"Forgive me for asking so many questions."

"An apology is not necessary, Bodo. The wise ask questions. Fools believe they have answers."

How wonderful it must be to read Hebrew from Abraham's Torah and the collection in this vast library instead of Latin *biblia*. Inaccurate translations were common and created different meanings.

During the next several weeks, Bodo learned some basic prayers at the Sabbath meals and celebrated with Abraham and his family Rosh ha Shona, the Jewish New Year. He also attended sermons given in Francique by Abraham's friend, Rabbi Sedechius, at the Aachen synagogue, a small plain wooden structure devoid of images. Many clerics, even Drogo and Hugo, and certain nobles and their families came often to hear them.

Rabbi Sedechius, large, round-shouldered, and grey bearded, whose genial expression made him seem accessible, was present during one of Bodo's lessons in Abraham's library. He emphasized that intensive study of a biblical passage was itself an act of prayer to the glory of God.

"Before you begin any exegesis, you must pray for the Holy Spirit's presence and guidance. All other steps follow in His light. Know that you cannot produce a definitive interpretation of any passage, but you can make it coherent and useful for teaching or preaching. There is no one right exegesis, but there are many wrong ones. Do not allow erroneous commentaries to sway you from the search for truth."

"How can I know which to choose, Rabbi?"

"After much practice, you will learn to select the most correct, but try to be original where you can. Of course knowledge of Hebrew is desirable if not a necessity. The Greeks and Romans were not always accurate with their translations. In essence, you must convey God's relationship with humanity. How does God relate to us in the selected passage? How should it affect individual members of the congregation? Ask yourself what Word of God did you hear in the selected passage?"

"I have so much to learn."

"Yes, it takes a lifetime of study, and until the day we die, we are students."

34. Count Bernard of Septimania

Bodo genuflected before Judith in the empress' antechamber at the Aachen palace. She sat on a high back chair cuddling her restless son, and he took his turn paying homage to Charles on the occasion of the prince's first birthday.

"His Highness is large for his age and handsome too."

"So everyone says, Bodo. He will surpass his namesake and be the greatest ruler the empire has ever known. That is what the Astronomer promised after he cast my Benjamin's horoscope, and you shall be at my son's side to advise him when he becomes king."

Bodo wanted to say he could be Charles' *camerarius* without serving in the clergy, but he backed away from the empress for others in line to pay their respects. Many prelates and nobles outside the immediate family had come to Aachen with gifts for the little prince.

Bodo moved through the crowded room closer to Abraham, who conversed with three men he remembered seeing at the Pageant of Favorites:

Bodo the Apostate

Viscount Taurus of Roquemaure, the merchant's nephew, Count Bernard of Septimania, and Viscount Meinrad of Béziers, a broad shouldered Saxon. They spoke a mix of Roman and Francique, two of several languages Bodo now understood.

He focused his attention on Judith's most powerful lay ally attending her this day, the emperor's cousin and godson Bernard, Count of Septimania, Count of Barcelona, and Margrave of the Marches on both sides of the Pyrenees. Bernard's wife had died three years earlier after giving birth to a girl who survived. In less than two weeks on the twenty-fourth day of June in the Aachen palace chapel, he would wed Lady Dhuoda of Uzès.

Bodo remembered Bernard's overt interest in Judith at the Pageant of Beauties and had since heard much about the greatest warrior and most controversial man in the empire. The Lotharians hated the count for replacing their allies with his vassals in the Marches of Hispania. They seldom referred to Bernard by his given name. Instead, they called him *Naso* because of his prominent nose and to remind all of the count's Jewish origins and position of *Nasi,* Prince of the Jews.

Lotharian nobles and clergy often challenged each other to create metaphors for the size of Bernard's nose:

"It is a nose larger than that of Abul-Abbas, Charlemagne's elephant."

"His nose precedes him by a mile."

"When he inhales, all air disappears from the room."

"It is the prow of a Roman trireme."

"It combines all the noses of Israel's Ten Tribes."

Count-Abbot Wala held a visceral hatred for Bernard even though he wed the count's older sister, Rolinde. Bodo had yet to learn if it was envy because Louis favored Bernard or for a more personal reason.

The Lotharians also detested Judith, and nothing short of the empress' banishment or death would satisfy them. They spread rumors that Bernard preferred Judith's company to that of Dhuoda, and despite Prince Charles' Carolingian complexion and features, continued to assert he was the boy's father.

Now closer to Abraham and the three men, Bodo listened to Bernard whisper:

"This cannot be known beyond the four of us. If Dhuoda cannot give me a son, I shall see to it my daughter Dulciorella marries Charles. I believe I can persuade Judith to agree to the union. My lineage is greater than the

Welfings. Who else can prove descent from both the House of David and that of Arnulf, father of Charles Martel?"

Bernard paused and gripped Bodo's shoulder "Have you been spying on us? Who are you, boy? Speak up."

"Calm yourself, Bernard," Abraham said. "We have nothing to fear from him. He is Bodo, kin to both the emperor and empress. Count Welf is his uncle, and his great-aunt Good Queen Hildegard was Louis' mother."

Bernard released Bodo and spoke in Francique. "Did you understand everything I said?"

Bodo rubbed his shoulder. "Yes, I did."

"You had best not repeat a single word. Swear you shall not."

"I so promise."

"Easy for him to say, Abraham, but can he be trusted?"

Bodo stiffened and coated his tone with prideful indignation. "Count Bernard, I never violate my given word."

Bernard's good humor returned. "Oh, but you will, yes you will violate many oaths sworn when you are older, as we all have done."

"Not I. Never."

On Saint John's Day, the twenty-fourth of June 824, Bernard wed twenty-two year old Dhuoda, the only survivor of a noble and wealthy Septimanian family that perished during feuds and civil war. Dhuoda had much in common with Judith. She could speak, read and write Latin, Greek, and several languages of the empire. Bodo thought Bernard's bride had strong almost mannish features when contrasted with the symmetrical feminine countenance of the empress.

Those who hated Bernard spread a malicious rumor: Dhuoda's mother had been one of Charlemagne's *concubitae*, which made her a half-sister of Emperor Louis. Some said she was baptized Daouda, a female variant of David, the name Charlemagne took for himself. Dhuoda's facial bone structure and coloring did suggest consanguinity with the royal family.

Bernard's brothers Gaucelm and *Magister Judaeorum* Evrard and cousin Eudo served as groomsmen. Their wives and the count's attractive surviving sister Gerberga, a nun who had been placed in a convent while still a girl, attended the bride. Dulciorella, Bernard's three year old daughter by his previous wife and three year old Princess Giséle preceded Dhuoda and spread rose petals before her.

Bodo the Apostate

Giséle had her mother's coloring and potential to be as attractive. Dulciorella held Bodo's attention for a moment, a strange tiny little creature with eyes too large for a small face that reminded him of a little owl. Of more interest to Bodo, Viscount Meinrad did not take his eyes from Adeltrud, nor she from his.

35. Viscount Meinrad

After the wedding, all went to the great hall to congratulate Bernard and Dhuoda. Bodo followed Meinrad close enough to hear the Saxon's conversation with Abraham, Bernard, and Taurus.

"Who is that pretty woman to the right of the empress next to Lady Gerberga? I have been admiring her from afar since my arrival at Aachen."

Abraham saw Bodo and smiled. "She is the Lady Adeltrud, a first cousin of the empress and daughter of Count Gunzo the Strong. Her mother was a Hunfriding."

"Excellent pedigree. I find her desirable enough to make her my wife."

Abraham beckoned Bodo closer. "Then you must meet Lady Adeltrud's brother."

After formal introductions, Meinrad took Bodo aside. "I want to speak to you about your sister, Lady Adeltrud."

Bodo preferred to hear from Adeltrud if his sister was likewise attracted to Meinrad. "It is too crowded and noisy here, and the banquet is about to begin. I know a place where we can meet tomorrow."

Was the Saxon worthy of Adeltrud? Bodo wished it to be so, for his sister had passed her eighteenth birthday and should have been wed by now. He used the remainder of the day and well into the evening to learn all he could about Meinrad.

The viscount had a reputation for bravery, and, of equal importance, a worthy lineage. He was a Hornbach from a noble Saxon family Charlemagne converted to Christianity by the sword about four decades earlier. Meinrad's aunt Guiberc married Bernard's father Count Guillaume of Gellone, the second *Nasi* of Narbonne, which made them first cousins on their Saxon maternal side. That explained in part why Bernard made Meinrad his viscount of Béziers.

In the morning outside the thermal pool, Meinrad extolled Adeltrud's beauty and grace, reputation for kindness and charm, and confessed his love. "I must know, Bodo, does Lady Adeltrud look upon me with similar favor?"

"My sister has confided she does."

"She has? Then I implore you to arrange a meeting so I may tell fair Adeltrud of my love."

"And your intentions?"

"I would wed her this day were it possible, with your approval of course."

"You have it, but you and Adeltrud must speak to each other in private. After you meet, I will speak again to Adeltrud. If she agrees to accept you for her husband, we shall so inform the empress. Because Adeltrud is one of the empress' ladies and her cousin, you must make a formal appeal to Her Majesty for her consent to wed my sister."

Bodo had no idea how Judith might react. The empress could be selfish, even cruel, or most generous.

After Adeltrud met with Meinrad, she told Bodo of her willingness to become the viscount's wife. Together they went to the empress' antechamber. Adeltrud told Judith about Meinrad's offer of marriage, extolled his virtues, and described their love for each other. Bodo affirmed his approval of the viscount.

The empress smiled. "Cousin Adeltrud, Viscount Meinrad has already asked us for permission to wed you." The empress' ladies squealed and giggled until Judith commanded silence. "One more time we ask you. Is that your wish?"

Adeltrud blushed. "Yes, Your Majesty."

"Then we give assent to your marriage. Even though we shall miss you, it pleases us, dearest cousin, that you shall be Meinrad's wife."

Adeltrud kissed the hem of Judith's mantle. "I am eternally grateful, Your Majesty."

Bodo embraced his sister ahead of the other ladies in attendance. "You shall be a viscountess."

Bodo the Apostate

Judith gestured toward a page. "Find Viscount Meinrad and bring him to us."

A small celebration for Adeltrud and Meinrad followed in Judith's suite with wine, cheeses, and fruits attended by Louis, Welf, Countess Heilwig, Hemma, the empress' brothers, and her ladies.

Judith announced she had enough of the excessive pomp and gluttonous feasting that took place at Bernard's marriage a few weeks earlier. The empress arranged for a more intimate wedding to be attended by family, her ladies, and a select few palace officials.

"Adeltrud, those jewels and garments you inherited from your mother and placed for safekeeping in our father's house when you arrived in Aachen … they are inadequate. You are first cousin to an empress. We cannot allow you to marry and depart in so low a condition. Bodo, go to Count Abraham and bring him here. We shall prepare a list for him to array your sister as fits her lineage and rank of viscountess. Also Adeltrud, we will not allow a mere priest nor any Lothairian bishop to wed you and Viscount Meinrad. Bishop Drogo of Metz is still at Court. He shall perform the Sacrament of Marriage."

Bodo met Adeltrud alone in the royal chapel a day before her wedding. "Sister, forgive me for seeming to ignore you at times these past years at Court."

"There is nothing to forgive, Bodo. I have been aware that Louis and Judith have demanded all your time when you have not been studying."

"But I have never thanked you for raising me with all the love of a mother before we came to Aachen."

"Then I shall give you a mother's advice before I depart for Béziers. More than anyone, I am aware how disappointed you are to have been forced into the clergy, but consider this. Their Majesties, especially Judith, have made plans for you anyone would envy. If they honor their promises, you shall be the most powerful and influential man in the empire after Charles when he becomes emperor."

"So I have been assured."

"Then forget your dream of knighthood and holding a petty county when you can have an empire."

"I cannot."

"But you must do so to be happy. Judith graciously provided tutors who taught me to read and write Latin. Therefore, I shall continue to mother and advise you in my letters."

"I look forward to receiving them. I shall miss you more than I can express."

"I miss you already, Bodo. I pray you will visit us often in Béziers."

"I would like nothing better."

Abraham did not disappoint. He obeyed Judith's commands and provided fine array for Adeltrud including a powder blue silk tunic trimmed in gold thread and a darker blue velvet mantle for her wedding dress with matching shoes. From his treasures, the merchant gave Adeltrud a gold hairband encrusted with gems of all colors, belts, bracelets, a necklace of matching pearls, and perfumes.

Before the wedding ceremony, Judith presented Adeltrud with a small gilded box and a gold key. "Our parting gift to you, sweet cousin."

Bodo stood beside Adeltrud when she opened the box. The empress had filled it with gold coins.

While Drogo conducted the Sacrament of Holy Matrimony, Bodo never took his eyes from Adeltrud. His sister's eyes and complexion glowed, and he reminisced about Adeltrud's early mothering and in recent years how she had been his confidante, an extra pair of eyes and ears, so necessary to have at Court. That left Priscus as the only person Bodo could trust. Count Abraham might be another, but the merchant often absented himself from Court.

Who else, who else?

The answer came. Somehow, he had to find a way to bring Strabo to Court.

36. Physical Changes

After Adeltrud's wedding and departure, Bodo's reputation as a gifted lector grew. Word spread that the emperor preferred his exegeses to those of much older and more experienced men, and Louis often

Bodo the Apostate

assigned him specific topics to research and upon which to expound.

On the first Sunday of February 825, Bodo faced a full congregation in the palace chapel that included the emperor and empress, Welf and Heilwig, cousins Hemma, Conrad and Rudolf, King Lothair and his Queen Irmingard, King Ludwig, Arch-Chaplain Hilduin, Priscus, and Einhard. When he expounded on a passage from Kings II, his voice alternated between the familiar high-pitched sweetness of a male child and the croaking of a frog.

Other physical changes affected Bodo over the next several months. Bones ached at night. Manly hair sprouted on his body. A downy suggestion of a mustache appeared above his upper lip.

Between preparing his lectures and serving the empress, Bodo swam in the Bodensee, lakes, and across rivers to increase his stamina and speed. Over subsequent months at the gymnasium and fields where knights and tyros trained, he ran faster, threw ax and spear farther with more accuracy, and wielded the heaviest swords with ease. Bodo practiced until he gained the ability to leap onto a horse in full armor. As a result, his torso and limbs developed a noticeable musculature.

A growth spurt during the summer of Bodo's thirteenth birthday brought his height to eye level with Conrad whose body had softened because of excessive dissipation. Kings Lothair and Ludwig, several knights, and the Masters of Arms told Bodo he could be a great warrior and leader were he not destined for the clergy.

A different physical change surprised and embarrassed Bodo at inappropriate times, an uncontrollable tumescence. It occurred whenever he saw an appealing girl, a desirable young woman, or read in the archives writings by Petronius, Catullus, Ovid, and Martial forbidden to all but a few.

From observation and overheard conversations Bodo knew what choices to make that would give him relief. He could take pleasure from a willing female, and many at Court had let him know they would welcome his attentions. He could satisfy himself or struggle with abstinence.

In the archives Bodo read specific references in both Old and New Testament Pslaters and writings of the Church Fathers relating to copulation, marriage, and celibacy. "Be fruitful and multiply," demanded the Lord in Jewish scripture. Nowhere did Judaism forbid their priests of yore and currently its rabbis to wed and have children.

In the New Testament Christ himself blessed a wedding at Cana. Yet, Orthodox Christian theology demanded its clergy resist all carnal temptations and never to wed. Denial of natural urges seemed unnatural to Bodo and to many bishops, abbots, and parish priests who had wives, *concubitae*, or who fornicated at random.

The foremost example of the latter was Bishop Drogo, whose well-deserved reputation for hedonism was so widespread Lothairian clerics referred to his episcopal palace at Metz as a vile abyss of sin. Their condemnations did not stop Louis' half-brother from wallowing in pleasures of the flesh. Once when Drogo over indulged in wine, Bodo heard the bishop rant that celibacy was aberrant behavior best suited for men who hated women and mankind. He went on to say that minor penances were preferable to self-denial.

Bodo still had two years ahead before he took an oath of celibacy instead of being knighted. To whom could he appeal? He knew Judith's answer, and Louis would defer to the empress. Bodo decided to confront Welf with cogent arguments why he should be a knight and not a cleric.

37. Welf's Lessons

Too late for Bodo, at the advanced age of sixty Count Welf died in his sleep without warning signs of illness or any diminishing of mental acuity. Louis decreed an extended period of mourning, but Bodo did not grieve for his uncle, a complex man who schemed each waking hour and succeeded in every endeavor.

No one else in the empire surpassed Welf's accomplishments and good fortune. Bodo remembered that evening in Aachen when his uncle plotted with Abraham to make Judith Louis' empress. After they wed, Welf became Duke-Regent of Bavaria for Ludwig and continued as such after the young king came of age. He laid the foundations for Hemma to marry Ludwig and one day become Queen of Bavaria. He secured a county and an abbey for Conrad with the same awaiting Rudolf when he came of age.

A confluence of fortunate circumstances also played a part in Welf's successes:

Bodo the Apostate

Queen Irmingard's unexpected death.

Abraham's advice that Judith wed the emperor instead of Welf's choice King Lothair.

The merchant's proposal for a Pageant of Beauties.

That Judith was the most beautiful and best educated young woman in the empire.

The death of Bodo's father Count Gunzo allowed Welf to give the Bodman home to the emperor and plan for Conrad to have The Aargau.

Had Gunzo lived, he would have prepared his only son for knighthood never the clergy, and perhaps Adeltrud and not Hemma would be Queen of Bavaria.

Despite long-held resentments toward his uncle, Bodo conceded Welf always behaved toward him and Adeltrud with kindness and generosity. He had the best education possible at the Palace Academy, resided at the seat of imperial power well fed and clothed, and his sister lived well as one of Judith's ladies until the day she wed Viscount Meinrad.

Yet, from the day they arrived in Aachen, Bodo sensed something offputting about his uncle and with good reason.

Welf's family aggrandizements continued after death. Although bereft of her father's counsel, Judith prevailed upon the emperor to make her mother Abbess of Chelles. Countess Heilwig thus succeeded both Charlemagne's mother and sister as head of that most prestigious sanctuary for women from families of ancient noble lineage.

Upon Rudolf's fifteenth birthday early in May of 826, Judith's younger brother underwent rituals and ceremonies of knighthood, and Louis gave him the County of Ponthieu in Picardy and Jumièges Abbey near the mouth of the Seine.

Welf's other counties and holdings reverted to the Crown to be held for Charles until he came of age. On the day his grandson became king and possibly an emperor, Welf would have achieved his greatest triumph of all.

His uncle's accomplishments taught Bodo three important lessons: Always be circumspect, have a well-conceived strategy to fulfill one's aspirations, and accumulate likeminded influential friends.

Bodo faced the grim reality it was too late for those lessons to help him achieve his three goals: leave the clergy, become a knight, and regain his father's lands.

Judith was unwilling to release him from his blind promise.

Trapped into the Minor Orders and destined for the higher clergy, Bodo could not become a knight.

He had lost his father's lands forever. Welf gave Gunzo's home at Bodman to the emperor for a summer palace. The Aargau belonged to Conrad, and Hohentwiel became part of Charles' future kingdom when the boy came of age.

Still, it was difficult for Bodo to forget his dreams.

Bodo needed to think long term, a salient lesson he learned from Welf. By example, his uncle showed him the necessity of having allies at Court to whom the emperor listened, men cultivated over many years.

But why rely on others? Better yet, why should he not become one of the emperor's most trusted advisors before Charles came of age?

Bodo assessed his current position at Court. Favored by Judith, he had easy access to the empress who shielded him from enemies and rivals in the clergy. Recently, Bodo had come under Louis' notice because the emperor preferred his exegeses. He now had the prospect of becoming more important and perhaps over time indispensable to the emperor. It would take several years before that happened and much planning and patience on his part.

Bodo did not forget the positive aspects of his life at Court aside from being well clothed and fed while living in the center of imperial power. He had the freedom to read in all archives and libraries in the empire, and he had time to hone his stamina, strength, and martial skills at the gymnasium and training fields.

Yes, if he had no other choices, why not rise in the clergy and eventually be given an abbey or an episcopal see while serving as Charles' *camerarius*? Bodo startled himself when he realized his beloved father, Gunzo the Strong, never held so high a position in the empire.

But to what end? What did he really want? Those were the conundrums for which Bodo had no answer.

A final lesson learned, Bodo did not forget the role Dame Fortuna played in contributing to Welf's successes. Did the goddess favor him as well, or was it more likely that a prepared man made his own luck?

All in all, a daunting future for a young man one month away from his fourteenth birthday.

38. The Danes

Another letter arrived from Strabo, whose scholarship and poetry had become renowned throughout the empire. Even so, the Abbot of Reichenau sent the young monk away from his *Felix Augia,* happy isle, to Fulda where its esteemed Abbot Hrabanus Maur could provide a better education.

Strabo also described his most recent extended poem, *Versus de Beati Blaithmaic vita et fine,* about the martyrdom of Irish Saint Blaithmaic, an evangelist slain by the Danes two years earlier on the altar steps of Iona Abbey. Strabo did not yet know that Louis and Danish King Harald Klak agreed to an alliance. The Danes promised to convert to Christianity and become a buffer ally against the Vikings, and Louis would defend Harald's right to be their King against any usurper.

Fulda was less than a week's journey from Mainz where the conversion would take place. If Strabo came to witness the conversion, how might the gentle scholar react to hundreds of wild Danes?

Strabo never left Fulda, but his Abbot Hrabanus Maur came to Mainz to help baptize the Danes and to visit the Abbey of Saint Alban where he once taught. Bodo took an instant liking to the short chubby abbot, who had the rosy face of a cherub and a pleasant mien. He asked the abbot about Strabo and was gratified to hear Hrabanus praise his boyhood friend's dedication, scholarship, and botanical knowledge.

King Harald Klak of the Danes arrived at the head of a caravan with his wife Imhild, son and heir Gotfrid, several brothers, and more than four hundred nobles of both genders and all ages. While Louis and Judith hosted the royal family at the administrative palace, the greater number of Danes stayed at Saint Alban's Abbey on a hill to the south of the city or pitched their tents in the surrounding meadows and fields where they celebrated their last Midsummer's Eve festival as pagans.

On Saint John's Day 826 in the grand Church of Saint Alban adjacent to the abbey, the greatest nobles and clergy of the empire filled its interior to celebrate another triumph for *Orthdoxia* Christianity, the conversion of the Danes. Bodo sat in the row behind Countess-Abbess Heilwig, Conrad, and Rudolf. Priscus conversed with Court officials across the aisle. No surprise, Abraham absented himself from the sacrament.

Would the Danes pay attention to paintings along the walls created to instruct the illiterate masses? They represented the Garden of Eden, Cain's murder of Abel, Noah's ark and the flood, the first Patriarch Abraham, Joseph, the Exodus, the giving of the Law to Moses, Joshua's victories, Solomon's temple, and Christ's life from the Annunciation to the Ascension. Others from pagan and Frankish history emphasized royal power and Louis' lineage: Romulus and Remus, Cyrus of Persia, Alexander the Great, Constantine and Constantinople, Charles Martel, Pepin the Short, and Charlemagne.

Horns blared. Louis' half-brothers Archbishop Drogo of Metz and Abbot Hugo of Saint Quentin and Laubachon marched along the center aisle to assist Archbishop Otgar of Mainz and Abbot Hrabanus at the baptismal font. More horns sounded. The royal mace bearer marched ahead of Louis, with Chamberlain-in-Name Fridugis, the emperor's foster brother Archbishop Ebbo of Rheims, Arch-chaplain Hilduin, and Abbot Helisachar trailing half a step behind. Louis wore cloth of gold crusted with precious gems for the occasion instead of his usual somber garb. Lothair and King Harald followed the emperor. Judith appeared next with Danish Queen Imhild escorted by Hugh of Tours and Matfrid of Orleans, which confounded Bodo.

Why had Louis bestowed such honors on those virulent Lotharian enemies of the empress? Was it an attempt to win their loyalty?

The procession continued. Lothair accompanied Harald's heir, ten year old Prince Gotfrid. Pepin of Aquitaine walked beside King Harald's brother Hemming, Ludwig with Eggihard, Count of Harald's palace, and Judith's sister Hemma with a Danish princess. More candidates for baptism followed until the aisle filled with Danes and their sponsors with more waiting their turns outside the doors.

During the interminable baptismal ceremony, Louis became Harald's godfather. Judith sponsored the Danish queen, and Lothair the same for Prince Gotfrid. Otgar and Hrabanus baptized the remaining Danes by rank.

Communion and High Mass followed. Well into the night, Louis prayed with Harald, and hordes of monks and priests taught groups of Danes the Lord's Prayer and the Apostles' Creed. Hilduin assigned Bodo to instruct the Danish children.

Bodo the Apostate

At daybreak wearing shirt, trousers, and boots for the hunt, Bodo stood on the deck of the royal galley, which was festooned with royal standards, pennants, flowers and ribbons. He enjoyed the cacophonic chaos on the Mainz docks while Louis' Court, clergy, and Danish converts boarded a flotilla of floral decorated boats and barges waiting to transport everyone to Rettbergsaue, an island three miles downriver, one of many game preserves throughout the empire.

The island of dense forests of ash, elm, pine, fir and willow, said to be the largest in the Rhine, was about two miles long and a quarter mile wide. It often split in two depending upon the current. Wild falcons attacked a variety of native and migrant birds fleeing before the landing parties.

Prince Charles' preceptor, an elderly monk Markward from the Abbey of Tours, had trouble controlling the rambunctious boy while they disembarked, and Judith beckoned Bodo. "We want you to watch over our son this day."

Louis intervened. "No, we promised Bodo he could participate in the hunt. Markward can manage Prince Charles."

Judith was not pleased but Louis kept his word. He told the weapons bearers to provide Bodo with sword and spear and the stable master to give him a fine steed.

When Judith mounted a powerful stallion, Bodo thought she resembled descriptions he read about legendary pagan warrior queens of old. The Danes rode bare-chested, and their hairy torsos glistened with sweat under the bright sun despite the early hour. Would these fierce warriors show the fury of berserkers in the hunt? Perhaps they might be mistaken for animals. Their scent was the same. Best to stay upwind from them in the searing heat of day.

Horns sounded. Hounds bayed. A row of beaters preceded the hunters. Their drums and horns terrified animals forcing them to flee from the woods toward a meadow where ladies and men too old or too timid to hunt filled the stands.

Franks, Alamanni, Saxons, and Danes shouted and charged after their prey. Bodo rode with the royals and speared a majestic stag. Lothair slew two bears in succession with his sword. Nearby, Louis skewered a wild boar with his spear and brought down a bison with bow and arrow. Harald swung a great ax and felled all prey within reach.

Bodo rode near Judith. He enjoyed a petty moment of triumph when Conrad missed a spear-thrust at a bison and fell from his horse. After the empress dispatched a deer with an arrow, she dismounted at the stands where Charles in the front center seat shouted and laughed at the great slaughter of animals. He struggled to break free from Preceptor Markward.

"*Mutti, mutti*, I want to hunt."

"Hush, my handsome son. You are too young."

Charles screamed louder on the verge of a tantrum, and the empress appealed to Bodo. "Do something. Catch that young doe for my Charles."

Bodo ran toward the female and raised a hand at the nearest hunter. "No. This one is for Prince Charles." He seized the shaking doe and carried her to Charles. "Here, Your Highness, your first animal so you can begin to have a zoo like your father."

Markward lifted the excited prince from the stand and handed him to Bodo. He led Charles to the doe. "A pet for Your Highness."

Instead, on Judith's command a huntsman roped and restrained the helpless creature. Laughing, Charles stabbed the fawn with his small dagger until she died. Courtiers praised their prince's courage.

Bodo regretted he delivered the helpless doe to so wretched a death. It was well he did not give voice to his disappointment. Judith invited him to sit beside her in the stands.

"The hunt is over. Our son likes you. Bodo, come, sup with us. Markward cannot control Prince Charles. You must sit with our son. From now on, we shall arrange for you to see more of him."

Bodo dreaded the empress might make him Charles' tutor. Best he found someone better qualified to teach the prince, and soon.

39. Challenges

The hunt stimulated Bodo's appetite and thirst. He went with the royals and highest ranking nobles to a grove where kills roasted over fires, butchers skinned more game, and cooks prepared them. Under green arbors, tables were laden with freshly baked bread, fruits, nuts, and vegetables. All drank ale or wine while they awaited the meats. Those of lesser rank sat on the grass or lounged under shady trees to escape the intense heat of the day. Bodo sat between Charles and twenty-two year

Bodo the Apostate

old King Ludwig, known by all as the Alaman. The youngest of the three kings had a muscular body and resembled Lothair, except for a ruddy complexion made more rufic from drink.

An army of servants brought a bountiful meal to the tables on enormous platters and filled cups with wine, beer, or ale. The Danes preferred to drink from long horns in one gulp. They attacked the meats with great energy and threw bones everywhere unconcerned if they struck another person. Bodo's modest belching could not match their prodigious eructations.

The Danes mingled by rank with Louis' nobles. King Pepin conferred with the Unholy Trinity of Counts Hugh, Matfrid, and Lantbert. Bodo amended that first impression. Not conferring, conspiring would be the more accurate word.

Danes and Court ladies who kept pace drinking with the men lost their inhibitions. They sat on laps and allowed themselves to be kissed and fondled. Several younger desirable ladies signaled with their eyes and gestures they would welcome Bodo's attentions. Perhaps he ought to taste an apple offered by some Eve before it became forbidden fruit. Still a member of the minor orders, Bodo had not yet sworn an oath of celibacy.

Charles fell asleep during the feasting, and Preceptor Markward carried the boy to a tent for his nap, which freed Bodo. Ludwig leaned closer so they could speak above the noise.

"Bodo, you often attend my stepmother. I know it has been arranged for me to wed her sister, whom I adore. But I must know … does Hemma favor me?"

"Yes, from the moment she first saw you."

"Is that true? You are not flattering me?"

"On my word of honor. Lady Hemma wishes you and she were already wed."

"As do I."

Bodo touched goblets with Ludwig. "To your success."

After the feasting, Bodo watched the Danes, Louis' sons, and many knights compete in running, bow and arrow, and throwing the ax despite the stifling midday heat.

Lothair gripped Bodo's arm and brought him to King Harald.

"Despite his age, this young man here is our best with the ax."

Harald squinted at Bodo in the bright sunlight. "Good height. Remove your shirt." Bodo complied. "Well-muscled, but still beardless. Shall we shorten the distance for this boy?"

Bodo understood most of Harald's accented north Saxon. "Sire, the distance need not be changed."

Lothair slapped Bodo's back. "Well said. Now do us proud."

Harald gave Bodo an ax. "Ours are heavier than your puny Frankish toys."

Bodo held the weapon and felt its weight. The Danish king had not exaggerated. It was weightier. Bodo balanced the ax in his hand and studied the target, a tree trunk with the head and body of a man outlined in chalk.

Harald beckoned his largest warrior, a hirsute redhead half a head taller than Lothair. "Olaf, show this beardless youth how a Dane throws."

Olaf complied. The Danes cheered when its blade embedded inside the outline where a man's heart had been drawn.

Both beer and the midafternoon heat affected Bodo. Legs unsteady, perspiration drenching his eyes, face and body, he uttered a short prayer to the Thunderer and aimed. Bodo's sweaty hand released the ax sooner than he intended. It flew higher than his aim. Was it a sudden breeze or a gift from the Thunderer? He would never know. The blade struck the middle of the target's face and a grain of wood, splitting the trunk in half.

Lothair embraced Bodo. "Well done, cousin. This is how legends are born. The bards will sing your praises."

The Danes also acclaimed Bodo and stung his back with powerful slaps. Harald saluted Bodo with a jeweled horn and drank from it while his subjects counted. After the king finished he threw it to Bodo.

"Here, my horn is yours if you can empty it faster."

Bodo filled the horn from the nearest hogshead of beer and drank the brew in one draught.

"Not bad, Bodo," Lothair said, "but two counts more than King Harald."

"As it should be."

Lothair lowered his voice. "Tell me the truth. You lost the drinking challenge deliberately?"

"I thought it best."

Bodo the Apostate

"Strength and wisdom for one so young."

A Dane farted, and King Harald congratulated him. "Thunder worthy of Thor."

Lothair shouted over the Danes' repeated breaking of wind, "Come now men, let us show our guests we Franks have stronger entrails."

After listening to so many variations of the *bumbulum*, Bodo thought the most sulfurous came from the silent successes. Before he could escape, Lothair shook his shoulder. "We have yet to hear from you."

"That is because my attempts have been discordant and puny when compared with the fragrant music composed by great kings and knights."

Bodo left when their attention turned to a new challenge, who could hurl a hogshead of beer the farthest, and walked through an oak grove to the edge of the Rhine to refresh himself and swim. After he undressed, giggling came from behind an oak.

"Who is there?"

"A *veneficia*, a witch of the woods."

The voice was young and female, childish too, but then witches and sorceresses were said to be protean, able to appear in many shapes. Best to challenge her.

"You are no witch. You are a girl."

"I am for now, but I may turn into an ugly toothless hag with a hairy wart on the edge of my nose."

Bodo walked toward the oak. "I think not."

"Or, I may become a lamia and devour you."

Bodo enjoyed the banter. "Lamias are demons that devour children, and I am not a child."

"You are tender enough for me, handsome Bodo."

Her voice and laughter aroused him. "How do you know my name? Who are you?"

"Find me if you can."

Bodo searched around several trees and stopped surprised at the sight of a naked young woman he recognized, who had wed in a ceremony at Court several months earlier at age thirteen a decrepit elderly magnate.

"You are no ugly witch, Countess Sigrada, but you have bewitched me."

"Well spoken. Now, Bodo, take me in your arms, your young and strong arms."

After Sigrada left, Bodo washed and swam in the river. He looked ahead to more pleasurable encounters with the young countess and other agreeable ladies. Bodo's conscience did not trouble him regarding the Seventh Commandment. Not he, Sigrada was the married partner.

Bodo returned to the Mainz palace with the hunting party. Hordes of servants carried slain animals that had not been consumed. Eating and drinking continued while officials distributed the carcasses. Bodo sat between Charles and Priscus. Chamberlain Fridugis called for silence. Judith embraced Imhild, and the Danes cheered when the empress presented their queen with farewell gifts, all of gold, many supplied by Abraham: a tunic heavy with precious gems, a necklace with a large cross, a chaplet encircled with gems, armbands, and a cincture studded with jewels, to wear around the waist. Last, Judith draped a cloth of gold mantle over the Danish Queen's shoulders.

Louis gave the Danish King a tunic cinched by a belt decorated with jewels, white chamois gloves, and a golden bejeweled baldric. The emperor's final gift surprised all in attendance.

"Harald Klak, King of Jutland and the Danes, I bestow upon you the eastern *Gau* of Rüstringen in Frisia."

Bodo turned to the Astronomer. "Priscus, why did our emperor give him that province?"

"To further ensure Harald will be better positioned to defend against our mutual Viking enemies."

"Although these Danes are now baptized, they are Christian in name only and still pagans at heart. And what about their greater population?"

"Many monks will accompany the converts to their homeland and instruct them in their new faith."

"With King Harald's sword to ensure they succeed?"

"Ever the skeptic, Bodo."

While the Danes departed laden with gifts and an abundance of carcasses from the hunt in a procession stretching over several miles, Bodo recalled the oft-repeated homily: faith is mightier than the sword. Better said, faith was mightier with the sword.

40. Discontent

After the Danes' conversion, Bodo accompanied the emperor and empress throughout their annual summer of fishing, autumn of hunting, and presiding over regional Diets. He might have participated more often in the chase, but Judith demanded he attend her and Charles during most days. At night, the emperor summoned Bodo to discuss biblical exegesis and sing verses from the Old Testament about the travails of Kings Saul, David, and the successors of Solomon.

One evening after a hunt in the Vosges, Bodo sat alone with Louis in the emperor's thatched hut illuminated by a single candelabrum. Instead of discussing Kings I and II from the Old Testament, he listened aghast while Louis questioned his own ability to rule, complained about recurring episodes of gout and debilitating headaches, and confessed he might yet abdicate and retire to a monastery.

The emperor spoke of his difficulties beginning with the unbridled ambitions and desire for more independence of his three sons by Irmingard. The bishops sought Church supremacy over the Crown, and nobles schemed for more regional autonomy. All ignored Louis' capitularies for reforms. Peasant grievances remained unaddressed, and they continued to live in abject poverty under tyrannical landlords. Clerical reforms had not taken place. Most priests, bishops, and abbots lacked discipline and purpose. The Norse raided at will in Frisia, along the Breton Coasts, and to the far south in Aquitaine. Pagan tribes in the east pressed against the empire's borders for land and food.

Worst of all, the Spanish March was aflame. Christian sons and supporters of the counts Bernard replaced had allied with a rebel Visigoth chieftain and Muslim Saracens. They swept through the counties of Cerdegne and Valles south of the Pyrenees pillaging, raping, and slaughtering whole populations and livestock.

While Louis lamented and prayed, a messenger arrived from Barcelona with Count Bernard's request for more soldiers. The emperor refused.

"Not at this time. Tell Count Bernard that Priscus has forecast an early winter. There will be no raids or fighting until after the spring thaws.

We shall postpone any decision to send reinforcements to Barcelona until our advisors join us at Court for the winter."

Louis dismissed the messenger and turned to Bodo. "You have given us solace. Now let us pray together and get some sleep, for we ride at daybreak to the chase."

Bodo now believed Louis never allowed any crisis to interfere with his seasons of hunting, not even a flaring of his gout. Only during the forty days of Lent through Easter Sunday did the emperor abstain from his favorite activity. Instead of leading an army to the south, Louis prayed to God for Count Bernard to prevail and for Priscus' reading of the heavens to be accurate.

Again, Bodo questioned if God answered any prayers.

Bodo delighted in the Lotharians' frustrations. The gods of war favored besieged Bernard. Winter weather arrived early fulfilling Priscus' prediction. Heavy snows and powerful blizzards in the Pyrenees prevented the war from continuing. Severe weather in the Ardennes and Vosges ended Louis' season of hunting.

Bodo returned to Aachen with the emperor's Court. Religious observances before and after the Nativity competed with revelries. In Judith's suite, Bodo played the lute and entertained all with melodies he composed to the bards' heroic tales of Teutonic heroes of yore. He also indulged in carnal pleasures wherever and whenever opportunities arose. Confessors gave admonitions for the venial sin of fornication rather than harsh penances. Nearly all clergy except the most ascetic monks, nuns, and a few zealot bishops recognized that celibacy was unnatural for men and women. Bodo did not confess his sins of fornication because he had never been caught, not even in the chapel's sacristy.

At Aachen, the Lotharians angered Bodo when they made no secret of their plans to destroy Louis' favorite, Bernard. They referred to the count not by name, but as *Naso* to emphasize the third *Nasi*'s Jewish origins and spread a new rumor:

After Dhuoda gave birth to a son in Uzès on the twenty-ninth of November, a bishop ally of Bernard took the newborn from his mother before he could be baptized. He brought the infant to Barcelona, a city dominated by Jews, and there *Naso* had his firstborn circumcised.

Bodo the Apostate

Obsequious before Their Majesties, the Lothairians continued to repeat canards that Judith was a sorceress and Bernard the natural father of Charles even though the prince had Louis' features and none of the count's. They repeated Agobard's turgid sermonizing that in His Majesty's palaces "cuckoldry, sorcery, and sordid filth prevail. Worst of all, Louis' Court is the nexus of heterodoxy and moral degeneracy."

Why did Louis, Judith and their allies not confront and punish the Lotharians for their rising tide of calumnies? If they continued their slanders unchallenged, Bodo foresaw Their Majesties' adversaries becoming emboldened enough to rebel.

41. Risen in Rank

After King Ludwig wed Judith's sister Hemma in the spring of 827 at Regensburg, Louis moved his Court to Bodman for several weeks of hunting and fishing. This day in the empress' pavilion on the grassy field outside the royal palace at Bodman, Bodo wrestled gently with Prince Charles while six year old Princess Giséle proclaimed to all she would wed him one day. No one paid attention to the pretty little blonde who resembled her mother.

"Prince Charles has natural strength for a boy soon to be four, Your Majesty."

"Yes, but that is enough, Bodo. Charles is now tired enough to fall asleep for his afternoon nap." Judith hugged and kissed her son. "Our Benjamin is growing so fast. We cannot believe he is almost four years of age. Have you decided who will be the best tutor for our son?"

Bodo feared Judith might select him to be the boy's preceptor. "Priscus."

Judith gestured for Bodo to sit and commanded her servants to bring them honey cakes and wine. "Yes, he is the best choice, but the emperor will never allow that. His Majesty is too dependent upon Priscus. He wants the Astronomer at his side or at the charts."

"Other than exceptional knowledge, what other qualities and virtues do you demand for His Highness' tutor?"

"A good question, Bodo. As you know, we prefer someone like you, with your keen mind and many knightly attributes, but we have other plans for you." Judith handed her son, now asleep, to a trusted servant. "Take our Benjamin to his bed. We will see him later. Back to your question, Bodo. Prince Charles' tutor must have above all else absolute loyalty to the emperor and his family."

"I promise, your Majesty, I shall find you that scholar."

Bodo had decided upon Strabo, but Charles would not require a tutor for another three years. He thought it too soon to mention the scholar's name.

"He is too young."

On the morning of his fifteenth birthday in June of 827, Bodo stood beside Arch-chaplain Hilduin at the foot of the dais where Louis and Judith presided over palace clergy and officials in the great hall of the emperor's expanded palace in Bodman.

Judith glared at Hilduin and spoke for the emperor. "We disagree. Everyone knows that Bodo is qualified. Even you have praised his knowledge and mental acuity. Also know this, if the emperor can make Bodo a subdeacon, deacon, or bishop, he can also remove you from your Abbey of Saint-Denis this day if he so chooses."

Hilduin continued to protest until Louis silenced the arch-chaplain. "We reject your arguments. On Sunday, you will confer the subdeaconship upon Bodo. From that day, whenever we attend Mass, we expect to see Bodo serving at the altar. You will now prepare Bodo for his investiture."

"As you command, Your Majesty, so it shall be done."

Outside the great hall, Hilduin said to Bodo, "I am aware you know the duties of subdeacon, but I am obligated to enumerate them. You will assist the deacon at Mass. You will prepare the bread, wine, and sacred vessels for the Holy Sacrifice. You will offer the chalice and paten and pour water into the wine for the Eucharist. You will chant the Epistles and wash the sacred linen." The arch-chaplain paused and stared unblinking at Bodo. "I have not heard reports that you have succumbed to the abominable vices of the Court, but know this. From the moment of your ordination, you will be bound to celibacy."

"I shall be no less celibate than any cleric."

"I well understand your meaning. I warn you, Subdeacon Bodo,

Bodo the Apostate

beware of hubris, the sin of Pride. You have a natural arrogance and self-awareness Their Majesties favor you. You lack humility."

Hilduin's hypocrisy disgusted Bodo. Nothing could be more arrogant than to demand humility from another.

At the altar of the small Bodman palace chapel, Bodo faced Arch-chaplain Hilduin and the local deacon at an angle that allowed him to see the emperor and empress in the front row, Louis with a benevolent expression, Judith tense, unsmiling, eyes narrow. Priscus sat in the second row with other Court officials.

Hilduin placed Bodo's hand on a Bible chained to the altar and intoned in Latin:

"You must consider again and again the burden you are taking upon yourself of your own accord. Up to this moment you may yet choose the secular and carnal world, but if you accept this Order of the Subdioconate, it will be unlawful for you to turn away from your purpose. You will continue in the service of God, and with His assistance to observe chastity, bound forever in the ministrations of the Altar, and serve whoever reigns."

Bodo took his vows, and the arch-chaplain offered him a leather bound volume decorated with a cross of gold encrusted with precious gems. "*Yppodiaconum* Bodenum, take this Book of Epistles, a gift from Their Majesties. You now have the authority to declaim each one in the Holy Church of God for the living and the dead in the name of the Lord."

Hilduin recited more homilies while presenting Bodo with cruets to hold wine and water, an empty jeweled chalice; and a paten of gold used for the bread of the Eucharist. The arch-chaplain then covered Bodo with the tunicle of subdeacon, a white linen vestment.

Louis and Judith took communion from Hilduin assisted by Bodo. The congregation followed the emperor and empress, and afterward all congratulated the new subdeacon.

Two months after Bodo's installation, a monk from Fulda on his way to Paris delivered a scroll written by Strabo:

Ad Bodonem yppodiaconum

Haec tibi dat Strabo, carissime pusio Bodo,
 Paucula parva licet legenda tuus.

Quem fervore pari dudum defixiumus arvis,
 Surculus ad superos prodeat ille Nothos

Pura per assiduous surgat dilectio motus,
 Donec firma polos astraque adire queat.

Sis memor in precibus, reddia dum vota tonanti,
 Strabonis memo rest simper et ipse tui.

Quod domino, sectare, placet, quod iussit,
 amato, Quod spondet, speres,
 quod prohibit, fugias.

Dilege virtutes, vitiis procul omnibus esto:
 Praemia certa bonis, poena datur miseris.

Ad meliora tuos ducat dues omnia sensus Et tibi
 perpetuo munera magna ferat.

Candide, care vale, carissime semper ubique
 Pusio candidule, candide pusiole.

To Subdeacon Bodo:

Bodo dearest boy, your Strabo, gives you these few little words to read if you will. May the young shoot, which we with warm hope planted in the fields a short while ago spring to meet the high south winds. By diligent cultivation may pure love rise ever upward until it can approach the poles and the fixed stars.

When you pay your vows to the Thunderer, remember Strabo in your prayers as he always remembers you. Pursue what pleases our beloved Lord and what He has commanded, hope for what He promises, flee from what he forbids;

for certain reward awaits the good, but punishment comes to the wicked.

May God direct your feelings toward all the better things and evermore bring you great offices.

Farewell, dear fair one, always and everywhere most beloved, my little blond boy, my blond little boy.

Bodo read Strabo's poem perplexed by the affection showered upon him and puzzled by the Strabo's mention of the Thunderer instead of God or Jesus. He understood Strabo's "farewell" to mean that the scholar no longer thought of him as a "little lad."

42. De Facto Confidante

As Louis' personal subdeacon and newest confidante, Bodo supped often with the emperor, who provided private places for him to sleep within the royal apartments and others nearby when they traveled or hunted. Most evenings, Louis invited Bodo to his private quarters, tent or lodge to discuss passages from favorite books of the Bible.

An intimate of the emperor and present when Louis discussed policy with his advisors, Bodo was well informed about all travails facing the empire. In October 827, word arrived that the Saracens captured Caesaraugusta, which the Visigoths called Zaragoza and the Muslims Saraqusta. The emperor sent two Lothairian counts, Hugh of Tours and Matfrid of Orleans, to reinforce Bernard.

No surprise, Hugh and Matfrid dallied to ensure *Naso's* defeat, which left the Saracens and Visigoth Christians free to devastate the March and besiege Bernard at Barcelona. Those Frankish nobles gave no loyalty to Louis unlike the Alamanni and Saxons, whose tribal codes and customs dictated that to have order they must give unquestioning fealty to their leaders.

In February of 828 at a public assembly in the palace Council Hall, Louis removed Hugh and Matfrid from their counties because their disobedience and reluctance to aid Bernard caused unnecessary widespread destruction of fields and villages. He condemned both men to death, changed his mind, and spared their lives. Louis' harsh sentencing of treasonous subjects followed by generous mercies had a predictable rhythm no different from a liturgical chant or poet's meter.

Now that Bodo attended the emperor daily and often at night, he became more familiar with Louis' recurring ailments: gout, severe headaches, boils, and problems with eyesight. Without mentioning the emperor's name, Bodo intended to speak later in private with Zedekiah and ask the physician if those same plants and herbs caused one to vacillate and have nightmares.

Because the emperor had been expressing dissatisfaction with his ineffectual physicians, Abraham brought a cousin to Court, Zedekiah, who had served the emir of Cordoba. In his private quarters, Louis told Bodo, Abraham, and Priscus to stay while the young physician made a diagnosis and treatment of his gout.

Bodo liked Zedekiah, a robust man in his twenties, whose quiet manner and eyes that suggested perpetual merriment might reassure the most fearful patient. The physician eschewed bleeding and application of leeches or worms to an inflamed toe. He preferred the efficacies of colchicine, an extract from the autumn crocus long used by the Byzantines and Persians for gout, emphasizing its toxicity required careful measurement of doses.

Zedekiah questioned Louis about other medicines prescribed by his physicians explaining that certain regional plants and herbs used for healing might contribute to extreme changes of mood and mind. They could make one suspicious, inconsistent, or bring on hallucinations.

Healing plants and herbs, pain and suffering, or Louis' nature, for Bodo the causes of the emperor's repeated vacillations did not matter as much as their encouragement of treason throughout the empire.

Zedekiah applied a salve to Louis inflamed toe that brought instant relief, and his final prescription was for the emperor to rest and definitely not sit a horse until the flaring and pain dissipated. The start of Lent was a few days away, and Louis promised to give up hunting through Easter Sunday. He then appointed Zedekiah to be his principal physician, and commanded Bodo to stay so they might discuss Samuel I and II from the Old Testament.

The emperor turned to a page, squinted, and complained about his weak eyesight. He told Bodo to read aloud the story of King David's eldest and favorite son Absalom. Men who believed they could control the prince encouraged him to lead a rebellion against his father. Joab, one of David's generals, slew Absalom in the mistaken belief it would please the Israelite king.

After Bodo finished reading the passages, the emperor worried which son might be an Absalom to his King David. No matter what he did for each, all were dissatisfied with the *Divisio* of 817. Lothair aspired to be sole emperor. Pepin coveted Count Bernard's lands. And Ludwig wanted to add Alamannia to his Kingdom of Bavaria. Should one of his sons dare to rebel, Louis feared one of his loyal subjects might slay Lothair, Pepin, or Ludwig when he would offer forgiveness instead.

"Your reputation for being merciful is legend throughout the land, Sire. We are not Byzantium where patricide, matricide, and filicide reign co-equal with their emperors and empresses."

"Wisely said, Subdeacon Bodo. Now, sing for us one of David's psalms to lift our spirits."

Bodo did not miss an irony. Both Charlemagne and Louis named themselves David after the great King of Israel, but at this moment the emperor became more a tormented King Saul. And he, Bodo, assumed without intent the palliating role of young David, but with a lute instead of a harp.

43. Khazars

A letter from Adeltrud arrived in March 828 informing Bodo she gave birth to a boy in January baptized Guntrum, War Raven in the Alamannic language. He regretted not being present at the sacrament, but Adeltrud's last words cheered him. She had selected her "beloved brother" to be his nephew's godfather in absentia.

Bodo thought often of Adeltrud and hoped to visit his sister, but Judith's and Louis' demands prevented him from traveling to Béziers. He missed Adeltrud for a reason other than sibling love. She had been his most loyal confidante at Court and best pairs of eyes and ears.

Priscus interrupted Bodo's satisfying soaking in the thermal pool. "Dress quickly. His Majesty has delegated us to appear at Count Abraham's home and welcome two ambassadors from the east."

The merchant's eldest son Nathan had returned from a journey beyond Byzantium and brought the emissaries with him ahead of their caravan slowed by the severe winter weather. Byzantium, Baghdad, or some pagan tribe, Priscus did not identify their origins, and Bodo was content to wait until he met the ambassadors.

Abraham greeted Bodo and Priscus and led them to his library where Nathan and two strangers warmed themselves by a blazing fire. The merchant's firstborn had matured and resembled his father in features, build, and mannerisms. The ambassadors reminded Bodo of wild animals in their brown fur cloaks and hats of the same pelt, with bushy eyebrows and long untrimmed beards, one black the other flame red. Only their eyes and noses were visible.

Abraham introduced Bodo and Priscus as representatives of Emperor Louis come to welcome the emissaries in His Majesty's name. "Our guests are Gideon and Sabriel, ambassadors from the Jewish Empire of the Khazars beyond Byzantium and lands of the Bulgars and Rus. But we can speak further in more comfort, for it is time to take our midday meal and warm our innards."

No women and children sat at the table, and Abraham blessed the bread and wine in Hebrew. Without their fur outer garments the two Khazars projected a contrast in physical appearance. Black of hair and beard, Gideon was shorter, slight of build with coloring similar to Abraham and Nathan. Sabriel more than a head taller than his companion and carrying much girth had pale skin filled with freckles, blue eyes, saddle nose, and red hair and beard. Khazaria must indeed have as great a mix of peoples no less than the empire.

Gideon and Sabriel did not speak Alaman or Francique but did know Hebrew, Arabic, Greek, Latin, and numberless regional languages. All agreed Greek would be the preferred language spoken at the table.

Abraham told the Khazars that Priscus was Louis' Royal Astronomer, and trusted advisor on military strategy and tactics. He described Bodo as kin to the emperor and empress, a gifted scholar skilled at biblical exegeses, and confidante of His Majesty.

Although Bodo always enjoyed the flavorful food at Abraham's table, this day the conversation impressed him more. The ambassadors were

Bodo the Apostate

genuinely interested in Priscus' views of natural astrology and how Bodo had become Louis' confidante at so young an age.

Bodo relished most the personal exchanges between Abraham and the emissaries. The merchant had not seen Gideon and Sabriel since his last trip to Khazaria about ten years earlier. Unlike Court banquets and intimate meals with Louis and Judith, there was no talk of war, factions, or religion. Instead, the men exchanged anecdotes about their families with much humor, and each expressed pride in their children's successes. Unlike the coarse laughter brought on by excessive drinking at feasts and banquets, their merriment came from the heart.

Were all Jewish families the same?

Afterward in the library, Nathan told of the difficulties they faced traveling from Khazaria through hostile lands and across great rivers, foul marshes, and mountain passes to the empire. Gideon and Sabriel described the history of the Khazar Empire and revealed the purpose of their journey.

The world held more diverse kingdoms, tribes, and populations than Bodo had assumed. How wonderful it would be to travel and visit them all or at least as many as Abraham and Nathan had seen.

Bodo and Priscus returned to the palace and had a private audience with Louis and Judith who listened with keen interest to all they learned about the Khazars. Khazaria extended from Georgia in the Caucasus Mountains, westward to lands bordering the Pechenegs and Magyars, far north beyond Kiev and Kursk to Bolgar, and to the east beyond the Caspian and Aral Seas to Karakum. Their capital Itil was located near the mouth of the Volga River at the north shore of the Caspian Sea. The weakened Byzantine emperors, Rus, Bulgars, and Pechenegs paid heavy tribute to their Khagan, emperor.

The Khazars were an amalgam of tribes that migrated westward and settled where the Volga River emptied into the Caspian Sea. Fierce warriors, they conquered adjacent lands. Their pagan religion had vile and licentious rites. The Khazars sacrificed humans and even sold their own children into slavery.

About a hundred years before, the Byzantine Emperor Leo made a decision that benefited Khazaria. When he demanded all Jews in his empire convert to Eastern Christianity, large numbers fled to the Khazars who persecuted no religions. Those Jews were physicians, interpreters, traders, scholars, and rabbis. The Khazar elite valued their knowledge and skills. Their Khagan Bulan made several his royal counselors and officials.

After Bulan defeated the Saracens in battle and conquered Armenia, he yearned to know the best way to worship God. Monks from Constantinople and Imams from Baghdad came to the Khagan's court with gifts and attempted to convert Bulan and his subjects to their religions. Unsure which faith was best, Bulan summoned the most learned Jew, Byzantine bishop, and Muslim sage and challenged each to convert him.

The Khagan gave much thought to all they said. He selected Judaism because it was the foundation for the other two religions, which he deemed unnecessary. Bulan and four thousand of his nobles submitted to circumcision and converted to Judaism, and with them their families.

Unlike Christian and Islamic rulers, Bulan did not convert his subjects to Judaism by the sword. He allowed freedom of worship except for the old practices of human sacrifice and selling one's children into slavery. The Khagan insisted, however, that his successors must be of the Jewish faith.

The ambassadors had come to Aachen to sign a treaty of friendship with the empire against their Rus, Bulgar, Pecheneg, and Byzantine foes. They also planned to visit Cordoba and make a limited alliance with Abd al-Rhaman II against his dynastic rival the Abbasid Caliphate that encroached on both the emir's North African lands and those of the Khazars.

The Khazar's and Nathan's caravans arrived, and Bulan's ambassadors appeared at Court. Abraham served as translator during Louis' welcome. Their gifts for the emperor included lush furs from white ermine to dark sables, rare gems, spices, oils, perfumes, cloths and carpets of woven silk.

Next, four strong men carried a roll of shiny brown leather into the Great Hall so large that nobles and clergy alike had to step back to make room. Louis and Judith left the dais for a better look after the ambassadors gestured for it to be unrolled.

Bodo watched the reactions of certain clergy that ran the gamut of awe, interest, and blatant hatred when the great leather jeweled map showed the vastness of Khazaria in relation to all of Europe, North Africa, and lands of the Abbasid Caliphs. More than its size, about twenty feet square, what was on the map caused gasps. The Khazar Empire, Byzantium, Baghdad Caliphate, Louis' Empire, lands of the Pope and Emir of Cordoba had been painted in vivid colors and their borders outlined with tiny precious gems. Larger stones marked their capitals: a magnificent blue diamond for Itil, capital of the Khazars, vivid green emeralds for Baghdad and Cordoba, a sapphire for Constantinople, glistening white diamond for Rome, and, an enormous ruby for Aachen. Most striking of all, a huge six pointed Star of David in pure gold stitched into the leather with gold thread dominated the center of Khazaria.

The Empire of the Khazars appeared vaster than Louis' domains. Bodo recognized the contours of the Black Sea, Anatolia, and the Byzantine Empire from other maps he had seen, but nothing else to the east and north. Abraham translated the Hebrew writing of cities, rivers and mountains, all unfamiliar names.

Bodo had much to digest and remember. Priests and bishops often sermonized that the Jews had lost political sovereignty because they rejected Jesus as the Messiah, The existence of a Jewish empire much larger than Solomon's kingdom of Israel at its peak contradicted Orthdoxia Church dogma. Bodo also had a question about the Jewish religion for which he had yet to receive an answer, and it was one he thought best to research on his own.

44. Heretic?

The Khazars left for Hispania, and Bodo's comfortable routine continued at Court. He performed duties as subdeacon during Mass, attended Their Majesties when summoned, taught Prince Charles rudiments of sport and arms, rendezvoused with diverse ladies, and enjoyed the stimulating company of Priscus and Abraham.

One afternoon in the merchant's library, Bodo stood over something he had not seen before atop a small table. A square ivory board divided into sixty-four equal squares held small carvings of what Bodo guessed to be two armies, one in gold, the other of silver.

Abraham explained it was a gift from the Khazar ambassadors, a challenging amusement from India called Chatrang-namak. Unlike knucklebones and other games of chance, it challenged one's mental acuity with absolutely no factor of luck. He touched each golden piece identifying the king, his counselor beside him, each flanked by an elephant, horse and chariot. Eight identical pieces in front of them were foot soldiers, and the silver pieces an opposing army.

"I have yet to translate its rules from the Persian, but I assure you, Bodo, you will be the first to read it after I do and learn the game. Then, perhaps, you shall teach Their Majesties after I present it to them."

By the end of Lent, Louis' symptoms of gout, headaches, and other ailments disappeared because of Zedekiah's medicines. After celebrating his fiftieth birthday in April, the emperor returned to his favorite pastime of hunting. Louis dithered the same as his sons and counts who disobeyed and did not send reinforcements to relieve Bernard at Barcelona.

During the annual spring royal progress to the important cities of the empire and between hunts, Bodo searched through manuscripts hidden or long-forgotten in abbey and episcopal archives about the origins of the religion he served. All he read validated his belief that Trinitarian dogma promulgated by the Roman Church deviated so far from the original teachings of Jesus, the Apostles, and early church fathers it had become indistinguishable from pagan practices. For those and other reasons, Bodo saw himself more a fraud than a hypocrite while assisting at Mass, reciting exegeses, and discussing the Bible and writings of church elders with the emperor.

One heterodoxy appealed to Bodo, Adoptionism, which flourished during the reign of Charlemagne and lingered after Louis became emperor throughout Muslim Hispania, the Midi, Septimania, and Aquitaine. Bodo reduced the concept to its essence.

Adoptionists believed one must differentiate between the human and the divine aspects of Jesus.

Christ the man was the "adoptive" and not the natural Son of God born of woman. The human Jesus could not be said to be God, but instead God by adoption and grace, a true mortal son exclusive to his divine nature.

Adoptionism contradicted the Roman dogma of Trinitarianism, that God the Father, Jesus the Son, and the Holy Spirit were One.

Hilduin and other ranking palatine clerics refused to discuss heterodox beliefs out of fear or ignorance. They left all questions to be decided by Church councils and never by individuals. Priscus also refused to discuss the schisms or the question that had tormented the Christian faithful from their religion's beginning: was Christ human with divine attributes or divine with human attributes?

    A crisis shook the foundation of both Empire and Church in late spring of 828. A delegation of prelates headed by Louis' foster brother, Archbishop Ebbo of Rheims, Bishop Agobard of Lyon, and Arch-chaplain Hilduin arrived at Bodman with calamitous reports. Throughout Aquitaine, the Midi, Septimania and Provence, people of all classes, even clerics, had been seen offering sacrifices to the old gods at forbidden enclosures, groves, trees, and monoliths. The bishops also feared a return to licentious Dionysian rites at autumnal harvesting of grapes.

    Bodo understood why so many Christians were embracing the old ways. The Church had failed to provide adequate food during recent famines. It could not satisfactorily explain why floods, earthquakes, and storms killed innocent children and loved ones, why livestock died, and why winters had become longer and more brutal. Because no true miracles occurred, many returned to the old gods and unproven superstitions.

    Louis listened without comment when Agobard warned that the increasing number of people returning to paganism was like a plague spreading throughout the empire. After other prelates offered their recommendations, Hilduin demanded permission to lead an army and put to death each transgressor.

    Louis objected. Instead he ordered the bishops to go forth with priests, exorcists, and soldiers representing both ecclesiastic and secular authority so that when they preached to the flocks it would be in the names of both God and Emperor. He approved the bishops' decree to be posted through the empire condemning magic, sorcery, witchcraft, divination, charms, and belief in dreams. The prelates added a list of severe punishments for anyone caught serving Satan or practicing "the blatant remnants of Paganism."

    Bodo believed such decrees and threats could never obliterate all pagan practices. Instead, the synods were likely to subsume them in church ritual and teachings with threats of force to ensure that Roman Orthodox Trinitarianism would prevail.

After the bishops departed, Bodo gathered berries and walked in the woods after mushrooms, and brooded over one thought and one question at the base of his Tree of the Thunderer: the Trinitarian faith, which he preferred to use instead of Roman, was no less false than those the pagans believed. Was there indeed a true faith? Bodo found a possible answer when he sorted in his mind the Christianity he preferred:

No praying to icons, images, or relics.

Jesus had separate natures, human and divine.

Celibacy was unnatural and not one of the Ten Commandments.

Free will allowed one to make choices that would earn salvation.

Bread and wine of the Eucharist did not become Christ's flesh and blood. They were symbolic.

By Donar's hammer, Bodo realized he had described himself as an Adoptionist, a damned to hell Adoptionist.

"Are you truly dead, Donar Great Thunderer, or will the resurgence of pagan beliefs awaken you?"

As if in reply, the sky blackened. Sounds of a summer thunderstorm rumbled in the distance. Then silence prevailed until a pleasant female voice penetrated Bodo's mind:

"Such thoughts will do you no good, Bodo, son of Gunzo."

Absolute silence returned until Bodo awakened to familiar sounds of the forest. A little owl. A little owl, less than a foot high that Priscus once identified as *Athene Noctua,* perched on a branch high above. It stared at Bodo unblinking, immobile. The sun began to set. Had so many hours passed? Bodo sensed he experienced several visions, and as before he could not recall them. Bodo thought he had heard a female voice but could not remember what she said.

45. At the Empress' Command

The year 829 brought another severe winter, and fires blazed in the empress' apartments where Louis and Judith watched Bodo play with Charles, and she spoke over her son's laughter, "Have you

Bodo the Apostate

given much thought to who might be the best tutor for Prince Charles?"

"Yes, Your Majesty, Walafrid Strabo, the renowned scholar."

"We have read his verses and are aware of his impeccable reputation." Judith whispered with Louis, who nodded agreement. "Bodo, we wish you to leave for Fulda immediately. Decide on our behalf once you have absolute certainty Strabo is truly worthy to become tutor to our Benjamin. If so, bring him with you upon your return to court."

"As you command. Prince Charles is intelligent for his age, and with Strabo, he will have the best possible tutor."

"Bodo, we want you to assist Strabo whenever you can, for our son takes pleasure in your company, as do we all. It is essential that our Benjamin is comfortable with you, has confidence in you, so that when the time comes he will agree with us that you above all should be his chief counselor, his *camerarius*."

"I am honored and shall be more than delighted to obey your command."

The climb to so much power was not so easily achieved when other men aspired and conspired to reach the same heights. Many years would pass before he became second man in the empire, and by then Judith might change her mind about his suitability.

"Take care," Louis advised, "for the weather is foul, and Priscus says it will become worse." The emperor snapped his fingers. A servant left, and several returned bearing weapons and armor familiar to Bodo. "You must be able to defend yourself well against wild animals who will be ravenous and men who are starving."

Assisted by servants, Bodo removed his mantle and accoutered himself in his father's armor. With reverence, Bodo held Gunzo's sword forged by Saxon armorers renowned for their skill in iron working. Its hilt had a carved representation of Donar's hammer and on the blade an inscription in Latin asking for the Thunderer's aid in battle.

After Bodo collected his father's spear, bow, arrows and quiver, Judith said, "The purpose of your journey is twofold. We trust you above all to carry this donation to Abbot Hrabanus. And here are the coins your father bequeathed to you. You shall be well-provisioned with food and drink for your journey."

"Now I can purchase a horse."

"No, that will not be necessary." Louis rose from his chair and beckoned Bodo. "Come with us, and we shall give you a choice of several mounts, one to be your own."

At the stables, Bodo selected a powerful black Frisian horse with about ten years of age named Amalric he often rode in the chase. In full armor, he jumped over its rear and settled in the saddle, satisfying himself that no knight could have better accomplished it.

The winding road between Aachen and Fulda covered more than two hundred miles, and winter conditions slowed Bodo's progress, during which he grew more beard and hair that covered his tonsure. Almost a month later on a sludgy trail in a snow covered forest Bodo heard children screaming in the mist ahead. He kicked Amalric to a faster gait on the treacherous path and reached a quartet of snarling wolves circling two peasant boys who had been gathering wood and setting traps for animals. They held the ravenous pack at bay with sticks and a small ax.

Bodo shot an arrow at the wolf nearest the boys. It fell dead in the snow. A second wolf leaped toward him, and he skewered it with his spear. Shouting curses, Bodo dismounted, drew his father's great sword, and used a two handed grip to behead the pack leader. The survivor fled.

Exhilarated, Bodo wished Louis had seen him dispatch the wolves. The emperor always praised the best hunters after a chase.

"Good steed." Bodo patted Amalric, rode to the two trembling malnourished boys, and spoke Saxon. "Where is your home?"

The oldest, whom Bodo estimated to be about eleven, pointed. "Over there, Sire, about a mile away."

"Then let us take these wolves to your parents. Their fur will keep you warm throughout the winter, and their meat will fill your bellies."

Bodo secured one carcass across the back of his mount and followed the boys who dragged another. They left the decapitated wolf behind.

When Bodo reached a thatched hut, the boys' parents emerged from the doorway with two small girls and another son he guessed to be no older than three. Their father approached and groveled before Bodo.

"I am Bertwald, forester for the local landowner. My lord, we thank you for rescuing our precious sons and your generosity."

"I am no lord, but a subdeacon of the emperor's palace on my way to Fulda Abbey."

Bertwald looked toward the shrouded sky. "It must be close to midday. You have much time to arrive before darkness. May we offer you hospitality?"

Bodo the Apostate

The stench of the peasants and the sounds of grunting and cackling from inside the hut banished any appetite he might have had. Bodo thanked Dame Fortuna for being *geboren* and favored by Louis and Judith, whereas foaled peasants like Bertwald and his family existed no better than animals and barely survived.

"I thank you, forester, but I must hasten." Bodo recognized a wooden replica of a human leg dangling from a bare tree branch. "Is someone injured?"

"My eldest son broke his leg and is abed. I made that limb and hung it so he will heal."

Bodo turned Amalric toward Fulda without comment. Lingering superstitions were no different from the belief in healing qualities of holy relics.

46. Fulda Abbey

During previous travels with the Court and along his journey to Fulda, Bodo disliked most staying in monasteries and abbeys with their bleak, gloomy atmospheres and humorless inhabitants. Fulda Abbey did not surprise him when it loomed though a mist ahead gray stone, grim, and typically constructed after the original Basilica of Saint Peter in Rome.

Bodo rode past monks shoveling snow away from broad fields that had been cleared from the surrounding forests. When he dismounted at the front steps of the abbey, several black hooded monks approached. "We welcome and bless you, stranger," their leader said. "Have you come for food and shelter?"

"I am Subdeacon Bodo, sent here on a mission to Abbot Hrabanus by the emperor and empress."

"Then please, come with me."

Bodo followed the monk up two dozen steps through a gated arched entry and bell tower into a large atrium with a fountain in the center. A group of boys stood nearby listening to their teacher. When Bodo threw back his hood, the monk genuflected and called out to another. "Brother Albrecht, ring the bells. Send another to our abbot and tell him that we are visited by His Majesty King Lothair of Italy."

Monks and students bowed despite Bodo's protestations and declarations of his true identity. Before he entered the transept, Strabo appeared. A year and a half had passed since Bodo last saw his childhood friend.

Strabo assured the disappointed monks and students the stranger was not King Lothair and greeted Bodo with a broad smile. "Subdeacon, how delighted I am to address you by your title. How you have grown so tall, sturdy, but that beard covers too much of your handsome face."

"It seems you shall always be half a head taller than I, squinty-eye, and you are lean as a migrant wading bird."

"I often forget to take my meals when I write and study. But why are you so heavily armed?"

"To defend against wild beasts and brigands."

"Of course. What brings you to our abbey? Have you come to study under the great Hrabanus Maurus?"

"My visit here is official and to be of short duration and for reasons I will disclose later."

In the rectory, Strabo prevented Hrabanus Maurus from genuflecting. "No, Your Reverence, he is not King Lothair but my childhood friend, Subdeacon Bodo, who has come from Aachen."

"Of course. We met during the conversion of the Danes, and Strabo has often spoken well of you. I welcome you to our abbey, Subdeacon. May I ask why you honor us with your presence?

"To bring you this donation from Her Majesty."

Hrabanus weighed the bag of coins in his hand. "The empress is more than generous."

"I shall report your gratitude to Her Majesty."

"For how long do you intend to enjoy our hospitality?"

"No more than a few days."

"We are at your service. Strabo, attend to our guest and see that he has the run of our abbey."

Strabo led Bodo to an upper floor in the clerestory above the transept and crypt to a small study filled with manuscripts. "Here is where I write and sleep. There is an adjacent cell where you can rid yourself of your armor and retire in private tonight."

Bodo the Apostate

They reminisced about their childhood. Bodo spoke of having lost Bodman forever to the emperor who transformed his home to a palace.

"Alas, my parents died in December. I do not know when I can visit their graves."

"I shall lay flowers there when I am next in Bodman."

"I thank you. Is Adeltrud well?"

"Happily married and now a mother. I am an uncle and godfather of a boy named Guntrum. But tell me, how are you?"

Strabo spoke of his happiness learning and writing with all the freedom he wished at Fulda. "But, I shall always yearn most for a return to Reichenau, forever my happy isle."

"Perhaps you may see it sooner than you think."

"Tell me. What is it that you know?"

"Not yet. First, I want to see your great library for which Fulda is renowned."

Strabo complied and took Bodo to a large room that held several thousand manuscripts, many original from the Greeks and Romans. The adjacent scriptorium was no less impressive, better lit than the one at the palace with more comfortable seating. Identical, however, were the copiers bent over their manuscripts. Bodo thought the monks and scribes, although well fed, lived a life of drudgery no better than peasant families like the forester Bertwald's.

No different from Aachen, monasteries, and other abbeys Bodo visited during the emperor's progresses, scribes grumbled about bad ink, tired eyes and hands, and hemorrhoids. He read their coarse complaints on manuscript margins in cursive Latin, his favorite being: "I have written enough. Fool that I am, why did I give up ale and wine for Lent?"

Darkness came early, and Bodo supped between Strabo and Hrabanus at the head table in the great dining hall perpendicular to several benches filled with monks, oblates, and students. Bodo's bowl contained a tasteless Lenten gruel of grains, milk, and vegetables boiled to unrecognizable color and taste. He recalled the thirsty monk in the scriptorium when he drank weak ale.

Bodo postponed revealing the second reason for his coming to Fulda until the morrow and decided to leave for Aachen the day after. He also chose not to discuss and question the orthodoxy of the Carolingian Church. Conversation and the abbots' lectures confirmed for Bodo that Hrabanus and Strabo were devoted to the Trinitarian faith. That was further brought home when Hrabanus declared to a gathering of students:

"Neither latent paganism nor the all too seductive appeal of the Jews, no not they ... the greatest threats to Orthodox Christianity are heterodoxies that came from within our Church and lead to schisms by those who misinterpret the Bible, which only an enlightened few should be allowed to read."

During his stay at the abbey, both Strabo and Hrabanus impressed Bodo with their knowledge of ailments, diseases, and their cures. Unlike most clerics and much of the laity who believed all afflictions were God's punishments for lapses and sins, they asserted that conditions of one's blood caused phlegm and bile, which led to melancholia, the same opinions held by Priscus. The Astronomer and Strabo had much in common.

After the midday meal, Bodo asked for a private meeting with Hrabanus and Strabo. They sat in the abbot's office lit by one candle, more Lenten denial.

"Your Reverence, I have brought more than a donation from Their Majesties. Here is a command from the empress for Strabo." Bodo handed the stunned scholar a scroll sealed in wax with the imperial mark. "Yes, it is for you, my friend, a summons from Empress Judith. She has appointed you to be royal tutor for Prince Charles. You are to leave with me for Court on the morrow."

"Is it true?"

"Of course I would never jest about so important a matter."

Hrabanus congratulated Strabo. "I would rather you stay here at Fulda, but you cannot refuse the emperor and empress. Of all in the empire, you are best qualified to teach Prince Charles."

Strabo read the summons. "I am speechless to have been honored so, but I do not understand why they have chosen me."

"Your poems and scholarship are renowned throughout the empire."

"Even so, Bodo, I suspect you may have had something to do with my appointment."

"When Their Majesties asked whom I would recommend, I had no choice but to tell the truth and extol your piety, scholarship, and virtues."

Bodo the Apostate

"I am humbled and shall spend the night praying that I may be worthy of so great a trust."

Bodo looked forward to having another reliable friend at Court.

In Strabo's study on the morning of their departure, Bodo waited for his friend to return from the chapel. He saw some papers on a nearby table. Curious, he read the top page expecting it to be an allegoric poem. Instead, it was a draft of a letter Strabo addressed to someone named Luitger:

> My dearest, you come suddenly, and suddenly too you leave; I hear, I do not see. Yet I do see inwardly, and inwardly I embrace you even as you flee from me in body but not in devotion. For just as I have been sure, so am I now, and so will I always be, that I am cherished in your heart, and you in my mind.
>
> May passing time never persuade me or you of anything else. If you can visit me, it will be enough to see you my dear one. But at other times, write me, write me anything; I have known your sorrows and reflect on them with grief. Grief is the world's province.
>
> The things you consider bright and happy flee all the faster into clouds and sad shadows. Like a bird that hovers above the world, now climbing, now falling, so is the wheel of the world in its turning.

Had Strabo violated his vow of celibacy with another male? Bodo turned from the desk when he heard his friend approaching. "I thought you would be here."

Strabo placed a manuscript on top of the letter. "Bodo, did you sleep well, or have our conversations filled your head with thoughts that left you awake through the night the same as I? I prayed in the chapel for God to give me the wisdom and strength to be a worthy tutor for Prince Charles."

"And so you shall."

"Is it true what I have heard about unspeakable vices occurring at the emperor's palace in Aachen?"

"Rumors spread by the Lothairian faction. You shall soon see with your own eyes how false they are."

"I pray it is so, Bodo, for there are always temptations of the flesh."

Bodo resisted glancing toward Strabo's letter. "In monasteries too, I have been told."

"Yes, we are continually tested."

"Have you strayed from your monkish vows?"

"In mind and heart, but not in body. I confess I am drawn to the beauty of symmetry, which all can see I sorely lack. As the Lord has created plants and flowers, so has He created men and women of perfection in features, body and mind ... as you are so blessed. That is why I worry about you, Bodo. It is easier to resist carnal desires here in the cloisters, but in a secular world with so many temptations, it seems that only a very few who have taken the vows are blessed with the strength to remain celibate."

Bodo understood Strabo suspected he had read his letter to Luitger and was both defending himself and imparting advice.

47. The Tutor

Bodo returned to Aachen with Strabo and sent a servant to notify Judith that Charles' tutor arrived. He led the scholar along the Stone Corridor toward the steps leading to the royal apartments amused by his friend's childlike awe at the sights and sounds. From age seven, Strabo led a cloistered life in abbeys away from the real world of the laity. How might the gentle scholar adapt to his new life amidst the royal family and palace intrigues? True, Strabo was more than four years older, but Bodo believed he must now become his naïve friend's mentor and alert him to the pitfalls of Court life.

At the entrance to Judith's suite, Strabo stopped and gaped at the statue of Nike until he found his voice. "Can any living woman equal such great beauty? Was there one who posed for it centuries ago, or is this statue an ideal of a sculptor's imagination?"

Bodo did not reply. He preferred Strabo see Judith to form an opinion of her beauty and guided him into the empress' antechamber. Judith sat on a chair attended by her ladies. Prince Charles played with carved knights in a corner of the suite supervised by his Preceptor Markward. Eight year old

Bodo the Apostate

Princess Giséle cried out Bodo's name, ran to his side, and clutched his hand as if taking possession.

Strabo blushed open mouthed when he approached Judith. Bodo gave the empress Hrabanus' letter, and his nudge reminded the scholar to genuflect. "Your Majesty, here is Prince Charles' tutor, the eminent scholar Walafrid Strabo."

"And our empire's most renowned poet. Strabo, you may rise. Markward, bring Prince Charles here and inform His Majesty our son's tutor has arrived."

Bodo enjoyed watching Strabo's reaction to Judith. Sustaining his deep blush, the scholar could not hide his awe of the empress' beauty. He must have been comparing the empress to the statue of Nike, and Judith, used to receiving effusive compliments, had to be pleased by the eloquent silence of her son's tutor.

"Strabo, here is your pupil, Prince Charles. In two months he will be six years of age. Subdeacon Bodo believes he is not too young to learn the Latin alphabet and memorize the Lord's Prayer and Apostles' creed. What do you think?"

"Y-y-your Majesty, I taught Subdeacon Bodo the very same when he was that age."

"Excellent. You will spend Prince Charles' waking hours at his side and sleep in the same room."

Markward returned to the antechamber. "His Majesty comes."

Louis entered alone and bade Strabo rise. "We have received only favorable reports of your piety and scholarship. We have enjoyed reading your salutary poems as well. You shall be a shining example for our son to emulate. But your robe, so dusty and soiled, and you so thin. Subdeacon Bodo, take Strabo to the clerical wing. See that he refreshes himself, receives new clothes, and sups to his fill."

"Yes, Sire."

"And good Markward, you have served us well. There is a vacancy in the Abbey at Prüm. You shall be its new abbot."

While Markward knelt and kissed Louis' hand, Judith watched one of her ladies overturn an hourglass on a nearby table. "Subdeacon Bodo, familiarize Strabo with the palace. Bring him back the hour after nones."

"I want Bodo to be my tutor."

Judith beckoned Giséle to her side. "Bodo is too busy to be your tutor."

Outside Judith's antechamber, Strabo stopped again at Nike. "Bodo, more than this statue, the empress ... never have I seen such beauty and symmetry in any human. Such perfection of face, form, and soul. It is Judith Augusta, not Helen of Troy, who could make men do great deeds, write paeans to her beauty, and launch a thousand ships."

"Strabo, you may yet become her favorite poet."

"I shall try. To think I may gaze upon her beauty every day."

Bodo did not discourage Strabo by recounting how other clerics competed to praise Judith, many of them also renowned scholars. The flattery began from the day of her marriage to Louis.

The monk Ermoldus Niger wrote the empress into several scenes in his *In Honorem Ludovici* and praised Judith as *pulcra induperatrix*, the beautiful empress. Thegan, provost of the Monastery of Saint Cassius in Bonn, surpassed Niger when he described Judith as *eminem pulcra valde*, truly exceedingly beautiful.

In appreciation for Judith's literary patronage and expansion of the Court Library, Strabo's mentor Abbot Hrabanus dedicated two biblical commentaries to the empress, one on Judith, "your equal in name," and the other on Esther, "your equal in dignity." Other admirers compared Judith to Rachael, Moses' sister Miriam, and Bathsheba, but none to any woman from the New Testament or a saint.

Bodo looked forward to reading Strabo's efforts, which he expected to be the most effusive paeans honoring Judith above all others.

Shy Strabo blushed again at the warm greetings and fulsome praising of his poetry from monks and priests in the clerical wing. After the scholar washed his face and hands and donned fresh garments, Bodo showed him the royal archives, and scriptorium.

"So many books and manuscripts. A veritable scholar's paradise. Here is where I shall tutor Prince Charles."

The bells of sext tolled, and Bodo led Strabo to the royal chapel for prayers.

"But now, I have an appetite. Will we be dining with the clergy?"

"Not today. We shall share our midday repast with someone I want you to meet, Priscus who mentored me."

"I look forward to it. You praised him for his knowledge in every letter."

Strabo did not blush when Bodo introduced him to the Astronomer. "I believe we have mutual interests in healing plants and herbs."

Bodo the Apostate

"So Bodo has told me, and I have been impressed by the quality of your verses."

Throughout the midday meal of hearty pottage and wine brought by servants from the royal kitchen, Bodo listened to Strabo and Priscus discuss their mutual interests in botany and medicine pleased they were getting on well.

Strabo gestured toward Priscus' chart of the Zodiac hanging on a wall. "There is a question that has long bothered me. I hope I will not offend you if I ask it."

"Of course not."

"If one can predict the future by charting the positions of the constellations and planets, does it not mean our lives are predetermined and we have no free will? Is that not contrary to Church dogma?"

"My new friend Strabo, the stars do not compel. They impel. Their alignments offer warnings to be heeded or disregarded. Each man may still alter his course through free will. Regardless, God knows all the choices we make, for if He is not omniscient and omnipotent, then He would not be God."

Bodo did not participate in their conversation. He divined the future by observing men not from reading the stars.

48. Lothair Revealed

Shortly after Strabo's arrival at Court, Count Bernard broke the siege of Barcelona without reinforcements and drove the Saracens and their Christian allies from the Marches of Hispania. Louis proclaimed a day of celebration and for all at Court to offer prayers of gratitude. Invigorated by Bernard's victories, the emperor called for an Imperial Diet at Worms on the Rhine and summoned Lothair, Pepin, and Ludwig.

As a confidante of both Louis and Judith, Bodo became the only one privy to what the emperor planned to announce at the Diet. Judith had at last prodded Louis to guarantee her Charles a generous share of the empire in violation of the 817 *Divisio* even though the boy was not yet seven. Louis' sons and the Lotharians also did not yet know that the emperor removed

Fridugis as his *camerarius* and gave him leave to return to his duties as Abbot of Tours.

A day before the assembly began, a page brought Bodo a request from Lothair to appear at his encampment outside the town. A month away from his seventeenth birthday, Bodo had grown to six feet with more musculature, a full mustache, and a trimmed beard similar to those of Louis and Lothair. The weather was mild, and he wore shirt, trousers, boots, and cap when he rode Amalric to Lothair's encampment.

At the perimeter, guards genuflected and others scratched their heads confused when Bodo passed. The same had happened when he arrived at Fulda and again when he dismounted and went to Lothair, who drank with his knights outside a tent at a table laden with food.

Lothair laughed and pointed at Bodo. "Everyone, look at him. Study each feature of Bodo's face, sturdy frame, and coloring. Cousin, looking at you I see my reflection. If you served me, I could be in two places at once."

Lothair's sustained flattery made Bodo feel uneasy. What was it he really wanted?

Lothair pushed against the knight at his right. "There, I have made room for you. Come, Bodo, sit beside me. Eat and drink your fill. And tell me. I know why my father summoned me to the Diet, but I want to know exactly what he has in mind for me. Surely you must know. Is it not true what everyone says, that you are his confidante?"

Bodo asserted he had not been privy to Their Majesties' plans because they had sworn him to silence. "Sire, there is one thing I can tell you. His Majesty is disappointed that you disobeyed his command to reinforce Count Bernard at Barcelona."

"Yes, I know. That is why he summoned me. But I have an excuse. My wife was ready to give birth. I could not leave her."

Bodo almost spit his wine at the unexpected reply. Lothair had not been present earlier when his wife gave birth to a son and another time a daughter. More than the flimsy excuse if not an outright lie, Lothair's whiney tone disgusted Bodo.

"Sire, is that what you would have me tell the emperor?"

"No, of course not. I know His Majesty loves me. I am his first born and favorite, superior to my brothers in every quality. Tomorrow at the assembly, I expect one of my father's reprimands. Perhaps he might decree some minor punishment, which he will rescind upon further reflection as he always does, and offer forgiveness. Unless ...."

Bodo the Apostate

Lothair's expression became grim when he paused to quaff from a goblet of ale. "Unless that sorceress stepmother uses her incantations and seductive ways to convince my father otherwise."

Lothair then went into a long rant against Judith, which disgusted Bodo, and accused the empress of witchcraft, every evil carnal and impious act, and creating potent brews to bend Louis to her will. He called Judith a Jezebel, a Delilah, and the Whore of Babylon. He said her goal was to destroy all three of Louis' sons by their mother Irmingard so that Bernard's bastard Charles alone could inherit the imperial throne.

"Bodo, the worst day of our empire was when my father wed that woman. It was unnecessary. He did not need another wife and heir. He could have ... should have ... taken any other woman as his *concubita* instead."

Bodo perceived weakness of character in Louis' eldest son, whom he had thought to be as bold of purpose as he was fearless in battle. Lothair was incapable of unifying all factions and holding the empire together, nor were Pepin or Ludwig up to the enormous task. No man living could fill that role, alas, not even Louis.

After Lothair emptied another goblet of ale, he smiled at Bodo, his tone unctuous. "I remember that you preferred knighthood to the clerical life and how my *veneficia* stepmother misled you into the clergy. If you agree to serve me, I promise you this. I can and I will influence the Pope to free you from your vows, and I shall knight you myself."

A tempting offer of everything Bodo had once wanted but no longer desired. By now he mistrusted Lothair's ability if not intent to keep his word whatever the promise.

"Sire, you honor me, but I have given my word to serve only Their Majesties."

"You may yet find cause to change allegiances at an appropriate moment. Remember this, Bodo. In life there are those who win and those who lose. I intend to win, so choose wisely."

Lothair's behavior saddened and disillusioned Bodo. The fierce warrior's words and comportment were ordinary, not noble, and no different from the lowly supplicants, those wheedlers and schemers who came to Court begging and bribing for sinecures and information.

Louis' eldest son did not have the temperament or the ability to unify the empire. More likely, it might not exist for much longer given the Lothairians' persistent conspiring and the conflicting aspirations of Kings Lothair, Pepin, and Ludwig.

49. New Division of Empire

Bodo's certitude that rebellion might be imminent did not change during the Imperial Diet at Worms where he watched and listened in a state of detachment. Kings Lothair and Ludwig, nobles and prelates filled the assembly hall of the royal administrative palace. Resplendent in imperial regalia, Louis and Judith sat on throne chairs atop a dais. Six year old Charles and Strabo stood at the emperor's right.

Although Pepin sent a message that illness prevented him from attending the Diet, Louis chastised his second son in absentia for disobedience. Bodo saw Ludwig smiling. Based upon previous conversations with the young king, he surmised that Louis' ambitious third son expected to acquire more of his brothers lands whenever each lost favor.

The emperor next addressed Lothair. "Despite your cowardice and bad faith, Count Bernard ended the siege of Barcelona and chased the traitors and their Muslim allies from the March across the Ebro River into Hispania. Therefore, we, Hludovicus Caesar, give our son Charles all Welf lands in Alamannia, Rhaetia, and Burgundy, vassal to no man save our self. When he is of age, he shall be king of those same lands."

Lothair's face reddened, and Ludwig's turned ashen. The Lothairians in attendance grumbled. The atmosphere in the hall became tense, hostile.

Louis had more to say. "Know this and so let it be recorded. Lothair is no longer co-emperor. We have removed his name from all imperial edicts and charters. Lothair, we now banish you to your kingdom in Italy where we expect you to rule with justice tempered by mercy."

While Louis lectured Lothair how to be a better king, Bodo wished the emperor had not moved so soon and draconian to decree a new Division of Empire. Because Charles was so young, Louis should have waited several more years before he gave the boy a kingdom, and he might have were Judith not the stronger in purpose of the two. Unfortunately both were blind to reality. Why could they not see that many nobles and prelates once loyal to the emperor had been switching to the Lothairian faction.

After Louis ended the Diet, men who had not been friends clustered together. Their angry expressions alerted Bodo that more were certain to defect to the Lothairians.

Bodo the Apostate

Louis spent late summer and fall hunting and fishing, while at a synod of bishops, Count-Abbot Wala and Arch-chaplain Hilduin fulminated against what they called The Sins of Emperor Louis. They prepared a letter to remind him of the Papal *Gelasium Dictum*, an Episcopal Order asserting supreme authority of the Orthodox Church over any king.

In late October at an assembly in the Aachen palace Council Hall, Hilduin read the *Gelasium Dictum* aloud to Louis and Judith. He exhorted the emperor to promulgate reforms suggested by the bishops, end regional feuding and bloodshed, and appoint qualified men to carry out all royal commands.

Louis' cousin Count-Abbot Wala of Corbie took his turn to speak. "Leave all sacred things of God to the bishops and priests …."

Louis raised his hand to command silence from Wala, and he stifled protests from Hilduin and other prelates. "We have been patient. We have listened. Now, you shall hear us. We assert that our authority comes directly from God, not from any Pope or bishop. Furthermore, we have summoned Bernard of Septimania from the March of Hispania, and he has arrived."

Angry murmurings and the pejorative *Naso* came from the Lothairians before Bernard strode into the Council Hall accompanied by his brothers Gaucelm and Evrard, cousin Eudo, and four viscounts including Meinrad.

Louis rose and beckoned Bernard to stand on the dais beside him. "Here is Count Bernard. Like his heroic father, the great Guillaume of Gellone, he drove the rebels, Moors, and Saracens from the March of Hispania alone, without any help from our disloyal sons and treasonous nobles. Here is the man who shall from this moment be Imperial Chamberlain of Affairs. Here is the man who shall be the protector of our son Charles. This assembly is ended."

Louis, Judith, and Bernard left leaving most of the assemblage stunned. Bodo lingered to observe the Lothairians. Count Lantbert of Nantes, the one member of the Unholy Trinity not to lose his county, conferred with Wala and Hilduin. Also significant to Bodo, Ludwig and Lothair left together, less as brothers and more as fellow conspirators.

50. Family Reunion

"Bodo, has it been almost four years? How you have grown, tall and strong like our father. You have indeed become a man. For a moment I thought you were King Lothair."

"A common occurrence."

Meinrad had brought Adeltrud and Guntrum to Aachen where they lodged at one of the nobles' homes Bernard appropriated for his viscounts. There after the assembly, Bodo greeted his sister, still beautiful and more womanly now that she was both wife and mother. He renewed his acquaintance with Meinrad and met Guntrum, who would be two in January.

Both well covered for the chilly weather in heavy woolen garments, Bodo sat with Adeltrud by a fire in the great hall of the manse. She described the pleasant climate and her daily routines in Béziers, typical of all noblewomen, managing her household and estate whenever Meinrad was away on military campaigns, caring for Guntrum, and embroidering. Adeltrud reassured Bodo that Meinrad's love for her had not waned, but she wished he did not have to be away for so many months each year battling Saracens and Visigoths.

Bodo described his position at Court as Louis' subdeacon, traveling and hunting with the emperor, researching and always learning, and Judith's plans for him one day to be Charles' *camerarius*. "Have you seen the empress yet?"

"No, it was more important for me to see my brother. Oh, Bodo, why have you not visited me in Béziers?"

"As I wrote often, my obligations to Their Majesties prevent me from leaving. Now, let me take you to Judith."

Outside the empress' suite, Adeltrud hesitated at the statue of Nike. "Bodo, I remember when it was discovered after the great earthquake. Is Judith unchanged as well?"

"Better I leave that for you to judge."

Bodo the Apostate

Judith acknowledged Adeltrud with imperial reserve as if she had never been one of her ladies or even a cousin. Instead, she summoned Strabo to bring Charles. "You must see how handsome and intelligent our son is."

When Strabo entered with Charles, Adeltrud ignored the boy. "Walafrid."

"Lady Adeltrud?"

Judith interrupted their reunion. "Lady Adeltrud, tell us. What do you think of our son?"

The empress did not wait for a reply and spent the entire audience extolling Charles' accomplishments and courage. "When he is King, our son shall surpass Alexander, Caesar, and Charlemagne."

After they left the empress' suite, Adeltrud shook her head when she passed the statue of Nike. Bodo did not need to ask what his sister must be thinking.

Throughout November, Bodo became better acquainted with Meinrad while they exercised with weapons or dined. He liked his brother-in-law and could not have been more pleased when Louis raised Meinrad from Viscount to Count of Béziers and Agde. He took great delight whenever someone addressed his sister as Countess Adeltrud.

One blight, Judith reprimanded Bodo for preferring the company of Adeltrud and Meinrad over Charles. She demanded Bodo devote all his time to her son when he was not serving the emperor or researching for his next sermon.

One Sunday in November after Mass, Adeltrud waited for Bodo to change out of his vestment, and they walked together along the Stone Corridor.

"You are troubled, sister?"

"I was wrong. I cannot explain it, but Judith has changed. It is as if she has become that statue of Nike, cold as the marble, with no heart and soul."

"Judith must be imperious as befits her position."

"It is more than that, Bodo. It is her obsession to raise Charles above Louis' other sons. Meinrad worries that the emperor's new Division of Empire will lead to rebellion. You are well placed here at Court. Do you think my husband may be right?"

"I have discussed that likelihood with Meinrad. He told me he wants to return to Béziers well before the spring thaws. I wish you could stay longer."

"I must confess I am eager to return home. Like Judith, everything has changed for the worse. Bernard behaves as if he is emperor not Louis, and Judith encourages him."

Bodo agreed with Adeltrud. The Court had become unrecognizable after Louis made Bernard his *camerarius* and de facto emperor in his name. Instead of restoring order to the empire and strengthening it through reconciliation, emboldened and arrogant Bernard peremptorily replaced palace officials, even those loyal to Louis, with his favorites and two of the emperor's close advisors with his brothers Counts Evrard and Gaucelm. He offended clergy of all factions when he brought from sunny Septimania to the palace more musicians, actors, jesters and mimes than had been seen before in Aachen.

Arch-chaplain Hilduin and other remaining palace clergy complained that festivals and revelries at Court turned night into day and day into night and Saints' Days became excuses for feasting and revelries instead of prayer: Martinmas on the eleventh of November, Saint Andrew's Day on the thirtieth, Christmas, Saint Stephen's Day on the twenty-sixth of December, Saint John the Evangelist the following day, Holy Innocents Day on the twenty-eighth, and the remainder of the Twelve Days leading to the Epiphany on the sixth of January.

More scandalous, Bernard resided in the palace, and he installed his wife, daughter, and sister, the nun Gerberga, in a nearby convent. Dhuoda should have become friends with Judith because both women were well educated, but Bernard's wife avoided the Court and stoically bore her husband's frequent private meetings with the empress and the vile rumors circulating about their adulterous behavior.

Louis antagonized all factions by raising Bernard and his family higher yet. The emperor transferred all lands of ousted Hugh of Tours to Bernard, Provence too because its count died. Louis appointed Bernard's brother Gaucelm Margrave of Gothia, which included the counties of Conflent, Rasez, Roussillon, Girona, and Ampurias, and he gave their cousin Eudo Matfrid's former county and Diocese of Orléans. The emperor also made Bernard's youngest brother, *Magister Judaeorum* Evrard, Count Palatine. Bernard then assumed without Louis' authorization the title Duke of Septimania and spoke of his lands as a kingdom.

Bodo the Apostate

During celebrations of the Nativity, Louis suffered recurring nightmares followed by insomnia. Zedekiah's potion brought deep tranquil sleep to the emperor but listlessness when he was awake, leaving Bernard and Judith free to administer the empire.

The Lothairians had enough of Bernard's arrogance and Judith's scheming for Charles. Separately or in small groups they left Court to meet with their fellow conspirators in Paris. Bodo could well surmise what form their plotting might take. Before the inevitable tribulations began, he decided to lose himself in pleasures of the flesh and seasonal fetes.

51. The Poet

Because Louis was unwell, Bodo spent added time with Charles and, as a result, he saw Strabo more often than Priscus and Abraham. The Astronomer consulted daily with Zedekiah about the emperor's health, and the Merchant of the Palace always distanced himself from Court during celebrations of Saints' Days from November through the Nativity to the Epiphany.

Despite the many hours Strabo tutored Charles, no other poet surpassed his prolific and hyperbolic praise for Judith. One morning after lauds, he asked Bodo to stay until the other clergy left. Strabo opened a page of his *vademecum*, personal handbook he carried at all times and showed it to Bodo.

"I cannot control what my mind conceives and my hand obeys. I confess that when I cannot see the empress or hear her voice, I worry. I despair. I fear. Have I displeased or pleased her? Dare I show this to Her Majesty?"

Bodo read the poem and resisted an inclination to smile. Naive Strabo appreciated beauty in both genders, but this effort approached *laesae majestas*.

>When out of your sight.
>And away from your voice
>I suffer between hope and fear.
>Do you love me not,
>Or do you love me?

"Your expression, Bodo. You do not like it?"

"Strabo, read it again and consider how it might be misinterpreted."

Strabo did as Bodo suggested. "You may be right."

Strabo changed the subject and revealed all thoughts and feelings that accumulated since his arrival at court, some identical to Bodo's. Strabo never lived so well as now in the palace. He repeated how much he adored Judith and confessed his difficulties resisting the Deadly Sin of Gluttony. Although he enjoyed teaching Charles who was bright and a quick learner, Strabo would give it all up for the life he wanted: to be left alone to contemplate, compose verse, pray, and tend to his botanical gardens at Fulda or better yet Reichenau.

What bothered Strabo most was the divide between the emperor and his eldest son and what might happen if they did not close it. He thrust a leather parcel at Bodo. "That is what motivated me to write another work I completed last night. Will you read it? You know how much I respect your opinion."

Bodo left Strabo and went to a quiet corner in the archives. He lit a candelabrum and read what he believed to be Strabo's greatest epic. *De Imagine Tetrici*, was based on a vision recorded by the monk Wettin about the cruel Ostrogoth conqueror and Arian heretic, Theodoric, whose equestrian statue in the palace courtyard came to life.

Strabo included many hidden meanings in his masterpiece. The divide between the emperor and Lothair distressed Strabo most. He compared Louis to Solomon and Caesar and named him the New Moses. He likened Lothair to Joshua, Ludwig to Jonathan, Charles to Benjamin, Hilduin to Aaron, and Einhard to Bezaleel. He gave Pepin of Aquitaine the fewest lines and no comparisons.

Of greatest interest to Bodo, Strabo described Judith in thirty-five lines. He equated the empress with Rachael who gave birth to Benjamin, to Miriam both prophetess and musician, and to the biblical Judith who slew the Assyrian General Holofernes to save her people. He compared the empress' erudition, compassion, and gifts in the Arts with the Hebrew prophetess Hulda and a poetess, Sappho of Lesbos.

Strabo's dedication to Judith concluded with:

Whatever the deficiency of your gender took from you,
an educated and disciplined life awakened your natural abilities
in which we see much to be admired.

Rich in dogma, powerful in reason,
chaste with piety, valiant spirit,
eloquent in speech, sweet in love,
strong in mind,
charming in conversation,
reclining contented,
may she be happy sitting,
may she be made cheerful rising,
and made blissful when she is
placed in the seat of heaven.

Lover of peace, Friend of Light Who protects all good things
Kind one accept these, my writings.

Bodo searched in vain for any comparison between Judith and women from the New Testament or a female saint. He looked forward to discussing the reasons why with Strabo another day.

52. Judith Invites

At the end of January 830, Bernard summoned Bodo, Meinrad, and Priscus to a meeting of his inner council in the camerarius' chambers with his brothers Gaucelm and Evrard. The men discussed how best to deal with the Lothairians and their new allies now defecting from the emperor in greater numbers. Arch-chaplain Hilduin, other disaffected palace clergy, and minor officials had already departed for Paris where the Lothairians were forming an army.

A proven brilliant tactician, Bernard expected an insurrection to begin after the spring thaws, and he planned to strike first at the emperor's foes. Because the putative Duke of Septimania could not be in two places at once, he delegated his brother Margrave Gaucelm and cousin Meinrad to raise an army in the south and be ready by the end of Lent to march on Paris or against Pepin if the King of Aquitaine joined the Lothairians.

Bernard had sent a message to his cousin Count-Bishop Eudo of Orleans to build another army for an attack on Paris and expressed confidence that he and other advisors could motivate the emperor to lead an army from Aachen. With Bernard at Louis' side, they would crush the Lothairians.

Bodo and Meinrad encountered a page waiting for them outside the emperor's antechamber with a summons from Judith. The boy had instructions not to reveal what she wanted but under questioning from Meinrad he confirmed that Adeltrud and Guntrum had been with the empress for over an hour.

When they entered Judith's chambers, Bodo paused and took in the entire room lit by dozens of candles with one sweeping glance, astounded by the chaos of unusual activities. The cheerful young empress whom Bodo remembered had returned.

Near a blazing fire, Judith sat on the floor beside Adeltrud in the center of a circle of children, her ladies, and Bernard's sister, the nun Gerberga. Toys and dolls lay scattered around them. Servants distributed sweet pastries. Strabo hovered over Charles who helped Guntrum celebrate his second birthday by opening the toddler's presents, most prominent a detailed and painted carving of an armed knight on horseback. Bernard's strange dark daughter Dulciorella watched Giséle play with an extensive collection of dolls, and as usual, Dhuoda had absented herself from the palace.

After Judith told her ladies to help the children hold hands and form a moving circle, she strummed a cither and sang a children's song. When Giséle saw Bodo, she broke away from the circle and ran to him.

"Bodo, Bodo, when I am older, I shall marry you."

"Your Highness, I am most honored, but I can never wed you."

Giséle, who resembled Judith, pulled at Bodo's sleeve. "You shall. You shall. My mother and father will force you."

Judith called to her daughter. "Giséle, listen to me. Bodo is not allowed to wed because he is of the clergy. When you are older, we will find a suitable husband for you."

"No, no, I want Bodo or I will never wed."

Bodo and Meinrad joined everyone on the floor. Judith handed her cither to a lady and calmed Giséle, giving her daughter the most attention since the day of Charles' birth.

Adeltrud whispered to Bodo that if they did not leave before noon, their departure would have to be delayed for another day. "But Judith has been so kind. She ordered from the kitchen all those sweet pastries, gave

Bodo the Apostate

Guntrum so many gifts, and for me that magnificent sable cloak there on the chair."

Over the noise and gaiety, Meinrad taught Guntrum the names of each garment and weapon on the carved knight. Bodo posed riddles for Charles that brought on the prince's laughter. Judith plucked the strings of her cither again and sang in harmony with Bodo and Adeltrud as they had years before. Giséle forgot about her dolls, ignored Dulciorella, and clung to Bodo.

"Count Bernard."

The page's announcement ended the informal party. Judith's regal demeanor returned. On command, two ladies helped the empress to her feet. All rose with the empress, and the children quieted.

Judith told Strabo to take Charles for his daily lessons, sent her ladies and Giséle away, and commanded the servants to clear the room. Strabo pleased Bodo when he bade farewell to "Countess" Adeltrud.

Judith took a few moments for an abrupt and formal goodbye to Adeltrud and Meinrad, who gathered the heavy hooded cloaks they had shed. Bernard waited impatient and grim of expression waiting for Gerberga and Dulciorella to leave.

Bodo lifted Guntrum astraddle on his shoulders and accompanied Adeltrud and Meinrad to the palace courtyard whipped by a frigid north wind. Under a sky bleak as worn stone, a groom held the reins of Meinrad's steed, and another waited beside a cart horse attached to a covered wagon.

Adeltrud raised her hood and gripped Bodo's arms. "My cherished brother, I fear I may never see you again."

Bodo had the same presentiment but instead reassured Adeltrud he would visit Béziers, perhaps within a year. A groom helped Adeltrud onto the cart beside the drover, and Bodo lifted Guntrum to his mother. A final wave goodbye and he watched until they passed through the gate.

Before Bodo entered the Stone Corridor, he stopped at the statue of Theodoric. Would Louis heed Strabo's metaphoric caveats in *De Imagine Tetrici*?

... ever the lover of peace and friend of stability, the emperor always sought not only for his sons but also for his enemies to be one with him in charity.

The Anonymous

Part Three
Bodo, the Disillusioned
830-835

53. Blunders and Disasters

During the winter months in the palace, factions schemed, Louis prayed, and Judith hosted banquets and entertainments attended by Count Bernard, and Bodo wallowed in carnal pleasures. On a blustery night early in February, he warmed himself with Countess Sigrada in the sacristy of the royal chapel. They entwined against a wall between hanging liturgical vestments of all colors reeking of dried sweat and a second time on a table he swept clean of cruets, chalices, ciborium, paten, altar linens, and vials containing Holy Oils.

After their liaison, Bodo carried a torch to the unattended thermal pool. He disrobed and swam unable to avoid dwelling on the troubles Louis faced.

Aachen, the empire, and lands beyond suffered through a winter so severe even the Nile in faraway Egypt froze.

Basques, Bretons, Saracens, and Slavs pressed against the marches.

Vikings raided the coasts.

Louis' three older sons blamed Judith for their loss of lands.

Bishop Agobard of Lyon and his allies feared and resented freedoms and powers given to Jews, which threatened their Church.

Great magnates led by the "Unholy Trinity" of deposed Counts Hugh, Matfrid and Lantbert sought to regain their lands. Former administrators like Wala requested restoration of their honors and prominent positions at Court. All hated Bernard for his arrogance and Judith's brothers for their insolence.

The common folk, who demanded redress of abuses by their clergy and lords, believed Lothair would be the unifier and reformer, not Louis.

Lothairian nobles and clergy persuaded Wala to take the lead in thwarting Judith's ambitions for Charles. Their demands were:

First, Louis must be forced to restore the division of 817 and make Lothair heir to the empire with Pepin and Ludwig his vassals.

Second, Prince Charles must never be given any land and instead be banished for life to a monastery.

The hostile Lothairians spread new rumors that Bernard planned to be more than a ruler of the empire through Louis and Charles. *Naso*

Bodo the Apostate

intended to do away with Louis, marry Judith, and wed Charles to his Jew-face daughter, Dulciorella. Agobard spread fear with his most recent calumny: Bernard's ultimate goal was to convert the empire to the religion of the Jews.

In his screed titled *Concerning the Superstitions of the Jews*, the relentless Bishop of Lyon blamed them and their allies in the palace for causing all evil afflicting the empire. Monks and bishops preached daily that Count Bernard planned to murder the emperor and make it appear he died of some illness. They called the palace a brothel where an adulteress was queen an adulterer reigned, and Bernard dominated Louis through the use of soothsayers, diviners, seers, and interpreters of dreams and entrails. Agobard sermonized that the empress had turned to lasciviousness, first secretly and now without shame causing young men to snicker, elders to grieve, and great nobles to call her behavior intolerable.

The three kings preferred to believe those unfounded Lothairian rumors as truth, and Hilduin was of like mind. The arch-chaplain declared nothing was more unfortunate than the day the emperor summoned *Naso*, whom he called a manifest Antichrist. He blamed Judith's lust for Bernard and her *maleficia* for bringing the count to Court.

Exhausted from his extensive swim, Bodo rested at the edge of the pool. In the torchlight, steam rising from the water formed an unnatural mist that obliterated visibility. Bodo thought he made out the form of a female approaching in the mist and hovering above the water.

The shape dissolved in the mist, and Bodo continued to sit confused at the edge of the pool. No light from the torch. How much time had passed? What did these visions mean? Why could he not remember?

As Bodo foresaw, King Confusion and not the emperor reigned. He would forever remember the weeks of Lent and the month after as a time of avoidable blunders.

First Blunder: During Lent of 830, Louis' inaction allowed the Lotharians to scheme and sow unrest throughout the empire. Because the populace believed the dissident clergy, Counts Gaucelm and Meinrad could not raise an adequate army in Septimania, nor could Count-Bishop Eudo build a sizable force at Orleans.

Second Blunder: Count Bernard and Judith convinced Louis that the Bretons were not waiting for the spring thaws to assert their independence from the empire and he should form an army and conquer those bothersome vassals for good.

Third Blunder: Two weeks before Easter Sunday Bernard showed Louis reports that the margraves had secured the border against the Bretons. He urged the emperor to march on Paris instead and punish all disloyal counts and clerics. Louis refused to believe his subjects would rebel and instead decided to conquer the Bretons.

Fourth Blunder: Bernard prevailed upon the emperor to begin the march from Aachen on Holy Thursday, second to Easter as the holiest of days, which impelled prominent clergy to proclaim the emperor *quibusdam praestigiius deluseum,* delusional without ability to reason. They called Bernard a blasphemer at best and at worst a Jew who disrespected Christianity. When Louis ordered his army to move out, the Franks refused and threatened mutiny. Loyal Alamanni and Saxon contingents supported the emperor and forced the march.

Fifth Blunder: Judith and Count Bernard did not accompany the emperor. That mistake gave further credence to rumors about their adultery.

Sixth Blunder: When Louis' army reached Rennes at the border of Brittany on the Armorica Peninsula, messages confirmed that the conspirators were waiting in Paris for Lothair and Pepin to arrive with reinforcements. Yet, Louis decided against riding to Paris ahead of his sons and instead returned to Aachen.

Seventh Blunder: At Aachen where Louis hoped to regroup, Bernard announced they were too weak to attack the Lothairians or defend the capital. Louis gave Bernard permission to return with his family to Septimania and recruit a large army.

Eighth Blunder: Louis agreed to the Lothairians' demand that he attend a Diet in Compiègne.

Ninth Blunder: Louis sent Judith with Charles, Giséle and Strabo to the Convent of Saint Mary at Laon for asylum, and he told Count Evrard to defend the palace with a small number of soldiers.

Bodo worried the emperor had indeed become delusional. How could Louis believe Judith and his children would be safe in any convent, church, or abbey? If men broke their word more than once to God and their emperor, why would they honor the canon of Sanctuary?

Bodo the Apostate

Unable to sleep the night before he left with Louis for Compiègne, Bodo reviewed a list of allegations and new demands Wala signed and sent to the emperor.

The Lothairians accused His Majesty of violating the Constitution of 817, having given large areas of Lothair's and Pepin's lands to Charles.

They accused the emperor of removing senior officials without a fair hearing.

They accused the empress and Count Bernard of adultery.

The conspirators demanded that Louis abdicate and retire to a monastery.

They demanded Judith be confined for life in a convent, Charles imprisoned unto death in a monastery and Princess Gisélé placed in a convent until she wed or not at all.

Wala decreed if Bernard did not die during battle he would be executed if captured.

Why did Louis not reject those absurd and disrespectful demands, flee to his loyal Alamanni and Saxons, and raise a new army? Did the emperor believe he could sway the Lothairians away from their harsh goals with rhetoric?

Perhaps Louis understood that except for a collective desire to restore the Division of 817, his foes had conflicting goals.

Lothair aspired to be sole emperor, but Pepin and Ludwig wanted more autonomy.

Great Magnates led by the Unholy Trinity wanted to control their domains without interference.

The Church sought to assert its supremacy over temporal rulers and institute widespread reforms.

Wala and other former officials, who wielded power during Charlemagne's last years, sought revenge against Louis for confiscating their titles, lands, and most of all for imprisoning them.

And what were Bernard's true motives? The insurgents feared *Naso* because of his deserved reputation as a victorious general. An army led by Bernard, even if outnumbered, might have caused the rebels to disperse. What scheme did he have in mind? Would the self-proclaimed Duke of Septimania form a large army and come to Louis' aid? Did he intend to create a separate kingdom during the chaos of rebellion? Or, did Bernard have a more audacious scheme, the one his enemies described: murder Louis, wed Judith, and rule the empire through Prince Charles.

Louis had not revealed why he accepted Wala's demand to appear at Compiègne. The emperor might be indecisive, but he could be cunning.

54. Compiègne

Bodo enjoyed previous seasonal hunts with the emperor at Compiègne in Picardy where nearby dense forests of beech and oak provided ample deer, wild boar, and rabbits for the chase. This day outside the assembly hall beside the royal residence on the west bank of the Oise, Bodo felt more like prey when he and Priscus walked behind Louis between two lines of soldiers holding back a hostile mob.

Louis wore plain tunic and mantle and bore no arms, nor did Priscus, but Bodo carried sword and dagger. Before they arrived at Compiègne, he acceded to the emperor's request not to draw his weapons no matter what transpired.

Inside the hall, Lothair sat crowned on his father's throne holding orb and scepter. Pepin and Ludwig sat on either side in lower chairs. A crescent of ranking archbishops, bishops, and abbots stood below the dais. Wala, Hilduin, Agobard, Ebbo, and Helisachar glared at Louis, and Bodo regarded each with disgust. What kind of Christians were they who violated oaths sworn in the name of the Lord?

Bodo turned his attention to the three kings. Lothair might be wearing imperial regalia, but he seemed unsure of himself and drank from a jeweled goblet. Pepin had an odd expression, neither one of pity nor triumph, eyes unfocused, jaw slack. Ludwig fidgeted, unable to look at his father.

A commotion interrupted Bodo's musings when four soldiers brought Conrad and Rudolf in chains to Lothair and forced Judith's brothers to their knees. Cuts and bruises marred both faces, eyes swollen and discolored.

Count-Abbot Wala, who presided over the Diet, beckoned Abbot Helisachar. "I give you the honor of tonsuring these overweening Welfing pups and the choice of confining them in separate monasteries where they may reflect upon their sins until the day they die."

Bodo the Apostate

"I have already selected their prisons." With a dagger, Helisachar pulled, cut, and shaved Conrad's and Rudolf's hair the way hunters skinned game after the chase. Blood from the abbot's slashes flowed down their faces.

After the soldiers dragged Conrad and Rudolf from the hall, Matfrid of Orleans led Count Evrard before Lothair bound in heavier chains than Conrad and Rudolf.

Bishop Agobard confronted the prisoner. "This blaspheming criminal is *Naso's* brother. We all know he has championed Jews over Christians in my Diocese of Lyon. For his many crimes and violations of canonic laws, he must be put to death."

Wala whispered to Lothair, who nodded agreement and gave the Count-Abbot permission to speak. "No, not death," Wala shouted. "Evrard shall be blinded and exiled to a dungeon cell at the Monastery of Monte Cassino in Italy."

Louis did not protest, but Bodo saw the emperor's jaw muscles tighten when two henchmen forced Evrard to his knees, and Matfrid of Orleans brought a heated blade into the hall. One man gripped Evrard's hair and pulled the count's head backward until it was face up and immobile. Matfrid, a protégé of Agobard, forced open his victim's right eye. Bodo's scrotum contracted at Evrard's agonized screams when Matfrid pressed the flat of the heated blade against his eyeballs and seared them.

"*Majister Judaeorum*, no more," Agobard proclaimed. "Never again shall you vex me. Take this dog away."

"Were *Naso* here, I would deal with him myself," Wala declared as soldiers carried Evrard away and Lantbert of Nantes pushed Judith into the hall.

Unnaturally pale, her coarse robe torn and soiled, Judith pointed at Matfrid and Lantbert and accused them of violating the Law of Asylum when they abducted her, Prince Charles, and Princess Giséle from the convent. Over loud objections, the empress described how Matfrid and Lantbert promised a painful death by slow torture unless she agreed to go to a convent and tell the emperor he had no choice except to abdicate, submit to tonsure, and become a monk.

Those had been Wala's demands, but Louis faced Lothair instead, his posture straight, tone of voice authoritative. "Before this assembly, we give our empress leave to retire to a convent."

That was not enough for Wala. He confronted Judith with all the self-righteousness of an Old Testament prophet. "Oh, wicked Jezebel, you are no longer empress and are hereby banished to Poitiers. There at Saint Radegunda's Convent of the Holy Cross, where Louis cruelly and without just cause exiled my sister fifteen years ago ... there you shall take the veil and spend the rest of your life in contemplation for your many sins."

Judith ignored Wala and spoke to Lothair. "We demand to see and speak to our Charles."

Wala intervened. "No. Never again shall you see him."

Bodo admired Judith for her regal bearing and courage amidst so many enemies and shouts from the mob outside demanding her death. The empress' comportment did not change when two servants carried the detached head of Nike's statue into the hall, its nose broken away, and Wala swung a mallet smashing it to pieces.

"Thusly, I destroy this pagan representation of a vain sorceress. Take that woman to Saint Radegunda. Give the witch no comforts."

Monks escorted Judith from the hall, and the empress cried out Charles' name when she passed Lantfrid returning with her children and Strabo. Eight year old Charles seemed confused and frightened. Giséle placed an arm around her younger brother's shoulder and held his hand no less defiant than her mother.

Lothair raised his scepter for silence. "No harm shall come to the children at this Diet. It is for me alone to decide their fate at a later time in Aachen. Gentle Strabo, you may accompany Charles and still tutor the boy. Perhaps you can teach him to be a better man than his father."

Wala glowered at the emperor. "And now you. Do you confess to all accusations and agree to each of our demands?"

Louis did not flinch, posture still erect, tone of voice stentorian. "We have read them all. We gave our consent that the empress may retire to a convent, but we shall not abdicate and go to a monastery. You, my eldest son, you must commit patricide, and you, Wala, you must commit regicide to have your way. But we solemnly avow that never again shall we do anything without your counsel. We therefore decree and will that the empire continue as formerly ordained by the *Divisio* of 817 and constituted by us with your consent."

Bodo almost applauded Louis for wresting the initiative from Lothair and Wala. Confused, the Count-Abbot deferred to Lothair for a decision. Louis' eldest son drank from his goblet and stood.

"Now, I want all present to bear witness to this." Lothair gestured,

Bodo the Apostate

and two priests carried a heavy Bible to Louis. "Place your hand on this Holy Writ." Louis complied. "Do you recognize I Lothair, King of Italy, as your co-emperor and your sole heir to the empire?"

"We do."

Bodo saw both Pepin and Ludwig frowning at Lothair's demand to be sole heir of their father. Did Louis see their reactions? The emperor had confided on several occasions how well he understood his sons' ambitions and the venality of men. Would Louis apply the dictum *divide et impera*, divide and rule?

Lothair continued, "Do you agree to restore all lands to me and my brothers that you gave to Charles?"

"We do."

Not only the Lotharians, even Louis was capable of swearing false oaths with hand on the Bible.

Lothair confirmed Pepin's claim to Autun and other lands seized from Bernard, but he added nothing to Ludwig's Kingdom of Bavaria. Bodo suspected Ludwig, who coveted Alamannia, must now be worrying how far to trust his brother. He also remembered the expression of anger on Pepin's face when Louis confirmed Lothair as sole heir to the empire. His Majesty might yet be able to induce both brothers to turn against Lothair.

Hilduin spoke. "What shall be the fate of these two adherents of Louis, Subdeacon Bodo, who is his confidante, and Priscus, who practices judicial astrology, which is a pagan practice banned by our *Orthodox* Church? I recommend their banishment to monasteries."

Lothair beckoned Bodo and Priscus to the foot of the dais, and the astronomer said, "I have served both Charlemagne and my emperor as Royal Astronomer, and I deny any and all accusations that I practice judicial astrology. I chart the heavens solely to determine the weather and to aid physicians in their diagnoses, of which the Church approves as natural astrology."

Lothair interrupted Hilduin's protest. "Priscus may continue as royal astronomer."

"Then what about Bodo? His negligible tonsure and blasphemous questions are an affront to our Church."

"Bodo shall attend me, arch-chaplain. One last thing. I command all present to continue respecting my father as co-emperor, and he shall accompany me to Aachen. And now, I declare this Diet, ended,"

During the ride to Aachen, Bodo summarized in his mind all that had occurred. Lothair vacillated no less than his father. He should have tonsured and banished Louis and Charles to a monastery and sent Giséle to a convent, which Wala had wanted. Not Lothair or either of his brothers, not Judith, and not Count Bernard, Count-Abbot Wala might have been the one individual to hold the empire together, but that could never be. Bodo longed for a return to the old Alamannic tribal tradition of men electing the strongest and wisest to be their chieftain.

55. All for Naught

At Aachen, Lothair confined Louis in the emperor's apartments, moved into Judith's suite, and quarantined Charles, Giséle, and Strabo in Welf's home. Priscus resumed his duties in the observatory, and Bodo carried out his obligations as subdeacon. Lothair requested Bodo attend him at hunts and palace banquets repeatedly tempting him with promises if he forsook Louis. Lothair gave his word that Bodo could obtain a release from his clerical vows and be knighted with the titles Count of Hohentweil, Count of Bodman, and Count of the Aargau.

Bodo no longer aspired to transient titles bestowed and taken away at an emperor's caprice. Having reached the age of eighteen and an inch over six feet with the bearing of a noble knight, he enjoyed life at Court as a favorite and could not resist a whim to style his mustache and beard identical to Lothair's. Whenever Bodo wore clothes suitable for the chase and a cap that covered his tonsure, palace officials and guards often mistook him for the co-emperor.

Lothair assigned Bodo and several monks to harangue Louis and persuade his father to accept the monastic life. He also appointed Bodo to discover what happened to the greater portion of the palace treasury. All gold and silver coins and the most valuable gems and artifacts had disappeared. Louis accused the rebels of looting. The Lothairians suspected *Naso* may have taken the treasures when he fled with his family to Septimania.

After Bodo heard complaints that Abraham's home and warehouse also had been emptied of valuables before looters arrived, he deduced that with the emperor's consent the merchant had sequestered the greater portion of Louis' imperial treasury in anticipation of an insurrection and took his family and personal wealth to an undisclosed location.

Whenever they met, Bodo read and discussed the Old Testament with Louis, mostly Psalms and about the reigns and conduct of Israelite kings. He assured the emperor that Charles and Giséle were not being mistreated while living with Strabo under guard at the Welfings' home.

Not long after he arrived in Aachen, Bodo cultivated a friendship with Gundbald, a Saxon from a noble family and one of the monks Lothair assigned to sway Louis toward a monastic life. Over several evenings of drinking with Bodo, Gundbald described how he resented his parents for giving him to the Church at age ten as an oblate. A young man in his early twenties, Gundbald disdained the monastic life and divulged his grandiose aspirations to Bodo, who believed the short ambitious man could be brought to Louis' side with proper inducements.

Bodo spoke to the emperor about Gundbald. "If you promise the monk an impressive reward, he will come over to your side."

"What price does he ask?"

"To be your *camerarius* in place of Count Bernard."

"So great an appetite for one so small and slight. Well, why not? Although we prefer Drogo to be our next *camerarius*, we shall, for the time being, promise Gundbald that place he covets, provided the monk succeeds at any task we assign him."

Two months after the Diet at Compiègne, Bodo sensed Lothair's growing insecurity after the co-emperor's soldiers, noble and clerical allies dispersed to their farms, estates, abbeys, and sees. Because he had no access to Louis' treasury, Lothair could not pay for a sufficient force of mercenaries.

Then Gundbald sent word to Bodo of his success with Louis' other sons. Enticed by the monk's promises in the emperor's name and their mistrust of Lothair, Pepin gathered an army in Aquitaine and Ludwig the same in Bavaria to rescue Louis. By then, a large contingent of loyal Saxons and Alamanni commanded by Drogo and Hugo approached Aachen and forced Lothair to flee.

When Lothair sent a message asking to meet with his father, Louis agreed but issued specific conditions:

Lothair must appear with each dissident noble, bishop, and abbot at a Diet in Nijmegen. They could bring no more than a single retainer. None should wear armor and carry arms.

The emperor forbade Hilduin, Helisachar, and Ebbo to appear.

Bodo appreciated why Louis chose Nijmegen. Built along the Waal River, a tributary of the Rhine, the town was adjacent to loyal Saxony where Ludwig's army of Bavarians augmented the forces led by Drogo and Hugo while Pepin approached from the south.

Wearing crown and jeweled robe, holding the orb and scepter of imperial authority, and Charles standing at his side, Louis welcomed Lothair with honor in the assembly hall of the Nijmegen administrative palace. Bodo had a good vantage point on the floor between Priscus and Strabo.

Hilduin accompanied Lothair in full armor and bearing weapons contrary to the emperor's terms. Louis showed all he had regained control of the empire when he commanded Hilduin to leave Nijmegen or suffer dire consequences. The erstwhile arch-chaplain and abbot obeyed without argument or defiance.

Louis introduced Gundbald to the assembly as his presiding official. The monk's air of self-importance was made more ridiculous by his high-pitched voice. The pompous little man might make an innocuous comment about some food or the weather and yet seem offensive.

Gundbald screeched the names of the rebel leaders. "Each man shall be taken to Aachen for confinement and trial. King Lothair shall be confined to the palace." He paused, faced the conspirators, and then the assemblage. "In the matter of Her Imperial Majesty, Judith Augusta, you shall acknowledge that you imprisoned the empress unjustly and illegally without trial."

All Lothairians including the Unholy Trinity obeyed, and Gundbald again rapped his staff of authority. "The empress shall be brought to Aachen, where according to law, anyone who accused her of sorcery, witchcraft, and other crimes must either offer proof of those charges or defend himself by judicial combat. Furthermore, Count-Abbots Conrad and Rudolf shall have their lands and titles restored."

Gundbald declared the Diet closed, and Louis summoned Bodo to his apartments. "Lead an escort of suitable rank and pomp for the empress, and bring her to Aachen where we shall winter."

After a five hundred mile journey to and from Poitiers that took several

Bodo the Apostate

months, Bodo escorted Judith into Aachen with fanfares and a guard of honor. He scorned the mob lining the streets. Months earlier, crowds had raged and threatened the lives of Their Majesties. Now, men and women of all classes cheered and shouted welcomes at the former "Jezebel empress."

The palace came to life. Celebrations and rejoicing followed even though Judith could not yet cohabit with Louis. The empress needed Pope Gregory's approval to be released from her religious vows and to remove the veil. She contented herself by doting on Charles.

A week after Judith's return, Louis informed his council that a message arrived from Count Bernard who requested restoration to *camerarius* but did not explain why he failed to come to the aid of Their Majesties as promised. The emperor asked for advice how best to refuse that proud, ambitious, and unpredictable warrior.

Bodo, whom Louis added to his inner circle of advisors, agreed with Drogo, Hugo, Priscus, and Judith's brothers that Bernard must never return to Court. The count was the main if not the only cause of the rebellion through misuse of office and sweeping removal of the emperor's former advisors. No one mentioned Bernard's presumed adultery with Judith or Louis' abrogation of the 817 Division of Empire as contributing factors.

The emperor considered all they said. "We are aware of Bernard's failures. For those reasons we have decided that never again shall he be our *camerarius* or invited to Court. The monk Gundbald has asked to be our Imperial Chamberlain, and we did promise him high rank if he served us well, which he has. He is in the antechamber awaiting our decision. Subdeacon Bodo, bring Gundbald here."

56. Another New Division of Empire

The next Imperial Diet took place in the Council Hall of the Aachen palace. Bodo doubted Louis would be strong and decisive. Men might have free will, but few had iron will.

The emperor sat on one throne, the one beside him empty. Charles stood beside his father, Lothair, Pepin, and Ludwig at one side below the dais. All rebel leaders who had been captured, tried, and convicted genuflected before the emperor. Only Archbishop Ebbo was missing. Louis could not bring himself to punish his foster brother, yet another repeated blunder.

Chamberlain Gundbald pounded his staff of office on the floor. "His Imperial Majesty, Hludovicus Caesar, will now speak."

Louis rose, stared at the prisoners, and pronounced punishments Bodo had long desired to hear. "We hereby sentence all of you to death for treason and *laesae majestas*." Over gasps from the assembly, Louis demanded of his sons, "Do you concur?"

"Yes, Your Majesty," each said.

Louis disappointed Bodo yet again.

"But, we can be just and merciful. Therefore, we hereby commute all sentences from death to banishment. Laymen shall be tonsured. Appropriate monasteries shall be the future homes for all traitors with certain exceptions I have decreed."

Louis sat and Gundbald read from a scroll. "Helisachar, you are hereby deprived of all abbeys and benefices. Leave now for your home.

"Hilduin, you have already lost your position at Court and the Abbeys of Saint-Denis and Saint Medard. Furthermore, you shall spend the winter in an army hut at Paderborn to reflect on your ingratitude and hubris. Take him away.

"Hugh of Tours, Matfrid of Orleans, and Lantbert of Nantes, you are forever dispossessed of all titles and lands. Matfrid and Lantbert, you are fined for violating the Canon of Asylum when you abducted Empress Judith, Prince Charles, Princess Giséle, and Walafrid Strabo from their sanctuary. The penalties are thirty-six solidi to be paid to the Church and forty solidi to be paid to the authorities for violation of the law and for each person taken. Remove them."

Gundbald requested Lothair place his right hand on the palace Bible. "Do you swear never again to usurp the emperor's authority over his realm?"

"I so swear."

Gundbald unrolled a scroll and read in a sonorous pompous monotone, "His Majesty has issued a new *Divisio Imperii* to replace the *Ordinatio* of 817."

The assemblage fell silent. Louis' three sons tensed. Less than a year had passed before Louis violated his oath at Compiègne to uphold the original *Divisio*.

Bodo the Apostate

"King Lothair, you have forfeited all lands except your Kingdom of Italy. You no longer are co-emperor.

"King Pepin, you are now co-emperor in Lothair's place. In addition to your kingdom of Aquitaine, you shall have rule over all lands between the Loire and the Seine, and north of the Seine the counties of Chalon, Meaux, Amiens, and Ponthieu to the coast."

Face flushed, Gundbald paused, took a deep breath, and screeched, "However, King Pepin, you will have no rule over Autun, Septimania, Gothia, and the March of Hispania. Count Bernard, who is *in absentia*, will be notified of the following: He shall be vassal to the Crown with the understanding that Their Majesties will have direct rule over all counties until their son Charles is of age. Then they shall be his."

Gundbald coughed to clear his throat. "King Ludwig, for your loyalty, his Majesty generously adds to your Bavarian lands Thuringia, Saxony, Flandria, and Frisia."

Bodo foresaw seeds of a new uprising being sown in the Council Hall. Despite having been raised to co-emperor, Pepin coveted more lands, specifically Septimania and Gothia. Lothair would not be satisfied being a mere King of Italy. Ludwig wanted Alamannia.

"We shall speak now." Louis rose again from his throne. "We restore to our son, Prince Charles, Alsace, Alamannia, Rhaetia, and his portion of Burgundy. We further give Charles King Lothair's lands on the Meuse and Moselle, Rheims and its surrounding county. He shall rule over those lands ... and Provence, Septimania, Gothia, and the Spanish March as in my name when he comes of age."

Louis softened his voice. "If any one of our three sons behaves with overt obedience and good will towards Almighty God and, secondly, toward our self, it will delight us to confer upon him yet greater honor and power. We will increase his portion of lands at the expense of any brother who shall have displeased us."

The emperor paused and made a sweeping gesture. Servants opened doors. Horns blew an extended fanfare, and Judith appeared resplendent in a jeweled mantle with a crown atop her head accompanied by Conrad, Rudolf, Giséle, and her ladies. Louis offered his hand, and the empress stepped onto the dais beside him. Gundbald held a parchment for the assemblage to see.

"Pope Gregory IV has released Empress Judith Augusta from all illegal vows forced upon her. Who present here and now wishes to repeat the false and vile charges against Her Majesty?"

No one met the challenge. Judith placed her hand on the Bible, swore she was innocent of all accusations, and sat on the throne beside Louis.

Gundbald faced Wala. "Because you led the rebellion against Their Majesties and because you imposed harsh sentences upon the blameless, you are hereby stripped of all honors and authority. You shall be taken to the mountains above Lake Leman. There, a cave shall be your home. There, you may live the remainder of your life as a hermit to contemplate and learn from your sins."

Bodo had been present when Judith inveigled Louis into decreeing Wala's harsh punishment. She hated the Count-Abbot most for leading the rebellion, spreading vile rumors about her and Bernard, and his insistence the Division of 817 be enforced, which would have deprived her precious Charles of all lands.

Gundbald rapped his staff. "It being the second day of February in the Year of our Lord 831, His Majesty commands that we begin celebrating the Feast of the Presentation. This assembly is ended."

But not the ambitions and resentments of certain men.

Because of Louis' vacillations, Bodo foresaw an inevitable second rebellion looming on the near horizon. As before, the emperor paid no heed to his councilors' warnings while former Lothairian counts, dispossessed clergy, and dismissed administrators plotted with the emperor's dissatisfied sons to reclaim their domains, titles, and benefices.

Ludwig still desired Alamannia more than any other province. Co-emperor Pepin wanted to add Charles' lands, Septimania, and the Midi to his Kingdom of Aquitaine. Lothair would not rest until he reclaimed his domains also given to Charles and replaced Pepin as co-emperor.

Despite the overt conspiring, Louis inexplicably called for an Imperial Diet at Ingelheim on the Rhine. May 831 in the administrative palace where Charlemagne died in 814, the emperor granted amnesty to all banished Lothairians and restoration of status to a select few. Louis reinstated Helisachar to his abbey in Picardy and Hilduin to the Abbeys of Saint-Denis and Saint Medard. Louis did listen to Judith and his advisors and moved Wala, farther from Lothair's Italy to Noirmoutier Monastery on the Bay of Biscay.

Bodo the Apostate

Bernard presented a problem. The "Duke" of Septimania never explained why he failed to come with an army and support Louis, yet in several letters he expressed his desire to return as the emperor's *camerarius*. Their Majesties did not reply, and their silence prompted Bernard to arrive uninvited at a subsequent Diet in the Alamannian town of Diedenhofen on the Moselle. Louis and Judith refused to meet with the count, and without comment Gundbald in the emperor's name commanded Bernard to leave immediately for Septimania.

During those Diets and assemblies, Bodo became aware of a strange phenomenon at Court. Everyone showed him respect as a man of great importance and sagacity and sought his opinion on a variety of problems and the current most perplexing question:

Rebuffed and disrespected by Louis, what might Count Bernard do when the next rebellion began: support the rebels out of spite, aid the emperor, or wait to see which side was the victor before committing his forces? One man whose opinions Bernard valued most might dissuade him from taking arms against Louis, but would the count's kinsman Abraham return to Court in time?

Then word arrived that Abraham had crossed into the empire with a caravan and emissaries from Baghdad. Well in advance of their arrival, Louis summoned the three kings to join him for the elaborate ceremonies and signing of a treaty. Lothair and Ludwig obeyed, but Pepin did not. Furious, Louis sent another command for his second son to appear at Aachen.

57. A Wider World

Early in October 831, Abraham and his eldest son Nathan returned to Aachen with two emissaries from Baghdad, cartloads of presents from Caliph al-Mamun, and luxury goods from the east for sale to the nobles. Both ambassadors, Mutasim and Wathiq, were the caliph's nephews, and the princes pitched their enormous colorful and lavish tents on a broad field provided by the emperor outside Aachen near the Brandenwald.

Louis sent Lothair, Ludwig, Bodo and others of his council to welcome Mutasim and Wathiq, who invited the delegation inside their tents. Colorful woven carpets of silk and fine wool with designs of rosettes, stylized animals and trees covered the ground and hung on the sides. Plush pillows formed divans upon which to sit or lounge around low tables laden with bowls filled with fruits and nuts. Some carpets had designs shaped as arches on which the Muslims prayed in the direction of Mecca in Arabia five times each day.

Formal and distant, the princes bore their status with the same ease as one might wear a mantle. At the slightest gesture, their servants crawled to their masters, awaited a command, and scurried away on their knees, eyes always on the ground. Mutasim, the eldest, spoke Greek and wanted to know when they might present the emperor with the caliph's gifts. Bodo, the most fluent in that language in Louis' welcoming party, told the ambassadors that His Majesty looked forward to greeting them the following day at mid-morning.

Each envoy's harem of veiled women carried by strong men on elaborate litters enclosed by silken draperies fascinated all, but the princes' advisors, soldier escorts, servants, and slaves interested Bodo most, for they illustrated what Priscus had told him about faraway peoples. So many varieties of humans, all presumably created in God's image, came from lands conquered by the Saracens or purchased from beyond. Some had strange slanted eyes and were yellow of complexion, others from Africa black of skin, and the rest every shade of brown to pale white, with noses small as a button to those large as Abraham's, and hair of every color and texture.

Throughout the envoys' stay at Aachen, Bodo wanted to learn everything about their lands and customs. One of the princes' bodyguards spoke Greek and let him test the feel and balance of the *saif*, their impressive curved sword of steel. He told Bodo that many who served the caliph were multi-lingual.

So much wider had the world become. So small the empire and so confining his comfortable life at Court now seemed, and less civilized, after Bodo learned more about the culture of Baghdad. Abraham's and Nathan's description of the Caliph's court and capital seemed more mythological than real, but others in the emissaries' party confirmed all they said and stoked Bodo's desire to visit one day. Was rival Cordoba as fabulous?

Bodo the Apostate

Inside the crowded Council Hall, Abraham stood between Louis and Judith on the dais and translated during a formal presentation of fabulous gifts and expressions of peace and friendship between Caliph al-Mamun and the emperor, the same as had happened almost thirty years earlier between their predecessors Haroun al-Rashid and Charlemagne. The ambassadors' servants placed in front of the dais fine textiles, jewel encrusted objects of gold, and boxes of rare spices including nutmeg, cardamom, aniseed, tumeric, sumac, cinnamon, cloves, and pepper.

A parade of animals destined for the royal menagerie awed and entertained the Court: Monkeys garbed as humans, flamboyant peacocks, striped and spotted cats weighing more than a full grown man, but no elephants. A pair of camels had died along the way.

Louis invited the princes and their escorts to a pheasant hunt in the Brandenwald where they exchanged gifts of stallions and mares, a pair of Arabians for the emperor and two Frisians for the caliph. Beaters led the hunting party, and Louis gave Mutasim and Wathiq the honor of releasing their prized fierce falcons and hawks. They did not disappoint. Pheasants fell by the dozens. Yelping hounds retrieved them. Cooks collected the birds and tossed them into carts to be taken to the palace kitchen. The emperor commanded his falconers and nobles to release their raptors, and hundreds more pheasants were killed.

At a grand banquet in the Council Hall attended only by males. Abraham, Nathan, and Zedekiah sat with the ambassadors on either side of Louis and translated for the emperor and Court officials. The Saracens had their own cooks, who ensured meats, fish, and pheasants were prepared separately according to their dietary law of *Halal*. Deferring to the Muslims, the palace cooks served no pig or boar. All courses went as planned until roasted pheasants arrived at the table on golden platters decorated with the fowl's colorful tail feathers. For the Christians, the birds' skins had been larded with bacon and innards filled with butter. Although the Saracens' pheasants were seasoned only with spices, many became nauseated by the aroma of bacon on nearby plates. Abraham mollified the Muslims with apologies on the emperor's behalf.

If Bodo's instincts were correct, the Merchant of the Palace performed another more valuable service for Louis of which few were aware. When the emperor delegated Abraham to supervise and inventory the caliph's gifts Bodo observed more barrels, packages. and bundles than Mutasim and Wathiq had given the emperor being carried by servants to the treasury. Other than the emperor, no one except Bodo guessed Abraham had secreted the royal treasury before the first rebellion began and returned it mixed with al-Mamun's presents. A successful outcome, but how soon would it all have to be sequestered again?

While the emperor entertained and conferred with his guests over the next several days, Louis' alliance with the Baghdad Caliphate distressed Lothair, Ludwig, and the more intolerant nobility and clergy. They had not forgotten ninety-nine years earlier on this same day, the tenth of October, Charles Martel defeated the Muslims at Tours, thus saving Western Europe for the *Orthodox* Church. Following his victory, Charles "the Hammer" and successors Pepin and Charlemagne drove the Saracens and Moors southward beyond the Pyrenees. Why, the Lothairians asked, must a Christian monarch sign an accord with so far away a Muslim ruler?

Bodo explained for the Lotharians, not always with success, that faith mattered not when it came to dynastic rivalries. Baghdad warred against Cordoba over who should be caliph and disputed land in North Africa. The empire battled the same foe along the Marches of Hispania. Bodo quoted a saying Abraham had translated for him from the Arabic language to justify Louis' treaty with the caliph, "The enemy of my enemy is my friend."

Duplicities came with alliances. Had the emperor abrogated his pact of friendship with the Khazars who warred against the Baghdad Caliphate? No, Abraham told Bodo. Louis had not betrayed the Jewish empire, nor was there any mention of the Khazars in the Treaty of Renewal, which the merchant read and translated before the emperor signed and placed his seal on the document.

The day before they departed, Mutasim and Wathiq invited Louis, Lothair, Ludwig, and the emperor's favorites to a feast in front of their tents. Carpets atop carpets covered the grass in front with pillows for seating. Several elderly councilors had difficulty adjusting their legs to sitting so low. Their Muslim hosts served roasted sheep and goat, and while they supped, the princes' horsemen amazed all with acrobatics on horseback and deadly accuracy with bow and arrow while riding.

58. Petty Insurgencies

The princes departed for Baghdad laden with the emperor's gifts for their caliph, and a courier arriving from Septimania reported that Bernard made an alliance with Pepin. Again Louis and his advisors discussed the problem of the haughty count. Abraham explained why he no longer influenced Bernard. Still the third Jewish Prince (*Nasi*) of Narbonne, Bernard believed through his royal blood from the Houses of David and Arnulf and great military victories he was more entitled than any other man in Europe to rule an independent kingdom if not an empire. A second rebellion offered the best opportunity to achieve his goal.

Would Meinrad support Bernard or the emperor? Bodo's brother-in-law faced a dilemma. Meinrad was Bernard's maternal cousin and vassal, but under the new Division of Empire, Louis held direct rule over Septimania and Gothia. If Meinrad chose the losing side, what might happen to Adeltrud and Guntrum?

Bodo's concerns for Adeltrud prompted him to address the emperor, "Your Majesty, perhaps if you lead an army to Septimania and defeat Bernard before he has a chance to form a large army ...."

"That will not be necessary, Bodo. We have already sent word to our loyal vassals in the Midi to do precisely that."

Early in 832 Louis' vassals from the Midi and County of Toulouse surprised Bernard with a mid-winter invasion of Septimania and took Roussillon, Conflent, and Elna. At the same time, Matfrid of Orleans, unaware of Bernard's defeats, encouraged pliable young King Ludwig to invade the Alamannian lands the emperor had given to Charles on the assumption Louis would be too preoccupied with Bernard to resist. Matfrid and Ludwig miscalculated. Louis decided to lead an army against his youngest son by Irmintrud.

Before Bodo left with the emperor, Judith summoned him and her brothers. "Deliver to us Matfrid's head. He must pay with his life for violating our sanctuary. We want our sister brought to us in chains. We shall make Hemma do penance for encouraging Ludwig to take our son's lands. Were the emperor of like mind, we would demand Wala's death. He has been treated too well at Noirmouitier. We have, therefore, ordered him removed to Saxony where he can do no harm."

Judith's smugness contradicted reality. Any mistreatment of Wala short of execution for treason would fail. The Lothairians believed the Count-Abbot was the one man who could make Lothair sole emperor and bring both unity and peace to the realm.

Louis reached Lampersheim on the lower Rhine in Alamannia near Ludwig's encampment sooner than his son anticipated. The young king fled to Augsburg in Bavaria. The emperor's army gave chase. Ludwig surrendered without giving battle, and Matfrid escaped to Lothair's court in Italy.

Ludwig vowed never again to wage war against Louis or listen to anyone who advised it. The Emperor reprimanded his wayward son and commanded him to stay in Bavaria. Judith would not have Matfrid's head or see her sister Hemma in chains.

In October, the emperor's vassals defeated and captured Bernard, his brother Gaucelm, and King Pepin. They brought the prisoners to Louis at Limoges, a town built on Roman ruins in west-central Frankia. In a makeshift assembly hall at his villa residence, the emperor spared all lives. He chastised Pepin, removed him as co-emperor, and imprisoned his son in comfortable circumstances at Trier.

After Bernard apologized and expressed remorse for his alliance with Pepin, Louis punished the count and Gaucelm with loss of all lands and titles in Septimania and Gothia, which he bestowed upon the loyal vassals who defeated them. The emperor also rusticated Bernard to Autun in Burgundy where the erstwhile count had a family estate.

Bodo did not dwell upon Louis' mercies because Count Meinrad died from an infected wound. No longer Countess of Béziers, Adeltrud faced a destitute future. After speaking to Judith on his sister's behalf, the empress gave Bodo a scroll summoning Adeltrud back to Court. He sent Judith's message and a note of his own with the next courier to the south urging Adeltrud to leave Béziers immediately.

Bodo the Apostate

In October, Louis summoned all Court officials to the Council Hall. "Pepin has escaped to Aquitaine where he is raising another larger army. Therefore, we hereby dispossess him of Aquitaine, with the concurrence of King Lothair. Our beloved son Charles is now King of Aquitaine and so he shall be addressed as Your Majesty. We shall rule directly over the Aquitainians until King Charles comes of age."

That evening Bodo entered Louis apartments expecting to discuss relevant passages in the Bible. Instead, the emperor again confided in him.

"Bodo, we know you believe we are too lenient with those who would tear asunder the empire. You prefer we execute the traitors or chain them in dungeons for the rest of their lives. But we are not Byzantines. Although our sons have disappointed us, we cannot murder or tyrannize them. They must be taught severe lessons though. Promise us you will not divulge to anyone what we are about to say."

"I promise, Your Majesty."

"We are not well. There are worse ailments than gout, but we hope to live until Charles reaches his fifteenth birthday and we make him co-emperor. But that is still six years away. After Charles is securely in power, we shall then retire to a monastery."

Bodo foresaw the three kings uniting to defeat Charles. "I pray you do not."

Louis slouched in his chair and beckoned Bodo closer. "The empress has made it known to us that she intends for you to be our son's *camerarius* when he becomes co-emperor, and we concur. For that reason and for your loyalty and honesty, if we live long enough, you may yet become our *camerarius* and so be best prepared to serve Charles."

"Your Majesty ...."

"Subdeacon Bodo, we see by your expression we have surprised you. No need for you to say more. Now, sit beside us and read from the Book of Job. And then we shall discuss how we Christians and the Jews have differing interpretations of Satan."

In May of 833, Bodo walked along the bank of the Rhine at Worms and brooded over Louis' miscalculations during the past six months. They began the previous autumn when bishops and abbots in Saxony honored and deferred to Wala contrary to Judith's commands. Short of assassination the most respected man in the empire would continue to be the de facto leader of the Lothairians. Louis rejected Bodo's proposal and instead allowed the empress to write a decree ordering Wala returned to Corbie reduced to an ordinary monk without any position of authority.

Led by Priscus, who predicted an early winter, the council unanimously advised the emperor to deal with the Aquitainian insurrection after the spring thaws. Prodded by Judith to protect their son's added portion of the empire, Louis rejected the Astronomer's warnings and led an army toward Aquitaine to pacify the kingdom unprepared for Pepin's two formidable allies: unfamiliar terrain that allowed the rebels to make surprise raids, and brutal weather. Heavy autumnal downpours caused massive flooding. Early snow, slush, and ice blocked the roads forcing a retreat to Le Mans on the Sarthe River. Instead of regrouping his army, Louis spent the season of the Nativity hunting before he returned to Aachen. By then, Lothair and Ludwig allied with Pepin against Louis.

Throughout the early months of 833, while the size of armies on both sides increased, Lothairian bishops, abbots, and nobles, to whom Louis had granted mercy, repeated old lies about the empress. They fulminated in sermons and letters that Judith alone ruled the empire through sorcery and surrounded herself with advisors worse than Bernard, who, "like the Four Horsemen of the Apocalypse, trampled underfoot truth, justice, peace, and harmony."

"Ruined" was a better description than "ruled," and Judith used no sorcery nor did she listen to any advisor. The empress was so obsessive about Charles' inheritance she would destroy the empire to ensure her precious son gained a large portion of its corpse. Not any of the Lothairians and not Louis' three sons, Judith had become the greatest traitor of all.

Bodo believed that the emperor's inconsistencies and merciful nature caused all ills afflicting the empire except those brought on by Nature. Louis gave and took away kingdoms and counties at whim. He decreed severe punishments and then rescinded them. He desired clerical reforms but did not follow through with promulgating them. Better that Louis ruled like a Byzantine tyrant and executed all who conspired or warred against him.

Now an advisor to the emperor and privy to all that went on in the empire, Bodo suffered great distress because he and other councilors could not persuade Louis to attack while they outnumbered the Lothairians and before Lothair arrived with an army from Italy. Throughout May and into June while the emperor negotiated with Pepin and Ludwig, the Lothairians freed popular Wala from his exile at Corbie and made him their nominal leader.

Again, Bodo considered what might happen if he left Louis' Court to serve Lothair. He would despise himself. That, an unshakeable sense of loyalty, and instinct Lothair could not be trusted prevented Bodo from betraying Louis. No matter the outcome, he would honor his oaths and promises to Their Majesties according to Alamannic custom and his conscience.

59. Papal Plop

Word arrived Lothair crossed the Rhine with a large army accompanied by Pope Gregory IV, who sent messages to Louis of his intention to mediate a satisfactory solution between father and sons. Having the Pope at his side was enough for Lothair to convince the populace and many in Louis' army that His Holiness and, by implication, God favored the three kings.

Louis led his army south to Colmar in Alsace to meet with the Pope. He encamped by the Lauch River between the Vosges Mountains and Upper Rhine. Below a hill venerated and named by the Alamanni Siegberg, Mountain of Victory, the emperor faced the combined forces of his three sons several hundred yards away on a vast meadow known as Rothfeld, the Bloody Field.

Louis' soldiers voiced their reluctance to do battle against His Holiness. Unlike the great magnates and knights who sought honors and glory, freemen, tenants, and lesser nobles armed with spears, axes, and crude clubs preferred to be home with their families rather than risk death or maiming for nothing more than an exchange of rulers.

When Louis asked Priscus what the Astronomer divined from the planets and constellations, Bodo almost spoke out that the recent past not the heavens provided a better map of the future. Did no one else foresee an inevitable repeat of Louis' surrender in 830? That the emperor brought Judith, Charles, and Giséle with him also confounded Bodo. So did the empress' silence. How could Louis not realize he was placing their freedom and lives in jeopardy?

It mattered not to Bodo that the Vicar of Christ came as a man of peace if Lothair could intimidate Gregory through secular authority and implied force. The Pontiff had been coerced by such threats before. When Gregory was proclaimed Pope in 827, Louis imposed a delay for the consecration because, according to the Imperial Constitution of 824, as emperor he had to be convinced the Papal election was valid. Gregory complied. Thus, the Pope conceded that the emperor held supremacy over the Papacy.

Nothing good ever came from a Pontiff's meddling. Bodo never forgot Louis' humiliation at the feet of a previous Pope in 822 when Paschal I penanced the emperor for blinding his nephew Bernard, imprisoning innocent men, and violating the Division of Empire.

Neither side wanted to attack the other. Gregory IV summoned Louis' loyal bishops to attend a Mass in the field and for a parley afterward. Although the emperor preferred mediation to battle against his sons, he rejected the Pope's request. Archbishop Drogo wrote a reply that the bishops could not obey His Holiness because Louis had not ordered them to do so, thus continuing to assert His Majesty's primacy over the Papacy.

Bodo offered to deliver the bishops' response. He wanted to judge for himself the quality of the current spiritual leader of the Orthodox faith. Louis assented, and Bodo rode Amalric across the field through rows of knights, prelates and soldiers. Many bowed mistaking him for King Lothair.

Attended by cardinals, bishops, and lower ranking clergy, Gregory IV sat outside his white silken tent on a gilded throne resplendent in Papal finery but less impressive to Bodo than the Baghdad princes' grand display. Lothair, Pepin, and Ludwig stood on one side of the Pontiff, Wala, Agobard, and the emperor's ungrateful foster brother Ebbo, whom he raised to Archbishop of Rheims, on the other.

Bodo genuflected, kissed the Pope's ring, and handed His Holiness the bishops' response. While Gregory read the scroll, Bodo studied the

Bodo the Apostate

clean-shaven Pope said to be of noble birth. Soft of body, more amiable than dignified in appearance, those were mere externals. Was Gregory his own man?

Lothair answered Bodo's unspoken question with a disrespectful action. He snatched the parchment from the Pontiff's hand before Gregory finished reading, thus confirming for Bodo he dominated the Pope. Lothair told Bodo to wait and led Pepin, Ludwig, Gregory, Wala, Agobard, and Ebbo inside the Papal tent. After several hours, a priest emerged and without a word thrust the Pope's answer at Bodo, who carried it to the emperor.

Louis almost wept when Bodo told him Ebbo had joined the Lothairians. He recovered from the shock of his foster brother's betrayal and read the Pope's message aloud:

> "Do you not know that the rule over souls committed to us, a pontiff, is higher than the rule of emperor, which lasts but for a brief time? If I did not accuse the emperor of sinning against the realm, I should be committing perjury.
>
> You bishops say the Division the emperor made in 817 has now been altered by him because of timely need brought on by changed circumstances. This assertion, I say, is blatantly false. Not in season is the change, but out of season, for it is the cause and origin of tumult and discord, of turbulence and robbery, and more evils than may here be told."

Bodo pondered a theological conundrum. If His Holiness violated the Constitution of 824 in which Papacy conceded supremacy to the emperor, did it not set a precedent that released all Christian men from their vows whenever they chose to do so? Popes, bishops, abbots, kings, and nobles broke with predictable regularity God's Seventh Commandment by taking His name in vain. Why should he not to do the same?

Honor forbade. So did Bodo's yearning for an order that seemed no longer possible. At least he could be a fixed point of consistency in a chaotic world as an example to others.

60. "Field of Lies"

Three days after Bodo's twenty-first birthday, the twenty-fourth of June, and Day of the Feast of Saint John the Baptist, Pope Gregory broke the stalemate after Louis' loyal bishops refused to obey his repeated summons. Heralds blowing horns, drummers beating, cymbals clanging, and a choir of chanting monks and priests carrying Papal banners marched across the field to the emperor's camp. Escorted by cardinals and bishops and lesser clerics in their official robes, Pope Gregory followed in a gilded litter borne by eight strong men.

Each man in Louis' army dropped to his knees when the Pope passed and blessed them. Louis met Gregory outside the royal tent with all proper respect but rejected the Pope's terms. Negotiations continued. Pontiff, cardinals, and priests passed back and forth between the camps each day. Nobles, bishops, and soldiers on both sides mixed. Vatican officials and Lotharian magnates encouraged and bribed Louis' supporters to defect. A significant number did.

A priest approached Bodo. "You have been pointed out as the subdeacon said to be favored by the emperor and empress."

Bodo did not respond and waited for a predictable inducement from Lothair: release from his Holy vows, knighthood, and a county.

The priest did not disappoint. "King Lothair would favor you more than the emperor. He invites you to join his court. For that he would have His Holiness release you from your vows this day. He would make you Count of Hohentwiel, Bodman, and the Aargau, the same offices held by your father, Gunzo the Strong. He also would give you Princess Giséle to wed when she is nubile, or one of his own daughters. If you prefer to remain in the Church, he will bestow upon you a bishopric or abbey, with many lands and benefices."

Bodo gave much thought to Lothair's added enticements. "Tell King Lothair I thank him for his generosity, but I have sworn inviolable oaths to the Lord and to the emperor." Bodo no longer asked himself why he persisted in honoring his vows when other men, tempted by false promises and bribery or fearful of going against the Pope, deserted by the dozens to the other side.

Bodo the Apostate

Six days of negotiations passed before the Lotharian tactics succeeded. By the thirtieth of June, most nobles, bishops, and the greater part of the emperor's army defected. The Pope sent a priest to deliver a list of generous terms provided Louis surrendered.

The emperor decided he had no choice except to capitulate because most of his soldiers, clerics, and nobles had changed sides. Bishop Drogo spoke for all councilors and recommended they retreat east of the Rhine and gather a new army of loyal Alamanni and Saxons.

Louis slumped in his chair exhausted. "We believe our sons have accepted a compromise that will benefit all."

Drogo advised Louis to send Judith, Prince Charles, and Princess Giséle to Fulda. Abbot Hrabanus, always loyal to the emperor, could guarantee better sanctuary than what happened previously at Poitiers, and the Saxons were capable of defending the abbey. Louis rejected Drogo's recommendation and Conrad's and Rudolf's offer to escort their sister, nephew, and niece to Fulda.

The emperor held a scroll for all to see. "We have the written word of His Holiness that Her Majesty and our children will not be separated from us. If you wish, we give you leave to go to your estates, sees, and abbeys."

Bodo stepped closer to the emperor, "I shall never leave Your Majesty's side."

"Nor I," Priscus, Drogo, and Hugo shouted together.

Bodo rode with the imperial family and their few remaining adherents across the field to meet His Holiness in front of the Pope's tent. After they dismounted, Judith maintained a grip on Charles' shoulder. Eleven year old Giséle followed her mother. Conrad and Rudolf voiced their fears of being tonsured again.

Relaxed on his throne wearing a vivid red velvet cap and an ermine stole over silk robes. Gregory exuded benignity and held his hand low for each to genuflect and kiss his ring. Harsh expressions lined each of the three kings' faces even when they perfunctorily embraced their father. Wala seemed more worried than triumphant. That did not augur well. Not surprising, the disposed Lothairian magnates and clerics glared at Louis and Judith with palpable hatred.

Lothair interrupted the Pope's speech welcoming Louis and pointed at Judith. "Place that woman in the custody of King Ludwig, who shall take her to the convent at Tortona in Italy. There she shall stay for the remainder of her life."

Pope Gregory gulped for air like a fish out of water. His Holiness' distress appeared genuine.

Judith held Charles against her body and accused Lothair of treachery. Two monks pulled the empress from her son. Guards threatened Louis and his retinue with spears if they attempted to intervene. Another pair of clerics prevented Charles from aiding his mother.

Gisèle clung to Bodo for protection. No guard came near them. Bodo awaited a repeat of the same sequence of what happened during the first rebellion three years earlier. Except this time, harsher treatments of the emperor, empress, and Prince Charles seemed likely.

Lothair forced Louis to reaffirm the Constitution and *Divisio* of 817. "As co-emperor, I banish your son Charles to the monastery at Prüm and placed in the custody of his former preceptor Abbot Markward. Although the boy shall not be tonsured, he is now shorn of all lands. Henceforth, he shall be known throughout the empire as Charles the Bald."

Lothair waited for laughter to subside before he addressed Louis. "You shall be confined to Saint Medard Abbey in Soissons and there be penanced for your many sins and transgressions."

Bodo focused his attention on Pope Gregory. Yes, the Vicar of Christ had misread Lothair's intentions. Deceived by Louis' eldest son, His Holiness did not protest anything Lothair said or commanded. The words dupe, fool, and worse came to mind. The Papacy was no less corrupt and flawed than the Trinitarian Church it led.

Lothair rusticated instead of executing or imprisoning Louis' few noble supporters. He also allowed Drogo to retain the Diocese of Metz, Hugo his Abbey of Saint Quentin, and gave Louis' *camerarius* Gundbald leave to retire to a monastery of his choice. He chose a different outcome for Conrad and Rudolf.

"I prefer the look of these peacocks' previous shearing. Tonsure that woman's brothers and take them to the most remote monasteries, this time for good. Strabo, you may accompany Charles to Prüm. Priscus, you will continue to be Royal Astronomer. Princess Gisèle, stop your weeping. No harm will come to you. You will be taken to Chelles where your grandmother is Abbess. Subdeacon Bodo, we are kin, and I repeat my offer. It would please me to have the best ax man in the empire at my side."

"I thank you, but I cannot abandon my emperor, Hludovicus Caesar."

"As you wish. Perhaps you may yet have a change of mind. In the meantime, you will accompany my father and perhaps yet influence him to accept the tonsure and a life better suited to his nature than emperor. I also restore Hugh of Tours, Matfrid of Orleans, and Lantbert of Nantes to their honors, lands, and titles. I shall rule over Septimania and the Midi through my vassals."

Pepin and Ludwig looked at each other. They had not mistaken Lothair's intention to rule as sole emperor if their father abdicated and became a monk. Bodo believed they might yet be separated from Lothair, who again showed weakness and indecisiveness by not imprisoning or executing the emperor's loyal councilors. While they prepared to depart Rothfeld, Priscus took Bodo aside.

"They say His Holiness is distressed by Lothair's decisions. He had expected a true reconciliation."

"Pope Gregory has been used and cowed by Lothair. He does not deserve to be head of any church. His Holiness should be named His Irrelevancy."

"You may be right, Bodo, but do not repeat that within anyone else's hearing. Did you observe Wala's expression throughout the proceedings? It is obvious he disapproved of the betrayal."

"He offered no objections. His silence is the same as approval. Priscus, I shall always think of Rothfeld as a site of infamy. Better yet, it should be named *Campus Mendacii*, or *Lügenfeld*, the Field of Lies."

61. Louis' Nadir

At Soissons sur Aisne in Picardy, Lothair imprisoned his father in Hilduin's grim Abbey of Saint Medard at the town's outer boundary. He delegated all matters of Louis' confinement to the abbot, who forbade Bodo and physicians access to the emperor. Day and night Hilduin's monks and priests harangued Louis to confess all sins and abdicate of his own volition with no success.

Lothair gave Priscus permission to leave for Aachen. A vanguard he sent from "the Field of Lies" to take command of the treasury returned from the capital and reported the room had been emptied. Hilduin wanted to torture Louis and Bodo until they divulged where it was sequestered. Lothair refused. When questioned, Bodo responded with the truth. He did not know what happened to the treasury.

Lothair resided in the abbey when he was not hunting or carousing. Bodo chose to sleep each night in a tent. The less contact he had with Hilduin the better. Neither hostage nor a prisoner, but more as booty taken from the emperor, Bodo assessed his status at Soissons. Loyalty to Louis prevented flight to Alamannia or Saxony, which would have been tantamount to deserting the emperor.

Throughout July and August into mid-September, Bodo took advantage of his favorable standing with Lothair and relative freedom. Invited to the chase, meals, and drinking bouts, he also exercised Amalric, trained with weapons, and swam back and forth across the Aisne to release tension.

Seething with animus toward the Lothairians, Bodo mastered his emotions. Not by voice, not by facial expression did he reveal the contempt and disgust he felt for the traitors. Bodo's glacial aloofness created an unreachable barrier that prevented unwanted conversation, His intimidating skill with weapons and physical strength discouraged challenges.

By the first day of autumn, Bodo read Lothair as easily as the Latin alphabet. A vacillator like his father, Lothair lacked the resolve to depose or execute the emperor. Physically courageous but a moral coward, he took no responsibility for his actions and blamed others when confronted. A poor administrator, Lothair allowed himself to be ill served by venal supporters. No one advised him to consolidate his power at Aachen, declare Louis incompetent, and rule as de facto emperor.

Unlike Louis, who prayed and conversed about passages from the Bible after the chase, Lothair spent the remainder of the day into the evening drinking and wallowing in the Seventh Deadly Sin of Gluttony. Another dissimilarity, Louis never rebelled against Charlemagne.

Bodo remembered his own father. Inconceivable he would have abused Count Gunzo the way Lothair humiliated Louis. And the son was not through with the father. Lothair sanctioned a plan conceived by the bishops to solve for all time the problem of Louis' abdication.

On the Calends of October 833 Lothair brought his father to a Diet organized by the bishops at Compiègne about forty miles from Soissons.

Bodo the Apostate

In the assembly hall of the administrative palace, Lothair sat between Pepin and Ludwig. His brothers seemed more ornamental than kings of importance. Lothairian clergy and nobility at the forefront included: the Unholy Trinity of Hugh, Matfrid, and Lantbert; Abbot Wala of Corvey; Bishop Agobard of Lyon; Abbot Hilduin of Saint Denis and Saint Medard; Archbishop Otgar of Mainz who had baptized the Danes; the most traitorous of all, Louis' half-brother, Ebbo Archbishop of Rheims; and Bodo, whom guards placed between Wala and Hilduin as if to imply for the emperor that his favorite and confidante had gone over to Lothair's side.

Black monks led Louis into the hall. The hair shirt of a penitent covered the emperor's torso. He lost much weight, his face drawn and pale, beard untrimmed. Louis limped because of his untreated gout, yet he sustained a natural gravitas looking neither right nor left, seeing no one, not even when the monks forced him to kneel at the base of the dais.

Ignoring his father, Lothair restored to Pepin and Ludwig the boundaries of Aquitaine and Bavaria and added to his own kingdom all Frankish lands that had been given to Charles including Alamannia. He rewarded Archbishop Ebbo with the Abbey of Saint Vaast in Arras, appointed Matfrid of Orléans his *camerarius*, and added Wala, Hilduin, Hugh of Tours and Lantbert of Nantes to his council.

How many of the Ten Commandments had Lothair and his supporters broken? Kings, nobles, and clergy violated oaths, thus taking the Lord's name in vain. Lothair, Pepin, and Ludwig dishonored their father. All bore false witness. All coveted more lands and honors.

Having finished with temporal affairs, Lothair deferred to the bishops' authority regarding his father's abdication. He might well have washed his hands in a bowl of water like Pontius Pilate in the Four Gospels.

Agobard fulminated at Louis, and the Bishop of Lyon seasoned each word with venom. "Oh, man of weak will, you allowed wicked Jezebel to deceive you. Why did you not see and prevent that woman's numberless treacheries, manslaughters, adulteries, and incest? Woe to the empire for the extensive ruin she caused. For all that, you must and shall do penance. Because you are a failed king. You must abdicate."

Ebbo took his turn. Instead of offering gratitude and loyalty for all the emperor had done for him, the Archbishop of Rheims heaped scorn upon Louis:

"Through this man's short-sightedness and neglect, the empire has sunk so low as to be regarded by its enemies with mockery and derision. He is adjudged, therefore, to have forfeited the temporal rule."

Lothair thus conceded to the Church its supremacy over the Crown, contrary to Charlemagne's and Louis' precedents. Still that was not enough retribution for the Lothairian clergy. Monks dragged Louis outside and again forced him to kneel on a carpet of haircloth on the front steps of the assembly hall.

Before the great magnates, prelates, and the local population, Ebbo earned his added sinecure no less than Judas his thirty coins of silver. Enumerating each offense, the archbishop accused Louis of sacrilege, murder, and disregard of canonic law. He exhorted Louis to confess all offenses against God and Church and beg forgiveness or face eternal damnation and forever lose his soul.

"Now, take this scroll and proclaim your transgressions so all may hear."

Louis read the parchment before he recited in a monotone:

"We truthfully declare our self to be guilty of crimes against our brothers, sisters, and to our nephew Bernard whom we blinded and whose death we caused in the year of our Lord, 818.

"We confess to destroying the unity of the empire by the Act of Division of 831.

"We confess to violating Holy Thursday when we ordered the army to march.

"We confess to rising against our sons contrary to the common peace.

"For those and all other impious and cruel acts, we pray for forgiveness."

Although the emperor's use of first person plural instead of the singular implied Louis rejected the bishops' authority, Ebbo declared him deposed a second time by episcopal fiat.

"Such is the emperor that was."

What happened next surprised and dismayed the Lothairians. The mood of the populace changed. Some shouted disapproval and others wept over Louis' degradation. The expression of horror in the faces of many in attendance, including individual bishops and nobles, heartened Bodo. The Lothairians had miscalculated. Their excesses engendered sympathy for Louis and ensured his eventual if not imminent restoration.

62. Louis Rising

Lothair moved to Aachen for the winter, occupied Louis' suite, and confined his father to a small room in the palace with straw for a bed, small table and chair, candle, and the emperor's favorite *biblia*. Throughout December and into January of 834 pairs and trios of clerics harassed Louis to abdicate and retire to a monastery without success.

During the Feast of the Epiphany, Archbishop Otgar of Mainz complained to Lothair about Louis' stubbornness. "Your father shuts his ears and claims that he is still king and emperor bound by the will of Heaven. I do not know what more we can do. He must be imprisoned in a monastery or executed for crimes against God, the Church, and the empire."

"You go too far, Otgar, asking me to commit both regicide and patricide." Lothair turned to Bodo. "My father will listen to you. For the good of the empire, tell him that he must accept the tonsure. You shall benefit from your success. Once my father has taken his vows, you need not keep yours."

Bodo did not reply. Lothair's word differed not from counterfeit coinage.

Louis greeted Bodo with a rare smile. "At last, a friendly face."

"I have been ordered to succeed where others have failed, Your Majesty."

"Subdeacon Bodo," Otgar interrupted, "he is merely the emperor that was. Lothair is emperor now."

Bodo unleashed all the contempt he felt for Otgar. "Hludovicus Caesar Augustus His Majesty still is and always shall be, Your Grace, for unlike prelates such as you, I violate no sworn oaths to God and man. Have you no conscience? Have you no fear of God, of eternal damnation?"

Otgar recoiled at Bodo's vehemence. "How dare ...."

"Our subdeacon has our permission to dare. You can do no good here, Otgar." Louis softened his voice. "Loyal Bodo, have you any word of the empress and our son and daughter?"

"None, I regret to say."

"Lothair has set you a useless task."

Bodo spoke in an Alamannic dialect alien to Otgar, who was a Frank. "The populace is outraged over your mistreatment. Kings Pepin and Ludwig, Count Bernard, certain nobles and bishops too are having second thoughts about Lothair."

"What language are you speaking?"

Louis ignored Otgar. "If you can escape, do so and go to Ludwig." The emperor switched to Francique for the archbishop to understand, "Very well, Subdeacon Bodo, harangue me if you will."

After several hours, Bodo and Otgar reported to Lothair.

"Have you persuaded my father to accept the tonsure?"

Bodo spoke. "I believe he is weakening. Let him consider my arguments through the night. I believe I shall succeed after several more sessions."

"Archbishop, do you agree?"

"I must confess, Your Majesty, Subdeacon Bodo did so well, he almost convinced me to retire to a monastery."

"Perhaps you should. Very well, Subdeacon Bodo, try again."

"Without Archbishop Otgar present?"

"Yes, yes, however you wish, provided you succeed."

Bodo met with Louis alone and whiled the time with his emperor playing Chatrang-namak. He moved an elephant two diagonal squares and took one of Louis' foot soldiers.

The emperor moved his counselor piece one diagonal square and captured Bodo's knight. "Surely you are not allowing us to win. You know we have forbidden it."

"I have much on my mind. I am unable to concentrate and plan ahead."

"Planning moves ahead. Yes, that is what this game teaches, to plan ahead, a most necessary skill for a ruler. You must teach it to Charles …." Louis laughed aloud for the first time in Bodo's presence. "But never to our other sons."

Bodo chose to sleep most nights in Priscus' observatory. The Astronomer charted the heavens and concluded they augured well for Louis. Bodo preferred to assess reality. A tide of sympathy surged in favor of Louis throughout the empire as word spread about Lothair's despicable mistreatment of his father at Soissons, Compiègne, and now at Aachen. No Gundbald was needed this time. Reports reached the palace that after Ludwig sent Pepin a description of Lothair's continuing cruel treatment of their father at Aachen, the King of Aquitaine conferred with Bernard. Both men believed Lothair would be a worse emperor than Louis, and they allied with Ludwig against the Lotharians.

And at Aachen, the defections began.

63. Louis Restored

Night fell, a bitter cold winter night. Soaking in the thermal pool, Bodo heard shouting and the sound of horses neighing. He dressed and ran to the stone corridor. Terrified servants and clerics scurried in all directions carrying torches. Bodo stopped the first man he encountered, a scribe.

"What is happening?"

"King Lothair and his knights have fled to Paris with the emperor. King Ludwig is approaching Aachen at the head of a large force of Austrasians, Saxons, and Alamanni."

"Amalric."

Bodo hurried to the stables. Soldiers, clergy, clerks, and servants fought over the horses. A priest sat upon Amalric but could not control the stallion. Bodo drew his sword, and whistled. Amalric reared and threw the cleric who cracked his head on the cobblestones. Bodo seized the reins, and calmed his horse. "There, there, good Amalric, no other shall ever sit you again."

Through the thick grey mist of morning, Ludwig and his army entered Aachen. Outside the palace, Bodo and Priscus greeted the King of Bavaria, Bishop Drogo his military advisor, and Abbot Hugo.

The size of the force impressed Bodo. "Sire, King Lothair absconded with the emperor and fled to Paris."

"When?"

"Two nights past."

Ludwig, Drogo, and Hugo dismounted in the palace courtyard

and conferred with Bodo and Priscus in Louis' suite where a blazing fire warmed them. The thirty year old King of Bavaria stood with his back to the flames.

"We must inform our allies. King Pepin is marching from Aquitaine, and Bernard is gathering an army of Septimanians and Burgundians." Ludwig summoned two of his knights. "King Lothair has fled to Paris with the emperor. You, ride to King Pepin, and you, ride to Bernard. Tell them we shall converge at Paris."

"Sire, what shall be done about Prince Charles and Princess Giséle who are imprisoned at Prüm Abbey?"

"I prefer to leave my half-brother there forever, but the emperor would never forgive me if we did not free the boy. Prüm is about fifty miles to the south. Bodo, lead a troop of soldiers to the abbey, free Charles, and then join us on the march toward Paris."

At Prüm Abbey, the Lotharian guards surrendered without resisting and released their prisoners. Bodo reassured Charles the emperor was safe and thought it odd the boy did not ask about Judith.

He embraced Strabo. "You are so wan and more skeletal than ever, my friend, we must fatten you."

"The times have been trying. Abbot Markward treated me well enough, but each day he and the monks described as truth for Charles the vilest calumnies against Judith concocted by the Lothairians."

"We can discuss that another time. Now we must hasten away."

Abbot Markward provided mounts for Charles and Strabo. The scholar sat insecure on the saddle. "So high a horse, Bodo. I have ridden only mules before. I fear I may fall."

"By the time we reach Paris you will be an expert horseman."

Winter weather slowed progress, and Bodo caught up with Ludwig at Chelles less than ten miles from Paris. At the convent, he reunited Charles with Giséle and their grandmother, Countess-Abbess Heilwig.

Severe blizzards delayed Bernard's army, and Pepin could not cross the Seine because Lothair's soldiers destroyed all bridges and sank every boat they could find. Ludwig waited outside Paris until his allies arrived and boats could be built.

Bodo the Apostate

Lothair and his staunchest minions retreated to Hilduin's Abbey of Saint Denis, one of the most venerated shrines in all the empire, where Bodo attended Mass with the emperor during each progress in Paris. What he deemed a legend, the credulous believed to be a miracle. After the Romans beheaded Denis, the first Bishop of Paris, he carried his own head to a site for burial. Denis became the Franks' patron saint, and over the centuries they built a church, later an abbey, and inside placed a reliquary containing Denis' remains for the faithful to venerate.

To help pass the time, Bodo took daily walks along the Seine. Paris had left him unimpressed each time he visited during Louis' progresses. He knew its history. Clovis, the Merovingian King of the Franks who converted his people to the *Orthodox* Church, made Paris his capital in 508. The city later became vulnerable to Viking raiders who rowed their longboats along the Seine and sacked Paris. Successor kings built and improved a defensive tower on an island in the Seine but Pepin the Short moved his court to Aachen, and Charlemagne made it the new capital city of the empire for more security and pleasures of the thermal springs.

This day, Bodo walked with Strabo. "At Prüm you said the monks slandered Judith to Charles. It seems they were effective. Charles did not inquire about his mother when we freed him, nor has he since, unlike Giséle."

"I did not want to believe it to be so, but now I fear they succeeded in convincing Charles the empress is the most evil woman who ever lived. He is not yet eleven. Boys are impressionable at that age. We must do all we can to convince Charles they are pernicious lies."

Strabo had not taken into account that many in the palace clergy hated Judith and believed the empress was a sorceress. It might be impossible to keep all such priests and monks away from Charles. The boy if not later the man must decide for himself the truth about Judith.

Not until the fifth Saturday of Lent did the armies of Ludwig, Pepin, and Bernard converge outside Paris. Freed from their prisons by the King of Aquitaine, Conrad and Rudolf had not yet recovered from a poor diet. Their clothes fit loosely over their malnourished bodies. Fresh scabs ringed their heads where their captors tonsured the brothers.

Drogo included Bodo and Priscus in his delegation to negotiate Louis' freedom in the Abbey-Church of Saint Denis, an impressive construction about two hundred feet in length with a crossing tower and long apse over a large crypt. Lothair's listlessness, slack jaw, and darkly ringed eyes, gave him the appearance of a defeated man, which contrasted with the defiant hostility emanating from the Lothairians.

Drogo confronted Lothair. "As God is our judge, surrender the emperor to us, or we shall attack all who resist."

Lothair whined, "No one has suffered more than I because of my father's calamity. No one rejoices more in his good fortune. His confinement and penance is not of my doing. All was ordered according to episcopal judgment."

"You dare blame the bishops for Louis' maltreatment and deposing, which you alone could have and should have prevented? If you do not surrender the emperor to us, prepare for battle. If any harm befalls His Majesty, you alone shall bear all responsibility."

"You will have my reply within the hour."

"One hour, or we attack."

When they returned to confer with Pepin, Ludwig and Bernard, Bodo urged an immediate attack on Saint Denis because the Lothairians could not be trusted.

"Bodo is right." Priscus unrolled an architect's rendering of Saint Denis. "Here is a copy of the original floor plan I took from the palace archives. Look here. That is the sanctuary. I believe this part of the wall opens to a tunnel. They can use it to escape with our emperor."

The kings, Bernard, and their commanders concurred with Bodo and Priscus and attacked Saint Denis. The few monks and soldiers offered no resistance. They said Lothair and his followers fled after the parley through the sacristy tunnel without the emperor.

Outside Saint Denis with Charles at his side, Louis addressed the three armies. "Our sons and loyal subjects, you have asked us to don imperial regalia and formally take the throne in the Church of our patron, Saint Denis." Louis raised a hand to silence their cheering. "Let us wait until the morrow, it being Sunday. Steadfast Bodo, step forward. We raise you to Deacon of the Palace so you may conduct Mass for us and our family. And, we also appoint you to be our personal chaplain, answerable only to us."

Bodo genuflected. "Your Majesty, words fail me."

"Perhaps, but never has your fealty wavered."

Bodo the Apostate

In the Church of Saint-Denis, Louis attended Mass in imperial robes and made an odd assertion before the congregation: "Henceforth, I am Emperor by Divine Mercy repeating itself."

Ignoring the foul weather outside, the multitudes cheered and rejoiced. Then the skies cleared and the winds abated to a gentle breeze, signs all took to portend well for their reestablished emperor. During the celebrating that followed, Ludwig, Pepin, Drogo, and Bernard urged Louis to pursue, capture, and mete just punishments to Lothair and certain nobles and clergy.

"We must allow Lothair time to reflect and confess his faults and crimes so we can forgive him."

Bernard kneeled before Louis. "Sire, I petition you for the return of my lands and titles."

"Because of your alliance against us, brief as it was, we must give the matter further thought. For the time being, I restore to you your family estates at Autun and Narbonne."

"Your Majesty, may I be given leave to rescue the empress from her prison?"

"We thank you for your offer, Deacon Bodo. Because we also fear Lothair's allies may harm her out of spite, we have already dispatched a large force to Tortona for that very purpose. Now, hear this, one and all. We shall go to Aachen."

Raised to Deacon and appointed Louis' personal chaplain, Bodo doubted he could preach a religion in which he did not believe and yet seem sincere. Dissembling did not come easily.

"One more thing Deacon Bodo, go to Chelles with a suitable escort and bring Princess Giséle and Countess-Abbess Heilwig to Court."

64. Lessons not learned

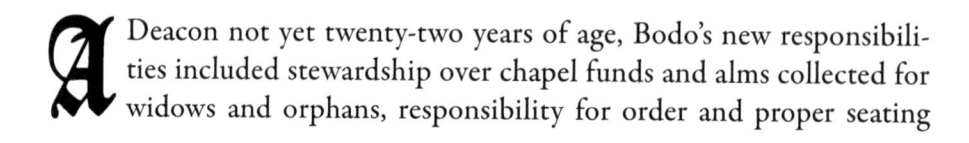

A Deacon not yet twenty-two years of age, Bodo's new responsibilities included stewardship over chapel funds and alms collected for widows and orphans, responsibility for order and proper seating for services, reading the Gospels, preaching, and assisting during the Sacrament of Baptism. He hunted with Louis, Pepin, and Ludwig during Lent and fulfilled his dioconate obligations with a detachment no one noticed.

After Easter Sunday of 834, Abraham led a long column of covered horse drawn carts escorted by soldiers into Aachen. In the Council Hall, the Merchant of the Palace gave Louis a bound plain dark brown leather covered ledger. "Your Majesty, here is the inventory of your treasury."

"Good friend Count Abraham, how can we best reward you for your indispensable service?"

"My second son Judah needs further secular education in the Trivium, Quadrivium, and mastery of arms."

"How old is he?"

"Thirteen, Your Majesty."

"We grant your wish. He is close in age to Prince Charles. May your Judah serve our son with the same loyalty you have given to us. Deacon Bodo, we charge you to arrange for Count Abraham's son to take lessons with Prince Charles from the Master of Arms and palace tutors."

"It shall be my pleasure. Count Abraham."

"And I congratulate you, Deacon Bodo, for your loyalty to the emperor and your new office."

Judith arrived at the palace several weeks after Abraham. Harsh imprisonment at Tortona and difficulties of the long journey from Italy altered the empress' appearance, her shorn hair not completely regrown, cheeks sunken, and dark shadows under the eyes.

Louis greeted Judith with warmth and affection. When she embraced her son and lavished kisses on his face, the boy stood stiff and unsmiling. Doting Judith was oblivious to Charles' coolness during celebrations in honor of her return. Strabo faced a daunting task to convince the boy his mother was innocent of all vices and crimes described by the monks and priests at Prüm. Lothairian nobles and clergy would be repeating those accusations to Charles.

Abbot Hrabanus of Fulda gave the empress an effusive welcome in the Council Hall before a great assemblage. "Your Majesty, I offer and dedicate to you this Book of Esther, which has been translated word for word from the original Hebrew. Most noble empress, God omnipotent, who roused Esther to save her people from extermination by the Persian emperor's evil advisor Haman, that same God shall lead you to similar glory."

Bodo the Apostate

After Judith settled into daily Court routine, she seldom smiled, and with good reason. Each day the empress failed to sway Louis to pursue and slaughter the men she hated most: Wala for his lies and screeds against her; Matfrid and Lantbert, who violated the Law of Sanctuary when they abducted her and Charles from the convent of Saint Radegunda.

Instead, Louis moved his Court to the dense forest of the Vosges. Bodo had less contact with Judith than before. He hunted with Louis, Pepin and Ludwig, and served as Louis' deacon and chaplain even though he was not a priest and thus could not hear confessions and absolve the emperor.

On Pentecost, couriers reported that Lothair had established a defensive position at Vienne on the Rhône south of Lyon, and recalcitrant Lotharians led by the Unholy Trinity were building a new army. Despite advice to the contrary, the emperor sent too small a force against the rebels. The insurgents ambushed and slew Bernard's brother Eudo, Count-Bishop of Orléans, and all other commanders.

Forced to end his season of hunting, Louis commanded Ludwig and Pepin to join him in defeating the Lothairians once and for all. He sent a message for Bernard to secure Septimania and Burgundy.

Bodo did not doubt that after victory, the emperor again would forgive Lothair and show mercy to the dissident nobles and clerics. Nothing changed, lessons never learned.

Early in August at an abbey near Dijon, Louis received reports that Matfrid, Lantbert, and Hugh were fleeing toward Chalon-sur-Saône about eighty miles to the south, and Lothair was marching from Vienne to join forces with them.

"We are confident Count Gaucelm and several other loyal local magnates will have successfully fortified the castle there as a refuge and bulwark. We weary of these rebellions. We do not want to waste more lives in battle, which is why we prefer to send a trustworthy emissary to Lothair. That man is you, Deacon Bodo."

"I am honored to be chosen, Your Majesty. What words have you for King Lothair?"

Louis handed Bodo a scroll. "Our terms for Lothair's surrender and reconciliation are listed here. You leave immediately." Louis showed Bodo a map. "Here is your route."

Chalon-sur-Saône lay about eighty miles to the south, a four day ride Bodo calculated. He armed himself and mounted Amalric, proud the emperor entrusted him with so significant a mission.

65. Chalon-a-Saône

The stench of death greeted Bodo when he reached Chalon. Scavenger birds, vermin, and feral dogs gorged on the dead, homes and shops reduced to charred embers, the town's churches and tower gutted by fire. Grieving survivors described how Lothair's army slaughtered much of the population sparing neither gender nor age while they pillaged and torched the town.

Bodo's questions about Count Gaucelm's fate were answered when he reached Lothair's encampment several miles to the south by the Saône. Many of Louis' vassals hung from trees. The heads of three counts rested atop stakes, Gaucelm's the highest, jaw slack, mouth open, eyes gouged. Evrard, Eudo, and now Gaucelm, did the Lotharians intend to slay all kin of Bernard?

Ahead in bloodstained armor, Lothair faced a chained woman in nun's attire. Gerberga, Count Bernard's sister, prayed while soldiers forced her into a weighted empty wine cask. Deposed counts, abbots, and bishops sat at a long table jeering at her impending fate. Nearby a stake had been erected for the next victim.

With Lothair's consent Hilduin pointed at Gerberga. "You woman, *Naso's veneficia* sister, you have been rightly judged guilty of sorcery ... of using witchcraft, to enchant and bend men to their will, as Eve seduced Adam to commit Original Sin ... and plotting to poison all who stand in your brother's way. I sentence you to a witch's death."

Soldiers sealed the cask and tossed it into the Saône to the accompaniment of cheers and curses. It sank to the bottom.

Bodo had fond memories of Gerberga. Impossible for her to be guilty of *maleficia*. He threw back his hood and approached Lothair.

"Deacon Bodo? What are you doing here?"

He gave Lothair Louis' scroll. "I am the emperor's emissary, and here is his message to you."

Bodo the Apostate

Lothair read aloud Louis' terms. The insurgents shouted and shook their fists.

"Treachery."

"A trick."

"Lies and falsehoods."

"I agree." Lothair tore the scroll into small pieces. "Return to my father. Tell him I reject his terms and shall be pleased to meet him on the field of battle. How far away is he?"

"I left the emperor four days ago while he was marching from Dijon."

"Still several days away. How big is his army?"

Bodo scanned Lothair's encampment. Much larger than yours."

"So you say. Well, before you return to him with my reply, come, sit beside me and feast. Perhaps I may yet induce you to join us."

Lothair shoved aside a sullen Matfrid to make room for Bodo on the bench. "Bring forth the next prisoner."

Two knights went into an adjacent tent and dragged a young female in chains to Lothair. Although Bodo had not seen the girl in years, he recognized Bernard's daughter Dulciorella. Not yet nubile and clad in a diaphanous shift, the girl faced her captors with dignity. That this child was their next victim horrified Bodo.

After conferring with his bishops and abbots, Lothair approached the girl. "Dulciorella of Septimania, daughter of the criminal Bernard, more appropriately known as *Naso* you have been accused of sorcery. Through Jewish guile and evil intent, you have practiced black magic to turn men away from the Savior and to serve the Devil. You have caused crops to fail, livestock to become sick and die, men to become ill. What have you to say in your defense?"

"I am innocent of false charges."

"Your words have no value. We have traditional ordeals to decide the guilt or innocence of accused witches and sorceresses."

Dulciorella's calm defiance and lack of fear impressed Bodo. So far, she had not recognized him. He rose and left the table without asking Lothair's permission. "I will speak for the Lady Dulciorella. She is no witch."

The Lothairians shouted threats at Bodo, but none drew dagger or sword.

Lothair commanded silence. "Deacon Bodo, have you gone mad?"

"No, not mad, I am merely a humble servant of the Church. Lady Dulciorella, do you remember who I am?"

The girl nodded she did.

"Sire ..." Bodo added scorn to his tone of voice "... most noble lords and devout bishops and priests ... I repeat ... Lady Dulciorella is no witch. She has been falsely and maliciously accused solely because she is the daughter of Bernard of Septimania. You have blinded her uncle Evrard. You have slain her uncle Gaucelm and cousin Eudo. You have drowned her falsely accused aunt, gentle Gerberga. I cannot allow you to murder an innocent child."

"She is a sorceress, a poisoner," Hilduin screeched.

Bodo threw his gauntlet to the grass. "I shall prove Lady Dulciorella's innocence through Trial by Combat. Who will pick up my gauntlet?" Bodo walked the length of the bench. "You, Abbot Hilduin, who wears armor and poses as a warrior? You, Archbishop Otgar, who wanted our emperor executed? You, Lantbert and Matfrid, despoilers of sanctuaries so bold to carry away a woman when no one is there to defend her?" Bodo placed his fists on the table and confronted Hugh of Tours. "Or you who shouted the loudest and whom Bernard rightly calls *Timidus*?"

Hugh of Tours heaped curses upon Bodo for the insult but did not leave his seat.

"Is there no hero in this august company of men who have despoiled cities and slaughtered the defenseless to risk his life against me?"

Silence prevailed. Lothair conferred with his advisors. Otgar spoke for them. "Deacon Bodo, you have taken Holy Orders. To defend a witch, to shed blood for this sorceress, that will condemn you to eternal damnation."

"To save the life of one who is innocent will guarantee my salvation. It is you who should fear being damned for all eternity. All of you, what afterlife do you face for having sworn falsely more than once to oaths declaring allegiance to your emperor before God, and again falsely that this maiden is guilty? Free Lady Dulciorella now or fight me with any weapon of choice."

Lothair took Bodo aside so no one might hear. "I admire your courage, and I have always been fond of you. In truth, this girl means nothing to me, but my subjects here have such hatred for Bernard, they will do what they can to slay him and all of his blood. My bishops and abbots also demand her death. I could not rescind the verdicts of their tribunal

Bodo the Apostate

of judges for the beheadings and drowning of Gerberga. No, not I. Why should you bother to save one of Bernard's blood. Are you expecting some great reward from him?"

"I serve only Their Majesties and want nothing from Bernard."

"By the Thunderer, Deacon Bodo, I believe you. I shall give this girl her freedom, place her in your charge, and you may do what you will with her ... unless one here accepts your challenge and you lose the combat." Lothair addressed his followers. "Which of you will take up Bodo's gauntlet?"

No one accepted the challenge.

"A county to any knight or soldier, an abbey to any cleric, who will fight Deacon Bodo and win the combat."

A voice came from the far end of the table. "I will pick up the gauntlet."

"Well done, brave Berald. May you be landless no longer and do honor to your older brother, Count Matfrid. Which weapon do you choose?"

Berald retrieved Bodo's gauntlet. "Sword on foot."

Bodo measured his opponent. Berald was no older than seventeen, an oddity of nature, a head taller and considerably wider with much blood smeared over his armor from the massacre in Chalon.

Bodo whistled for Amalric. The horse obeyed and trotted to his side. Bodo removed his robe, attached his helmet, and reached for the shield. At that instant, Berald shouted curses and attacked before Lothair signaled the combat to begin.

Bodo turned in time to block a powerful blow that dented his shield and sent him reeling backward against Amalric. He parried Berald's second slash so powerful he almost fell. His oversized opponent had momentum and the higher angle of a slope for advantage.

Swinging his sword, Berald drove Bodo toward the river to cheering and encouragement from the Lothairians. By now, Berald's blows had dented Bodo's shield to uselessness and brought unbearable pain to his left arm and shoulder.

At water's edge, Bodo remembered lessons from the Masters of Arms. Single combat had its own rhythm like the hypnotic beat of a drum. Strike, raise shield, and defend, strike, raise shield and defend.

Bodo sought to regain and maintain his equilibrium. Enraged by the unknightly attack, he broke the rhythm. Bodo threw the useless shield at Berald and circled to the right of his opponent's sword arm. His tactic forced Berald to turn, an awkward move.

Bodo feinted a slash from above. Berald lifted his shield to defend. Instead, Bodo thrust underneath and penetrated his opponent's exposed armpit. Berald screamed and fell.

No hesitation, Bodo raised his sword high and brought it down splitting leather and metal supports of Berald's helmet and the bone of his opponent's brainpan.

Breathing heavily, Bodo faced Lothair. "Sire, I have won this combat on behalf of the Lady Dulciorella, thus proving her innocent of all accusations."

Matfrid raged at Bodo and demanded his death. Clerics promised Bodo an eternity of torments in hell.

Lothair silenced them. "Count Matfrid, your brother disrespected us. He did not wait for our signal and attacked Deacon Bodo in a most cowardly manner. Berald twice shamed you, for his unknightly behavior and for losing the combat."

Lothair ordered his soldiers to release the girl. "Well done, Deacon Bodo. I shall keep my word to you. Take her to *Naso*, or better yet, make her your *concubita*."

"Will you also give me my father's counties?"

"Yes, if you join me, but do not wait too long."

Bodo covered Dulciorella with his cloak and placed her side-saddle upon Amalric. He sat his horse behind the girl and rode northward.

66. Dulciorella

Bodo looked behind. No one pursued. The shortest route to Louis led past burned manses and farms into death-stenched Chalon where vermin and carrion still devoured corpses. Amalric raced through the vile creatures until they reached the town's outer boundaries.

A few miles past Chalon, Bodo chose to rest at a secluded clearing by a cove on the Saône where they could not be seen from the busy river. Dulciorella had yet to speak a single word, which pleased Bodo. He disliked idle chatter.

The heat of combat dissipated. Pain shot through Bodo's left arm and shoulder as he helped Dulciorella dismount. It worsened with each

Bodo the Apostate

movement when he shed baldric, sword, and armor and lifted the saddle from Amalric. Bodo turned the horse loose to drink from the river and graze on the clearing.

Bodo and Dulciorella also drank. Sated, she removed the cloak he gave her and spread it on the grass. Bodo noticed Dulciorella's wrists and ankles had been abraded by her captors' chains.

She turned her back to Bodo and removed her shift. "I have not bathed in more than a week."

"While you wash, I will search for nettles. Mixed with mud, they can be a balm."

Bodo carried his saddlebag into the woods. He listened for animal sounds while gathering the stinging plant, fruit, and nuts.

Bodo returned to the cove and fed Amalric some wild apples. Dulciorella sat on his cloak plaiting her wet hair.

Bodo opened the saddlebag. "I found some things to eat."

Dulciorella accepted an apple and watched Bodo make a poultice. While she applied the palliative to her sores, Bodo bared his arms and torso. He saw bruises from Berald's powerful blows and scratches from dents in the shield that absorbed them. No broken bones though.

Bodo finished undressing and plunged into the Saône disappointed it was not cold enough to ease his discomfort. After a brief washing, he put on trousers and boots, and Dulciorella spread balm over his contusions.

"Deacon Bodo, I am beholden ...."

"It is not necessary to thank me. Had I arrived earlier, I might have saved Gerberga."

"I loved my aunt. Gerberga harmed no one. They murdered her and beheaded my Uncle Gaucelm out of hatred for my father. What can you tell me about Prince Charles?"

Bodo did not reply to Dulciorella's abrupt non sequitur and waited for the girl to continue.

"No, please forget I asked. I do not want to know."

Bodo chose not to press Dulciorella. With less than an hour of daylight left, he cut some branches for a fire.

Night fell. A crescent moon shone undulating patterns on the river.

Wolves howled far away across the other side. Not any animal, diverse thoughts kept Bodo awake. He was responsible for Dulciorella until he brought her to Louis and Judith in a day or two..

Bodo remembered his early impressions of the strange child when Bernard wed Dhuoda, and again at Aachen during those months her father misruled in the emperor's name. Dulciorella had not changed in all that time. She spoke few words out of necessity, never for conversation. Bodo could not recall seeing Dulciorella laugh or smile, so different in every way from another girl her age, Princess Giséle, whose liveliness and beauty presented a marked contrast to Bernard's dour daughter.

Yet, Dulciorella's graceful movements and gestures, even how she tilted her head, fascinated Bodo. So did her features and darker coloring that contrasted with the blonde, fair-skinned, blue eyes of most Alamanni, Saxon, and Frankish women. Dulciorella's hair shone raven black, enormous dark brown eyes enigmatic. One feature of the girl intrigued Bodo most. Her father's nose resembled a hawk-like promontory. Shaped the same, Dulciorella's was smaller, narrower, and more refined more like that of a small bird.

Bodo recalled Dulciorella's odd question about Charles and made sense of it. One Lothairian rumor about Bernard might be true after all. He was scheming to wed his daughter to Charles.

Bodo kneeled at the river. While washing off the nettles and mud, he relived his combat with Berald. From early childhood Bodo had looked forward to knighthood and winning glory in battle. Today, he slew a man but did not feel the same exhilaration of warriors who bragged about their victories. Bodo had no remorse for taking the life of a defeated foe. It had been necessary and just. Berald attacked him from behind. The coward deserved to die. Best not to dwell on it.

A star flew above the moon. An owl hooted, and a low protean vapor swirled wraithlike over the stream, an evanescent human form one moment, a diaphanous veil the next. Bodo recalled with sudden clarity his fantastic dreams in the forest outside Bodman and at the thermal pool. He stared at the miasma transfixed until it dissipated.

An owl, ephemeral water vapors, a crescent moon, and a flying star, all were natural occurrences at night, yet Bodo believed they portended something significant he had yet to divine.

67. Squandered Years

A two day's ride north of Chalon at an hour before sunset, Bodo and Dulciorella reached Louis' army encampment. In a field between a manse and the Saône, they rode past soldiers eating at cooking fires, sharpening weapons, and washing sore feet.

Bodo dismounted at the manse, helped Dulciorella from Amalric, and told the Master of Horses to feed, groom, and shoe his horse. He led Dulciorella into the noisy great hall toward Louis. The emperor supped with Prince Charles between Judith, King Ludwig, Drogo and others of his imperial council at the main table beneath typical trophies of hunts past. Military commanders, nobles, clergy and Court officials sat at lesser boards according to rank.

Louis called for silence. "Rise, Deacon Bodo, we expected you to return sooner and feared Lothair took you hostage. And who is this barefoot girl you have brought before us?"

"Lady Dulciorella, Count Bernard's daughter."

Bodo described the carnage he witnessed at Chalon, Lothair's rejection of Louis' conditions for surrender, the drowning of Bernard's sister Gerberga, and how he prevented Dulciorella being burned at the stake. Bodo concluded with an assessment of Lothair's army.

Louis sighed. "So much unnecessary cruelty. We know our son. If Lothair believes he is outnumbered, he will retreat until surrender is inevitable."

"Sire, Lady Dulciorella needs the care of a physician."

"Of course. Lady Dulciorella, we place you in the care of Her Majesty."

Judith told her ladies to move closer to each other and beckoned Dulciorella. "Come, child, sit and sup."

"We see that your left arm troubles you."

"Merely some bruising, Sire."

"Our physician Zedekiah will attend to you as well." Louis leaned forward to see Priscus farther down the table. "Astronomer, make space for Deacon Bodo."

Louis and Judith met alone with Bodo in the manse's small family chapel and asked him to repeat what he said earlier in more detail. After Bodo again described how and why he slew Matfrid's younger brother, Judith applauded. "Well done, Deacon Bodo, but we wish it had been that vile traitor Matfrid in his stead. Now tell us. Is Dulciorella unsullied?"

Bodo reassured Their Majesties that no one in Lothair's camp raped the girl, and as best he knew she was *virgo intacto*. Dulciorella's and now Judith's question convinced Bodo that the empress discussed with Bernard the prospect of his daughter and Charles marrying.

Judith turned to Louis. "With your consent we will send Dulciorella under escort to Chelles Abbey, and there she shall stay with Princess Giséle under our mother's protection until we can reunite her with Count Bernard."

The emperor assented. "You have served us well, Deacon Bodo. For that, we shall honor you after we defeat Lothair."

At daybreak, Bodo learned that Dulciorella had already left for Chelles. Not giving another thought about the girl, he rode with Louis and Ludwig, whose armies pursued Lothair's scattered forces through Autun, Orléans, and Le Mans. Pepin's Aquitainians came from the south, and they surrounded Lothair on a grassy field near Blois at the confluence where the Cisse flowed into the Loire.

Louis yet again preferred to avoid battle against Lothair and offered instead generous terms if he surrendered. While Lothair walked across the field and kneeled in submission, Bodo gave much thought to the emperor's repeated mercies. Perhaps it was more a type of madness that caused one to repeat the same mistakes in expectation of a different outcome each time.

After four wasted years of futile rebellions and turning points that failed to turn, the emperor yet again forgave Lothair after his eldest swore fealty and promised never to rebel again. Louis restricted Lothair to the Kingdom of Italy. With atypical resolve he removed Agobard from the Diocese of Lyon, and prepared to mete harsh punishments for all traitors. Too late, Agobard had fled to Italy with Wala, the Unholy Trinity, and other steadfast Lotharians.

Louis allowed treacherous Ebbo to retain the see of Rheims until Judith at last prevailed upon the emperor to take action against his disloyal and malicious foster-brother. Louis removed Ebbo from the diocese

Bodo the Apostate

of Rheims, forced the former archbishop to recant all lies before a synod of bishops, and imprisoned him at Fulda.

Yes madness, and Louis was not the only one to be so afflicted. It would be best if Judith demanded less for her son. Otherwise, Pepin and Ludwig were likely to ally, perhaps with Lothair too, and prevent Charles from taking one handful of soil from their lands.

Darker thoughts prevailed after Louis and Judith repeated their promise to make Bodo second man in the empire. What empire? Did no one else see it no longer existed except in name? Despite Louis' hopes and Judith's schemes, Bodo foresaw one outcome and no other: fragmentation into warring kingdoms, independent dukedoms, and petty counties.

Bodo hunted with the emperor until the Court returned to Aachen in late autumn of 834. Throughout those months he preferred solitude to the company of others. Discrete liaisons with agreeable ladies left him unsatisfied. Feast days and celebrations of the Nativity and New Year of 835 gave him no joy.

One bone chilling wintry day shortly after the hour of sext on his way to the thermal baths, Bodo encountered Strabo in the Stone Corridor.

"I have been seeking you."

"It must be a serious matter, Strabo. You are so solemn."

"I? It is you who appears so heavily cloaked in gloom."

"It shows?"

"Yes, but why? You are the most favored by our emperor and empress, a Deacon at age twenty-one. Soon you will be a bishop. What could weigh so heavily?"

"Indecision over a most important matter consumes me."

"Perhaps if you spoke to me or Priscus about it."

Bodo knew what their advice would be. "Another time, Strabo, another time."

His brief conversation with Strabo alerted Bodo to conceal better his discontent. He must be no less shrewd than his Uncle Welf. Having at last decided what he must do, the next problem to solve was how best to do it and when.

After Easter, the Court moved to Bodman. Thinking about his

future kept Bodo awake the first night in his boyhood home. Bells from Reichenau Abbey tolled the Midnight Vigil. A full moon illuminated the field and forest beyond. Planets and constellations appeared closer than ever. Priscus sat at the edge of the Bodensee charting the heavens.

Bodo wanted to be alone. Carrying a boar spear, a small amphora filled with wine, a cut of dried beef, and a block of cheese in a saddlebag, he walked to the tree in the woods where he had long ago carved his name with Strabo's assistance. As was his habit, Bodo sat at the great oak's base drinking wine, eating cheese and dried beef, restless, unable to concentrate. He closed his eyes wishing for another misty apparition.

An owl about two inches less than a foot of height surprised Bodo when it alighted on his wrist. Its talons gripped enough for balance but not deep enough to draw blood. Bodo moved his arm and brought the unblinking predator closer to his face.

A handsome little creature, unafraid of humans too. "Have you come to impart your great wisdom that I so desperately need?"

Bodo offered the owl cheese and dried beef. It preferred the meat. He stroked the top of the small raptor's head. "I would give you a name, but I do not know if you are male or female."

He fed the owl more pieces of beef while visualizing how certain men and women resembled birds and animals: the falcon-like faces of Abraham and Bernard, porcine prelates, vulpine and lupine nobles, saurian schemers, rodentine prevaricators, feline women, canine scholars and servants, and leonine Carolingian rulers. But who most resembled an owl?

Bodo closed his eyes again unable to focus on a single thought. Had he imbibed too much wine?

Bodo opened his eyes when the bells of Reichenau Abbey tolled an Hour of the Vigil, and three more. Four had passed like a grain of sand. He could not remember if he dreamed.

Surrounded by a low, swirling early morning mist, Bodo stood and stretched. Was that a human form he espied disappearing in the hazy distance?

The owl clung to Bodo's wrist. Had it kept him company those four hours while he slept?

Bodo the Apostate

"Come with me, my wise little friend, and tell me how best to accomplish what I must do."

In response, the tiny raptor flew away, and Bodo's laughter resounded throughout the woods when he remembered who most resembled a little owl.

Decisiveness is often the art of timely cruelty.
      Henri Becquirel

Part Four
Bodo, the Decisive
835-838

68. Old and New Alliances

The emperor cut short his time at Bodman and ordered an assembly to be held at Crémieu near Lyon two hundred and fifty miles from the Bodensee to decide if Bernard should again have rule over Septimania, Gothia, and the Marches of Hispania. More relevant for Bodo, an adversary arrived at Court. Hincmar, whom he thrashed years earlier for spreading vile rumors about the empress, sat out the rebellions at Saint-Denis instead of joining his mentor Hilduin and the Lothairians. The venomous priest had become corpulent with an added chin, typical of well-fed bodily inactive clergy. Hincmar's return spurred Bodo to speak to Judith about Charles in her suite before the assembly began.

"Your Majesty, you are aware that Hincmar has long been your enemy. I worry Prince Charles might fall under his pernicious influence."

"We thank you for your concerns, Deacon Bodo, but be assured, our son is forever loyal to us. No one, certainly not Hincmar, can break the bond of love between mother and son. We believe the priest may be a positive example for our Charles, whom you have neglected of late. And Hincmar has kept all his vows."

Bodo ignored Judith's rebuke. He no longer cared if he lost the empress' favor or truth be told, were Hincmar to become Charles' *camerarius*.

In the assembly hall, the emperor proclaimed a significant change at Court that pleased Bodo. He made his devoted half-brother Drogo chamberlain.

Dame Fortuna favored Louis. Bernard's principal rival died on the way to the assembly, which spared the emperor from making a decision certain to anger one party or both in the dispute over who should rule Septimania and the Marches of Hispania. Louis forgave his godson, restored all former lands and honors, added those of Toulouse, and bestowed additional titles. Bernard was now Count of Barcelona, Margrave of Gothia and Duke of Septimania.

Bodo tried to understand Bernard. The count showed no grief over the loss of siblings and kin. He did not demand the death of those responsible

Bodo the Apostate

for the blinding and subsequent death of his brother Evrard, beheading of another brother Gaucelm, drowning of his sister Gerberga, and the death of a cousin. Bernard lacked the attribute of honor common to the Alamanni.

Before the assembly ended, Judith brought Dulciorella to Bernard, who did not offer his daughter the slightest indication of affection. The girl reacted with similar indifference to her father. Bernard neither thanked Bodo for saving Dulciorella's life nor acknowledged his presence. The girl also ignored Bodo. Had he misjudged Dulciorella's character? Despite her admirable stoicism when threated with death, she may have inherited the flaw of ingratitude from Bernard.

After the Court returned to Aachen in the autumn of 835, Judith summoned Bodo for a private conference, and they sat facing each other. "Deacon Bodo, our son is but twelve. His Majesty's health is declining. As you well know, he has become frail in body and afflicted with gout and other ailments. Charles needs loyal and strong allies at Court and throughout the empire. That is why we have negotiated a marriage between Princess Giséle and Eberhard, heir to the Dukedom of Friuli."

Bodo viewed the marriage as another of Judith's schemes to strengthen Charles' position in the empire. Aside from the Dukedom of Friuli, Eberhard's family held many titles and great estates north of the Seine in the area of Tournai.

"A wise choice, Your Majesty."

"We expect you to officiate as principal witness during their sacrament."

"I shall be most honored and pleased to do so."

"But an alliance with Friuli is not enough. We have asked our self this question. Of Charles' three half-brothers who will be his best ally? Always the answer is the same. Ludwig is weak and easily swayed by Hemma who lacks judgment. Pepin is going mad and likely to die soon, which means our Charles will have Aquitaine. That leaves Lothair, who has always been the strongest of purpose and most able of the three."

Bodo understood why Judith believed she must reconcile with Lothair, who three times rebelled against the emperor and twice sentenced the empress to harsh confinement and mistreatment. Louis' deteriorating health intensified Judith's fear he might die before Charles came of age.

"I agree, Your Majesty, it should be Lothair."

Let the empress follow Louis' policy of forgiving treasonous stepsons, nobles, and bishops who accused her of the vilest sins and conduct. Let the madness continue.

Continue it did. One evening instead of discussing a portion of the Bible with Bodo, Louis expressed concerns over what might happen should he die too soon. Obsessed with ensuring that Charles kept his lands, Judith induced the emperor to invite Lothair to Aachen.

Louis rationalized no son more than Lothair was better able to confront the never ending assaults against the empire. Saracens and rebel Bretons, Basques, and Visigoths pressed against the Marches and Aquitaine. The Norse raided Frisia and adjacent lands at will looting and carrying away women and children for slaves. Pagan tribes encroached along the eastern frontiers. The Rhaetians either rebelled or committed brigandage against travelers passing through the Alps.

Louis lamented, "It is not only the depredations of man, Deacon Bodo. We agree with Priscus who said, 'It is as if God himself has abandoned all to the Devil who sends severe flooding, terrifying eclipses of sun and moon, awesome northern lights, scorching heat out of season, destructive earthquakes, preternatural thunder and lightning.'"

Priscus' reference to the Devil puzzled Bodo. The Astronomer usually regarded such phenomena as unexplainable occurrences of nature. Bodo comforted Louis with the Jewish interpretation of Satan's role.

"If Satan is causing so much devastation, God may be testing you, Sire, through his servant the Hebrews called *ha-Satan,* as is written in the Old Testament Book of Job."

"Thank you, Deacon Bodo, for you have given us hope that like Job we shall endure all travails."

Louis might be emperor until his last breath, but the empire would die with him.

69. Guntrum

Mid-morning in the archives, Bodo searched through passages in various *biblia* and commentaries piled on a table for the subject of his next sermon. None inspired him. Bodo closed

Bodo the Apostate

his eyes lost in thought until he became aware of a presence. A timid clerk brought a young servant and a boy in filthy worn clothes.

"Forgive my interruption, Your Reverence, but he says you are his uncle."

Bodo left his chair and went to the boy. He recognized nothing of his sister in the child's appearance.

"Your name."

"I am Guntrum, son of Count Meinrad and your sister Countess Adeltrud."

The weight of a heavy stone filled Bodo's stomach. Adeltrud had no reason to stay in Béziers and would have come to Court with her son.

"Where is your mother?"

"She died of fever. So did my younger brother."

Bodo never grieved in front of others. "May they rest in peace. You must be about seven years of age."

"Almost eight."

"You are also a Hornbach. You could have gone to your father's family."

"They are far away in Saxony, and my mother said you would be as my father."

Bodo had no choice but to accept responsibility for the boy, whose clothes, face, and hands were covered with filth accumulated on his journey from Béziers. He turned to the clerk. "Find fresh clothing for my nephew. We shall be at the baths."

Outside the archives, Bodo sent another clerk on a second errand to bring food and drink for Guntrum. "Take his servant with you and see that he is fed in the kitchen."

Bodo interrogated his nephew while the boy soaked in the thermal pool. Excepting Meinrad's absences, Adeltrud had led a happy life. Guntrum had good size for his age. Obedient and respectful too. Adeltrud raised the boy well.

The clerks arrived with Guntrum's clothes, a bowl of mutton stew, and a flagon of ale. Bodo watched his nephew eat and drink on one of the marble benches. What to do with Guntrum? Bodo had little time for the boy at Aachen. He decided to speak with Priscus about placing Guntrum in the Palace Academy. If his nephew found favor with Judith Augusta, she might give consent for him to be one of her pages.

"Guntrum, after you finish eating and dress. I shall present you to the empress, your mother's and my first cousin."

Bodo led his nephew to Judith's suite where Strabo, Charles, and her ladies attended the empress. Bodo presented Guntrum to Judith. "I am now responsible for my nephew because Adeltrud is dead."

Judith offered pro forma condolences and beckoned Guntrum to come closer. "Your mother was one of our ladies in waiting. Adeltrud's death reminds us of our own tenuous mortality. May we live long enough to ensure and secure our Charles' portion of the empire. You are quiet, Guntrum. Have you nothing to say?"

"Your Majesty, my mother told me you were beautiful, but you are more beautiful than she described."

"Did you tell the boy to flatter us, Deacon Bodo?"

"No, Your Majesty."

"Of course you did not. If you had, he would have phrased it better. What plans have you for your nephew?"

"I will place Guntrum in the Palace Academy, and if Your Majesty is agreeable, he might also serve as one of your pages."

"The same as you were. Yes, we accept him to be our page. Guntrum, report here after lauds on the morrow for instructions. If he is half as bright and clever as you, Bodo, we shall be pleased."

Strabo asked for permission to speak, and Bodo told Guntrum the scholar was Prince Charles' tutor.

"Your mother was the dearest friend of my childhood. May she rest in eternal peace. I cannot imagine a world without her gracious presence. I shall recite many prayers for Countess Adeltrud."

Judith dismissed Bodo and Guntrum. When they descended the steps to the Stone Corridor, Bodo saw Abraham and Priscus leaving the Council Hall. He introduced Guntrum to both men and explained why his nephew had come to Aachen.

"I am sorry to hear of Countess Adeltrud's passing," Abraham said. "My daughter Deborah was very fond of her."

Priscus agreed to supervise Guntrum's education in the Palace Academy and switched to conversational Latin, which the boy did not understand.

Bodo the Apostate

"I doubt if he will learn so much so quickly and as well as you did. The Astronomer switched back to Francique. "Guntrum, come with me, and I will do for you what I did for your uncle his first day at the palace."

Guntrum hesitated, and Bodo sensed the boy's confusion at being disoriented in a strange place. "Go with Priscus. I will see you later in the day." Bodo walked in the opposite direction with Abraham "There is something I must discuss with you alone at a more convenient time and place."

"I am on my way home. Any time today will do."

"Thank you. I shall be there within the hour."

Bodo wanted to be alone to reflect on Adeltrud's death. She had been the only link to his father and mother. Now he was the last of their line. True, Guntrum was of the same blood, and although he had not yet warmed to the boy, Bodo had no choice but to honor Adeltrud's wish and look after his nephew from this day forward.

But why had Guntrum not asked any questions? Did he lack curiosity, or was he shy?

70. Royal Wedding

Late June the Court moved to Bodman, and Bodo familiarized Guntrum with the town and environs, reliving his childhood through the boy's wonder at the animals they encountered in the woods. As he had done with Charles, Bodo gave his nephew swimming lessons in the Bodensee.

Shortly after their arrival at Bodman, Lothair's envoy Wala arrived from Italy accompanied by Princess Giséle's intended husband, Eberhard, heir to the Dukedom of Friuli. Sixty-four year old Wala showed his age. Bent of back, he used a stick for support when he rose from his genuflection and for balance while upright and walking

Bodo pitied Wala, whose life exemplified how one might rise to high favor and power and be discarded in an instant by a king or emperor. Once Charlemagne's *camerarius* and de facto ruler of the empire, Wala lost all honors and benefices. Imprisoned by Louis, moved from prison to prison by Judith, and banished to Lothair's kingdom, a man of his years and poor health might not survive a return to Italy.

Louis forgave Wala for his conspiracies, and Judith received her former adversary with formal politeness. Bodo doubted the empress truly reconciled with the man she hated above all others and once demanded his execution.

Early one afternoon while Guntrum practiced with weapons on the field in front of the summer palace, Bodo followed his routine of swimming in the Bodensee, which helped keep his body lean and sinewy. He came out of the water, put on his trousers, white linen shirt and leather boots, before he saw Princess Giséle on the promontory above beckoning him. She must have arrived from Chelles during his swim. How long had she been watching?

Unattended, Giséle greeted Bodo with a broad smile when he reached her atop the promontory. He had not seen the princess since the second rebellion. Now the same age as Judith when she wed Louis, Giséle's features, identical to her mother's, emphasized how much the empress had aged and soured.

"Where are Their Majesties, Bodo? I saw only a few servants when my grandmother and I arrived from Chelles a short while ago."

"The emperor and empress took Wala and your intended husband Eberhard to Reichenau Abbey. Conrad and Rudolf are over there on the field practicing with weapons. The emperor and empress did not expect you for another week. Where is Countess-Abbess Heilwig?"

"Our journey fatigued my grandmother, and she went to bed. Now, tell me about Eberhard. They say he was a student in the palace academy, but I do not remember him."

"Eberhard is several years younger than I. He was a diligent student then, and now he **is** reputed to be a brave warrior, intelligent, religious, and of honorable character."

"Is Eberhard handsome?"

"He is manly, brave, and devout."

"I used to imagine marrying you when I was a child. So did Dulciorella. We laughed about it while we were at Chelles together."

Bodo could not picture Dulciorella laughing or even smiling. "Well, your Highness, I shall be marrying you anyway."

"What? I do not understand."

"I have been given the honor to officiate as principal witness at your wedding."

Bodo the Apostate

Giséle's nuptials took place on a Sunday in the royal chapel at the Aachen palace. Music from the organ in the choir above filled the hall as if it came from Heaven, and boys sang hymns with the sweet tone of angels.

Wearing the dalmatic of his diaconate, Bodo marched behind Bishop Drogo to the altar at the head of priests, lectors, and altar boys. All Court officials, great magnates, and prelates of the empire filled the chapel according to rank. Abraham, his sons Nathan and Judah, and the royal physician took their places at the rear of the chapel. Ludwig and Hemma arrived from Bavaria to attend the nuptials, but neither Lothair, ailing Pepin, nor Count Bernard. Louis and Judith sat on their throne chairs in the gallery above. Eberhard and his groomsmen stood before the altar and awaited a procession of court ladies strewing flowers and escorting Giséle through the hall.

Bride and groom kneeled at the altar, and Drogo invited all present to pray. Lectors read passages from the Old and New Testaments, and a priest intoned a Psalm. Bodo's turn came to proclaim The Gospel of the Lord, and all present responded, "Praise to you, Lord Jesus Christ."

The Rite of Marriage continued through exchanges of vows, and Bodo assisted Drogo with the distribution of the Eucharistic bread and wine to Eberhard and Giséle. Louis and Judith descended from the gallery and led all in attendance to the altar for their participation in the Eucharist. After more blessings, the ceremony ended.

All left the palace and went to the gymnasium field to congratulate Giséle and Eberhard, to admire her dowry and presents on display under canvases, and to celebrate with food and drink.

The day after Giséle and Eberhard wed, they left with their cartloads of gifts for Friuli. Wala accompanied the couple. Again, Bodo doubted the old man would survive the journey, but good for the princess to be away from her domineering mother.

71. Long Haired Star

From the Calends of September through Martinmas in November, word arrived each week naming those who died from a severe plague ravaging Italy. Judith praised God each time when those she hated most perished: Wala, Matfrid of Orleans and Hugh of Tours. Not the emperor, for whenever Louis learned of a death, he wept in the chapel, beat his chest, and prayed for God to be merciful to the deceased. Bodo spent much time consoling the emperor.

One evening he discussed the plague with Priscus, who referred to the Lothairians' deaths as karma, an unfamiliar word, which the Astronomer explained as a belief one's acts were repaid good with good, evil with evil.

"As the Bible teaches, what one reaps one sows."

"Something like that."

Bodo grasped the concept that karma offered comfort to the just and to those who had been wronged, provided one lived long enough.

Good Friday arrived on the first day of April 837, and instead of an eclipse like the one that took place during the Crucifixion, a different marvel occurred. At dusk atop the observatory roof, Bodo, Guntrum, Priscus and the royal family stared awestricken at a bright phenomenon crossing the night sky. Below, the entire Court watched the spectacle. Some shouted they saw a dragon, others believed it was Donar's hammer.

"Astronomer, we know this long haired star has not been seen by us in our lifetime."

"That is true, Your Majesty. I believe it may be the bearded star that is said to appear every seventy-five years."

"What does it portend for us, for the empire?"

"I must calculate its trajectory. On the morrow, I shall report all my findings. For now, I can tell you this, Sire. This star first became visible in the sign of Virgo, and now it is obstructing the constellations of *Serpens* and *Corvus*."

"Serpent and Crow? What does it mean? Astronomer, be accurate in your calculations. Everyone, follow us to the chapel where we shall pray and praise God for this warning."

While Bodo kneeled beside Louis, he speculated about the long haired star. Priscus said it appeared every seventy-five years. Unless empirical evidence proved otherwise, its appearance posed no eschatological meaning or warning for mankind. No astronomer, Bodo equated the star's movement across the sky identical to the Sun's rising and setting and cycle of the Moon, no more, no less.

"Deacon Bodo, we are in such awe of God's wonders, that we cannot remember if there is consolation in the Bible. "

Bodo the Apostate

"Your Majesty, in Jeremiah 10:2, the prophet says be not dismayed by signs in the sky that cause nations to tremble."

"You are right to remind us, Deacon, for we should fear only the Creator of both mankind and that heavenly body."

At daybreak, Louis summoned Bodo and every important palatine cleric and noble to the Council Hall. Judith sat beside the emperor, Charles standing at his father's right.

Louis spoke from his chair. "Although we are sinful beings, we cannot praise or marvel enough at God's mercy. He has granted us this wonder to see as an admonishment for our wicked behavior. Because it affects everyone, let us all follow a better road according to our ability and judgment, lest perchance, we are found unworthy of His forgiveness."

"Amen." The assemblage intoned.

Louis, Judith, and Charles took goblets of wine from their servants, who distributed more to each man and woman present. The emperor gave Bodo the responsibility of dispensing generous alms to the poor, monks and priests.

For twenty-five days, the bearded star traveled in retrograde, passing through the signs of Leo, Cancer, and Gemini. Bodo never asked Priscus what it portended for himself. Not the stars and planets, free will offered a choice of paths. One led to an uncharted forest of uncertainty. The other offered a familiar chaos of changing alliances, broken oaths, and betrayals. His status, nay, his entire existence depended upon the whims of Their Majesties and eventually young King Charles, all fragile reeds upon which to lean. Bodo sensed he must come to a decision soon or it might be too late.

72. Valediction

Late June of 837 when the Court moved to Bodman, Bodo visited his parents' graves frustrated he could not remember the faces of his mother and father. He no longer enjoyed spending weeks at the Bodensee in late spring or early summer. The ever expanding royal palace, Louis' banning all Midsummer's Eve festivities on the field, and deaths of old vassals, retainers, and tenants made his former home unrecognizable.

Preferring to be alone, Bodo filled a skein with wine in the palace kitchen, and walked into the nearby forest. Fortunate animals, he had not come to hunt this warm day. Bodo paused at what he had named the Lake of Swans. Here, when a child, he looked for naiads between the reeds and lily pads. Some still believed swans showed themselves each full moon night in the form of beautiful maidens.

Bodo left the lake and went to the great oak where he had carved his name with Strabo's assistance nineteen years before. Unbelievable so much time had passed since. Bodo sat against the trunk and drank heavy wine from his skein. The midday temperature rose. Sounds of beasts and birds harmonized a soothing melody. Immersed in a pleasurable lassitude, Bodo bade farewell to individual animals. Did they suspect his intentions never to return? But how, when, and to what destination?

While Bodo considered his many options, the sky darkened. Thunder in the distance heralded a storm. Instinct alerted Bodo to rise and step a great distance away from the oak. More thunder roared above. A great flash of lightning blinded Bodo for a moment and set the tree afire. Donar had not spared the great oak this day.

Bodo raised his skein to the flaming tree and drank to a perfect valediction for a life about to change forever.

When Bodo emerged from the woods, Guntrum left his lessons in bow and arrow in the open field by the palace and ran to him. "Uncle, our cousin Conrad said the empress wants me to enter the clergy and assist you in serving Prince Charles. Is it true?"

"The empress has said nothing about that to me. Perhaps Conrad was teasing you."

"I think he meant it. I want to be a knight the same as my father."

A familiar song Bodo also had sung. "I know that, Guntrum. Wait here."

Bodo strode across the field to Conrad. "Is it true what you said to Guntrum, that the empress has destined him for the clergy? You distressed the boy."

"He had to know sometime. You, Deacon Bodo, you better than anyone can tell Guntrum how wonderful a life one can have in the clergy, a life such as yours, to be so special you are favored above all by the emperor and even by my sister, the empress."

Bodo the Apostate

Conrad's bitter tone surprised Bodo. "You know I preferred to be a knight."

"And a count too. I have known all these years that you wanted your father's titles and lands." Conrad removed his cap and showed Bodo scars on his head where the Lotharians twice shorn him. "You suffered no such humiliation and pain when you were tonsured, no imprisonment and torture. Tell Guntrum how well you live, how the path to bishop and many benefices lie ahead for you. I am the empress' brother and the emperor's brother-in-law. Why should you be promised the office of second man in the empire and not I?"

Bodo chose not to respond to Judith's bitter and envious brother. He left for the woods with Guntrum acknowledging he had no complaints about the superficialities of his existence. All Conrad said was true and more. He lived a life of comfort, favored by Their Majesties, with opportunities to join in the chase, unlimited food, drink, and carnal pleasures with pliant women if he so chose.

Were he true to his personal code, he should despise himself for serving a Church that could not make up its mind about dogma, none of which he believed. A Church that sought supremacy not by enlightening men but with threats of death. A Church whose leaders seldom practiced what they preached. A Church he never wholly accepted in heart and mind.

Bodo saw himself no different from Jews and pagans who had been forcibly converted. They observed Christianity on the surface but practiced Judaism or worshiped their old beliefs in secret.

Bodo met with Judith who confirmed what Conrad said. Guntrum would enter the minor orders when he reached the age of ten in January. Bodo seethed but did not protest. He decided not to tell his nephew what Judith said until after the Epiphany in January so the boy could enjoy the feasting days. By then, he might be able to offer Guntrum another choice.

73. Seeds of Chaos

Late October, Louis and Judith presided over an assembly in the Council Hall at Aachen. Fourteen year old Charles in colorful finery at his father's right twirled the small ends of a downy blond mustache as if his efforts might speed its growth.

Bodo recalled the time he saw the emperor, so strong and handsome in 819. Now an old man of fifty-nine, Louis' beard and hair had become white, cheeks sunken, body frail, a gouty foot resting on a pillow, too painful for him to rise.

After Chamberlain Drogo called for silence, Louis read from a scroll. Shortness of breath made the emperor's voice soft and halting.

"Let this be heard and written by our scribes to be distributed throughout our empire. On this day, we give our son Charles rule over Neustria. Henceforth, he shall be addressed as Your Majesty. We further decree our beloved son Charles to be our sole heir and emperor upon our death."

No one except the emperor's closest advisors knew about those pronouncements in advance. Murmurings and expressions of both surprise and anger prevailed in the Council Hall because Louis again created a new Division of Empire.

Drogo raised a hand to silence the assemblage and spoke for Louis. "Each Neustrian noble, bishop, abbot present will now swear an oath of fealty to King Charles."

The Neustrians formed a line. While each man declared his allegiance with right hand on the Bible and genuflected before Charles, Bodo credited Judith for her success encouraging Louis to give her son rule over so large a kingdom that included Frisia, Paris, Troyes, Sens, and Auxerre, the greater part of Flandria, and all lands between the Meuse and the Seine. Lothair, Pepin, and Ludwig would never accept Charles as both king and the next emperor. Seeds had been sown for another rebellion.

Drogo's shouts interrupted Bodo's musings. "Make way, make way."

Doors opened, and soldiers escorted Hilduin and several disgraced Lotharian nobles who had been imprisoned to the dais. They genuflected and offered new loyalty to the emperor, empress, and to King Charles, after which Louis restored their former titles and offices.

Neither Bodo nor any of Louis' advisors had been prepared for what happened next. They watched aghast when exiled Agobard entered the hall, calm and confident, attended by his protégés, Florus Deacon of Lyon and the priest Amulo.

Abraham cursed for the first time in Bodo's presence.

Florus and Amulo praised Agobard's saintliness and demanded the removal of Amolar, a gifted theologian who had administered the diocese of Lyon since 835 and whose loyalty to Louis never wavered. They accused the scholar of heresies, degeneracy, corruption, and moral perversion.

Bodo the Apostate

Louis listened to their charges without expression. "We have heard all you said and agree. Agobard, step forward. We return you to your diocese of Lyon and raise you to Archbishop with all honors, benefits and authority."

Why did Judith acquiesce to Agobard's restoration? No one more than this prelate had described the empress using the vilest names and metaphors.

Despite his detachment, anger and sadness became Bodo's companions. Wrong became right. Traitors obtained rewards. Loyalty counted for nothing. Adversaries became allies then enemies again only to be forgiven. Of what value did vows sworn before God by such men have? How could he, whose oaths were inviolate, survive much longer in a chaotic world of repeated treacheries?

After the assembly Bodo, Strabo, and Priscus met in the Astronomer's observatory. All understood Their Majesties' haste to give Charles his portion of the empire but not why the emperor reinstated Agobard and Hilduin with Judith's consent.

Priscus gestured toward a chart on his desk. "The stars continue to augur much confusion. The seasonal rhythms have become chaos with more dark days ahead for the empire. Our emperor has of late manifested a benignity that typically occurs a few years before a man's time on earth comes to an end. The empress believes Louis' death is imminent and is seeking all the allies she can find to support her ambitions for Charles, even former enemies. I am no less distressed then you."

"I have my own concerns," Strabo said. "Charles prefers the company of Hincmar, who hates Her Majesty."

Bodo hoped there was one who might be become a counterweight to Hincmar. Although the priest succeeded in worming into the young king's entourage, for an inexplicable reason Charles had taken a liking to Abraham's second son Judah.

Bodo understood the reasons for Louis' mercies. The emperor wanted nothing more than peace within his empire and believed he could achieve that elusive goal by reconciling with all former adversaries. Bodo instead foresaw years of disunity and shifting alliances the moment Louis died:

Lothair and Ludwig allying against Charles and Judith with support of the clergy led by Hilduin, Ebbo, and Agobard.

Lothair and Ludwig vying against each other to replace Charles as emperor.

Pepin too ill and mad to be of significance, his sons too young and inexperienced to lead an army, and anarchy prevailing in Aquitaine.

Each noble ruling independent of imperial authority.

Ambitious Count Bernard coveting the Midi and lands in Aquitaine, if not the kingdom itself, and joining with Lothair and Ludwig against Charles to gain them.

Bodo attended a meeting in Judith's suite at which the empress expressed the same concerns to those she trusted most and decided upon a course of action destined to fail. "We have no choice. Lothair is Charles' godfather. He promised to defend our son's person and rights against all enemies at his baptism. We must, with your help, motivate the emperor to reconcile with his eldest son for that very purpose."

Had the empress forgotten Lothair's violations of oaths, his severe mistreatment of Louis and her own self, Charles and her brothers? Had not Lothair ignored Louis' overtures to reconcile? Yet Conrad and Rudolf approved her new stratagems.

Fools, all of them fools. Why could they not perceive the obvious? Lothair intended never to rest until he reclaimed his former lands at Charles' expense, nor would Ludwig who coveted Alamannia.

74. A Boon Granted

Bodo hunted with Louis in the Brandenwald several miles east of Aachen. After making Charles King of Neustria and forgiving traitorous nobles and prelates, the emperor's health improved, which enabled him to ride without pain during a weeklong chase. They slew enough boars, bison, and deer to fill the palace larders and accumulate an abundance of pelts and skins to keep weavers and clothes makers busy throughout a long winter.

The last night of the hunt during a feast in the emperor's trophy filled lodge, Louis thanked and distributed gifts to his coterie of trusted advisors for their skill in the chase and loyalty: jeweled weapons, fancy saddles, or bags of gold.

Bodo the Apostate

Bodo decided the moment could not be more propitious to make his request. Judith lay abed at the palace refusing to be seen because a severe tooth abscess swelled her cheek, thus unable to sway the emperor otherwise.

Bodo left his seat between Charles and Priscus, walked around the long table, and genuflected before the emperor.

"Your Majesty, before my turn comes, I want to say I need no material reward, but I do ask for a boon."

"A favor? It must be something serious. Tell us. What is it?"

"I beg you. Give me leave to make a pilgrimage to Rome so I may pray in its churches, visit graves of the apostles and saints, and read in the Vatican's great library."

"Rise, Bodo. A worthy request indeed from our Deacon. Of all at Court, we prefer your absence least. Still, we see advantages for the empire. When would you leave?"

"As soon as possible."

Louis turned to Priscus. "Astronomer, how portend the stars?"

"Another severe winter is imminent, and everywhere the weather is already foul. The Alps will not be passable until April of next year after the spring thaws."

Bodo did not want to delay his departure for so many months. "Because brigands roam freely in the Alps and the Rhaetians are in perpetual rebellion, I have chosen another route."

"And which is that?"

"The land route to Lyon, Sire. From there, I will travel by boat down the Rhône to Marseilles, where I shall sail to Ostia, the port outside Rome."

"That makes sense. You may set forth the day after the Feast of the Epiphany."

"I also ask permission to take my nephew Guntrum."

"Yes, it will do the boy good to see the center of our faith before he enters the Minor Orders. We wish we could go with you."

Bodo caught Priscus' stare. Was the Astronomer trying to read his mind? His mentor and friend may have succeeded.

After the feast, Bodo sat alone with Louis expecting another evening of prayer and Biblical commentary. Instead, the emperor rambled at length how he envisioned Charles ruling as a true Christian emperor, just, merciful, brave and wise.

Donald Michael Platt

"Deacon Bodo, as you know, both we and the empress have made it known that you shall be King Charles *camerarius* after we pass on and he becomes sole emperor. But this evening you asked for a boon, which we granted, before we announced the gift we intended for you."

"As I said, Sire, I have no need for any material object."

"It was ... it is not material. It is an obligation. We have discussed the matter with both the empress and Archbishop Drogo, and we are in agreement. We had planned to announce it earlier at the feast, but now that we have granted your boon, we must postpone your appointment."

"Appointment? I do not understand."

"Deacon Bodo, upon your return from Rome, you shall replace Archbishop Drogo and be our *camerarius* for the last years of our life. You shall then be second man in the empire."

Bodo kneeled. "Your Majesty, words fail me."

But Bodo's thoughts did not. Louis' word was not Judith's and Charles' word. Bodo well remembered salutary lessons learned from Wala's life. No one held more power than the de facto ruler of the empire during Charlemagne's last ailing years. Yet upon becoming emperor, Louis peremptorily dismissed and imprisoned Wala in an abbey. Charles might assert his independence and do the same to his *camerarius*.

The temptation of so much power and influence was not enough cause for Bodo to deviate from his plan.

75. A Revelation

Days took forever to pass. A full long month of December and a week in January still lay ahead before Bodo's pilgrimage began. The evening after Martinmas, a clerk brought Bodo a message from Priscus for him to come to the observatory. He found the Astronomer writing at his table. Priscus lit more candles, poured an extra goblet of wine from an amphora, and invited Bodo to sit beside him.

"Here is the chart the emperor asked me to draw and ascertain if your pilgrimage will be successful. Priscus lowered his voice even though they were alone in the observatory. "You will never reach Rome."

Bodo tensed. He worried Louis might forbid him to leave for Rome if Priscus said he should not go.

Bodo the Apostate

"Strabo is no less concerned than I. He wants to speak with you about a most sensitive matter, and we suspect you have been deliberately avoiding us these past several weeks. He also believes that despite your favored position, rapid rise in the clergy, and becoming the emperor's *camerarius* upon your return, you are discontented. Strabo and I both know you prefer a secular life."

And a life of order. "That has never been a secret to those who know me best."

Priscus poured more wine, "Your discontent is the same as my own unhappiness."

"You, discontented? Now it is my turn to remind you of your favored position at Court and how much the emperor relies upon you."

"I would exchange all that for ...."

Priscus' extended pause piqued Bodo's curiosity.

"No one, not even Abraham knows what I am about to tell you. Before I continue, you must promise never to speak of what I am about to say."

"I so swear."

"Let my example cause you to think rationally." Priscus drank from his goblet, and his eyes became unfocused while he spoke. The Astronomer began with a description of the emperor's well-known appreciation for a pretty face and a comely form. About age fourteen at the onset of manhood, Louis took a *concubita* named Theodelinde, who gave him within two years a son and nonentity he made Count of Sens after becoming emperor, and a daughter named Alpaïis. To prevent their marrying, Charlemagne forced Louis at age sixteen to wed Irmingard.

Louis continued to see Theodelinde and brought Alpaïis to Court when she was twelve. Already nubile, the girl was fair of complexion with dark hair and eyes a deep blue. Then fifteen, Priscus adored Alpaïis, and she returned his love. They met often in secret for a year until Louis' domineering wife interfered, which had nothing to do with their trysts.

Irmingard hated Alpaïis because she was Louis' and Theodelinde's daughter. She persuaded Charlemagne that the girl must either take the veil or wed an elderly man, and he selected aged Count Beggo of Paris to be Alpaïis' husband. Eleven years later and childless with Alpaïis, Beggo died. By then, Louis was emperor. Pressured by Irmingard who again wanted to make his daughter take the veil, he compromised and installed twenty-four year old Alpaïis as Abbess of Saint Peter at Rheims in 818.

That was the same year Irmingard persuaded Louis to blind Bernard of Italy and imprison without cause all potential rivals against her sons: the brothers Wala and Adelard, and Louis' bastard half-brothers Drogo and Hugo. Some might say that Irmingard died that year because of her sins.

Bodo had known about Priscus' annual visits to Alpaiis' abbey whenever Louis visited Rheims during his progresses, and now he knew the full reasons why. He also understood Irmingard's motives. She feared if Alpaiis wed again and gave birth to a boy, the emperor might favor Theodelinde's grandson over his queen's brood, as he eventually did with Charles.

Priscus concluded his tale. "Since then, I have visited Alpaiis whenever I can with no hope of our ever marrying. And so you must understand, Bodo, your disappointment is not unique in this world where the powerful decide one's fate."

"Why have you not found another to love?"

"Alas, Bodo, you have never loved anyone the way I adore Alpaiis. My love for her is so strong I cannot bring myself to take a wife or a *concubita*. True, I have satisfied my needs with certain women outside of Court, but I always felt the worse for it afterward, as if I betrayed Alpaiis."

Bodo thanked the goddess Aphrodite for not afflicting him with the pain of love. No lady of the palace, not even Sigrada stirred him with so strong an emotion. He did not envy the Astronomer.

Priscus opened a cabinet and showed Bodo a cushion of silk twill died the color of red wine from the Rhone with the name Alpheidinivus and words such as *honorenovo* woven into borders of gold and silver thread. "Alpaiis made this cushion for me. It is my most prized possession. Each time I look at it, each time I touch it, I am with my true and only love. When I die, it shall be buried with me."

76. A Surprise for Strabo

Close to midnight in the otherwise empty scriptorium, Bodo placed his torch in a sconce and dismissed the servant who had prepared a table with a candelabrum, an amphora of wine, two goblets, and a plate filled with honey cakes. When Strabo entered, Bodo motioned for his friend to sit. He poured wine into the goblets and offered Strabo a honey cake.

Bodo the Apostate

"Bodo, this is most unusual. Wine and honey cakes in the scriptorium? And at this late hour? Why have you asked to meet with me?"

Bodo described what transpired after he discussed with the emperor a passage in the gospels relating to the Nativity. Aware that Strabo's time as tutor was ending, Louis wished to reward the scholar for his invaluable service and comfort he gave Charles during "the recent difficult years," as the emperor expressed it.

Strabo interrupted as if Bodo's mention of the word "reward" had not penetrated his brain. "Yes, after Charles reaches his majority age of fifteen in June, he will have no use for a tutor. In truth, there is nothing more he wants to learn from me. Most likely, I shall be given leave to return to Fulda where I can at last write and study in an atmosphere of calm and tranquility, but as you know better than anyone else I would prefer my beloved Reichenau on the Bodensee."

Oblivious to Bodo's silence, Strabo continued "Yes, I would rather live in a warmer clime where the winters are less brutal than at Fulda or here in Aachen."

Bodo handed Strabo a scroll with Louis' seal. "Because I have known you so long and well, the emperor delegated me to bring you your reward."

Hands shaking, Strabo unrolled the scroll and held it closer to the candelabrum. His mouth opened but no words came until he finished reading. "Is it true. Is it really true?"

"I drink to Abbot Walafrid Strabo of Reichenau Abbey. No one ever deserved a benefice more."

Strabo read the scroll a second time. "I must thank His Majesty for fulfilling my greatest wish."

"You can do that tomorrow morning after lauds, and then you will be free to leave immediately for Reichenau."

Strabo looked at the ceiling, praised God, and faced Bodo. "Years before, you convinced the emperor and empress that I should be Charles' tutor. Did you do the same regarding my appointment as Abbot of Reichenau?"

Strabo did not wait for Bodo's reply and reminisced at length about their childhood at Bodman. He praised Bodo's intelligence so obvious at a very young age and how easy it was to teach him the Latin alphabet, Lord's Prayer, and Apostle's creed by age five.

"Do you remember when I helped you carve on the Tree of the Thunderer *I, Bodo, was here*?"

Bodo nodded he did. This was not the time to tell Strabo that the

Thunderer had obliterated the great oak, nor did he want to wallow in nostalgia and resurrect a past buried deep in the recesses of memory.

Strabo took a honey cake. "This was your favorite treat and mine as well. I never enjoyed a Midsummer's Eve more than that night you leaped over the bonfire. We shared so many happy times when we were young."

Strabo praised the great beauty of Bodo's mother and her kindnesses. He never forgot that during famines and severe winters she brought food and ale to his parents, honey too when they were ailing.

He was also grateful to Bodo's father Count Gunzo for recognizing his potential as a scholar and escorting him to Reichenau when he was a boy of seven.

Strabo idealized his years at the abbey where he learned from knowledgeable teachers, wrote his first poems, and tended the herbal and botanical gardens until the abbot sent him to Fulda. He promised to tend the graves of Bodo's parents.

Strabo eulogized Adeltrud for her sweetness and friendship and the extent to which he missed Bodo's sister. He also recalled the many times they had to chase after Bodo who always outran them through the woods.

Unaware Bodo had not spoken Strabo recounted at length his years at Court. "Bodo, we have come far since those days. You are a Deacon and I am Abbot of Reichenau. Odd, I remember when I first came to Court how much the empress' beauty affected me. Now, I no longer worry if I do not see her face each day."

Strabo sipped from his goblet still unaware of Bodo's extended silence. "I look forward to greeting you at Reichenau as its abbot after your peregrination to Rome, perhaps upon your return or whenever the emperor brings his Court to Bodman."

Bodo again raised his goblet to Strabo as if to accept his friend's invitation.

77. Complications

Louis and Judith may have reigned during the Octave of the Nativity on the Calends of January 838, but joy and laughter ruled during entertainments by jugglers, mimes, musicians, and jesters in the Council Hall. All laity in the palace wore their gayest apparel. Clergy in

Bodo the Apostate

attendance discarded their inhibitions and joined in the feasting and merrymaking. Bodo pretended to be amused by the performers while looking forward to his imminent departure.

In the middle of the banquet, Louis called for silence. "Deacon Bodo, step forward."

Puzzled, Bodo obeyed and genuflected before Their Majesties.

Louis bade Bodo rise. "We are saddened because our beloved deacon and cousin will be leaving us shortly for a pilgrimage to Rome, and yet we are gladdened his piety will be a shining light for all to follow. Deacon Bodo, we cannot allow our representative to appear before His Holiness in modest circumstances."

The emperor gestured. A fanfare of horns followed, and the doors opened. All in attendance gaped at a parade of treasures carried by servants: jeweled golden crucifixes and crosses, boxes of coins and rare spices, vestments of gold and silver threads, holy relics, many of them seized from Hilduin's great collection, and rare books, some illustrated, all bound with covers of gold and jewels, and gilded armor, shield and jeweled baldric, more ceremonial than practical for battle. So were a sword and dagger with handles and hilts of gold.

"Deacon Bodo, we entrust you to deliver our gifts for His Holiness."

Bodo stared dismayed at the largesse. He estimated the gilded burden would fill a cart and slow his progress.

Three servants approached Bodo. No deacon's garb, they carried a purple cassock with amaranth trim, a rochet, a purple skull cap, and a trio of miters, one of plain white silk and fringed lappets, a second of gold covered with precious stones, and a third of gold cloth with embroidered gold and silver edges.

"It is our pleasure to raise our beloved Bodo to Bishop of the Palace for his unblemished service, unfailing loyalty, and solace he provided us during difficult times. Bishop Bodo, we bestow upon you these vestments to wear when you have your audience with His Holiness, who shall upon our written request confirm you in your office of Bishop Palatine."

"Words fail me, Sire."

"Well deserved, Bodo, well deserved." Louis gave Bodo a leather scroll. "During your travels, you will carry this *tractorae,* which gives you authority in our name to request lodging and to forage provisions for your retinue and mounts."

"My retinue, Sire? I had intended to journey in the plain robe and sandals of a penitent."

"Bishop Bodo, we appreciate your humility and piety, but you must arrive at Rome in state as befitting our representative with servants for your needs, carters to drive the draft horses, and soldiers to discourage brigands. Before you leave, we shall prepare a message for you to deliver to Archbishop Agobard …."

Another annoyance. Bodo had intended to bypass the treacherous old bigot when he rode through Lyon.

"… and two others, one for His Holiness and another for King Lothair."

"As you command, Sire, so it shall be done."

Bodo responded to Judith's demand he appear before her posthaste. Unattended, the empress sat covered in fur on a throne chair by a brazier when he entered her antechamber. Frigid as the weather outside, Judith addressed Bodo as "Bishop" in a sarcastic tone and imperiously gestured for him to take the low stool opposite her.

"You have displeased us. Displeased us greatly."

Bodo tolerated Judith's rebukes without apologies or asking what he had done to offend her.

"We know you deliberately asked His Majesty for permission to go on a pilgrimage to Rome when we were ill. Had we been present we would have persuaded the emperor to deny your request. We also are convinced you knew the emperor was going to make you Bishop Palatine. You should have told us in advance of his announcement. We do not like to be surprised. Therefore, we warn you. Do not linger in Rome. Remember this. No one is indispensable."

Uncomfortable in the low stool with knees almost touching his chin, Bodo cared not about being replaced as Charles putative *camerarius*.

"Now, Bishop, to another matter. Count Bernard has again offered his daughter Dulciorella as a bride for King Charles. We have changed our opinion about the girl. She shall wed our son. Because you are taking the Rhône route from Lyon, you will be passing near Uzès." Judith handed Bodo a scroll with her seal. "You will deliver our response there to Count Bernard and Countess Dhuoda. We also charge you to emphasize for Dulciorella that the great honor we bestow is our command and your wish as well. She owes her life to you. Remind her of that. Furthermore, we know how well you excel at keeping secrets. Swear to us you shall not repeat to His Majesty or anyone of our decision. We shall let the emperor know when the proper time comes."

Bodo understood why the empress changed her mind about Dulciorella. Reliable reports confirmed Ludwig had suggested to Lothair they should ally and take the portions of Charles' lands each coveted. To protect her son against a pact between the two kings, Judith believed she must join forces with the one man capable of defeating both, Count Bernard.

Bodo swore to Judith he would not reveal to Louis her marriage scheme for Charles and left annoyed to have been placed between empress and emperor and be made a courier for both. Louis had given him gifts and a letter to be delivered to the Pope, an entourage, and more messages for King Lothair and Agobard. Now Judith added another unwanted chore and detour.

78. Mysterious Gift

Abraham invited Bodo to his home. Unlike Judith, he gave Bodo the warmest of welcomes. Like the empress, the elderly merchant sat in a fur robe by a brazier in a room Bodo appreciated more than any other after they supped. One day he intended to have a similar study.

That Bodo would never see Abraham after he left Aachen saddened him. Full of years, the patriarch needed to lean on a stick when he walked. His eyes were so weak that when he bent to read his nose almost touched the book or manuscript. Others times Abraham used "Aristophanes' Lens," a glass bowl filled with water that magnified the smallest letters.

Bodo recalled Abraham's repeated kindnesses, hospitality, and helpfulness when he asked about learning Hebrew. Bodo never forgot his first night at Welf's home when he overheard the merchant describe him as a prodigy. Of late, Bodo considered Abraham to be more than a teacher and friend, his second father.

"Bodo, I invited you for several reasons. One is a favor I ask of you. Will you carry a letter to my nephew Viscount Taurus in Roquemaure? It is on your route down the Rhône. He will be most hospitable and at your service no matter what you request. I have traveled to and from Roquemaure many times during all seasons. You should arrive there no later than mid-February."

"I shall be pleased to see the viscount again."

Abraham digressed and spoke of his many journeys. He closed his eyes and talked at length about Khazaria. He feared the Jewish kingdom might not survive into the next century because powerful foes surrounded it on all sides: Byzantium, the Caliphate of Baghdad, and pagan Rus and Slavs proselyted by Orthodox Christians from Constantinople. Bodo took Abraham's prediction of Khazaria's ultimate fate as a warning for him not to go there.

"Bodo I have watched with pleasure your passion for learning from the time you were a boy to now. I never questioned why you wanted to learn Hebrew because I knew the answer from the moment you asked. Now come, kneel beside me."

Bodo obeyed Abraham who placed a hand on his head. "Here is the second reason why I wanted to see you. I have come to think of you almost as a son of my flesh and blood. As I would for my sons and daughters, I now give you a father's blessing, the same as Jacob gave to Manasseh and Ephraim, the children of Joseph."

Abraham recited the benediction in Hebrew, reached into a drawer, and handed Bodo a small leather bag tied with a secure knot. "And now the third reason ... my parting gift for you. Do not open it before you leave Aachen, and after if you so choose, use it well."

Touched by Abraham's gesture Bodo almost addressed the elder as *Abba*, the Hebrew word for father.

79. To Lyon

Louis provided Bodo and Guntrum with amblers for riding, strong draft horses to pull one cart loaded with gifts for His Holiness and another filled with food and drink, and mules for soldiers and servants to ride. Bodo told the grooms to provide padded braces for the draft horses and attach them to the shafts of the carts for better traction and a faster pace.

Bodo the Apostate

Bodo surprised Guntrum with a baldric, a scabbard and a sword of proper size for a boy of ten to wield, and a dagger for his belt. He took his nephew to one of the amblers. "This mount is yours. You are of good height and strength for a boy your age. You shall be my *scutarius*, shield bearer, or as we say in Francique, *escuier*."

After Bodo next met his retinue, a manservant, two carters, and four veteran soldiers, all devout Christians who volunteered for the pilgrimage, he went to the stable and saddled Amalric.

"My trustworthy steed, we are about to embark upon a great adventure."

The royal family and entire Court gathered outside to watch Bodo leave. Despite the emperor's flaws, Bodo held a fondness toward Louis but none for Judith. She had changed from a lively and charming girl-empress to a ruthless mother obsessed with gaining a kingdom for her son Charles even if it meant the destruction of an empire. Bodo never forgave Judith for forcing him to stay in the clergy.

Along the route from Aachen to Lyon, Bodo took provisions as necessary from abbeys, diocesan, and priestly lands. The clergy could afford food and drink for men and horses well beyond freemen and tenants who lived marginally on their farms.

Storms and thick mud, into which cartwheels sank, slowed progress along the winding route of more than four hundred miles. They did not reach the environs of Lyon until mid-February.

The well situated city lay on the west bank of the Saône, a tributary of the Maas, at a confluence with the Rhône, which allowed Lyon to develop into a major center of trade and important water route to the Mediterranean for transport of food, salt, wine, and luxury items. A rich diocese, its vast holdings extended far beyond the city to the foothills of the Alps, the Jura mountains in the east, and the Massif Central in the west.

Bodo decided not to travel on the crowded Rhône and instead take the parallel road to Marseilles after he saw bargemen controlling rudders with long poles and floating their boats with the current down river needing to apply all their skills to avoid collisions. They were not always successful because logs too large in size for any river craft to carry often slammed into them. Across the river teams of mules, oxen, or slaves pulled ropes attached to loaded flatboats and rafts against the flow.

They rode past a long line of wretched humans chained to each other, whipped and herded toward the city by slavers. Veiled females rode in canopied carts.

"Uncle, so many are blond and fair like us. Should we not free them?"

"They are pagans, not Christians, so it is best not to interfere. Lyon is a center where slaves are auctioned or transported to Hispania."

Bodo approached a lean swart man on horseback who led the caravan and whom he marked as a Saracen. He raised his hand in a greeting. "*Salaam Aleikham.*" The man did not respond, and Bodo switched from his rudimentary Arabic to Francique. "Do you understand me?"

The slaver gestured for his men to halt the line. "Your Francique will do."

"From whence do they come?"

"Lands of the Norse, pagan Saxons and Celts from the western isles, others from the Rus, Bulgars, and tribes farther to the east. The choicest women are for the Emir of Cordoba's harem, the strongest men to be warriors for his army or to serve in the mines and galleys, the boys destined to be eunuchs. If you want to purchase a slave, attend our auction tomorrow."

"Are there any Christians or Jews?"

"None. Pagan infidels all."

"And what route are you taking?"

"The usual. Down the Rhône to Marseilles and along the coast past Narbonne to Barcelona, and then inland through Saraqusta to Cordoba. And what is your destination?"

"A pilgrimage to Rome."

"You are a priest, a monk?"

"I am Bishop Bodo from Emperor Louis' court."

"Then you are an important man. So am I. I am Achmed, purveyor of slaves to Emir Abd al-Rhaman II of Cordoba. That baggage in your carts, gifts for your Pope?"

"A few items. The rest are provisions for the journey. Nothing worth dying for."

"I understand your meaning."

After conversation with Achmed, Bodo returned to his escort. "No Christians, those slaves are pagans."

Bodo stopped outside the grand episcopal house beside the cathedral of Saint John the Baptist. He dismounted from Amalric, rapped on the great door, and told the servant who opened it to summon the archbishop.

When Agobard, his Deacon Florus, and protégé Amulo entered the vestibule, Bodo handed the prelate Judith hated and Jews feared the most Louis' Imperial Decree. "Emperor Louis has elevated me to bishop, Your Grace."

The three clerics' faces registered surprise, then hostility. Aged Agobard had the lined severe face of an ascetic disappointed by life. Approaching his seventieth year, the Archbishop of Lyon had failed in every attempt to limit the freedom of Jews and abolish all worship of icons. Still, the prelate succeeded in regaining his diocese despite choosing the losing side in both rebellions against Louis.

The harsh countenances of Deacon Florus and the priest Amulo suggested men who also disapproved of laughter.

Agobard returned the scroll to Bodo. "Why has the Bishop Palatine come to Lyon?"

"I am on a pilgrimage to Rome, and I carry for His Majesty a message and gifts for His Holiness. These men are my escort, and the boy is my nephew, Guntrum, son of my sister Adeltrud and Count Meinrad of Béziers."

Agobard waited to speak until after Guntrum and the men took turns kissing his episcopal ring. "Bishop Bodo, for how long will you avail yourself of our hospitality?"

"We depart at daylight on the morrow."

"And how is the emperor's health? I have heard he is in decline."

Bodo heard unchristian expectation in the Archbishop's tone. "He suffers as usual from gout." Bodo produced a second scroll and handed it to Agobard. "His Majesty requested I deliver this to you."

Bodo knew its content. Abraham had petitioned the emperor to reconfirm all capitularies protecting the Jews and his own privileges and possessions because of Agobard's renewed activities against the Jews. In response, Louis ordered his clerks to draft a restatement of the ordinances with both a reprimand and command for the archbishop to cease his proselyting, sermonizing, and writings against the Jews.

While Agobard read the missive, his scowl became more delineated, his complexion near purple, and veins pulsated on his forehead. The archbishop handed the scroll to Florus and Amulo. "The emperor has favored the perfidious Jews yet again. We shall discuss how best to deal with it later. Bishop Bodo, we sup after sext. Your mounts, mules, and draft horses will be watered, fed and shoed as necessary. I shall provide a cell for storage of His Holiness' gifts and another in the cloister for you and the boy."

Bodo arranged shifts for his soldiers to be posted outside the locked door where the Pope's gifts had been sequestered. The cold small stone room Agobard provided seemed no better than a dungeon cell with one candle on a small table, a stool, and straw for bedding. Bodo looked forward to resuming his journey in the morning after what was certain to be a long, tedious, and unpleasant night. He told Guntrum not to say a word when they supped no matter what he might hear.

80. Agobard Agonistes

Although Lent had yet to arrive, Agobard offered a spare meal of bread and gruel, the latter a porridge of groats boiled in milk without seasonings, water instead of wine, mead, or beer, typical of the archbishop's abstemiousness in all matters corporal. The archbishop sat on a throne chair flanked by benches at a long table, Bodo at the archbishop's right and Guntrum at his right side. Deacon Florus and Amulo faced Bodo across the spare table at Agobard's left. Priests, monks and others in the minor orders filled the remaining spaces on the benches and at other tables.

After prayers, all sat cheerless and silent except for some loud slurping while they ate. Bodo took a spoonful of the tasteless gruel and preferred to soak his trencher of hard bread in the murky liquid.

Agobard waited until the end of the meal to complain about all that distressed him. The archbishop surprised Bodo when he condemned all singing in church, which did not enhance worship in any way but instead distracted the flock with transient sounds pleasing to the ear. More than anything else, Agobard desired unity of the Trinity throughout the empire, which, he declared the emperor supported. Even though the archbishop conceded defeat in the battle to eliminate icons and other images, he vowed to continue waging war against Adoptionism and other heterodoxies.

Agobard included in his tirade an assertion also held by the more rational Hrabanus Maur, "The faithful must never be allowed to read the Bible or offer prayers wherever they wish. It must be only in an Orthodox Church where our Trinitarian faith is correct and the teaching proper."

Bodo the Apostate

Soon the conversation focused on Louis' health and the imperial succession. Deacon Florus, a distinguished theologian, spoke for Agobard when he asserted the rights and role of the Church the archbishop had written about in his *De priuilegio et iure sacerdotii* and in *De priuilegio apostolicae sedis*:

"No matter who becomes the next emperor, the Church must regain the supremacy of priests over laity and that of the Pope over the emperor. Our bishops must be elected by our synods and approved by His Holiness and not appointed by kings."

Bodo ignored Florus' gibe directed at him.

Agobard launched a virulent screed against the Jews from his writings and previous pronouncements.

"Jews are the greatest threat to both the unity of our Church and empire. They are mendacious, demonic, sons of the Devil, each one an antichrist striving to fulfill Satan's will. They wallow in worldly pleasures, spread heresies, and wish to kill Christians. They are the Antichrist's enablers because of their blasphemies. Merely by their presence, Jews harm Christians. That is why I oppose the baptism of any and all Jews over the age of eight. Such conversions always prove to be false. Thus, we can deny the perfidious Jews all benefits of salvation and instead ensure their eternal damnation. Here on earth, I want all Jews isolated from Christians so our flock will not be led astray by their pernicious false faith."

"I agree, Your Grace," Amulo said. "Jews are cursed and carnal. They are a threat to the spiritual health and welfare of the faithful under your jurisdiction here at Lyon and the empire. We must remind out flocks how and why God abandoned the Jews. They are as a cast away woman who turns to whoring."

"Well said, Amulo." Agobard fixed his gaze on Bodo. "Bishop, you know the Court is a nest of Jewish vipers. How best can we convince the emperor to remedy the situation? How can we persuade him to prohibit their building new synagogues contrary to bans from the times of emperors Honorius and Theodosius II four hundred years ago? How do we remind him of the ban that prohibits Jews from holding public office and proselyting?"

Before Bodo could reply, Agobard continued with yet more passion in his voice, "Although the human body and heretics are sources of pollution through the Devil, the inventor and cause of all evil, Jewish blasphemies and carnality, are the greatest pollutives of all. They defile and prevent our flocks from attaining a more spiritual life. Jewish blasphemies consist of beliefs in God's corporeality, the eternal nature of the Torah, and the absolute worldliness of Jesus. Through their carnal laws of *kashrut* Jews not only focus on the body, but prove their uncleanness, since all things are clean only through Christ, whom they persistently reject."

While Agobard paused to clear his throat, Amulo said, "Your Grace, it may take a bit more time, but I know that eventually we shall be adding to the Good Friday liturgy the guilt of the treacherous Jews in the crucifixion of Jesus. Better yet would be an empire without Jews, a world without Jews."

Agobard raised a hand to silence his protégé. "Bishop Bodo, you have not spoken, unlike Amulo and Deacon Florus."

"Your collective eloquence leaves me speechless."

Agobard frowned unsure of how to interpret Bodo's reply. "Our meal has ended. After prayer at nones, we shall continue our discussion."

Bodo's disgust intensified with each word spoken by Agobard. The archbishop described an ideal Christian society in which the body never controlled a person through its demands, desires, and wants, for those corporeal instincts prevented spiritual progress and drew individuals away from the proper love of God.

"Those who wish for wealth and honors and have lustful thoughts, even if they never fulfill them, by those desires alone, they become adulterers and enemies of God."

Bodo could no longer remain silent. "Then the thought, even if not acted upon, is as sinful as the deed?"

"Absolutely, Bishop Bodo, and our priests must be no less celibate than the monks, for they preside over the Eucharist and thereby have physical contact with the flesh and blood of Christ. That is why our clergy must be apart from the laity, deriving special status from its service at the altar, physical contact with the sacred, and reproducing itself by non-carnal means. Our clergy must have clerical purity and lead a vigorous spiritual life."

Agobard paused and looked at the beamed ceiling to suggest he was speaking to the Holy Trinity. "Worldliness harms the Church through secular confiscations of its lands to the point where clergy barely sustains their ministries, thus starving the Church and the poor they serve. Monarchs

Bodo the Apostate

and nobles driven by greed violate consecrated property because they covet what has become God's. Too many priests are more dedicated to rising rapidly through the hierarchy and with their own welfare than they are for the souls in their care. Christ becomes irrelevant in their quest for increased wealth and prestige. Those who love their lands and livestock more than God are not worthy of Christ."

"Then you advocate cleansing the Church of such bad priests?"

"Bishop Bodo, can you not understand this? Even bad priests are intrinsically superior to the laity because like property given to the church, priests are consecrated to God. Only priests, regardless of their own personal worthiness, may perform the sacraments through which everyone can be saved. Their consecration and ability to administer the sacraments, particularly Baptism and the Eucharist, give them an authority over the laity so they may learn God's commandments."

Bodo had not forgotten the priest Theobald. "And those who sin with children?"

"Yes, even they, if they are contrite and confess their sins. Now, Bishop Bodo, I shall speak of an important matter. It is what I shall ask you to convey to His Holiness Pope Gregory in a letter I shall prepare before you depart on the morrow. The Pope must remind Emperor Louis to love the heavenly kingdom more than his earthly empire and that those who separate themselves from Rome risk detaching themselves from the divine mysteries, and thus from salvation. Louis must be more concerned with not offending Pope Gregory than with losing the empire to his sons."

"Shall I repeat your advice to His Majesty after I return from my pilgrimage?"

Blood drained from Agobard's face. Bells rang. He turned over the hourglass on his desk and rose. "Let us go to the chapel for the First Nocturne of Matins."

After prayers, Bodo retired to the cell he shared with Guntrum. The boy lay awake.

"You cannot sleep?"

"The things they said at supper. Why are they so hateful?"

"They fear worldly temptations and that the religion of the Jews will turn their flocks away from Christ."

"But you are friendly with the Jews."

"Yes, I am."

"Then they cannot be so bad."

"Well said, Guntrum. Now let us sleep, for we have a long journey to resume at daylight."

Bodo lay awake distressed by all he heard. These Trinitarians preached a religion of love, yet they hated not only Jews but all mankind because of human frailties. Better they all should confine themselves to monasteries and leave the populace alone.

81. Roquemaure

The end of February Bodo arrived at Roquemaure, a thriving river port situated in the Rhône valley between limestone cliffs and hills covered by groves of olive trees and abundant vineyards. At several landings, laborers loaded river vessels with casks, hogsheads of beer and ale, and terra cotta amphorae filled with wine.

Bodo dismounted at one of the docks where a man of soldierly bearing greeted him. "Bishop Bodo, I welcome you to Roquemaure."

"Viscount Taurus, you addressed me as bishop. I am surprised word about me has spread so fast."

"That and more. A courier from my cousin Judah arrived ahead of you with a message I shall discuss with you later. Who is the handsome boy?"

"My nephew. Guntrum, this is Viscount Taurus, Lord of Roquemaure and domains on the other side of the Rhône."

"May I assume you are carrying gifts for Pope Gregory in those wagons."

"And provisions. You are well informed."

"They shall be secure here, and your horses and mules will be well cared for in my stables."

"Count Abraham asked me to deliver this to you."

Taurus took the scroll. "Thank you. I shall read it later. Now, come and let me welcome you to my home. You and your nephew will lodge in my villa. Those men, they are your escort?"

"Yes."

"A sullen lot, but they may share lodging and food with my servants and workers."

Bodo the Apostate

Bodo repeated Taurus' offer of hospitality to his entourage. Each refused to have any contact with Jews. "Then eat and sleep where you will. Be here at daybreak."

Taurus watched the men trudge away. "Unpleasant company you keep."

"The emperor meant well when he encumbered me with them. I had planned to travel alone with Guntrum."

Taurus told several of his own workers to cart the Pope's gifts to his villa. Bodo and Guntrum followed the viscount on horseback and dismounted at the stables. Taurus pointed to nearby ruins at the crest. "That is the foundation of a Saracens fortress. Several years ago, Abraham succeeded in advising the emperor to thwart Agobard and prevent the Church from using that site for a new abbey."

"That zealot is relentless."

"He is seventy. His days are short."

"I regret to say that Agobard will be replaced by men no better and more likely worse than he. Beware of the clerics Florus, Amulo, and Hincmar."

After they washed and put on fresh clothes, Bodo and Guntrum met Taurus' wife Flavia and four children ranging in age from five to nineteen in the great hall of the viscount's restored Roman manse near the ruins of a Moorish fortress. The table's largesse for their midday meal included meats, vegetables, olives, nuts, and fruits.

Bodo heard the same prayers in Hebrew recited at Abraham's home for the blessing of bread and wine. Similar to Abraham's meals, he observed much interplay and laughter between parents and children.

Taurus addressed Guntrum. "Did you know your father was a cousin of Count Bernard, whose mother Guiberc, came from a pagan Saxon family?"

"Yes, Sire. My father was a Hornbach. Did you meet my mother too?"

"I had that pleasure. Countess Adeltrud was a lovely lady, may she also rest in peace."

Throughout the remainder of the meal, Taurus described the complex genealogies of the *Nasim* of Septimania. After the last prayer, he dismissed everyone from the table except Bodo and told a servant to bring more wine. Both no longer addressed each other by their titles of Viscount and Bishop.

Taurus told Bodo that Bernard was in the Midi with his vassals gathering support for an invasion and annexation of Aquitaine, presumably on Charles' behalf.

Bodo did not miss Taurus use if the word "presumably." Although Bernard's extensive domain included Gothia, Septimania, the Marches of Hispania, and lands in Burgundy, the count, or duke as he styled himself, coveted the Midi, Aquitaine, and the Toulousaine.

"Marcus, my eldest, was knighted by Bernard. He is obligated to join the count's army for the spring campaigns."

Obligations. Except for his responsibilities concerning Guntrum and promise to deliver Judith's letter to Countess Dhuoda, he would soon be free of all such encumbrances.

"Bodo, do you know the content of the letter Abraham gave you to deliver to me?"

"No."

"He mentioned that the empress has accepted Dulciorella for Charles' wife."

"Judith commanded me to deliver an identical message to Bernard and Dhuoda at Uzès. The empress believes an alliance with Bernard through marriage will secure Charles' reign over Aquitaine."

"Is Judith truly so desperate?"

"She is obsessive, possessed by the demon of ambition for her son. You said the courier brought a message from Abraham's second son Judah."

"Yes, he wrote that my uncle passed on, may he rest in peace."

Abraham's death saddened Bodo. "When we said our farewells, Abraham was frail and unwell."

"He died after a courier brought word that his eldest son Nathan succumbed to fever in Constantinople."

"I shall miss Abraham's wisdom and friendship. He was a great man and of significant influence in my life. A man I still aspire to emulate. I truly mourn Count Abraham."

"Judah will become the next Merchant of the Palace."

"Yes, he is almost seventeen, a capable young man, and favored by Charles. Viscount Taurus, because you, your family, all your servants and laborers are Jews, I assume you have a synagogue nearby."

"My wine master is our rabbi, and we pray in a structure on my property, which serves as our synagogue. Why do you ask?"

"I came to think of Abraham as a second father. I have been told that in your religion when a father dies his sons honor him with a specific prayer."

Bodo the Apostate

"Yes, we call it *kaddish*."

"I would like to say your prayer for the dead in remembrance of Abraham."

"I can arrange that, but before I do, I want to discuss something else Abraham wrote about you." Taurus paused and poured more wine. "Bodo, you should know that in his letter to me, my uncle expressed his belief you had been long dissatisfied with the Church you serve and have no intention of continuing on to Rome. My uncle asked me to do anything and everything possible to be of assistance to you."

"Were I traveling with Guntrum alone, I would need no help."

"Yes, your escort. I believe I have a solution to that problem. The details need not concern you."

"As you wish."

"Now, I shall be direct. Is your destination Hispania as my uncle suspected where you will convert to our Jewish faith?"

Bodo showed Taurus the pouch Abraham gave him and removed its content for the first time. He recognized what it was and ran a finger over the intricate floral patterns and six pointed Star of David engraved on its gold and silver exterior.

"Abraham gave me this gift before I left. I had not seen it before. I do not reject it now. That is my answer."

82. Rubicon

After Bodo prayed for Abraham, he sat with Guntrum on the fortress ruins and took in the sweeping vista of the Rhône Valley below. He described for his nephew the significant history of Roquemaure, which he had learned from Abraham and Taurus. From the docks below, Hannibal floated his elephants on rafts across the Rhône before he marched through the Alps to devastate Rome. At the apex of their conquests, the Muslims built a bridge to the other side of the river since destroyed during the Carolingian reconquest of Septimania.

The Franks gave the site its name, Rock of the Moors, Roquemaure in Francique. More than a wine-shipping port, from Roquemaure the finest wares of the region were transported throughout Western Europe, to the Byzantine Empire and to Hispania.

"I wish to know your thoughts on many matters, Guntrum. My sister Adeltrud, you mother, was she a devout Christian?"

"I cannot say. She attended Mass but often called upon the Thunderer."

"And your father?"

"He never spoke of religion or much of anything. He was away at war most of the time. Uncle, what will happen to me after we visit Rome and return to Court? I do not want to be in the clergy."

"Guntrum, like you, I was not allowed to decide my future. I wanted to be a knight and warrior, the same as my father. My Uncle Welf, Emperor Louis, and Empress Judith chose the Church for me. I obeyed them and honored my oaths. Now, I am about to do something unheard of. That is why I am giving you the choice I was denied at your age."

"I do not have to enter the clergy?"

"Listen to me and do not interrupt. Three roads lie ahead for you. One is to return to Aachen and enter the minor orders in obedience to the empress now that you have reached your tenth birthday. Your second choice can be the same I am making. I shall no longer live a lie pretending to worship and carry out my offices in a religion I find to be false and unnecessary. After I deliver the empress' message to Countess Dhuoda in Uzès, I will go to Hispania."

"Why? I thought we were going to Rome."

"That was never my plan. In Hispania, I shall convert to the Jewish faith and submit to circumcision. If you join me, that will be your second road."

Guntrum stared at Bodo speechless.

"Have you nothing to say?"

"What is circumcision like?" By the time Bodo finished describing the ritual, blood drained from Guntrum's face. "I ... I need time to think. You said I had three roads. What is the third?"

"Return to Aachen and denounce me."

"I would never do anything so dishonorable. If I convert with you, must I be circumcised too?"

"Yes, and think about this. Once we convert to the Jewish faith, we can never return to the empire. We will have to take Hebrew names and lead a different way of life. We shall be hated and despised by all devout Christians and Muslims. Do you understand?"

"Can I be a warrior in Hispania if I am a Jew?"

"Yes, if that is what you want."

Bodo the Apostate

"Then I shall go with you."

"Swear now you will not speak a word of this to anyone."

"I so swear."

Bodo gripped his nephew's shoulders. "You are brave, Guntrum, and I am proud of you."

"What about the escort?"

"Do not worry about them." Church bells rang in the village. "The hour of nones. Soon our lives will never again be ruled by the canonical hours. We leave on the morrow. Obey whatever I tell you to do without hesitation, without any questions."

In the morning, Bodo wore armor covered with a hooded bishop's cloak and took Guntrum with him to the docks where he supervised the loading of the Pope's gifts onto the carts by his sullen retinue.

The viscount ignored the insult and exchanged farewells with Bodo. "The weather is fair, the sky clear. May it stay that way until you reach your destination."

Bodo rode ahead of the lead cart and Guntrum behind the last along the road. About ten miles south of Roquemaure he halted the column.

"It is time for our midday repast." Bodo gave his retinue individual amphorae of non-kosher wine and generous portions of bread, and cheeses. "Imbibe freely, feed well, and take time to nap before we continue toward Avignon and beyond to Marseilles"

Bodo and Guntrum sat on the bank away from the men. Bodo also drank wine with bread and cheese supplied by Taurus. He provided a light beer for Guntrum.

"Look, Uncle, they are falling asleep."

"Hush, Guntrum. Last night, we added powerful sleeping draughts to their wine."

"Are we going to ride away from them?"

"Yes, but not as you may be imagining. Good, all are unconscious. Gather their weapons and hide them over there behind the trees." After Guntrum returned, Bodo pointed up river. "Here they come."

Guntrum saw Achmed's barges and the column of chained slaves approaching. "Are you going to sell them to the Saracen?"

"It is either that or slay the men here and now while they sleep. There is no other choice. Give it no more thought. Look, here comes Taurus."

The viscount rode to Bodo with a quartet of armed servants and surveyed the drugged Christians. "If these pond scum have such hatred for Jews, let us give them more reason to do so." Taurus waved at the slaver who beached his barges and halted the column of slaves. "Ho, Achmed. Here is more merchandise for Hispania, as I promised you."

Taurus' men and Achmed's slavers finished chaining the Christians and dumped them in the barges. The effects of the drug had not yet worn off.

Bodo rejected a bag of coins from Achmed, and the slaver snapped his whip. "The mines always need fresh meat."

Bodo thanked Taurus for his assistance and told Guntrum to bring the viscount the weapons he sequestered. "To distribute amongst your men."

"Excellent quality. Again, I wish you a safe and successful journey."

Bodo watched Taurus and his servants ride toward Roquemaure until they disappeared from sight and turned his attention to the slave caravan and barges continuing down the Rhône toward Marseilles. His fortuitous encounter with Achmed had prevented him from breaking one of the Ten Commandments, Thou Shalt Not Commit Murder. No Commandment existed that said Thou Shalt Not Sell Anyone into Slavery.

Bodo believed like Julius Caesar he had cast his die and crossed a personal Rubicon when he sold the Jew haters to Achmed, which burdened not his conscience. But what about another Commandment, Thou Shalt Not Steal? Louis' gifts for Pope Gregory presented a dilemma no less challenging than the disposal of his escort.

Bodo took inventory of the cart filled with gifts for the His Holiness: coffers of gold and silver coins, jewels, precious manuscripts, goblets, crucifixes, and bolts of fine wool and silk, some of which had been placed in the second cart containing food and drink.

What should he do with them? Throw everything into the Rhône and travel light? Stop at an abbey and trust its abbot to send them to Rome? The best use of the Pope's treasure would be to ensure a comfortable life in Hispania and dispense alms as he saw fit.

Bodo held the scroll Judith commanded him to deliver to Count Bernard and Countess Dhuoda. If Uzès had not been near his route to Hispania, he would have tossed it into the Rhône. Bodo decided to bring

Bodo the Apostate

Judith's letter to Dhuoda and take extra provisions from the countess. He and Guntrum could hunt and forage for more food and drink along the route to Hispania after they ran out. Bodo looked forward to teaching his nephew how best to hunt.

83. Dhuoda

They stopped at a small stream along the road to Uzès and watered the horses. "Uncle, why are you removing your armor?"

"So I shall be welcomed with due respect by Countess Dhuoda." Bodo placed a purple skullcap over his tonsure and slid onto the third finger of his right hand a large amethyst ring set in gold. "Now, let us continue."

They passed through groves of fruit and mulberry trees. Ahead lay the impressive mountains of the Cévennes looming above Uzès. Bells tolled the hour of terce, and Bodo estimated from the number of houses and shops clustered around the church and abbey a population of at least five hundred.

Upon their arrival at a villa high above the town, a young female servant led Bodo and Guntrum to a library filled with books and manuscripts. Dhuoda, dressed in austere grey wool, stopped writing in a ledger on her desk. The countess rose, bent, and kissed Bodo's ring. "I welcome you to my home, Your Excellency, but your face is unfamiliar to me."

"I am Bodo. I was a subde-acon when last you were at the palace in Aachen." He showed Dhuoda the document from Louis. "The emperor appointed me Bishop Palatine."

"Now I remember. And who have you brought with you?"

"My nephew Guntrum. We are on a pilgrimage to Rome, and our carts outside bear gifts from the emperor to His Holiness Pope Gregory."

"They will be safe here. You are the most welcome of guests. Whatever you need, consider it done. Unfortunately, all our vassals and male servants are with Count Bernard save the elderly groom of the stables. He and his grandson will care for your horses. Of course, you may take whatever provisions you need."

Bodo thanked Dhuoda and handed the countess a scroll. "I bring you this message from Empress Judith for Count Bernard and for you."

Bodo perceived a brief flash of anger in the countess' eyes when he mentioned the empress.

Dhuoda tore the seal and read what Judith had written. "Count Bernard will be most pleased the empress wants Dulciorella to wed King Charles. My husband is in the Midi or perhaps in Aquitaine by now where there is talk of rebellion against the emperor. They prefer Pepin's son Pepin II to be their ruler, not Charles. Now, I must find someone reliable to deliver this message to my husband. Forgive me, Excellency. I have neglected to thank you for your rescue of my stepdaughter Dulciorella although, I regret to say, it may have been all for naught. That ungrateful daughter of Count Bernard told us she will never marry anyone we might arrange for her to wed. That girl has always given us trouble. Count Bernard was a young and foolish boy who acted on impulse when he married a Jewess. My lineage is far superior to that woman." Dhuoda shook the scroll. "I had intended to send Dulciorella to a convent until she complied with our wishes. Like any son, a daughter must honor her parents' commands. Now, I will show you and your nephew to your room. We dine after the bells of sext and recitation of psalms in my chapel."

Bodo washed his face and hands in a basin the countess provided for their room. He had not seen Dhuoda in nine years, not since the beginning of the first rebellion against Louis when Bernard fled from Aachen with his family. Her strong masculine features were of a type that never seemed to age, unlike Judith's.

"Uncle, does Countess Dhuoda have any sons?"

"A boy of twelve who is probably with his father."

Bodo heard many at Court question Bernard's motives for removing Guillaume from Uzès before the newborn's baptism and naming. They spread rumors he had the boy brought to Barcelona for his circumcision and Dhuoda had not seen her son during the past eight years.

"Countess Dhuoda is haughtier than Empress Judith."

"With good reason, Guntrum. Dhuoda considers herself and Count Bernard to be superior to all others after the emperor."

Bodo did not discuss a persistent but unverified rumor about the countess. Many nobles and prelates believed Dhuoda was an illegitimate daughter of Charlemagne raised by a powerful family. Perhaps it was so. The countess' strong features suggested consanguinity with the Carolingians.

Bodo the Apostate

Dhouda and Dulciorella awaited Bodo and Guntrum in the family chapel. Icons and crucifixes decorated the walls between candles secured in sconces. Dulciorella wore a modest unadorned tunic and mantle of grey wool similar to Dhuoda's. Slight and no more than five feet tall, Dulciorella had become more womanly during the three years since he last saw her. Bodo did not know the month of Dulciorella's birth and guessed her age to be between sixteen and seventeen. Still strange of features, with those enormous eyes, small avian nose, and darker of skin than the fair maidens at Court, she might not appeal to Charles.

Dulciorella perfunctorily kissed Bodo's ring while church bells tolled in nearby Uzès for the prayers of sext. After he led the reading of psalms and a portion of the Gospels, they ate a light Lenten meal. Dhuoda said she wanted to speak with Bodo alone and sent Dulciorella to her room. Bodo gave Guntrum specific instructions what necessities to take from the countess' larders and stable.

Dhuoda invited Bodo to her library and wasted no time with niceties after they sat facing each other. "Excellency, I wish to discuss with you my decision to write a handbook of advice for my son. I intend to provide Guillaume an ideal path for him to become the perfect aristocrat and knight exemplar. Perhaps you will be kind enough to offer suggestions and feel free to share any contrary opinions."

"I am honored to be privy to your thoughts." Bodo prepared himself for an extended monologue by the countess.

"I shall begin by telling my son that social order must begin with worship of God as a Christian of the Orthodox faith. I reject all heterodoxies. I shall teach Guillaume that after worship of God obedience to his father Count Bernard comes before obligations to any king or lord. After his king or lord, he must show respect for the priestly class. Alas, these days the understanding of proper order has fallen prey to the ambitions of venal prelates and the emperor's sons. Had they maintained their clear lines of obligation, there would have been no uprisings against the emperor or internecine wars. There is too much disorder in our land …."

Bodo could not agree more.

"… and yet the solution is so simple. What I propose is an ideal. The closer my son comes to it, the better example he will set for all. I pray each day and night I may live long enough to guide Guillaume to manhood.

Count Bernard has arranged for learned men to teach him, but they cannot have a heart as ardent as mine for my firstborn, nor are they of equal status to me. All is still in my head, ready to burst forth as a spring torrent onto the pages. I wish for my son to exercise the natural and specifically the Christian virtues, and to live the beatitudes, the gifts of the Holy Spirit, in order to be reborn each day in Christ and grow always in Christ. I shall instruct him in detail to live a life of prayer. He must emulate Christ as an ideal knight."

Mothers were all the same. Dhouda obsessed over her son's welfare and future no less than Judith did for Charles. "You are a wise and strong woman. I am sure with the Lord's help you will prevail."

"I thank you for your suggestions and for agreeing with me. Were you not resuming your pilgrimage to Rome so soon, I would further discuss my handbook with you. However, there is something you can do for Count Bernard and for me. Not only the males, but we of the weaker gender also owe the same obligations to our husbands and fathers after God. Dulciorella owes you her life. I believe you should be the one to tell her she must wed King Charles. Use the authority implicit in your rank and the gratitude Dulciorella has for you. Counsel her. Persuade Dulciorella to be obedient, to honor her father's wishes, and agree to wed Prince Charles."

Bodo had performed his obligation for Judith and did not want to speak with Dulciorella. "I intend to leave immediately. After we finish loading our provisions, we will leave for Marseilles. The weather is clear. The moon is full and closer than usual. It will light our way through the night."

"It should not take long for you to convince Dulciorella to wed King Charles." Dhouda showed Bodo the scroll. "The empress says you are to do as she commands. I shall tell Dulciorella to meet you now in the garden."

84. Departure

Bodo arrived ahead of Dulciorella in the garden of Dhuoda's villa where only perennials offered monochromatic green in the soft golden late afternoon sunlight. Branches, twigs, and other debris littered the bottom of a drained and tiled rectangular shallow pool with an image of Poseidon holding a trident. Despite a crispness in the air, Bodo

Bodo the Apostate

found the winter weather mild and pleasant farther south of Neustria, Saxony, and Aachen.

Dulciorella arrived wearing a heavy woolen cloak. A hood obscured most of her face. They walked together at a slow pace along the edge of the pool. Bodo waited in vain for her to speak.

"Lady Dulciorella, did Countess Dhuoda tell you why she wanted us to meet?"

"No."

"I detoured from my route along the Rhône toward Marseilles to bring your stepmother and Count Bernard a message from Empress Judith concerning you. She has had a change of mind. Judith wants you and Charles to wed."

Dulciorella stopped walking, turned and faced Bodo. "Why?"

"To ally with your father and ensure he will not desert Charles." Bodo almost asked Dulciorella if her large dark expressive eyes ever blinked.

"And the empress and my stepmother would have you convince me to agree to the marriage."

"Think well before you answer. You shall be a queen, possibly an empress."

"Do you believe I aspire to so great an honor?"

Bodo ignored Dulciorella's sarcasm. "It is both a royal and parental command."

"Did my stepmother tell you what will happen to me if I refuse?"

"You shall become a nun with permanent imprisonment in a convent."

"Yes, even my father would consent to that. Tell my stepmother she will have my decision in the morning. I want you to be present of course to hear it."

Bodo looked at the clear sky. "I told the countess I shall be departing after dark. The moon is full and will illuminate our way. I am most eager to resume my pilgrimage to Rome."

"Then let us say our farewells. One more time, I thank you for rescuing me."

Before Bodo could speak another word, Dulciorella hastened to the villa. He had no idea what she would tell Dhuoda in the morning. She revealed no emotion during their conversation, no rise and fall in tone of voice. Dulciorella's demeanor led Bodo to believe she would defy her parents regardless of their threats. Whatever her reasons, they concerned him not. Bodo satisfied himself he fulfilled his promise to speak with

Dulciorella, and he went to the stables to learn how soon they would be ready to leave.

Bells tolled the hour of Matins. Night fell. The moon shone sun-bright. Constellations and planets glittered. After he thanked Dhuoda for her hospitality, Bodo and Guntrum returned to the stables. The stable master and his grandson harnessed a fresh pair of draft horses to a long wagon with a leather covering. Bodo inspected its interior satisfied Guntrum had loaded the most valuable of the Pope's gifts beneath a false floor added by the stable master according to instructions. He told his nephew to tether their amblers to the rear of a second cart loaded with provisions.

Count Bernard had taken all mounts except Dhuoda's ambler. The other horses left behind were suitable only for drawing carts and for plowing. Bodo led the countess' ambler outside and tethered it to the side of the covered wagon opposite where he had tied Amalric. Three amblers would allow one to be spared the burden of saddle and rider at intervals.

Wheels had been well-secured and axels greased to Bodo's satisfaction. All horses had fresh shoes. He praised the stable master and his grandson for their assistance and gave each a silver coin. Both dropped to their knees and kissed his ring.

Bodo read a map he had taken from the royal archives. It delineated the best inland route through a pass in the Pyrenees leading to Ausona, gateway to the Emirate of Cordoba. Better they avoid well-traveled coastal roads to Hispania and the larger towns of Narbonne and Barcelona where he might be recognized by someone who had seen him at Court. They must hurry though before storms and thaws turned passable dry ravines into torrential streams and rivers.

"Guntrum, go to the cart. We leave now."

Bodo climbed onto the covered wagon and took hold of the reins. A mile or so from the villa, he stopped and exchanged his bishop's purple for soldier's garb and removed his ring. Bodo placed his father's sword in its scabbard, returned to his seat, and snapped the reins.

When they approached a bend in the road two miles from Dhuoda's villa, a familiar taste of honey cakes infused Bodo's palate and tongue. At the same instant, a little owl alighted on the seat beside him. Had it followed him all the way from Bodman? Or was it a portent? Ahead, he saw a hooded figure in the middle of the road and reined his draft horses to a stop.

Bodo the Apostate

Was it another vision?

The owl hooted and bolted. No vapors engulfed Bodo. The mysterious figure did not vanish or reveal herself as the mysterious apparition of his visions.

"Dulciorella."

85. Strong of Will

"Take me with you."

Bodo did not like surprises nor did he want more delays. "Impossible. Go back to the villa before Countess Dhuoda awakens."

"No, I will not." Dulciorella refused to move. "And I shall not wed Charles or anyone else my father and stepmother choose."

Guntrum joined them, and Bodo told his nephew to be quiet. "Dulciorella. Move off the road so we can pass."

"Then I will follow you on foot."

"Do as you will." Bodo snapped the reins.

Dulciorella climbed onto the wagon, threw her bag into the back, and sat beside Bodo. "You will be rid of me at Marseilles."

Bodo admired Dulciorella's resolve. "And what will you do there?"

"Board a ship or find a caravan that will take me to Barcelona. An uncle, my mother's brother, lives in Ausona."

Ausona lay on Bodo's route to Cordoba. She would learn his destination soon enough.

They made good time at night under the full moon. At daybreak, Bodo stopped at a junction outside Nimes about twelve miles south of Uzès. One road led to Arles on the Rhône. A second angled southward from Nimes to the coast. Bodo turned onto the third that faced due south.

"Stop. This road leads to Hispania."

Bodo reined the horses and hand signaled Guntrum to do the same. "I am not going to Rome."

Dulciorella did not seem surprised or ask why. She explained to Bodo why it was the wrong road to take this time of the year. She had spoken with many travelers. Impassable swollen wild rivers and deep gorges lay ahead. Bodo agreed to change course to the coastal road that would take them to the Marches even though he was more likely to be recognized along the way because it passed through important towns and counties whose lords had appeared at Court.

The coastal road meandered from the shore to about ten miles from the sea. On a good day Bodo averaged twelve to fourteen miles when he did not face one of several obstacles: heavy traffic in both directions; long waits at toll bridges and toll gates to towns; waiting for a barge to carry them across swollen rivers; rainstorms, the occasional wheel that came off in a rut; the need to purchase food or take time to hunt; and to find a local blacksmith to shoe the horses.

This was Bodo's first journey through Septimania. The same as when he was a boy traveling with the Court on Louis' royal progresses, he observed differences in regional food, clothing, and languages spoken. Roman replaced Francique as the dominant tongue in Septimania. Aside from the usual abundance of vineyards and groves of olives, rice fields and fruit orchards became more prominent.

Freed from the demands of Louis and Judith, Bodo traded away a pampered life for one of free choice answerable to no one. No longer did he have lesser clergy to do his bidding, fresh clothing awaiting him each week, meals prepared by cooks served at regular intervals, and thermal pools.

Bodo respected Dulciorella for her resilience, equanimity, and fortitude. Not once did she complain. She seldom spoke, which pleased him. Dulciorella bathed and washed clothes in streams chilled by thawed snow pouring from the hills and mountains. She out-bargained farmers for their chickens, eggs, fruits, vegetables, and wines and fishermen for fruit of the sea. On those rare occasions when Bodo stopped to hunt for game, Dulciorella helped skin the animals, lit fires and cooked the meat.

Through with the Orthodox Church, Bodo did not stop at any abbey or residence of a parish priest. He let hair, mustache and beard grow, and the hated tonsure disappeared forever. Fortune favored him. Conspicuous because of his height, blondness, and noble bearing, no one had yet recognized the emperor's former Deacon and favorite.

86. To Ausona

Late March of 838, they approached Béziers a town that rose above the Orb River on a small bluff about ten miles from shore. Guntrum led the way to his parents' graves at a church cemetery. The boy's weeping and praying annoyed Bodo. He left Guntrum at the headstones of Adeltrud and Meinrad but did not return to the wagon where Dulciorella waited. He required solitude. Bodo had mourned Adeltrud years ago, but seeing her grave severed the last link with a past forever buried with his sister if not in memory. To be sentimental about the past indicated weakness.

South of Béziers they reached Narbonne a town of some five hundred Jewish families and one of the great centers of Judaic learning. It was also the capital of Bernard's vast lands. Bodo had learned much about Narbonne's Jews from Abraham. Dulciorella related the same story about her great-grandfather Natronai of the Persian Bustanai family and a descendant of King David, whom Pepin the Short invited from Baghdad to rule as *Nasi,* the Jewish Prince, of Narbonne and gave his daughter as a bride. Dulciorella told Bodo she never saw her father, the third *Nasi,* practice Judaism even though Bernard's first wife and her mother was a Jew.

Dulciorella suggested they not stop because she had visited Narbonne with her father and might be recognized. Bodo agreed and they continued to the south through Gothia where yet another language was spoken. The same as in the northern and western counties of the empire, Francique, Roman and Goth dialects changed every ten to twenty-five miles.

South of Narbonne the terrain changed. On clear days they could see the high snow covered peaks of the Pyrenees. Closer to the Marches, they rode beneath granite cliffs and massifs.

Bodo veered off the road so their horses could rest and drink at a small stream trickling toward the sea. He dismounted when he heard Dulciorella scream Guntrum's name. She pointed at a crag above. Bodo saw his nephew climbing toward an Ibex, a magnificent mature male with great horns. Guntrum carried a spear too large for a boy his age to wield with ease.

Bodo chased after Guntrum and shouted his name. "Stop. Come back."

The Ibex bounded to a higher rock and leaped to a ledge above. Guntrum scrambled after it. When he reached the precipice, the mountain goat had disappeared. Unsure of his footing, the boy used the spear for balance while looking at his feet.

"Guntrum, behind you."

The Ibex sprang from the greater height, rammed Guntrum's back, and propelled the boy off the ledge. Bodo watched horrified as his nephew fell hard on the rocks below.

Dulciorella ran to where Guntrum lay and kneeled beside the boy. She shook her head at Bodo. "He is dead."

Bodo stood over Guntrum's broken body and recalled how the Church gave his father a Christian burial when Gunzo instead should have been better honored as an Alaman warrior. When the road brought them closer to the sea, he would cremate his nephew according to the tradition of their ancestors.

Bodo wrapped Guntrum in a blanket. Abandoned damaged carts littered the roadside, and he collected enough slats to make a raft while Dulciorella gathered dry scrub. When the shoreline became visible, Bodo walked down a trail to the sand where he found a cove. By the time he returned, Dulciorella had tied the slats with sections of rope and set dry scrub on the raft.

Bodo placed Guntrum atop the makeshift bier, mounted Amalric, and pulled it to the cove. As he had done for Bardulf, Bodo pushed the raft into the water, set it afire, and shoved the pyre farther out to sea with the receding tide.

Bodo watched Guntrum's cremation unsure to whom or to what he should pray. He believed in no Thunderer or any pagan pantheon, which included Trinitarianism. He had not yet converted to a religion of choice.

Early in April, they reached Girona, a town south of the Pyrenees well populated by Jews who spoke another strange language, a mix of vernacular Hebrew and the dominant regional tongue, Visigoth.

In Girona, Bodo sold the second cart, its pair of draft horses, and two amblers, which he no longer needed now that Guntrum had died. Everyone he spoke with advised him to wait for a caravan to form because brigands lurked along the road. Bodo disregarded their advice for several reasons.

Bodo the Apostate

Bernard's vassal administered the town. He wanted to rid himself of all responsibility for Dulciorella and reach the sanctuary of Muslim lands before inevitable word of her accompanying him reached her father, Dhuoda, or the Court.

Bodo rode Amalric, and Dulciorella drove the wagon along the eastern edge of the Guilleries, another granite massif, toward Ausona about sixty to seventy miles away to the southwest. At dusk in a clearing off the road, Bodo watched Dulciorella prepare a mutton and vegetable stew. As usual they did not converse, which allowed Bodo to plan ahead without interruption.

Dulciorella tasted the mutton stew and filled their bowls. A little owl startled Bodo when it settled on Dulciorella's shoulder. She did not flinch. From where had it flown? Had it followed them from Bodman or Uzès?

Bodo stared at Dulciorella and the owl fascinated by their resemblance. He cut and offered the small predator a piece of uncooked meat. It left Dulciorella's shoulder, swept the morsel from the tip of his dagger, and bolted into the night.

A week after they left Girona, Bodo and Dulciorella approached fog-shrouded Ausona one hundred miles south of the Pyrenees in the March of Hispania. The town lay in the center of a narrow sandy basin confined by rising hills to the west and south, the Montseny range to the southeast, and to the east the Guilleries.

Bodo knew from reports at Aachen that Saracen raids and local rebellions had depopulated and laid waste to Ausona, but according to what he heard in Girona, the town now had a growing and thriving Jewish population. They passed tents beside new homes being constructed. Sounds of carpentry and shouts of stone masons echoed through the streets.

At a market square filled with produce and farm animals for sale or slaughter, Bodo reined Amalric, dismounted, and approached a crowd of Jews at a stall filled with caged chickens and others defeathered with throats slit hanging upside down so their blood would drain. He asked if anyone understood Francique. Several did, and Bodo asked where Enoch bar Judah could be found. The men regarded him with suspicion. Bodo had anticipated their wariness. His height, blondness, and soldierly bearing caused him to stand out among these shorter and darker men.

One asked why he sought Enoch.

"I have been entrusted to bring his niece home to her uncle."

Over murmuring, the same man asked, "She is Count Bernard's daughter?"

Bodo did not reply. The men went to the wagon for a closer look at Dulciorella and conferred.

The boldest who had questioned Bodo spoke again. "Are Count Bernard or his vassals chasing after you?"

"I can assure you they are not."

"Enoch bar Judah now resides in the Jewish quarter of Saraqusta."

Better than Ausona, the border town was in Muslim Hispania and on Bodo's planned route to Cordoba. "Dulciorella, did you hear what they said about your uncle?"

"Yes."

"Then let us purchase some provisions and hasten to Saraqusta."

We may speculate that the source for the details about Bodo was news passed by word of mouth, that may have been embellished as it spread: "rumor spread the news," the text tells us.

    Frank Riess,
      From Aachen to al-Andalus, the Journey of Deacon Bodo, 823-76

Part Five
Bodo, the Apostate
Bodo-Eliezar, the Jew
838-848

... the correspondence with Pablo Alvaro is singular not only within the concrete conversion case of Bodo, but also valuable for the study of the phenomenon of Christian conversion to Judaism.

    Evina Steinova,
      The Correspondence of Bodo-Eleazar with Pablo Alvaro: A Rare Sample of Judeo-Christian Dispute from the 9th Century

87. Saraqusta

After a two hundred mile journey from Ausona, Bodo and Dulciorella washed at a stream and donned fresh clothes before they entered Saraqusta early morning on a mild sunny day in May. The frontier garrison town on the Ebro River was ruled by the Emir of Cordoba, who controlled all of al-Andalus, except for the County of Barcelona and Carolingian Marches at the eastern and central foothills of the Pyrenees, the tiny Christian Kingdoms of Navarre at the western edge of the great mountain range, the Asturias and the Basques beyond to the Atlantic and Bay of Biscay.

In Saraqusta, Muslim, Jew, and Christian lived in separate quarters, their Saracen style dress and homes indistinguishable from each other. After making inquiries, Bodo found a domed synagogue where men and women were leaving separately after morning prayers.

When Bodo dismounted from Amalric and Dulciorella from the cart, the congregation stopped talking and walking. Well aware his height and blond noble appearance caused people to stare, he said in Hebrew, "Peace be unto you, I seek Enoch bar Judah."

A short, rotund man approached Bodo and Dulciorella as a crowd surrounded them. "Unto you be peace. I am Enoch bar Judah."

"And I Bodo have brought your niece from Septimania."

Enoch studied Dulciorella's features and embraced her. "Yes, you are my sister Leila's daughter, may she rest in peace. But why have you come? Has something happened to Count Bernard?"

"I have come to Saraqusta to live as a Jew."

"Then we must celebrate." Enoch called for his wife to join them. "Hannah, this young woman is my niece, Dulciorella. Take her with you to our home where she may live as our own daughter. And you, who call yourself Bodo, you shall enjoy our hospitality as well. What are you? Frank, Saxon, Viking?"

"I am of the Alamanni."

"Why have you brought my niece to al-Andalus? Are you a vassal of Count Bernard?"

Bodo the Apostate

"All will be known to you when I speak with your rabbi. Take me to him now."

Enoch brought Bodo into the synagogue and introduced him to Rabbi Daniel, a vibrant young man, who led them into his study similar to those of Count Abraham and every Jew who offered Bodo hospitality over the years. He showed Rabbi Daniel and Enoch the document signed by Louis appointing him Bishop Palatine. Although kin to both the emperor and empress with so high a position in the Church, Bodo declared he had come to al-Andalus for the purpose of converting to Judaism. Anticipating one of their questions, Bodo described his longtime antipathy toward the pagan beliefs and hypocrisies of the Orthodox Church.

"When do you plan to convert?"

"Now."

"You must understand that according to our custom I am obligated to dissuade you."

The rabbi emphasized how Bodo's identity would change through conversion, with the added onuses of being hated and despised by all who wished to impose their religion upon Jews and drive into exile or murder those who refuse. He recited a long history of Jews wherever they resided forced to pay higher taxes, being denied ownership of land and freedom to be artisans, forced to wear clothing either marked to identify them as Jews or grotesque costumes to humiliate and differentiate them from the general population.

"Even when times are good for the Jews, as they are now in the empire and the Emirate of Cordoba, they may not last. Evil men might influence the next ruler to limit our freedoms and rights, or drive us to exile. Do you understand all I have said?"

Bodo told Daniel he knew about the bigotry Jews faced before and may yet again. He emphasized his decision to accept the Law of Moses was no sudden impulse, that from age of ten he read and prepared exegeses from Scripture, attended sermons by rabbis in their synagogues and heard them correct Christian bishops and priests in the meanings of passages.

"I am aware that to be a Jew I must acknowledge that God created the world, redeemed the Jews from slavery in Egypt, and gave them His Torah. All that I believe and accept."

"Then I shall now explain the rituals and instructions in the basic tenets of Judaism a gentile must go through before he can be accepted into the Jewish Nation. Are you willing to submit to ritual circumcision?"

"Yes, here and now."

"I am both rabbi and *mohel*, one authorized to perform the *berit milah*."

Bodo had feared placing his *membrum virile* in the hands of an elder with shaky hands. "How soon will I be circumcised?"

"First, I am required to instruct you."

Bodo surprised the rabbi with his knowledge of the six hundred and thirteen laws observant Jews followed and an understanding of *berit milah* and *mikvah*.

"Then I will perform the ritual in the morning. What Hebrew name shall you take?"

Bodo had given much thought to a new name. He believed his favored position at Court, introduction to Scriptural exegesis, and blessing of Abraham's friendship were gifts from God.

"I choose the name of Aaron's son and nephew of Moses, Eli'ezar, whom God has helped."

"A thoughtful choice. I must say your situation is unique. It is true that after the Muslims conquered al-Andalus, many descendants of Jews who had been forced to convert to Christianity by the Visigoths returned to Judaism and submitted to circumcision, even on occasion a Christian or pagan. But never in my experience and knowledge has so high-ranking a member of the Orthodox Church chosen to become a Jew."

Enoch resided a short walk from the synagogue, his home hidden behind high whitewashed walls. Dulciorella had left the wagon in the courtyard where servants fed and watered the horses. Enoch led Bodo into the tiled atrium of his new home constructed in a mix of Roman and Saracen styles, obviously a prosperous man. He took Bodo to a room with a comfortable bed, and a basin and ewer filled with water atop a table. Dulciorella had arranged for servants to bring into the room bags and chests containing the Pope's gifts.

After Bodo washed, he went to a large circular gathering room where Enoch awaited him. Dulciorella entered at the same time with her aunt, younger female cousins, and two boys. The women wore cotton robes in the Saracen style, hair coverings, but no veils. The boys had on floor length shirts with arms exposed and wore skullcaps same as their father.

Enoch again introduced Bodo to his wife Hannah, and then to his daughters Dina age fifteen and Chava age twelve, and sons eleven year old Elisha and five year old Reuben. Enoch and Bodo sat on Roman style chairs with crossed legs, the boys at their father's feet, the women on enormous silk pillows of vivid colors placed around a low circular table of carved polished wood. Servants brought wine, cheeses, and fruits, some of which Bodo did not recognize.

Enoch raised his glass and welcomed Bodo. "I thank you for restoring my niece to our family. Dulciorella's refusal to wed Charles and decision to flee is as astonishing as your intention to convert."

Bodo, ever curious and freed from Court protocol, returned to his blunt ways. "Why did you leave Ausona?"

While they ate and drank, Enoch explained his reasons for moving to Saraqusta. "After Bernard wed my sister, the count appointed me Viscount of Barcelona, I assumed the task of rebuilding Ausona and making it a Jewish town. Subsequently, my sister died giving birth to Dulciorella, and I later sided with Louis during Bernard's rebellion against the emperor. When Louis restored Bernard's titles and domains, I thought it wise to leave Ausona for Saraqusta where I have established a successful business provisioning the Saracen garrison. After your berit milah, will you reside here in Saraqusta?"

"No, I will leave for Cordoba immediately after."

"I suggest you postpone your journey until you heal well enough to sit a horse."

Bodo had not taken into account the time necessary for his recovery and hoped he was a quick healer.

88. A Practical Matter

In the morning as required, Bodo immersed himself in the *mikvah*, the ritual bath that washed away all sins he committed while a Christian. Gone were the oaths Bodo broke to a false religion and to Louis and Judith. The *mikvah* cleansed him of selling men into slavery, of breaking the Commandments prohibiting adultery with Sigrada and other ladies of the Court, and theft of the Pope's gifts.

Bodo had paid no attention to the days based upon the Roman Julian calendar during the months he and Dulciorella traveled from Uzès to Saraqusta. He found it ironic to be circumcised on the twenty-second of May 838, the day of the Vigil of the Ascension, which commemorated Christ's body returning to heaven forty days after the Resurrection, so the Christians believed. On that same day, he, Bodo, would die a Christian and be resurrected as Eliezar, a Jew.

Extra candles and lamps illuminated the great room of Enoch's home where adult males of the congregation gathered to witness the ritual. After what seemed to be an eternity of praying, Enoch offered Bodo a cloth. "To bite when you feel the pain."

Rabbi Daniel dropped to one knee. Between thumb and forefinger, he pulled Bodo's foreskin through a small loop extending from one of the instruments, recited a prayer, and cut it away.

Bodo bit hard on the cloth. Pain consumed his entire being as if engulfed by flames. Rabbi Daniel poured wine on Bodo's raw penis to cleanse the cut, wrapped it in clean linen, and recited more prayers concluding with "We welcome you, Eliezar bar Israel."

Bodo relaxed his body, satisfied he shed his identity of Bodo, the Christian, and had become now and forever Bodo-Eliezar, the Jew.

Enoch provided a feast to celebrate Eliezar's *berit milah*. The women of the congregation and their children joined the men. Suffering more from discomfort than pain, he sat in a chair beside Rabbi Daniel and drank wine.

"Before you continue on to Cordoba, I shall write a letter of introduction for you to Chief Rabbi Aaron there."

"Thank you. As soon as I am fit to travel, I shall leave."

"That may take a few weeks depending on how well you heal. Have you considered marrying? As you must know, a Jew is not a complete man until he has wed."

The rabbi had surprised Bodo-Eliezar. During all his planning over the past several years, he gave no thought to marrying and starting a family.

"There are more available young women and widows in Saraqusta and Cordoba than men. It will be a simple matter to arrange a marriage. A dowry can help you establish yourself in comfort within any Jewish community, where God willing, you will have many children."

Bodo the Apostate

The prospect of committing himself to a stranger in the emirate lacked appeal. That would be the equivalent of a blindfold purchase. Bodo-Eliezar recalled Louis "pageant of beauties" when he selected Judith to be his wife. He might be able to do the same here in Saraqusta or Cordoba but still would not know his choice's character or temperament until after the nuptials. Bodo-Eliezar disliked indecision as much as he hated disorder and spoke with Enoch alone after the last guests left.

"Rabbi Daniel lectured me that I will not be a complete man until I wed."

"That is true."

"I have made my choice. I shall marry Lady Dulciorella, if she agrees and if I have your blessing."

Enoch pulled at his beard deep in thought. "I cannot speak for my niece. As I have learned and you must know, Dulciorella is willful. I am still astounded that she fled with you and not only defied her father but also refused a royal command to wed King Charles. She could have been a queen, perhaps an empress. Although Saraqusta is under the emir's rule, Dulciorella is Count Bernard's daughter. We can never predict what that violent man will do once he learns you absconded with her. Nor can I predict what her response shall be to your offer of marriage."

"Dulciorella and I shall be far beyond Bernard's reach in Cordoba. Do I have your blessing?"

Enoch rose. "You have it. I shall now go and send Dulciorella to you. I will not tell her why."

While Bodo-Eliezar waited for Dulciorella in the great room, he remembered all the females he had known, how sated he became, and the great amount of time that passed since he had lain with one. Not once did he consider any of them in the context of marriage, and definitely not Dulciorella. Then why now should he choose that strange headstrong young woman? They had traveled together for three months, during which time he admired her calm and resilience in difficult circumstances. Yes, if he must wed, why not marry Dulciorella? He believed she could provide a well-ordered home to his satisfaction as a Jewish wife.

Dulciorella entered and sat in a Roman chair facing him. "My uncle said you wanted to speak with me."

"Yes. Did Enoch say why?"

"No."

"Lady Dulciorella, as you may or may not know, a Jew is not a man until he has wed." Bodo-Eliezar paused to gauge her reaction. Dulciorella's inscrutable expression did not waver, nor did she speak. "As a practical matter, I would select you for my wife."

"Why?"

Dulciorella's laconic question unsettled Bodo-Eliezar. It was not any of the responses he anticipated. "We traveled these past months together, and there was never any discord between us. I believe you will be a most satisfactory wife and mother."

"Have you any affection for me?"

Another unexpected question. Was Dulciorella asking for a declaration of love? Impossible. Bodo-Eliezar could not lie. "I have a fondness for you, and you have earned my respect."

"Fondness and respect? That is more than most brides are offered by their husbands. I could do much worse than choose you for my husband and perhaps no better. Yes, to repeat your words, as a practical matter I accept your offer of marriage."

"Then summon your uncle and his family so we may tell them of our decision."

Bodo-Eliezar and Enoch met with Daniel in the rabbi's study.

"You must wait ninety-one days from your betrothal to the day of your nuptials according to our law to ensure your bride has not been made pregnant by another man."

Bodo-Eliezar chose to use and emphasize the preferred Scriptural word. "No man has *known* Dulciorella, definitely not I, during the three months we traveled from Uzès to Saraqusta."

"My niece's menses began yesterday, which my wife can confirm."

Rabbi Daniel touched a thick volume on his desk. "I shall have to consult Scripture and the Talmud for guidance so I may make an exception given your long time together."

"Do so. We want to leave for Cordoba immediately."

"I understand your impatience to wed, but that cannot happen until you have healed from your *berit milah* and are able to consummate your marriage."

89. Budding Sweet Rose

Not yet used to his new name, Bodo-Eliezar resided with Enoch while he healed, studied Hebrew, and learned daily rituals: putting on the *tefillim*, phylacteries used for praying, and the *tallith*, a fringed prayer shawl. Rabbi Daniel taught him the meanings of holy days and celebrations.

Three weeks passed, and Bodo-Eliezar believed he healed enough to wed. Rabbi Daniel agreed to perform the ceremony. "Obviously, we must take into consideration your intended bride's monthly cycle, so both of you can be immersed in the *mikvah* before the nuptials and come to each other cleansed and pure, which also draws God and His blessing into your marriage."

"Then how soon can we wed?"

"I have made calculations. According to Enoch, Dulciorella began her cycle of menses three weeks ago. Her next should arrive in a week to ten days. Eight days after that, you may wed. That would be the fifteenth day of Tammuz."

Bodo-Eliezar calculated the Julian calendar equivalent. "The last day of June. And then at last, we leave for Cordoba."

Bodo-Eliezar observed a similarity in the homes of Abraham, Enoch, and other Jews who hosted him over the years. Each parent took joy, pleasure, and pride in their children. Unlike the noble Christians of the empire, no Jew would ever send his sons away at age seven to live with another family. Even after marriages, their married sons, daughters, and grandchildren resided in adjacent houses on the same property or in their parents' home if they lacked wealth.

Bodo-Eliezar intended to have many children with Dulciorella and a home filled with laughter, a home that embraced life instead of preparing for death and an afterlife. He also looked forward to the order and regularity of the Sabbath meal and other rituals. Bodo-Eliezar had long craved structure in his life, and the Law of Moses provided it with routines of daily prayers at home and synagogue, discussions over Scriptural meanings, the Talmud and Mishna, many of them heated, but with no ecclesiastic authority to demand conformity of thought and belief.

Enoch's wife Hannah taught Dulciorella how to organize three sets of cookware, plates, and serving bowls for meats, dairy, and Pesach according to laws of *Kashrut,* food considered fit and proper to eat. Until now, Dulciorella had never set foot in a kitchen although she had cooked game, fish, and vegetables during their journey from Uzès.

Rabbi Daniel explained *Kashrut* in more detail from Leviticus and Deuteronomy. Animals to be eaten must be slaughtered according to ritual and in the most humane way, with a slash across their throats to ensure a quick death and complete draining of blood.

Jews could eat any animal that had cloven hooves and chewed its cud, which included cattle, sheep, goats, deer and bison. Forbidden because they lacked those two qualifications were the camel, rock badger, hare, and all swine.

From the water, Jews were allowed to eat anything with fins and scales but shellfish were forbidden. Chicken, ducks, and geese were allowed, but scavenger birds and those of prey, rodents, reptiles, amphibians, and most insects were forbidden. So were animals from flocks and herds that died from natural causes, disease, or were killed by other animals. Milk, eggs, fat, organs, and nerves from forbidden animals should never be consumed, nor blood of a *kashrut* animal because it contained the creature's soul.

Jews could drink wine and other products from the grape only if processed by Jews and eat all fruits and vegetables but not any insect found on or inside them. Beer was allowed.

Meat and fish on the same plate was unhealthy. Fish and dairy could be eaten together.

Bodo-Eliezar thought about the life he could look forward to in what Christians called Hispania from what Enoch and Rabbi Daniel told him. The Muslim conquerors named the same land al-Andalus. They called Jews and Christians dhimmis, People of the Book, and allowed them to practice their religions, have their own courts, rights of residence, and equality to Muslims under general laws of property, contracts, and obligations.

Because Jewish and Christian males were not Muslims, they had to pay a personal tax called the jizyah after they reached puberty. More positive, the Emir of Cordoba did not enforce stricter laws of separation and debasement required of dhimmis common in other Islamic lands. Abd al-Rhaman II modeled his emirate after the similarly tolerant Persian inspired Caliphate of Baghdad.

Bodo the Apostate

Bodo-Eliezar improved his Hebrew, read the Talmud, learned *Halakha*, Jewish Law, and discussed commentaries. He prayed daily at the synagogue, and adapted to the Jewish calendar based on a lunar cycle with Hebrew names for the days, weeks, and months. The current solar year by Christian reckoning was 838 *Anno Domini*, from the accepted birth of Christ, but the Jewish year was 4598 dated from the Creation. Bodo-Eliezar decided to change his day of birth to the sixth day of *Tammuz*.

Nine days after his twenty-sixth birthday, Bodo-Eliezar stood beside Dulciorella in the synagogue under a *huppah*, a canopy decorated with colorful summer flowers supported by four men holding poles. After her *mikvah*, Dulciorella took the Hebrew name she received from her mother, Semadar, which meant sweet budding rose.

Bodo-Eliezar dressed in clothes made from bolts of cloth destined for the Pope that Semadar, with the help of her aunt and cousins, made for him. He wore over his white linen shirt and yellow velvet trousers, a golden mantle of the softest wool trimmed in pale blue silk that fell to his deerskin boots.

Dulciorella, Bodo-Eliezar could not yet think of her as Semadar, wore a Roman style dress of pale blue silk embroidered with gold thread. A gossamer veil held by a gold band covered her face.

Congregants filled the synagogue. Enoch stood beside the rabbi and held a large cedar box. A *hazzan* chanted prayers and began the betrothal ceremony with blessings over wine.

Bodo-Eliezar and Semadar drank from the same cup, and Rabbi Daniel spoke for all to hear, "Bodo-Eliezar, do you agree to wed Semadar of your own free will?"

"I do."

"And do you, Semadar, agree to marry Bodo-Eliezar of your own free will?"

"I do."

Enoch opened the cedar box, and Rabbi Daniel took from it a replica of the Great Temple of Jerusalem carved in wood to scale and covered with gold leaf with a golden ring attached to it, large enough for one to thrust a hand through its center.

"Eliezar, take Semadar's right index finger, place it on the ring, and recite after me, Be thou betrothed unto me by this ring in accordance with the Law of Moses."

After Bodo-Eliezar complied, the rabbi returned the temple-ring to its box and raised his hands over the bride and groom. "May you establish a loyal and fruitful house amongst the people of Israel." He recited more blessings, handed Semadar the *ketubah,* her wedding contract, and initiated the wedding ceremony.

The *hazzan* chanted the Seven Benedictions and again offered both bride and groom the wine. He placed an earthenware tumbler on the floor for the groom to shatter with his boot in memory of the destruction of the Holy Temple in Jerusalem. After Bodo-Eliezar complied, all present shouted congratulations and offered good wishes.

Bodo-Eliezar lifted Semadar's veil and kissed her. "My wife."

"My beloved husband."

Night fell. In the room they now shared, Bodo-Eliezar closed the door. By the light of a small candle, Semadar awaited him under the covers. Rabbi Daniel had instructed him in the commandments and carnal obligations of married men and women, which included specific rules for physical intimacy. While Bodo-Eliezar undressed, he asked himself how Semadar might respond to him. Would she be receptive or tense? He recalled many of the women with whom he had been intimate. Some like Sigrada were aggressive. Others had to be wooed to arouse their passion, and a few disappointed, often the most desirable, who let him have his way without any response. Women. The great mystery.

"I thought the wedding feast would never end."

Semadar opened her arms. "Now that it has, come to me."

Bodo-Eliezar snuffed the candle. Semadar did not disappoint.

90. Cordoba

Before they left Saraqusta, Bodo-Eliezar sold the last ambler and purchased a longer covered cart Semadar and he could use for sleeping and shelter. Again, he sequestered the Pope's gifts in a false bottom.

The day of their departure, Bodo-Eliezar made a donation of alms for the poor in the Jewish community, and they began a four hundred

Bodo the Apostate

mile journey to Cordoba along well traveled roads built by the Romans. Semadar drove the wagon, and Bodo-Eliezar rode Amalric beside her, alert to brigands and thieves.

The road accommodated much traffic. Individual travelers, entire families, and caravans of goods and slaves formed an unbroken line except when they had to move aside for companies of the emir's cavalry heading to and from Saraqusta.

Bodo-Eliezar and Semadar joined a mix of Jews, Muslims, and Mozarabs, Christians who adopted the Saracen dress, language and customs. Bodo-Eliezar found it of interest that Mozarabs generally preferred the doctrine of Adoptionism, some even Arianism, and were resented by the Trinitarian followers of Christ in the emirate.

They formed circles with their carts off the road around fires where they ate communally, conversed, and took turns standing guard. Bodo-Eliezar and the men hunted in thick woods or fished in rivers and lakes. Christians added wild pig to their diets. They also encountered inedible red foxes, wildcats and wolves smaller than those he killed during his hunts with Louis and Lothair. Bodo-Eliezar praised Semadar for how well she skinned the edible animals and carved their flesh for cooking. She also gathered brush and wood for the fires.

Depending upon the elevations, they passed through forests of cork, evergreen oak, firs and pines with undergrowth of myrtle, bramble, and rosemary. Along the rivers, they rode by woodlands of ash, willow, maple, and elms plus the usual reeds and bulrushes.

Bodo-Eliezar and Semadar bathed in rivers and lakes and drank water from clear springs or wells in small Muslim villages they passed. Farther south Semadar asked Bodo-Eliezar to stop when she pointed out a grove of almond trees in full bloom so she could gather some nuts.

He remembered what Strabo told him years ago. "Be careful to select only those from trees with white blossoms, for they contain the sweet nuts. Avoid those with pink blossoms. They can be poisonous."

After a harrowing descent from a jagged mountain range, they reached the Guadalquivir River and passed flour mills built along the strong current. The city loomed ahead. Bodo-Eliezar and Semadar crossed a thousand foot long bridge over the Guadalquivir of obvious Roman construction. A great wall surrounded the city, and they entered through one of the gates, passing a viable aqueduct and ruins of a Roman temple, theater, forum, amphitheater, statues, and palace of some long forgotten emperor.

By now, Bodo-Eliezar, and Semadar had been given a thorough description of Cordoba by their traveling companions who had not exaggerated. Lamps lined paved streets teeming with a noisy mix of tribes and races haggling with shopkeepers and vendors. They had been told Cordoba's population exceeded two hundred thousand with more people arriving in great numbers each day. Bodo-Eliezar lost count of the bath houses and mosques.

The city's cleanliness and construction impressed Bodo-Eliezar. The Saracens used stucco, stone, and marble to build their homes, shops, mosques, and palaces embellished with yellow and blue tiles. In the Jewish quarter, homes lay hidden behind whitewashed walls on streets lined by tall palms and cypress. Ahead Bodo-Eliezar saw a large domed structure with steps leading to pillars supporting an arched entrance. Neither mosque nor church, it had to be the great synagogue of Cordoba.

Bodo-Eliezar handed his letter of introduction from Rabbi Daniel to Chief Rabbi Aaron, an elder of fine physique who stood straight and had the energy of a man half his age. He welcomed Bodo-Eliezar and Semadar and found them an empty home one of his congregants had for lease.

That evening Rabbi Aaron introduced them to the congregation. Many regarded Bodo-Eliezar with awe because of his former position in the empire and commanding presence, Semadar with respect because she was, through her father Count Bernard, a descendant of the *Nasim* of Septimania and House of David.

Soon to arrive were the Ten Holy Days of Awe that began with Rosh Hashanah, the Crown of the Jewish Year, and ended after Yom Kippur, All Vows, the annual Day of Atonement. Bodo-Eliezar commissioned a scribe to create a Torah on parchment for personal use. He purchased land and designed a home in the Saracen style with the help of a builder recommended by Rabbi Aaron. He made sure it included a study similar to that of Count Abraham and scheduled its construction to begin after Yom Kippur.

91. The Ten Days of Awe

Throughout *Elul,* the month before Rosh Hashanah, Bodo-Eliezar took instructions from Rabbi Aaron on the requirements necessary to be an observant Jew. He became familiar with the Jewish calendar based on the lunar cycle. The first day of each month began in the evening at first sighting of a new moon.

Each weekday after morning ablutions, Bodo-Eliezar applied phylacteries and *tefillim*, then went to the synagogue for morning, noon, and evening prayers. He learned to recite the blessings of the *Amidah* while standing and facing Jerusalem. Each blessing began and ended with the phrase "Blessed art Thou O-Lord." Readings from the Torah, the Prophets, and chanting of hymns also were included in the prayer services. Bodo-Eliezar felt at home with the routine and order of daily synagogue prayers that began with the Shemah followed by the *Amidah* with no crucifixes, icons, statues, relics, and the Eucharist during which bread and wine supposedly became flesh and blood. The same as every Jew, he had a direct and personal relationship with the one and only indivisible God.

The Rabbi explained why the congregation had no *Siddur,* prayer book. Until recently there had been disagreement between two factions. One believed fixed prayers were not sincere petitions to God, and the other advocated for a universal prayer book to be used wherever Jews lived, which was being written at the Jewish Academy in Sura, Babylon, and likely to be completed within the next decade or two.

Each weekday after his morning ablutions, Bodo-Eliezar applied phylacteries and wore the fringed tallith. He went to the synagogue for morning, noon, and evening prayers. He recited the Shemah and Amidah, readings from the Torah, prophets, and chanted hymns. The synagogue had no crucifixes, icons, statures, or relics. No Eucharist either when bread and wine supposedly became flesh and blood. The same as any Jew, Bodo-Eliezar had a direct relationship with the one and only indivisible God.

The rabbi's explanation why men and women were separated in a synagogue either by partition or in a balcony made sense to Bodo-Eliezar. Although the tradition originated in part from the prophet Zechariah

12:12-14 regarding separation during mourning, it was more an understanding of human behavior. Physical separation brought about spiritual concentration to ensure one focused on praying and not on the opposite gender. Bodo recalled how often he had paid more attention to appealing ladies of the Court than any prayer.

During the month preceding Rosh Hashanah, Bodo-Eliezar and Semadar began a period of self-examination and repentance to end the following month after Yom Kippur. The *Tokea,* a skilled blaster, blew the *shofar*, a ram's horn, each morning at the synagogue alerting Jews to the coming days of judgment.

It was a time for introspection and reflecting upon one's mistakes and sins of the past year, to repent each and promise to be a better person, a Jew's final moment to atone for sins against God and man before He wrote in His books who would live and die in the coming year, and who would have a good or bad life. God sealed those books at the end of Yom Kippur.

Rosh Hashanah came on the anniversary of the creation of Adam and Eve, one hundred and sixty-three days after the first day of Passover, and on the first day of *Tishrei*. Because *Tishrei* was the seventh lunar month, many Jews called it the Sabbath of the Year

At the synagogue, religious services for Rosh Hashanah started with the blowing of the *shofar* in long, short and staccato blasts following a sequence described in the Torah, eventually totaling one hundred. Along with the regular daily prayers, ten verses each were recited regarding kinship, remembrance, and penitence.

Bodo-Eliezar and Semadar had their first traditional Rosh Hashanah meal at Rabbi Aaron's home, which included apples dipped in honey, to symbolize a sweet new year.

Each day at the synagogue between Rosh Hashanah and Yom Kippur, the congregation greeted Bodo-Eliezar and Semadar with the phrase "*L'shanah tovah tikatev v'taihatem*, may you be inscribed and sealed for a good year."

Erev Yom Kippur, Eve of the Day of Atonement, was the day preceding Yom Kippur corresponding to the ninth of *Tishrei* and observed with two festive meals, the giving of charity, and asking others for forgiveness.

Bodo the Apostate

During Yom Kippur, one prayer in particular, *Al Khet,* was repeated throughout the service. Congregants lightly beat fists against their chests at the mention of each sin and asked forgiveness for those they may have committed during the year.

Bodo-Eliezar preferred the Jewish view of sin over the Christian concept of Original Sin. Jewish offenses included hurting those one loved, lying to one's self, or using foul language that Judaism considered to be wicked. Sins were mentioned in plural form because even if someone had not committed a particular sin, Jewish tradition taught that every Jew bore a measure of responsibility for the actions of other Jews.

Bodo-Eliezar believed he wronged no one after his conversion, immersion in the *mikvah,* and *berit milah.* What he had done before no longer mattered. Still, he repented with the congregation:

For the sin that we have committed under stress or through choice;
For the sin that we have committed in stubbornness or in error;
For the sin that we have committed in the evil meditations of the heart;
For the sin that we have committed by word of mouth;
For the sin that we have committed through abuse of power;
For the sin that we have committed by exploitation of neighbors;
For all these sins, Oh God of forgiveness, bear with us, pardon us, forgive us.

During Yom Kippur, Bodo-Eliezar and Semadar observed the traditional prohibitions from the hour before sunset to the beginning of evening the following day, a total of twenty-five hours: No eating, no drinking, no working, no washing and bathing, no intimacies with one's spouse, no wearing of leather, and no anointing oneself with perfumes or lotions. It was a last chance to atone for sins against God and to reconcile and right wrongs committed against another person.

Rabbi Aaron and his wife Rebecca prepared a great feast to break the Yom Kippur fast and after that showed Bodo-Eliezar and Semadar how to celebrate two festivals that came later in the month: *Sukkot,* the week-long commemoration of the forty-years the children of Israel wandered in the desert; *Simchat Torah,* the completion of the annual cycle of weekly Torah readings, starting with Genesis 1, ending at Deuteronomy 34, and beginning again with Genesis 1 to remind all Jews the Torah was a never ending circle.

92. An Orderly Life

Bodo-Eliezar's new home built in the wealthiest section of the Jewish quarter had white and azure tile floors, arched windows with iron grilles, outer whitewashed stucco walls, and a tiled roof. All rooms opened to a large central patio covered by smaller blue and yellow tiles of geometric design, a border of vivid flowers, and a fountain in the center. Cypress, jasmine, and palm trees flourished on both sides of the wall. He said a prayer for Abraham when he attached the merchant's gift to the front doorpost, a *mezuzah*. Bodo-Eliezar added a small stable for Amalric, hired a groom to attend and care for it, and exercised the stallion each day in one of the many parks throughout Cordoba or along the Guadalquivir when he wanted to swim.

Semadar furnished the interior as she saw fit with cushioned divans, oversize pillows of the richest fabrics, colorful rugs, and furniture of the finest woods. Diaphanous white gauze hung from the canopy of their bed.

Bodo-Eliezar designed and personally furnished his study with ample shelving for the library he planned to accumulate and a lectern for the Torah he ordered from a scribe. He kept a heavy copy of Alcuin's vulgate Bible in old Latin and Greek filled with elaborate hand-painted images that had been destined for the Pope so he might use the New Testament portion for references when he wrote condemnations of Trinitarianism.

Semadar's new wardrobe included the *khimar*, a head covering, and *niqab*, a veil to wear in public with an *ishaba*, a wide embroidered and jeweled wide band to wear around her head. She purchased chemises of varying colors, embroidered cloths to wrap around her body, shirts that fell to her shoes, and a *rida*, a cloak worn over her shoulders.

Bodo-Eliezar's clothing included a *qamis*, a full length shirt with an embroidered collar and openings for his head and hands, a *durra'a*, a woolen and brocaded loose outer garment with sleeves slit in front, and a vest, the *shudra*.

Beneath the outer clothing and against their bare bodies, both Bodo-Eliezar and Semadar wore the *sirwal*, roomy drawers held by a sash, or the *tubban*, short drawers covering the navel to the knees. They had a wide

Bodo the Apostate

variety of *khuffs* from which to select: leather boots covering the ankle, and others rising to the middle of the leg, sandals, socks worn under the boots, some of silk or soft goat-hair, leggings for colder weather, and shoes of vivid colors and contrasting laces of black and red, yellow and black.

For headwear, Bodo-Eliezar preferred a skullcap at home and a turban for formal outer wear, which the Saracens considered to be the distinctive dress of a man. He found their clothing more comfortable than the robes of a Christian cleric and garments worn by nobles. In the emirate, only men were permitted to wear white garments.

One evening Semadar sat on the edge of their bed covered with a robe instead of awaiting him naked under the covers. She would not look at Bodo-Eliezar.

"I fear I may have done something you may not like."

He sat beside Semadar and held her hand. "How is that possible?"

"The women of the congregation suggested I do as they and follow a custom of the Saracens and other Muslim tribes. They call it *fitrah*."

"That is a word I have not heard before." Bodo-Eliezar turned Semadar's face to his. "For a moment I feared you tattooed your face like the Berber women. Your robe, have you marked your body?"

"I would never do that. The women and I, we sat around an incense burner and waxed away all our body hair."

"All?"

Semadar saw where his eyes focused. "Yes, even there."

Bodo-Eliezar stood and helped Semadar to her feet. He removed his wife's robe and stared at her hairless body. "Smoother than a marble Roman statue."

"You are not angry?"

"I believe *fitrah* is yet another Saracen custom I shall enjoy."

Bodo-Eliezar found smiths who could melt gold, silver crucifixes and other religious gifts intended for the Pope into ingots after their gems had been removed. He commissioned an artisan to create a menorah and wine cups of silver for the Sabbath meal, Pesach, and other holy days and festivities, and another to support and cover his Torah with two wooden shafts known as Trees of Life around which the hand-written parchment was rolled. Both extended ends were topped with crowns of silver. A sash was used to secure the Torah when not in use, and it was covered by a mantel of velvet embroidered with golden thread, and colorful beads with curvilinear designs and a Star of David. Bodo-Eliezar commissioned a silver breastplate for the covering to hang by a chain over the front of the mantel. The final accessory was the *Yad*, a silver pointer with a hand at the end, its index finger extended. When not in use, it would rest in an ark he designed.

Semadar added to the order Bodo-Eliezar sought. At home she provided a predictable routine for meals and comfort. She selected Jewish servants to clean their home, attend to all needs, and work in the kitchen where she enforced *kashrut*. Semadar more than fulfilled Bodo-Eliezar's expectations by the discipline and authority with which she ruled their household.

Each morning she went to the Jewish markets for fresh food. Her meals were a delight for the senses, visually, aromatically, and to Bodo-Eliezar's taste. Wines were available, and his only olfactory discomfort came whenever he passed Christian homes and markets where the aroma of pork reminded him of meats he used to enjoy now forbidden.

By the summer of 839, Bodo-Eliezar and Semadar acclimated to life in Cordoba. They spoke adequate Arabic, the daily language used by all in the great city, and learned to count with their numerals, an easier method than using fingers or the Roman method. Although church bells could be heard from the Christian quarter, they kept time by the muezzins' calls to prayer from the Great Mosque, its huge dome said to be supported by eight hundred and fifty marble columns.

Bodo-Eliezar the Jew achieved the orderly life denied Bodo the Christian. Each morning at the same time, he prayed at the synagogue. Afterward, he studied Torah, Talmud, and Mishnah, and discussed their meanings and nuances with the rabbis and other congregants. Several days each week, he hunted for books and manuscripts for his expanding library.

Bodo-Eliezar added another pursuit at home. Each evening at the same hour, he wrote searing polemics against the Trinitarians, ridiculing their beliefs as false and idolatrous.

93. Abd al-Rhaman

One evening after prayers, Chief Rabbi Aaron invited Bodo-Eliezar to the synagogue conference room. "As you know I represent our community as an official of the emir's council." He handed Bodo-Eliezar a scroll. "Emir Abd al-Rhaman II gave me this summons to pass on to you. He expects your attendance in the morning. The emir is curious why someone of your high station in the Christian Church and at the emperor's court converted to Judaism. Of more importance, he believes you may provide him with useful information about what may happen in the empire after Louis dies. Is it true the emperor is near death?"

"When I left Court, the emperor was unwell."

Bodo-Eliezar came to Cordoba to live as a Jew and to lead a tranquil orderly life, through forever with courts, rulers, and petty intrigues. He preferred not to meet with the emir but had no choice.

Rabbi Aaron and several Court Jews also members of the congregation prepared Bodo-Eliezar for his audience with the emir. He thought the men exaggerated when they said the emir surpassed even Charlemagne by bringing to Cordoba the most brilliant minds and talent in the sciences, learning, and commerce.

The rabbi praised Abd al-Rhaman II for offering education to all his subjects and building hospitals, public baths, and libraries filled with Arabic translations of Hebrew, Greek, Roman, and Egyptian writings. He added that not only the emir, but his Muslim subjects too, if they chose, could disregard much forbidden by their *Qur'an*, the Law of the Prophet. No longer austere conquering sons of the desert like their fathers and grandfathers, Abd al-Rhaman II and most of his Court imitated Babylonian and Persian ostentation and luxury, indulging in wine, music, dancing girls, and the hunt.

Bodo-Eliezar intended to judge for himself if the emir was so enlightened and tolerant a ruler.

Bodo-Eliezar's audience with the emir took place in a vast hall of marble and tile. Abd al-Rhaman, lean and sleek with a trimmed spade beard, lounged on a divan upholstered in golden silk with lush cushions of vivid stripes and floral design atop a dais. Imams and representatives of Jewish and Christian religions stood to one side below, court officials on the other. Two muscular guards held the chains of large spotted cats that slept on each side of Abd al-Rhaman's divan. Soldiers from his African and al-Andalusian domains guarded the hall. He saw intelligence in swarthy Abd al-Rhaman's wolf's eyes, suspicion and curiosity in those of the emir's Muslim and Christian advisors, and welcome expressions from his fellow Jews.

"You were the Christian Bishop Bodo who is now the Jew Eliezar."

The emir had spoken in Arabic, and one of the Court Jews translated. Bodo-Eliezar believed the emir spoke and understood several languages.

"We have heard much about you. You resemble more one of our Slav and Norsemen soldier-slaves."

"I am of the Alamanni and Saxons."

"And you have chosen to reside here in Cordoba."

"A veritable paradise."

"We try to make it so. Is it true you were the Frankish emperor's spiritual advisor?"

"Yes, I was his deacon, and he appointed me Bishop Palatine before I left."

"So high a rank, so well favored, and yet you converted to the religion of the Jews. Why?"

"I could no longer serve a false idolatrous pagan belief."

Abd al-Rhaman suppressed a smile, and with a wave of his hand the emir silenced angry murmuring from the Christians. "Now, we would like to hear and confirm much about our foes to the north from your knowledge of them. We invite you to dine with us."

"I am honored." An imam stepped away from the emir, and Bodo-Eliezar noticed a small table the cleric had obscured. "Your Highness knows Chatrang-namak?"

"Very well. I have never lost. And you?"

"I played often with Emperor Louis."

"Then we shall do battle against each other on the board another time. I can learn much about a man by the way he moves the pieces."

Night fell by the time Bodo-Eliezar returned home, and Semadar held a candelabrum to his face. "You are so late. What happened?"

"As you can see, my head still rests on my neck between my shoulders. My audience with Abd al-Rhaman went well."

Bodo-Eliezar described his impressions of the palace and the emir. Abd al-Rhaman II was a civilized ruler who loved luxury, music, poetry, and dancing. After an abundant meal with so many courses and foods he lost count, the emir and his military advisors questioned him extensively about Louis' sons, and the manner in which they waged war.

"Forgive me if I do not sup this evening, for I am sated with food and drink."

"Are you going to appear often at the emir's court?"

"Not voluntarily. Only when summoned. I did not turn my back on one court to exchange it for another."

"Then let us retire for the night."

When Bodo-Eliezar came to bed, Semadar greeted him with a kiss and an expression on her face he had not seen before. She did not speak and placed his hand on her belly.

The instant Bodo-Eliezar understood Semadar's meaning, he sat up in bed and stared at his wife in the light of the full moon slanting through the bedroom shutters. Semadar had never looked so beautiful. "You are with child."

"Yes. Are you pleased?"

"I never imagined myself becoming a father so soon. We must find more servants to attend you, the best midwife and physician."

"All that in time. Our child will not be born for another six months."

"In the morning, we must prepare a room for our firstborn."

94. Leila

So tiny and delicate, dark like her mother.

Nine Julian calendar months to the day he and Semadar wed, Bodo-Eliezar counted his daughter's fingers and toes while servants scurried about bringing fresh towels and warm water. The midwife reassured him that the newborn was healthy of normal weight with no deformities. She added that Semadar suffered no injuries or exceptional loss of blood and had an easy birthing. Before the midwife returned their daughter to Semadar, she cut the umbilical cord and began to wash the infant in a basin with lukewarm water.

Bodo-Eliezar sat on the bed beside Semadar. "Both our mothers died giving birth, but you lived. I thank God for that."

"I am strong. I will survive every birth. Are you disappointed I did not give you a son?"

"I am pleased we have a daughter born of a Jewish woman who will give us grandchildren descended from the House of King David the same as you. What shall we name her?"

"Leila, for my mother, may she rest in peace."

"Dark Beauty, and so may she become."

The midwife brought their daughter to Semadar oiled, scented and swathed in white cotton. When his wife began to nurse Leila, Bodo-Eliezar retired to his study. Unlike the noble women of the empire, Jewish mothers did not give their newborns to a wet nurse at birth. The Talmud recommended but did not decree that a mother should suckle the child for at least two years and up to five, but a wet nurse might be substituted at any time.

Bodo-Eliezar searched through his Torah and several manuscripts he had collected to learn what other rituals and obligations they must observe following the birth of a daughter. One fact he did know.

While a subdeacon, Bodo-Eliezar had learned the Jewish origins of the Christian celebration that took place on the Second of February. It was known as the Feast of Mary's Purification and Presentation of Jesus when she, as a devout Jewish woman, brought Jesus to the Temple in Jerusalem for ritual purification. According to Leviticus 12, a mother who gave birth to a male child was unclean for seven days, followed by thirty-three more days of impurity. That was when the mother took the male infant to the Temple and later to synagogues to be purified. But was it the same when she gave birth to a daughter?

Each day while Semadar lay abed, Bodo-Eliezar shared what he learned from his research and discussions with sages at the synagogue. According to the Talmud, the impurity of a woman who gave birth to a daughter lasted twice as long than if she had borne a son, a period of eighty days during which the mother foreswore all intimacies with her husband.

Semadar held firm opinions about suckling and abstinence from carnal relations for so extended a period of time. They had not observed the

Bodo the Apostate

required twelve days of separation with no affection during and after her menses, and she believed a month of breastfeeding after giving birth would suffice. Bodo-Eliezar agreed and found a wet nurse. They could always repent during the Ten Days of Awe and on Yom Kippur.

The detailed compilation of laws and precedents in the Talmud reinforced Bodo-Eliezar's impression that Judaism was as much a legalistic orderly way of life as it was a religion. He explained to Semadar what the Talmud said about a daughter. Unlike the formal giving of a name to a son on the day of his *berit milah*, no precedent or ceremony existed for a female infant.

"Then we shall begin our own tradition for the naming of our daughters."

Other than peasant women who often gave birth while working in a field and continuing to toil afterward, most noble women in the empire might lay in bed for seven to ten days. Not Semadar. She was on her feet in four.

The April weather was mild, and they established a routine, setting aside an hour each morning before the midday meal to sit with Leila under a canopy in the garden facing the fountain. Bodo-Eliezar held his daughter, let her play with his beard, and began to teach the first words he wanted to hear her say: *Abba* and *Eemah*, Hebrew for father and mother.

He also discussed with Semadar what the Talmud said about raising a daughter. Up to the age of twelve years she was a minor, a child under her father's absolute authority. During those years, he had the right to choose her husband.

Between the ages of twelve and twelve and six months she became a young woman, her legal status ambiguous.

At twelve years and six months a female attained adulthood, which ended a father's autocratic control. As an adult woman, Leila would have well defined rights based on legal decisions made and refined over the centuries. Bodo-Eliezar decided not to discuss them with Semadar until and when the matter in question arrived such as Leila's material support until she wed, freedom to accept or reject a father's choice of a husband, her Right of Dowry, and how she would be affected by laws of inheritance.

When Bodo-Eliezar looked ahead to the future, he had many questions. Would Leila be obedient like Adeltrud or strong willed the same as her mother? He decided to leave the rearing of their daughters to Semadar while he educated his sons yet to be born.

The best examples for raising children were those Bodo-Eliezar had seen in the homes of Abraham, Taurus, Enoch, and Rabbis David and Aaron where warmth and love toward their wives, sons and daughters prevailed. He did not know what love was, but his affection for Semadar had intensified, and for little Leila it had begun.

Another thought gratified Bodo-Eliezar. He had begun his own dynasty.

95. The Challenge

In the spring of 840, a Mozarab servant brought Bodo-Eliezar a letter in Latin addressed to his former name Bodo and signed by Paulus Alvarus. The bishops must have encouraged Alvarus to write him.

From the day they settled in their new home, Bodo-Eliezar had intensified his speaking and writing against Trinitarian Christianity with passion so eloquent their bishops and secular leaders became alarmed. He understood the Christian Bible and writings of the Church Fathers better than most clergy, and he was fluent in Latin and their Roman dialect similar to the languages spoken in Septimania and the Marches.

Alvarus' extensive harangue included typical Christian arguments *contra* the Jews Bodo-Eliezar had heard throughout his life in the Church: the identity of True Israel, invalidity of the Law of Moses, support for Trinitarianism and Incarnation, and an attempt to prove Jesus was the Messiah for whom the Jews had waited. Alvarus included predictable selected citations from Scripture and writing of the Church Fathers.

Bodo-Eliezar lost count of how many times he heard priests, monks, and bishops cite Jacob's blessing from Genesis 49:10:

> The scepter shall not part from Judah, nor the ruler's staff from between his feet, as long as men come to Shiloh and unto him shall the obedience of people be.

Paulus Alvarus wrote:

Bodo the Apostate

> Shiloh is Jesus, the True Messiah, for in our times Israel has neither Temple nor king.

Alvarus added more quotations with personal commentary from Leviticus, Hosea and Daniel 9:25 that he claimed had predicted the Second Coming of Jesus. He also identified himself as a Jew whose family converted to Christianity and concluded:

> I pray you may always enjoy good health, my most revered and most beloved brother by race but not by faith.

Bodo-Eliezar spoke about the contents to Semadar. "His appeal for me to reconsider my conversion is filled with homilies of so-called Christian love and false humility. My inclination is to burn the letter and forget about it instead of responding to his absurdities."

"Before you do, I suggest you speak with Chief Rabbi Aaron."

"You always well advise me."

Rabbi Aaron finished reading Alvarus' letter. "Yes, it is as you described, a polemic typical of what we have dealt with before. Yet, it appears to be less of an attack against our beliefs and more an effort to make you aware of your errors and convince you to return to your former faith."

"Then he is a fool. Who is this Alvarus?"

"He is a wealthy knight and influential leader of the Christians in Cordoba but not a priest. I believe it was Bishop Saul, their spiritual head, who encouraged Alvarus to challenge you."

"Rabbi, I prefer to ignore the letter and forget about that flea."

"I disagree. I am not surprised someone from the Christian community has contacted you. It is common knowledge the church authorities fear your cogent reasoning. Even before you arrived in Cordoba, they had been losing adherents to Islam and to heterodoxies from within. Now our people have an articulate champion in you."

The rabbi told Bodo-Eliezar the bishops had become more distressed after several Mozarabs, who read his condemnations of the Orthodox Church, converted to the Law of Moses. Their distress became panic when many Christians, whose Jewish forebears had been coerced into the

Trinitarian faith during Visigoth rule before the Muslim conquest, turned to Judaism. Well aware Bodo-Eliezar had been a prominent cleric, the bishops feared with justification that he might sway more of their susceptible flocks away from the Roman Church in al-Andalus with his polemics.

"I trust you will consult with me before sending a response. Although you are well versed in Scripture and their false New Testament and Church writings, I suggest you also become familiar with the wisdom of our rabbis who participated in earlier disputations against the Christians."

96. Bodo-Eliezar vs. Alvarus

Bodo-Eliezar followed Rabbi Aaron's advice and read several defenses of Judaism, which helped frame his response to Alvarus. Alone in his study, he took a fresh sheet of vellum, dipped a quill in ink, and began his response.

> First, you must address me by my true name, Bodo-Eliezar. Were it not for the urgent command of my rabbi and teachers, I would not have condescended to reply.

Bodo-Eliezar ridiculed and corrected Alvarus' mistranslation of *shebet* as sovereignty when it meant tribe, specifically that of Judah:

> More than that, you Christian Visigoths cruelly persecuted and attempted to eradicate all Jews in your kingdoms. That is why they welcomed the Muslim invasion. That is why many fled to the benevolence of the Franks. Now, you are equal to us under Muslim rule because both Jew and Christian lack sovereignty here in the emirate.

Next, Bodo-Eliezar used Alvarus' calculations from Daniel to prove the True Messiah had not yet come but would appear in twenty-seven years. He was pleased with himself for specifying the year of the Messiah's appearance. Bodo-Eliezar added it more to annoy Alvarus than for accuracy. No specific date existed in Scripture for the Anointed One's appearance.

Bodo the Apostate

He concluded his letter by asserting Jesus' sufferings and death on the cross were inappropriate for Israel's savior and redeemer, and Trinitarianism was a false dogma because God is One and indivisible.

Alvarus wasted no time responding. He wrote no salutation, suggesting that anyone named Bodo-Eliezar did not exist. Instead, he opened with a complaint and another mistranslation of a passage:

> Your writing desecrates the Name, and you have insulted me and my ancestors. Isaiah, 7:14, predicts a virgin shall conceive and bear a son.

Bodo-Eliezar made a note to instruct Alvarus that the Hebrew word *alma* had a broader meaning: young girl, maiden, and yes, virgin, but there was no mention of any divine penetration in that passage from Isaiah.

Alvarus replied to Bodo-Eliezar's prediction the Messiah would appear in twenty-seven years with a wager in his next letter that whoever was wrong would return to his original religion.

Alvarus then asked why he left Christianity.

In his second letter to Alvarus, Bodo-Eliezar addressed the Mozarab as a sententious mediocre compiler who lacked erudition and originality. He asserted Israel was God's Chosen People, who received the Torah on Mount Sinai and kept to this day its laws and statutes, without which there could be no redemption. Because Christians did not observe the commandment of the Torah and believed in a false Trinity, there was no salvation in Alvarus' religion. He then quoted Jeremiah 17:5:

> Cursed is the one who trusts in man, who draws strength from mere flesh and whose heart turns away from God

Bodo-Eliezar next answered Alvarus' question why he left the Church for Judaism, emphasizing he forsook a deceitful, despicable, and inferior faith. There was only Hebrew Scripture and no God-given New Testament. He asserted the story of Christ, belief in virgin birth, and creation of saints were variations of paganism borrowed from and inferior to those of the Greeks, Romans, and Alamannic tribes.

Bodo-Eliezar added:

But who could blame them? In the empire, if you get fourteen churchmen together, they will have fourteen different opinions about Christianity, the degenerate, abject, lying, accursed, detestable vile faith that prevails there.

Bodo-Eliezar described how Christians at Court violated oaths and tenets and recounted their moral laxity, conceding he was no better than any palatine noble and too many clerics regardless of his vow of chastity:

> ... ita ut passim per diversarum feminarum concubitos in temple nostro te glories dulces tibi habuere complexos.

> ... so here and there I had intercourse with diverse sweet and cooperative women, even in our glorious royal chapel.

Alvarus' next response took weeks to arrive and with good reason. It was the longest yet, and he addressed Bodo-Eliezar as Transgressor instead of by name. Alvarus cited Isaiah 43:18-19 to refute Bodo-Eliezar's statement on the observance of the Ten Commandments:

Remember not the former things.

He quoted Malachi 1:11 to disprove that only Jews are chosen by God:

For my name is great amongst the nations.

Nations meant gentiles according to Christian teachings.

Alvarus argued Jesus, not some non-divine man, would ensure that the House of David lasted forever. He defended the Trinity Doctrine of three-in-one and declared Jesus' death on the cross was not a reproach but an honor. Then, Alvarus went into a mad rant:

> In order that you, who call yourself Eliezar, may understand who I am, I am the one Alexander the Great declared

Bodo the Apostate

who must be avoided. I am the one who caused General Pyrrhus to shudder. I am the one Caesar feared.

Bodo-Eliezar suspected the boaster must be drunk and continued reading to the end of Alvarus' extended diatribe:

> Who is more worthy of the name Israel? You, Transgressor, who claims to have left the worship of idols and come to the worship of the supreme God, a Jew by faith, but not by race, or I, a Hebrew both by faith and by race?

"You have won a victory for our people, Bodo-Eliezar. That Alvarus showers personal invective upon you is the proof."
"I want to get on with the routine of my orderly life, Rabbi. This correspondence with Alvarus is taking valuable time away from my studies and my family, but I must write another response."
"And I will have scribes copy all you have written for distribution to our synagogues throughout the emirate and Frankland."
"That pleases me."

At home in his study, Bodo-Eliezar began a brief reply to Alvarus.

> You are a mad yapping dog, foaming at the mouth, who writes only what others have written before, all which is simple blathering....

Again, several weeks passed before Alvarus' reply arrived:

> You call me a yapping dog. Perhaps I am, but you are a snarling fox.

Alvarus next cited other miracles to prove virgin birth was possible and concluded with another hysterical attack against the Jews:

> The Jew is unable to understand the higher spiritual dimension of any argument and trapped in a lower plane

of spiritual existence. This position culminates in the association of purely physical and body functions to the Jewish view of reality. I curse you and all Jews for blindness. Judaism cannot see beyond the material existence of Christ's body.

The letter may have been written by Alvarus, but as Bodo-Eliezar continued to read, he heard Agobard's voice.

Your conversion was caused by desires of the flesh. Why not become a Muslim and taste as many women as you wish? You are a sexual animal who can only read the Law literally and not interpret it figuratively in a Christian sense. For if you wish to understand the Law as carnal, not only do you attribute limbs to God, but affirm that He is similar to you, and whilst you refuse to say that Christ is God, you make all men equal to God. We all know that you left our faith for pleasures of the flesh.

Furious over Alvarus' insults Bodo-Eliezar thought long and hard how best to create a response that would silence the bombastic fool once and for all. He researched more disputations in the rabbi's study and added them to his most blasphemous reply to Alvarus.

God never entered into marriage, nor did He create a son, nor was it possible for Him to have a partner to his sovereignty. As He said to Moses: *There is no God without me. I put to death. I make alive. I strike and I heal.*

Bodo-Eliezar next wrote a series of rhetorical questions:

Can God be man? Can He be born of woman? Can He be beaten and sentenced to death? Why did God have to suffer? God could have sent angels and prophets to save mankind, if indeed it was necessary, and He had many other means to achieve that goal instead of humiliating His flesh.

Bodo the Apostate

Bodo-Eliezar refuted each of Alvarus' assertions that Christ was unique and God joined with the Holy Spirit.

If Jesus had no earthly father, neither did Adam, so worship him too, and Eve, for she had neither father nor mother.

If Christ should be worshiped because he ascended to heaven, so did Enoch and Elijah before him. So add them to your pantheon with Christ.

You hold that Christ is God because he is called Son of God in the Gospels, but in the Torah, God calls the children of Israel my son, my firstborn, Israel. Thus the Children of Israel are God and so are Christ's brothers, and his Jewish disciples. Worship them too.

If you cite Christ's miracles to prove he is God, let me tell you about those who performed more wondrous things.

Elijah revived two dead people, one before and another after his death. He blessed a small amount of flour and a small amount of oil, and they lasted three years.

Elisha walked on the Jordan River the same as dry land and cured Naaman, the King of Aram's minister, of leprosy.

Nothing Christ did is more remarkable than anything done by Moses, peace be upon him, whom God sent to Pharaoh with ten plagues, who turned his stick into a snake, and split the sea and drowned Pharaoh and his armies.

Moses rescued the children of Israel and at Mount Sinai gave them the Torah. He made the manna and quails come down before them. He made water flow from the rock. He led them through the desert. Their clothes did not wear out. Their feet did not swell.

All that is more remarkable than what Christ did. So

worship Moses, for he is more noble than Christ, who did not do anything more remarkable than General Joshua who stopped the sun and the moon for almost an entire day and dried the River Jordan.

Compared with the deeds of these men, the deeds attributed to Christ are a fraud and a lie and worship of him is nonsense.

Bodo-Eliezar concluded with praise for God, who enlightened him, and for the Torah. He signed and sent his response.
He heard no more from Alvarus.

97. Lion

After Bodo-Eliezar's correspondence with Paulus Alvarus ended, he returned to the steady rhythms of family and religious life. He prayed daily at the synagogue, observed Jewish rituals, celebrations, and Holy Days, interrupted on occasion by a game of Chatrang-namak or participation in the hunt with Abd al-Rhaman.

Semadar ensured Bodo-Eliezar's privacy and quiet times when he read or wrote in his study. At the end of 841, she gave birth to a second daughter they named Gila, Hebrew for Joy, and a year later, she presented him with a perfectly formed son.

Semadar cuddled the newborn in the crook of her arm. "Now our daughters should meet their brother."

Bodo-Eliezar told the attending servants to bring the girls to their mother. One returned with two and a half year old Leila, and another carried year old Gila. He took Leila's hand and led her to Semadar's bedside. "Kiss your brother and welcome him to our family."

"Yes, *Abba*."

He lifted Gila and placed her beside Semadar.

"What name have you chosen for our son?"

During each of Semadar's pregnancies, Bodo-Eliezar gave much thought to the naming of a male child. He not could choose Gunzo or

Bodo the Apostate

Bernard. His father had no Hebrew name, and Semadar did not know which one her paternal grandfather gave to Bernard.

Bodo-Eliezar lifted their newborn's hand with his forefinger and liked how he gripped it. "I have decided upon a name, which I shall reveal at his *berit milah*."

Eight days later in the crowded central room of his home that opened to the patio, the men of the synagogue joined Bodo-Eliezar to witness his son's *berit milah*. Semadar, and the women of the congregation waited for the ritual to end in a separate room.

After the *mohel* recited the last prayer, Bodo-Eliezar held the newborn high for his male guests to see. "Give welcome to my son, Ariyeh bar Eliezar."

What more appropriate name could he bestow upon a male child than the Hebrew word for lion? While Bodo-Eliezar accepted congratulations, he resolved to control Ariyeh's upbringing with both a religious and secular education that included lessons in weaponry and horsemanship. Semadar must never become doting and consumed with blind ambition for Ariyeh the way Judith was with Charles, or didactic like Dhuoda tried to be with her son Guillaume.

While all celebrated with food and drink he provided, Bodo-Eliezar brought Ariyeh to Semadar in their bedroom where she sat awaiting his return with Leila and Gila attended by a wet nurse, female servants, and several ladies of the congregation.

"Here is Ariyeh bar Eliezar, our son,"

"Ariyeh," Semadar repeated and cradled the infant against her breast. "You have chosen the perfect name for our son, for he is descended through my father from King David whose Tribe of Judah was symbolized by the Lion."

"We are of like mind."

With three children in his home, Bodo-Eliezar added one dictum and one new addition to his daily routine. He told Semadar, their daughters as best they could understand, and the servants never to disturb him in his study unless it was of the utmost importance. He made time each day before and after meals to give attention to the girls and Ariyeh.

Bodo-Eliezar marveled at how fast his daughters grew. Leila took after Semadar feature for feature, but would Gila's hair remain blonde and eyes stay vivid blue or darken as happened to many children? He could not yet determine whom Ariyeh might resemble. Within a short period of time, everyone called him Ari.

First Leila, then Gila, now Bodo-Eliezar and Semadar waited for Ari to speak the same first words as the girls when they addressed him as *Abba* and their mother as *Eemah*.

98. Aluf

Several months after Ariyeh's birth, Bodo-Eliezar met with Chief Rabbi Aaron, other rabbis, and secular leaders of the community. They discussed a serious new internal threat to both the emirate and the Jews living in al-Andalus. Archbishop Eulogius of Toledo, a Trinitarian zealot, was urging his flock to become martyrs, rise against Muslim rule, and massacre all Jews. Eulogius also demanded the Mozarabs shed their Saracen dress, way of life, and cease speaking Arabic or they too would face extinction.

In Toledo, monks inflamed by their archbishop's rhetoric interrupted Friday prayers in mosques to preach and convert Muslims to Christianity. The authorities reacted with swiftness and severity. They held public executions of the fanatics.

Led by the emir's eldest son Muhammad, several of Abd al-Rhaman's Muslim and Jewish advisors including Bodo-Eliezar urged him to slay or imprison all Christian clergy and monks. The emir sided with those who voiced restraint because the majority of Mozarabs caused no trouble and opposed the zealots. Still, rumors spread that Eulogius sent several monks to Cordoba to foment an insurgency against the emir and to plan attacks against the Jewish quarter.

The rabbis and influential members of the synagogue debated how best to defend their community. No consensus emerged until Bodo-Eliezar suggested they create a trained militia.

Sabbath Eve at the synagogue Chief Rabbi Aaron informed the entire congregation that he appointed Bodo-Eliezar to recruit a Jewish

Bodo the Apostate

militia with the Hebrew rank of *Aluf*, commander, and declared him to be an Ornament of the Jewish Community for his polemics against the Orthodox Church. The rabbi also praised Bodo-Eliezar for his exchange of letters with Alvarus.

"You have heartened our people and strengthened our resolve. Each word you have written is being copied by our scribes and spread throughout the emirate, the Marches, Septimania, Aquitaine, and all of Frankland. Here and everywhere, the Orthodox Church is censoring your most cogent responses out of fear they will influence more Christians to forsake their false Messiah. Regardless of their efforts, our truth shall prevail."

Within the congregation, Bodo-Eliezar found a half dozen hardened veterans of battles in the Marches, who helped him train a troop of volunteers. Through donations, the synagogue outfitted the men with weapons, mounts, and provided colorful banners designating the Tribes of Israel attached to upright lances whenever they paraded with the emir's army through the streets of Cordoba. Rabbi Aaron might be the spiritual head of the Jewish community, but without trying or scheming, Bodo-Eliezar *Aluf* became its de facto secular leader, fulfilling the literal meaning of his Alamannic birth name.

Because Muslims, Jews, and Mozarabs united against the Christian zealots, no monk violated a mosque, and no mob attacked the Jewish quarter. One disappointment tempered Bodo-Eliezar's personal triumphs. His loyal steed Amalric approached his twenty eighth year and tired during marches and rides in the parks. After making inquiries, Bodo-Eliezar heard of a field where horsemen released their aging mounts among flocks of wild horses. He purchased a young mare of a breed preferred by the Saracens and known as Arabian. He named her Yaffa, a Hebrew word meaning beautiful.

After Yaffa became comfortable with Bodo-Eliezar, he led her and rode Amalric for the last time to a broad meadow by a brook where aged horses grazed and galloped in short bursts. He dismounted, removed Amalric's saddle and bridle, and attached them to Yaffa.

Bodo-Eliezar stroked his stallion. "Well, old friend, here is where you may frolic for the rest of your life."

Amalric angled his head and brushed it against Bodo-Eliezar's cheek. He slapped the Frisian's haunch. "Go and be free."

Amalric trotted into the meadow. Bodo-Eleazar mounted Yaffa and rode her to Cordoba. He did not look back at Amalric, the last link with his previous life in the empire.

But Bodo-Eliezar was mistaken. Late morning the week after Yom Kippur, he reacted with both surprise and dismay when the past breached the protective walls of his home.

99. The Anonymous

A servant escorted Priscus into the study. Stunned for a moment by a visitor from the previous life he forsook, Bodo-Eliezar experienced a simultaneous mix of emotions and thoughts: resentment that the past intruded into the present, unwanted nostalgia for the best of his former life, and affection for an old friend and mentor. He took Priscus' bag and staff and set them aside.

Lean and fit for a man in his early fifties, skin smooth as burnished brown leather, hair and beard gray, eyebrows dark, the Astronomer stared at Bodo-Eliezar's beard, long hair, robes, and skullcap. "Despite your Saracen garb, you resemble Lothair even more than before." He turned and peered at the titles of books and manuscripts filling the shelves. "You have become a bibliophile like Abraham."

"I am forever a student."

"I shall always remember you as the boy who asked more questions than there are stars in the sky."

Bodo-Eliezar did not want to reminisce. "How did you find me?"

"I asked about you at the synagogue."

A servant announced it was time for the midday meal. Bodo-Eliezar escorted Priscus from his study. "Come and meet my family."

In the central room, Priscus responded to Semadar's welcome with formal reserve and awkwardness toward the children. He did not recognize her, and Bodo-Eliezar thought his wife wise not to reveal herself as Count Bernard's daughter.

"Priscus and I will sup alone outside. We must not be disturbed."

Bodo the Apostate

Under a canopy of striped orange and azure silk, Bodo-Eliezar invited Priscus to sit with him on oversized soft cushions facing the garden of vividly colored flowers and a fountain flanked by cypress, palm, and jasmine. Bowls of fruit and nuts, plates of cheeses and savory meats, and an amphora with two matching goblets had been set on a round carved ebony and ivory table in front of them. The autumnal weather was mild, and a perfumed breeze wafted the sweet scent of blossoms.

Before they ate and drank, Bodo-Eliezar recited in Hebrew the blessings for bread and wine. "What has brought you to Cordoba?"

"In part curiosity. Before you left on your presumed pilgrimage, we had our last conversation. It was then I sensed, and your chart confirmed, you did not intend to return. I never suspected you would convert to Judaism. Did Abraham have something to do with it?"

"Indirectly. He never proselyted, but one might say he showed me the way through example."

"Did you ever think about the distress and turmoil your apostasy created at Court, throughout the empire, and to those who cherished you, especially Louis, Judith, Strabo, and myself?"

"Once I came to my decision, I did not look behind. I am no longer Bodo, the boy you mentored and young man you once knew. I am Eliezar, an observant Jew, married and a father."

"Then read this." Priscus reached into his bag and thrust a scroll at Bodo-Eliezar. "It is a copy of what the black monk, Prudentius of Troyes, wrote about you in the Court Chronicles, the *Annales Bertiniani, anno 839*.

Bodo-Eliezar unrolled the scroll.

> ... in the meantime, believable rumors caused all ecclesiastics of the Catholic Church to lament and weep. Deacon Bodo of the Alamanni, who was educated from early childhood by palace scholars in the Christian faith and secular learning, abandoned Christianity and turned to Judaism. The previous year he requested and received permission from the emperor and empress to make a pilgrimage to Rome. Laden with many gifts, he began his journey but was seduced by the enemy of the human race.

Of course Agobard's disciples would create any excuse to blame the Jews and refuse to recognize he had been raised to bishop.

> Bodo's first undertaking after planning his treachery and perdition with the Jews was a callous scheme to sell his retinue into slavery, except for one said to be his nephew, whom he took with him. Then, alas, he abjured faith in Christ and professed Judaism. After circumcision he let his hair and beard grow, took the name Bodo-Eliezar, donned armor, married the daughter of a Jew, and forced his nephew into similar conversion.

A lie. He never forced Guntrum to do anything, and his nephew died before any *berit milah*.

> Completely overwhelmed by hatred, Bodo entered Caesaraugusta, a city of Hispania, in mid-August. So monstrous and grievous was Bodo's apostasy to the emperor and empress, indeed to everyone saved by the Christian faith, it was apparent to all that the emperor refused to believe its truth.

Even if it was true he caused much anguish for Louis, it was insignificant when compared to all the emperor's ungrateful sons did to their father and to the empire.

"How and when did the Court learn of my conversion to Judaism?"

"After Lent in April of 839, Louis moved his Court to the palace at Bodman. There Abbot Strabo came from Reichenau and told Their Majesties what he had heard from a reliable source. You never made your pilgrimage to Rome. Instead you went to Hispania where you converted to Judaism and wed a Jewess."

Bodo-Eliezar had been listening to Priscus' narrative in a state of detachment, as if the Bodo the Astronomer spoke of were a stranger, but the mention of his boyhood friend prompted him to ask, "How is Strabo? Is he content at his abbey on Reichenau?"

"He was not at first. Upon Louis' death, Charles asserted independence from his father's and mother's advisors. He removed Strabo as

Bodo the Apostate

Abbot of Reichenau and exiled him to Fulda. A year later he reinstated Strabo as Abbot. Charles also replaced Drogo with the monk Grimald as chamberlain and returned to Ebbo the diocese of Rheims."

"He would have removed if not exiled me as well."

"I think not. But to your question, Strabo leads the life he always wanted as Abbot of Reichenau. Before I left, he said if I found you, I was to say he prays often to God for your immortal soul to be saved and for the Thunderer to keep you well."

How much better the Orthodox Church might have been if all followed Strabo's humble example.

"And because of your virulent writings and vituperative attacks against their Church in your letters to Paulus Alvarus, the bishops now believe you are Satan incarnate."

Bodo-Eliezar did not care what Agobard and his ilk thought of him. "You read what I have written?"

"I have. They are well reasoned, but I still do not understand your motives for leaving Court to become a Jew. You were more than pampered and favored. No one lived a better life. Louis loved you as a son and confided in you. Both Louis and Judith planned to make you the second man in the empire. But tell me the truth. Did you convert to Judaism out of sincere conscience and faith, or was it your hatred of the Orthodox Church?"

"Both."

The meal ended, and they strolled together in the garden around the fountain. Their silence hung heavily in the air. Bodo-Eliezar saw no point to reminiscing about the good times he shared with Priscus. He did not ask what happened in the empire and at Court during the years since his departure. Reports arrived with regularity, and he had been informed about the passing of Louis and subsequent internecine warfare between Lothair, Ludwig and Charles. He knew that Agobard died the same year as Louis and the archbishop's protégé Amulo became Bishop of Lyon.

Bodo-Eliezar assumed the Astronomer felt no less awkward then he. Yes, they could talk about the past and fond memories they shared, but after that what?

He did have one comment for Priscus. "I am surprised Judith allowed you to leave Court."

"She did not. She could not."

"Why?"

"Then you have not heard."

Priscus told Bodo-Eliezar that Bernard had a ward named Irmintrud, daughter of his cousin Eudo, Count-Bishop of Orléans, who died at the start of the third rebellion. After conniving with the count, Judith arranged for Charles to wed Irmintrud. Shortly after the marriage, Bernard allied with Pepin II of Aquitaine against Charles the Bald. That gave Charles an excuse to rid himself of his domineering mother. He declared Judith guilty of adultery with Count Bernard and a number of other crimes. He confiscated his mother's lands, wealth, and imprisoned her. Judith died shortly after her incarceration at Tours on the nineteenth of April 843 at age thirty-nine, the day before Priscus left Court.

Bodo-Eliezar did not pity the ruthless and obsessive mother the once charming Judith had become. Had she continued to dote on her ungrateful son until her death, proud she succeeded in making him King of West Francia?

"And your chronicle of Louis' reign. Did you finish it?"

"I distributed several copies while still at Court and signed it The Anonymous. No one at Court knows I wrote it."

Bodo-Eliezar did not ask Priscus why. Instead, he inquired about Count Bernard on Semadar's behalf and did not like what he heard. Not only Louis' sons, Count Bernard wanted more. He aspired to become King of Septimania, the Midi, and the Marches, vassal to no man, which was why he allied with Pepin II against King Charles.

"During my journey to Marseilles, I learned that His Majesty's soldiers captured Count Bernard. I have not heard what Charles will do with him."

"I must withhold from Semadar what you said about Bernard until I learn his fate."

"Why?"

"Before we wed, her name was Dulciorella."

"Your wife is Bernard's daughter? No one suspected as much up to the day I departed from Court, not Their Majesties, not even Bernard and Dhuoda. How did it come to be you chose Dulciorella?"

"It was a confluence of unforeseen occurrences." Bodo-Eliezar chose not to relate that long story. "For how long do you plan to stay in Cordoba?

Bodo the Apostate

I would like you to be my guest, stay as long as you wish, and introduce you to the emir. Abd al-Rhaman follows the planets and constellations no less than Charlemagne and Louis did through you."

"In truth I am not comfortable here. Everything about you confuses me. Your appearance is still that of an Alaman. Yet, you are no longer Bodo the boy I taught and the adult friend he became. The Bodo I knew and loved is dead. In his body lives a stranger to me, Eliezar the Jew. For that reason, I wish to leave now. I regret I came to Cordoba."

Bodo-Eliezar shared the same regret. He led Priscus back to his study. "Will you return to Court?"

"I am no longer welcome there. When Charles imprisoned Judith, I fell out of favor."

Bodo sensed Priscus' departure from the empire had more to do with Alpaiís, but if the Astronomer did not mention the abbess, neither would he.

"The planets and the stars told me not to come to Cordoba. I shall now resume my journey as they so advise."

Priscus did not mention his destination. Bodo-Eliezar believed it might be Baghdad or beyond.

Priscus reached into his bag and gave Bodo-Eliezar a manuscript. "This is my chronicle of Louis' reign."

Bodo-Eliezar placed it on his desk and escorted Priscus to the gate. He wished the Astronomer a safe journey and watched him walk away. Priscus did not look back.

Semadar stood beside him. "My husband, your expression ... Priscus' visit has caused you much sorrow."

"He belongs to a past I rejected."

Bodo-Eliezar still held much affection for his mentor and friend, a rare individual who had earned his trust. Yet, today it was as if he had been visited by a ghost.

"I am well out of it, well out of it."

Bodo-Eliezar did not repeat to Semadar what Priscus related about Bernard. That must wait until he learned more about her father's fate.

100. Vita Hludovici

Bodo-Eliezar returned home after evening prayers at the synagogue. In his study he lit a candelabrum for extra light, and began to read Priscus' chronicle of Louis' reign titled *Vita Hludovici*.

It revived more unpleasant memories he had buried with his past: the rebellions; hypocrisies of the clergy; ingratitude of the emperor's sons and those Louis raised high at Court; and the emperor's vacillations. The chronicle also elicited two questions he would have asked Priscus. Why did "the Anonymous" not mention the Jews? Why did Priscus not describe Bodo's apostasy and the reactions of Their Majesties and the clergy so prominently mentioned in the *Annales Bertiniani*?

Bodo-Eliezar read details he had not known about Louis' last days. On the fifth of April 840 a total eclipse of the sun terrified the emperor. Already bedridden, Louis made an oral will. Upon his death, Lothair would become emperor provided his eldest did not break faith with the portion of the empire promised to Charles.

> ... on the twentieth day of June, away from Judith and Charles, and with only Drogo, myself, and several priests present at his bedside, Louis shouted his last words, *"Hutz! Hutz!* Go away! Go away!"

Priscus wrote that the emperor must have seen an evil spirit. Bodo-Eliezar believed Louis had a final vision of the nephew he blinded, Pepin, King of Italy, who had haunted the emperor's dreams for two decades.

Well into the night Bodo-Eliezar dwelled upon all Priscus wrote and imparted during his visit, some of it new, some confirming much he heard from official reports, travelers, and rumor. He also read the excerpt from the *Annales Bertiniani* a second time. Led by Agobard the bishops accused Bodo of avarice, the evidence being his sale of devout Christians to pagan

Bodo the Apostate

slavers, and of conscupience, desire for carnal pleasure, the proof being his marriage. Yet they did not accuse him of stealing the Pope's gifts.

After Louis' death, the emperor's sons warred against each other. Intra-dynastic rivalries and breaking of oaths continued for more than two years until the great nobles and prelates on all sides had enough. They forced Charles the Bald, Pepin II of Aquitaine, Ludwig, and Lothair to accept a truce and negotiate a final treaty at Verdun. The new Division of Empire created three kingdoms: West, Middle, and East Francia.

Charles the Bald, became King of West Francia, all lands west of the Rhine, with suzerainty over Aquitaine and his vassal rebellious Pepin II. He gave another vassal, Count Bernard, rule over Septimania and the Marches south of the Pyrenees.

Lothair, who became a more nominal than actual emperor, took Frisia, Flandria, Lorraine, Alsace, Burgundy, Provence, and the Kingdom of Italy plus Aachen and Rome. His lands became known as Middle Francia and later Lothairingia.

Ludwig the Alaman acquired East Francia, all lands east of the Rhine including Alamannia, Bavaria, Saxony, and the Marches to the north and east of Italy.

Thus ended the empire Charlemagne created and which Louis the Pious inherited and failed to hold together. It lasted a mere forty-three years, beset by too many pressures from without and within to survive. Although Louis had been weak and inconsistent, Bodo-Eliezar believed the emperor tried his best.

He rose from his desk. He had given enough of his time to Priscus and remembering the past. Sentimentality was weakness. His own iron will had brought him to a better present and brighter future.

Several months later in his study, Bodo-Eliezar held Semadar's hands. "Today I confirmed news of your father that I had been keeping from you. Bernard wanted more than what Charles gave him at the treaty of Verdun. He allied with Pepin II of Aquitaine and made war against King Charles. Defeated in battle, they were captured. Charles executed your father for treason and *laesae majestas* because he declared Count Bernard guilty of adultery with Judith." Semadar did not react. "Did you hear all I said?"

"Yes, I was thinking of the Fifth Commandment. How can I mourn and honor a father in death, whom I seldom saw, who had no affection for me, and who treated me only as merchandise to be bartered for lands, titles, and power?"

Bodo-Eliezar had no answer for Semadar.

"Odd, although Countess Dhuoda also held no fondness for me, her passing last year affected me more than my father's death. I am grateful to my stepmother for being strict in educating me to read, write, and learn the classics, which I shall pass on to our children."

101. A Man of Importance

Bodo-Eliezar reviewed his relationship with God before the final Yom Kippur prayer and the All Mighty closed His books for the year 4607 since the Creation, 847 being the Christian count. From the day of his conversion to this moment, he committed no sin against the Lord, followed without exception the six hundred and thirteen laws, and obeyed all Commandments.

He had been righteous in dealings with his fellow men and had no need to correct wrongs or apologize for anything he might have said, done, or failed to do. Bodo-Eliezar also praised God for bestowing upon him a life of order with a loving wife who made their home a sanctuary from the outside world, and gave him four healthy children.

Without seeking honors, Bodo-Eliezar had become a man of importance in the congregation. More than *Aluf*, he became the Jewish community's secular leader. His wealth had increased dealing with Semadar's Uncle Enoch and through friendship with Viscount Taurus of Roquemaure. He imported *kashrut* wines from the Rhône for both the congregation and Abd al-Rhaman and left the accounting to Semadar who was a genius for numbers.

Four years had passed since Priscus' visit, and Bodo-Eliezar contrasted his life as a Jew in Cordoba with his favored position at Court in the empire serving a weak ruler, an obsessive empress, and a false faith. He thanked God again for giving him the strength and wisdom to escape from that morass of petty intrigues, idol worship, and unnecessary rebellions to lead a life of choice and tranquility with one unavoidable exception.

The emir liked Bodo-Eliezar and appointed him to his council. Having learned much from previous experiences at Aachen, he avoided

Bodo the Apostate

being drawn into the quicksand of Cordoban court machinations yet established a bond with the emir similar to his relationship with Louis. They played Chatrang-namak and hunted together. Both were scholars and bibliophiles and enjoyed discussing the classics and poetry.

After the Yom Kippur services ended, Rabbi Aaron beckoned Bodo-Eliezar and requested they meet after morning prayers on the morrow. He inferred from the rabbi's expression the subject might be more serious than the usual requests for donations or what to do about individuals who violated laws and commandments.

Rabbi Aaron handed Bodo-Eliezar a manuscript sent by the Chief Rabbi of Lyon. It was a screed against the Jews written by Agobard's protégé and successor, Bishop Amulo, and distributed throughout Charles the Bald's kingdom, titled *Epistola seu liber contra Judeos ad Carolem regem*.

The first paragraph began: "Detestable is the belief of the Jews ...." Bodo-Eliezar dropped the manuscript on the rabbi's desk. "No need for me to continue reading. Amulo has merely plagiarized Agobard's writings, and it is filled with the usual Christian venom, bombast, hyperbole, and misinformation. What is its significance?"

Rabbi Aaron turned to a page and returned the manuscript to Bodo-Eliezar. "Amulo mentions you here."

> There was an incident, the like of which we do not recall. A palace deacon, of noble birth and noble rearing, trained in the Orders, and held in high esteem by the emperor, was so diverted and seduced by diabolic inducements that he abandoned the palace, his fatherland and his kin, and absolutely rejected the kingdom of Christians.

> Now in Hispania amongst the Saracens, he has been persuaded by wicked men to deny God's Son Christ, to desecrate the grace of baptism, to undergo corporeal circumcision, and to change his name. He who was once Bodo is now called Eliezar. The complete Jew in belief and garb, bearded and wed, he daily frequents the synagogues of Satan and with others blasphemes Christ and his church.

Another unpleasant reminder of the past. "You may burn it for all I care."

"This is but one example of what is happening in West Francia."

Rabbi Aaron expressed concerns that a greater number of Jews than before were arriving in the emirate from Charles the Bald's kingdom. He repeated the immigrants' tales of woe and the bishops' vicious attempts to persecute the Jews.

Archbishop Amulo of Lyon and Hincmar, who replaced the deceased Ebbo as Archbishop of Rheims, had called for a synod of bishops at Meaux near Paris, ostensibly to reclaim spiritual power over royal authority and demand an end to lewd and gluttonous behavior by too many in the clergy. Their main intent was to restore and apply the traditional canonic laws and secular restrictions against the Jews previously enforced by Constantine and his successors in the Roman and Byzantine empires, the Visigoths in Hispania, and the Merovingian Franks. They demanded that Charles the Bald revoke all capitularies by Charlemagne and Louis the Pious favoring the Jews.

No Jew could hold a position in government or obtain honors. No Jew could engage in trade or own land. No Jew could be a judge, collect taxes, or appear in public during Easter Week. Jews must show respect to Christian clergy. Converts who continued to observe Judaism would have their children taken away. Jewish rites, circumcision, and observance of their Sabbath and Holy Days must be banned. Jews could be flogged and executed for offenses by civil authorities. Jews must pay ruinous taxes. Jewish property could and should be confiscated. Jews were to be baptized by force.

Charles the Bald responded by dissolving the assembly of bishops and rejecting all the bishops' new regulations against the Jews. He stated his intent to enforce Louis' capitularies.

Amulo and Hincmar resumed their scheming and haranguing. They issued a directive for all priests to include in their Easter sermons the canard that the Jews killed Jesus, which aroused hatred and caused violence against the "Christ killers" in their dioceses at Lyon and Rheims. In al-Andalus, Archbishop Eulogius of Toledo advocated the same by Bodo-Eliezar's former adversary, Paulus Alvarus.

Bodo-Eliezar felt his face afire with rage. "Rabbi, I know better than anyone here and despise with all my being the false faith of the Trinitarians.

Bodo the Apostate

The more distance the Orthodox Church travels away from its Jewish origins, the more vicious it becomes toward our people because we remind them their religion is one of idol worship and belief in a false Messiah.

"It is a bogus faith for a second reason. They appropriated the gods and festivals of the Egyptians, Greeks, Romans, and my Alamannic and Saxon forebears. They made them saints and holidays with different names.

"Also, the pagans enjoyed life, and we Jews celebrate it. To the contrary, the Orthodox Church promulgates a religion of death and hatred of mankind for something they call Original Sin. It would have every man, woman and child ruled by harsh monkish dicta.

"The Orthodox Church also preaches the lie it is not pagan. How can it claim to believe in One God and yet believe in Trinitarianism and the worship of icons and relics without it being a lie?

"Christians like Amulo and Hincmar want to extinguish all Jews. We cannot reason with such men.

"Now, here is what I shall propose to the emir. For what Amulo has written and all that the Trinitarian bishops wish upon the Jews, I shall tell Abd al-Rhaman what I would like to see done to the Christian population in his emirate. I would do unto those foaled Visigoth vermin no less than they have done to the Jews in the past and would do again if they could. Every restriction against the Jews Amulo and Hincmar passed at Meaux should be applied to the Christians here in al-Andalus. Better yet, I would give them a choice. Convert to the Jewish faith or Islam. If anyone refuses, he dies."

Bodo-Eliezar's tirade left Rabbi Aaron speechless.

At home for his midday meal, a desire to protect his family from Trinitarian bigotry consumed Bodo-Eliezar. He gave more attention and affection than usual to his lively children: Leila now seven and identical to Semadar in every way; fair and blonde Gila, who resembled Adeltrud and inherited his and Good Queen Hildegard's unusual eyes; Ari soon to be four, dark like Semadar with his father's features; and six month old Joshua whose face had yet to be delineated.

Afterward in his study, Bodo-Eliezar thought about what Rabbi Aaron and the *Bet Din* told him about the Trinitarian threat. Were it in his power, he would take up the sword and smite the idol worshippers same as the Israelites did during the Scriptural eras of Judges, Kings, and Prophets.

102. Harsh Proposal

Muhammad, Abd al-Rhaman's eldest son, sole heir, and general of the emirate's army returned from an inspection of the Northern provinces. At a meeting of the emir's council, which Bodo-Eliezar attended, the twenty-four year old described a deteriorating situation. The Christian kings and bishops along the border were encouraging their co-religionists in the emirate to rise against the Muslims with promises of aid from Charles the Bald. Worse, several local governors were not to be trusted. They had been making plans to hire Christian mercenaries, declare independence from Cordoba and establish petty *taifas*, kingdoms. Muhammad executed the traitors and replaced them with military commanders.

Abd al-Rhaman asked each advisor to opine how best to prevent rebellion and invasion. Bodo-Eliezar preferred to speak with the emir and Muhammad alone so the Christians would not hear what he had to say.

Abd al-Rhaman dismissed the council and invited Bodo-Eliezar and Muhammad to his chambers.

Bodo-Eliezar and Abd al Rhaman sat on chairs facing each other over a table and board for a game of Chatrang-namak. Muhammad stood behind his father. Servants and slaves waited to refill goblets with wine and bowls with fruits and nuts.

The pieces on the ivory board differed from the set Abraham had gifted Louis. Those in gold topped by crescents represented the Muslims, and opponents in silver with crosses the Byzantines. Towers replaced chariots at the far ends of the back row. Instead of elephants, rectangular representations of imams moved diagonally for the Muslims and bishops for the Christians. The emir called his most important pieces also of abstract non-human form caliph and vizier, and those for the Byzantines, emperor and chamberlain.

"I look forward to defeating you this time."
"If you can, it will be a victory honestly earned."

Bodo the Apostate

"I do not expect any less from you." The emir turned to Muhammad. "Do I not often say that how a man plays Chatrang-namak reveals his true character? Here is a man who will speak his mind to me. Here is a man who has given me accurate information about the infidels to the north and whose advice has proven sound. Here is a man I can trust. Here is a man I shall listen to after our match."

Abd al Rhaman moved a Muslim foot soldier forward. Bodo-Eliezar did the same with his Byzantine. The emir launched clever attacks. Bodo-Eliezar's defenses held. Midway through the match they had lost the same number of pieces.

Their previous games had been hard fought, usually draws. Like Louis, the emir demanded an honest game. Bodo-Eliezar gave him one, and it ended in a stalemate.

Bodo-Eliezar first spoke how wise Abd al-Rhaman was to make his eldest son sole heir instead of apportioning the emirate to many sons who would want to rule as emirs. He cited the disloyalty of Louis sons as a reason why primogeniture was superior to the Salic Law of Inheritance. Bodo-Eliezar next described how Charlemagne and Louis moved administrators from county to county after a few years so they did not become too entrenched and powerful.

"That is what should be done with all your northern governors."

Abd al-Rhaman and Muhammad agreed that policy made sense, but Bodo-Eliezar had more to say and to phrase it in such a way as to include the Muslims. He called for the conversion of all Christians in the emirate to Islam or Judaism.

The emir rejected Bodo-Eliezar's proposal as unrealistic and likely to cause an unnecessary bloody uprising because the majority of Mozarabs had been quiescent. He also believed Charles the Bald would never go to war against the emirate.

"As you have said so often, Eliezar, King Charles of West Francia is too engaged on many fronts defending against repeated Viking raids, fighting the Aquitainians who want an independent kingdom, and repelling incursions by Basques and Bretons."

The emir gave permission for his eldest son and heir to speak. Muhammad sided with Bodo-Eliezar. He described Eulogius' seditions in Toledo and demanded at the very least the archbishop be arrested and executed as an example to all who dared to incite violence in the emirate.

The emir advised caution. Muhammad insisted their army needed to be strong enough to fight potential simultaneous internal rebellions and external wars against the Christian Kingdoms to the north of the Ebro and their allies in the Marches. He reminded Abd al Rhaman and Bodo-Eliezar that Mozarabs, freed slaves from Eastern Europe, and recalcitrant Christians outnumbered the Muslim and Jewish population in al-Andalus.

After further deliberation, Abd al-Rhaman gave Muhammad authority to increase the size of the army but to avoid making war on his Christian subjects unless provoked. "Remember this, my son, and you, Eliezar. A bad peace is preferable to any war."

Bodo-Eliezar had a sudden vision of a bloody Christian uprising in the near future and had no idea how to prevent it if the emir did not strike first.

103. Second Sight

Late summer of 848, Bodo-Eliezar attended his weekly meeting with the Chief Rabbi and the Bet Din to discuss and deal with religious and secular matters affecting the Jewish community. First on the agenda was how best to punish individuals who had broken one or several of the 613 laws. They passed appropriate sentences upon those men and women brought before them.

Next, the rabbis accepted or rejected petitions from individuals pleading their cases before them. One man, a newcomer from Lyon, submitted a request that Bodo-Eliezar cease his successful polemicizing and proselyting.

"They have provoked great fear within the Christian communities throughout al-Andalus and West Francia. So has his friendship with the emir. I have brought with me letters from several rabbis in West Francia who fear his diatribes will arouse the Christians to attack their communities."

Bodo-Eliezar rose and towered over the pusillanimous man. "I shall not be silenced."

The newcomer cringed but handed Chief Rabbi Aaron a small scroll. "I brought you this to bolster my case."

Bodo the Apostate

Rabbi Aaron handed the scroll to Bodo, who read: "This is a copy of an entry from King Charles the Bald's Court Annalist and Scribe, Prudentius of Troyes' for his Annales Bertiniani, Anno Domini 847. It seems they cannot forget you."

Rabbi Aaron read aloud:

> Some years ago Bishop Bodo deserted Christian truth and submitted to Jewish perfidy.
>
> He became so evil that he sought zealously to inflame the minds of Saracens, of the emir, and people alike, against all Christians dwelling in Hispania. His intention was that the latter should abandon Christian faith, cease practicing their religion, and turn to Jewish irrationality or Saracen madness, with the alternative to be death.
>
> Thereupon, the Christians in that realm sent a description of Bodo's malicious intent toward them to King Charles the Bald, his bishops, and other ranks of our faith. It was so poignant that it caused all who read it to weep. The Christians in Hispania requested that King Charles the Bald send a demand for the emir to extradite the aforesaid apostate so he would no longer be a threat to Christians residing there.

"Now they remembered I was raised to bishop."

The petitioners' naive expectation that he would cease polemicizing and proselyting amused Bodo-Eliezar. So did Prudentius' use of his former name. He doubted King Charles would agree to the Christians' request.

"Rabbi Aaron, although the emir never agreed to my proposal, I take much pleasure that at the very least I am causing the Christians much fear and perhaps many sleepless nights."

"I worry that our people will soon be facing much worse than loss of sleep in West Francia to the north. If those malevolent archbishops have their way, and I fear those bigots or their successors shall, there is nothing we can do to aid our suffering brethren. If they will not or cannot flee, our numbers are too few to prevent their annihilation."

During his walk home from the synagogue, Bodo dwelled on the distressing images Rabbi Aaron invoked of what was likely to happen to Jews in the former empire and lands ruled by the Byzantines. So lost in thought he was unaware the sky changed from grim grey to charcoal black. Bodo thought he heard an owl but saw none. No palms, no poplars, no cypress, the same as when a boy he ran again in the familiar thick forest beyond Bodman. Ahead and blocking his way stood the great oak on which he carved his name

A blinding flame.

The oak disappeared.

Silence, absolute silence followed.

A swirling mist replaced the oak

A gentle breeze wafted the vapor toward Bodo and engulfed him.

Unseen arms cradled him. He felt comforted and loved.

A familiar taste of honey cake lingered on his palate.

Something unseen carried Bodo through the mist until he stood at a house unfamiliar to him.

All previous dreams and visions now made sense. The amorphous apparition that had haunted Bodo from early childhood at last became known.

Eliezar the Jew opened the front door to his home where Semadar and the children awaited him in a sanctuary of order, routine, and love.

Author's and Historical Notes

In *Bodo The Apostate,* how much was fiction, how much was historical? The answers follow.

No detailed biography of Bodo-Eliezar exists. All that is known about him comes from the following documents that appeared in *Bodo*: Strabo's poem addressed to Subdeacon Bodo, brief mention in two Carolingian Court annals, a short screed by Bishop Amulo of Lyon, a few sentences in a letter by Archbishop Hincmar of Rheims to King Charles II, the Bald, and sixty-seven lines of Bodo-Eliezar's polemical correspondence that survived Church censorship. For obvious reasons, excluding Strabo's poem, one may conclude those writings are biased against Bodo-Eliezar.

Historians base Bodo's year of birth on Walafrid Strabo's poem, in which the scholar called him "my little blond lad." Consequently, they estimate Bodo was four or five years younger than Strabo, whose year of birth might have been 807 or 808.

To this date, no mention of Bodo-Eliezar's life in al-Andalus after 847 is extant. One exception may be that he is the "Eliezar of Hispania, *Aluf,*" who appears in records of the Babylonian Academy of Jewish sages at Sura. Scholars speculate he may have communicated with the rabbis from al-Andalus or moved to the Jewish community there in later years, ca. 876.

That same year in a letter to King Charles the Bald, Hincmar referred to Bodo's apostasy:

> Many Christians do not realize how dangerous contact with Jews can be even for theologians. My intent is to show how one should conduct himself in this matter in consonance with the tenets of the Church.
>
> Nothing like that Bodo incident happened before. The emperor's priest was led astray by Jews who enticed him with blandishments of Satan himself, so much so he forsook the palace of the emperor, the land of his birth and his parents to join the Jews of Hispania. Now he sits each

Bodo the Apostate

day in Satan's houses of worship, bearded, married, and profaning the name of the Nazarene and his church, even as do all Jews.

Christian martyr uprisings and invasions by Christian kings of the Asturias began in 852 and were put down by Abd al-Rhaman's son Emir Muhammad III, who then fulfilled his father's dream. He became Caliph and initiated Cordoba's brief Golden Age. There is no record to date of an Eliezar *Aluf* fighting against the rebels.

An Abraham is documented as Merchant of the Palace during the reign of Louis the Pious, and another named Judah was praised by Charles the Bald for his loyalty. I created their lineage and added the historical Ambassador Isaac as Abraham's father.

Abbot Walafrid Strabo of Reichenau drowned in the Loire August 849 on his way to a meeting with Charles the Bald. His life and writings are well-documented.

I gave both the fictitious name Priscus and identity to an unnamed historical personage known both as The Anonymous and the Astronomer. A polymath, he chronicled the reign of Louis the Pious to the emperor's death but did not mention Bodo's apostasy, the Jews, or attach his name to the manuscript. One can only speculate why he did not. His name, years of birth and death, family, and tribal origins remain a mystery.

No contemporary portrait or full physical description of Empress Judith exists. Her admirers and enemies praised her beauty, but the color of her hair and eyes are not known. That is why I decided to create the fictional discovery of Nike's statue after the historically documented earthquake of 823.

For those interested in reading about the Jewish Princes of Narbonne and Bernard of Septimania, I recommend the controversial book *A Jewish Princedom in Feudal France 768-900* by Arthur J. Zuckerman.

Bodo-Eliezar's Jewish wife is not named, nor are her origins and family, nor if they had any offspring. Hence, I created Dulciorella-Semadar and made her a daughter of Count Bernard.

No source mentions the name of Bodo-Eliezar's nephew or if he was the son of a brother or sister.

I found no description of the gifts intended for the Pope and what happened to them. Of interest, in all their condemnations of Bodo-Eliezar, the *Annales*, Amulo, and Hincmar do not accuse him of stealing those presents meant for His Holiness.

For story purposes, I created Bodo-Eliezar's lineage. All that is documented about his background and life appear in the aforementioned *Annales Bertiniani*, Amulo's screed, and exchange of letters with Paulus Alvarus I included in *Bodo*.

Bodo-Eliezar spoke for himself in his exchanges of letters with Paulus Alvarus, d. 862, also known as Pablo Alvar/Albar, available in translation by several scholars. Some historians believe Alvarus was not descended from Jewish converts and instead a Visigoth. I added Jewish arguments to Eliezar's letters from other sources because many pages of his replies to Alvarus are missing, having been expunged by the Church.

The motives given by scholars for Bodo-Eliezar's apostasy fall into two camps of speculation: either he was influenced by contact with the Jews over many years, or he decided to convert to Judaism on his way to Rome. My description of Bodo-Eliezar's journey from Christianity to Judaism may have value no more or less than theirs, but perhaps as the result of a novelist's instinct, it may well be the most accurate and definitive, until and unless proven otherwise.

Why did I write a novel about Bodo-Eliezar? Little-known historical individuals who led interesting lives arouse my interest. Sparse documentation about them gives me more freedom to create character motivation and an entertaining story line.

When I researched the family origins of Vicente de Rocamora, the historical protagonist of my published novels, *Rocamora* and *House of Rocamora*, I came across the story of Bodo-Eliezar, the Apostate. Despite different origins and centuries, their lives had striking similarities, which motivated me to write *Bodo*.

Documents confirm Bodo and Rocamora came from noble families. Both were educated to serve the Church. Both lived at their respective Courts. Each became close to the royal family. Each was a spiritual advisor to a royal personage. Both defected from Christianity and converted to Judaism. Both chose Hebrew names. Bodo became Bodo-Eliezar bar Israel, and Rocamora chose Isaac bar Israel.

The Church in its wisdom canonized Agobard as it did Vicente de Ferrer who, in 1391, instigated and led the murderous pogroms and forced conversions of Jews in Spain.

Bodo the Apostate

Bodo-Eliezar and Vicente-Isaac de Rocamora have differences. Church documents, which appear in the last chapters of *Bodo* and in Latin at the end, describe the effects of the scandal caused by Bodo's apostasy, whereas the Spanish Church is silent about Rocamora's conversion to the Law of Moses. Another is that Rocamora's life is relatively well documented after he converted in Amsterdam, but very little is known about him earlier in Spain. Much less is known about Bodo-Eliezar before and after his conversion.

Donald Michael Platt

Fictional Characters as They Appeared

*Referenced in Historical Notes.

*Adeltrud, Bodo's sister
Berend, a servant of Bodo's family
Engelbert, a shield bearer
Dachs, Count Welf's retainer
*Priscus, Bodo's mentor, based on an unnamed historical personage
Theobald, a pedophile priest
Rabbi Sedechius
*Dulciorella, based on an unnamed historical personage
Countess Sigrada
Bertwald, a forester, and his family
Gideon and Sabriel, merchants from Khazaria
Berald, Bodo's opponent in Trial by Combat
*Guntrum, based on an unnamed historical personage
Achmed, a slaver
*Viscount Taurus of Roquemaure and family, a composite of Jewish landowners
*Enoch, Dulciorella's uncle
Rabbi Daniel of Saraqusta
Chief Rabbi Aaron of Cordoba
Bodo-Eliezar's and Semadar's children

Bodo the Apostate

Original Latin

***Annales Bertiniani*, anno 839, pp. 17-18**
Interea lacrimabile nimiumque cunctis catholicae aecclesiae filiis ingemescendum, fama perferente innotuit: Bodonem diaconum Alamannica gente progenitum et ab ipsis paenae cunabulis in christiana religion palatinis eruditionibus divinis humanisque litteris aliquatinis inbutum, qui anno praecedente Romam orationis gratia properandi licentiam ab augusti poposcerat multisque donariius muneratus impetraverat, humani generis hoste pellectum relicta chrisitanitate ad iudaismum sese converterit. Et primum quidem consilio proditionis atque perditionis suae cum Iudaeis inito, quos secum adduxerat paganis vendendos, callide machinari non timuit; quibus distractis uno tantummodo secum, qui nepos eiusferebatur retento abnegate – quod lacrimabiliter dicimus – Chrisit fide, sese Iuaeum professus est. Sicque circumsis capillesque ac barba crescentibus, et mutate potiusque usurpato Eleazari nomine, accinctus etiam cingulo militarii, cuisdam Iudaie filiam sibi in matrimonium copulavit, coacto memorate nepote suo similiter ad iudaismum translato, tandemque cum Iudaeis miserrimam cupiditate devinctus Caesaraugustam, urbem Hispanae.mediante Augusto mense ingressus est. Quod quantum extiterit Augustis cunctisque christianae fidei gratia redemptis luctosum extiterit, difficultas, qua imperatori id facile credendum persuaderi non potuit, patenter omnibus indicavit.

Bishop Amulo's's *Espistola seu liber contra Judaeos* XXIII, ca. 845-46
Quid enim nunquam antea gestum meminimus, seductus est ab eis diaconus palatinus, nobiliter natus, nobiliter nutritus et in ecclesiae officiis exercitatus, et apud principum bene habitus, ita ut eorum diabolicis persuasionibus

abstractus et illectus, deseret patrium et parentes, deseret penitus Christianorum regnum; et nunc apud Hispaniam inter Saracenos Judaeius sociatus, persuasus sit ab impious Christum Dei Filium negere, aptismi gratium profanare, circumcisionem carnalem accipere nomen sibimutare, ut qui Bodo, nunc Eliezer appeletur. Ia ut et superstition et habitu Judaeus effectus, quotidie in synagogis Satanae barbatus et conjugatus, cum caeteris blasphemet Christum et ecclesiam ejus.

Annales Bertinani 847, pp. 34-35.
Bodo, qui ante annos aliquod christiana veritate derelecta Iudeorum perfidian Concesserat, intantum male profecit, ut in omnes chrisianos Hispaniae degentes tam regis quam gentis Saracenorum animos concitare studerit, quantenus aut relicta christianae fidei religion ad Iudeorum insaniam Saracenorumve dementiam se converterent aut certe omnes interficerentur. Super quo omnium illius regni christianorum petition ad Karolum regem regnique qui episcopos ceterosque nostrae fidei ordines lacrimabiliter missa est, ut memoratus apostate reposceretur, ne diutius christianis illic versantibus aut impedimento aut neci foret.

About the Author

Author of four other novels, *Rocamora, House Of Rocamora, A Gathering Of Vultures,* and *Close to the Sun,* Donald Michael Platt was born and raised in San Francisco. Donald graduated from Lowell High School and received his B.A. in History from the University of California at Berkeley. After two years in the Army, Donald attended graduate school at San Jose State where he won a batch of literary awards in the annual *Senator Phelan Literary Contest.*

Donald moved to southern California to begin his professional writing career. He sold to the TV series, *Mr. Novak,* ghosted for health food guru, Dan Dale Alexander, and wrote for and with diverse producers, among them as Harry Joe Brown, Sig Schlager, Albert J. Cohen, Al Ruddy plus Paul Stader Sr, Hollywood stuntman and stunt/2nd unit director. While in Hollywood, Donald taught Creative Writing and Advanced Placement European History at Fairfax High School where he was Social Studies Department Chairman.

After living in Florianópolis, Brazil, setting of his horror novel *A Gathering Of Vultures,* pub. 2007 & 2011, he moved to Florida where he wrote as a with: *Vitamin Enriched,* pub.1999, for Carl DeSantis, founder of Rexall Sundown Vitamins; and *The Couple's Disease, Finding a Cure for Your Lost "Love" Life,* pub. 2002, for Lawrence S. Hakim, MD, FACS, Head of Sexual Dysfunction Unit at the Cleveland Clinic.

Currently, Donald resides in Winter Haven, Florida where he is polishing a dark novel and preparing to write a sequel to *Close to the Sun.*